lolololol

S°Cute It Hurts!!

(>-<)

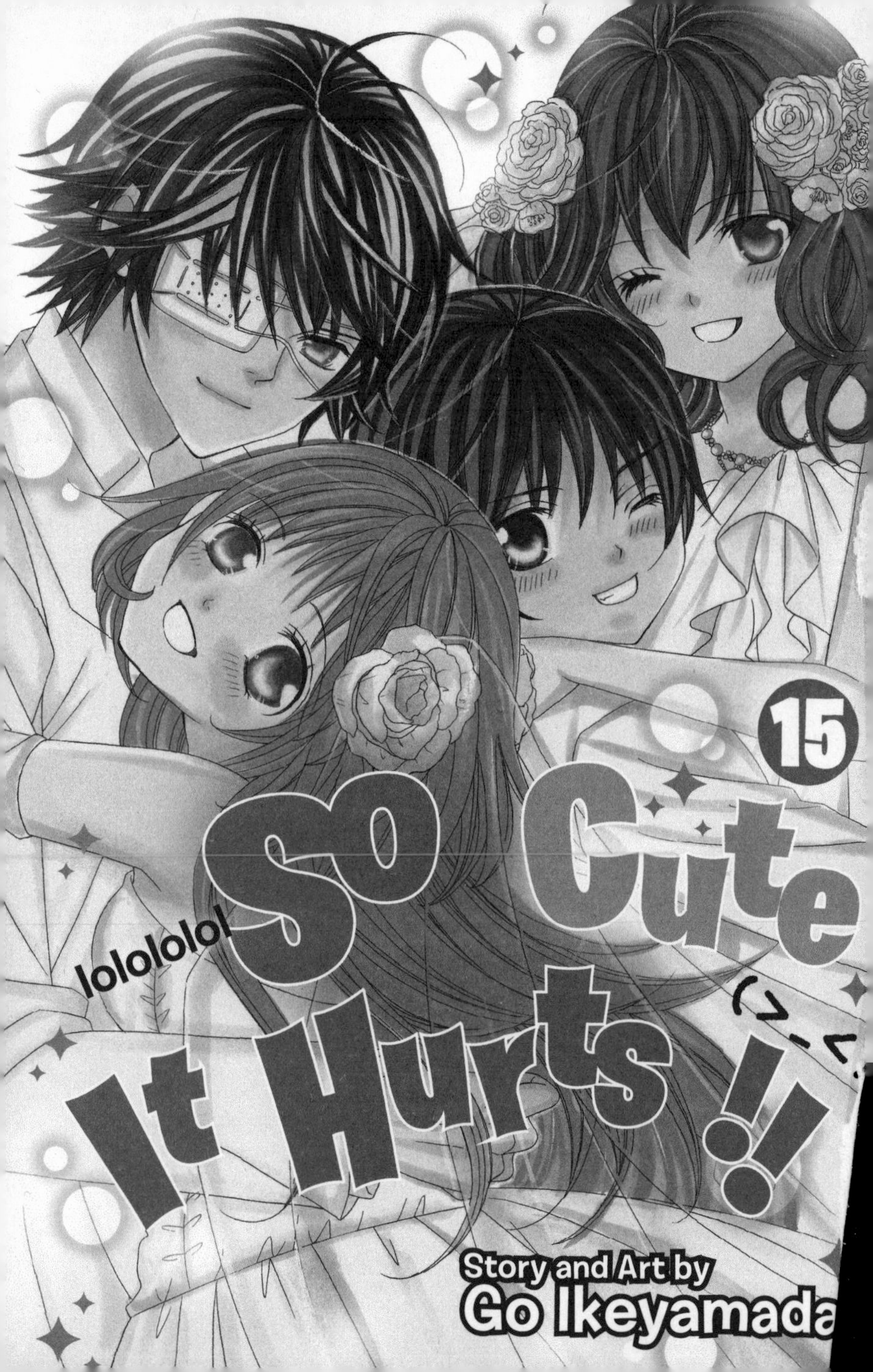
15
lolololol
So Cute It Hurts!!
Story and Art by
Go Ikeyamada

CHARACTERS

Cross-dressing as her brother!

Mitsuru wears bows! ☆

Nickname: Mego

Switched places at school!

Megumu Kobayashi (younger sister)
History nerd who loves video games. She likes Aoi.

Twins

Cross-dressing as his sister!

Mitsuru Kobayashi (older brother)
Starts going out with Azusa in high school.

Going out ♡

Likes him

Likes her

Half siblings

Half sisters

Aoi Sanada
Megumu's boyfriend. Marries Megumu while attending college.

Shino Takenaka
She's deaf and she's Aoi's younger sister.

Azusa Tokugawa
School chairman's daughter and fashion model.

STORY

★ Mitsuru and Megumu are twins. One day they switch places and go to each other's school for a week! That's when Megumu falls in love with Aoi. They begin a long-distance relationship when Aoi goes to Sendai for college.

★ Mitsuru and Azusa are engaged now. With Mitsuru's full support, Azusa decides to become the first female president of the Tokugawa Group.

★ On March 11, 2011, the Great Tohoku Earthquake hits Japan. Aoi encounters his mother, Yuki, in the ensuing chaos and is swept away by a tsunami while trying to protect her and her young son. Yuki later dies in an attempt to save Aoi, who is agonized by her death. Megumu and Aoi are finally reunited in the rubble of Sendai. Megumu decides to share Aoi's heavy burden and accepts his marriage proposal, becoming engaged at 18.

★ Four years later, Megumu and Aoi are having a wedding!

CONTENTS

Chapter 72 ⋯⋯⋯⋯⋯⋯⋯⋯ 5
Final Chapter ⋯⋯⋯⋯⋯⋯⋯ 42
Bonus 1 ⋯⋯⋯⋯⋯⋯⋯⋯⋯ 95
Bonus 2 ⋯⋯⋯⋯⋯⋯⋯⋯⋯ 128

Special Interview ⋯⋯⋯⋯⋯ 131
The Goddess Never
Turns Back?! ⋯⋯⋯⋯⋯⋯⋯ 136
Afterword ⋯⋯⋯⋯⋯⋯⋯⋯ 182

Chapter 72

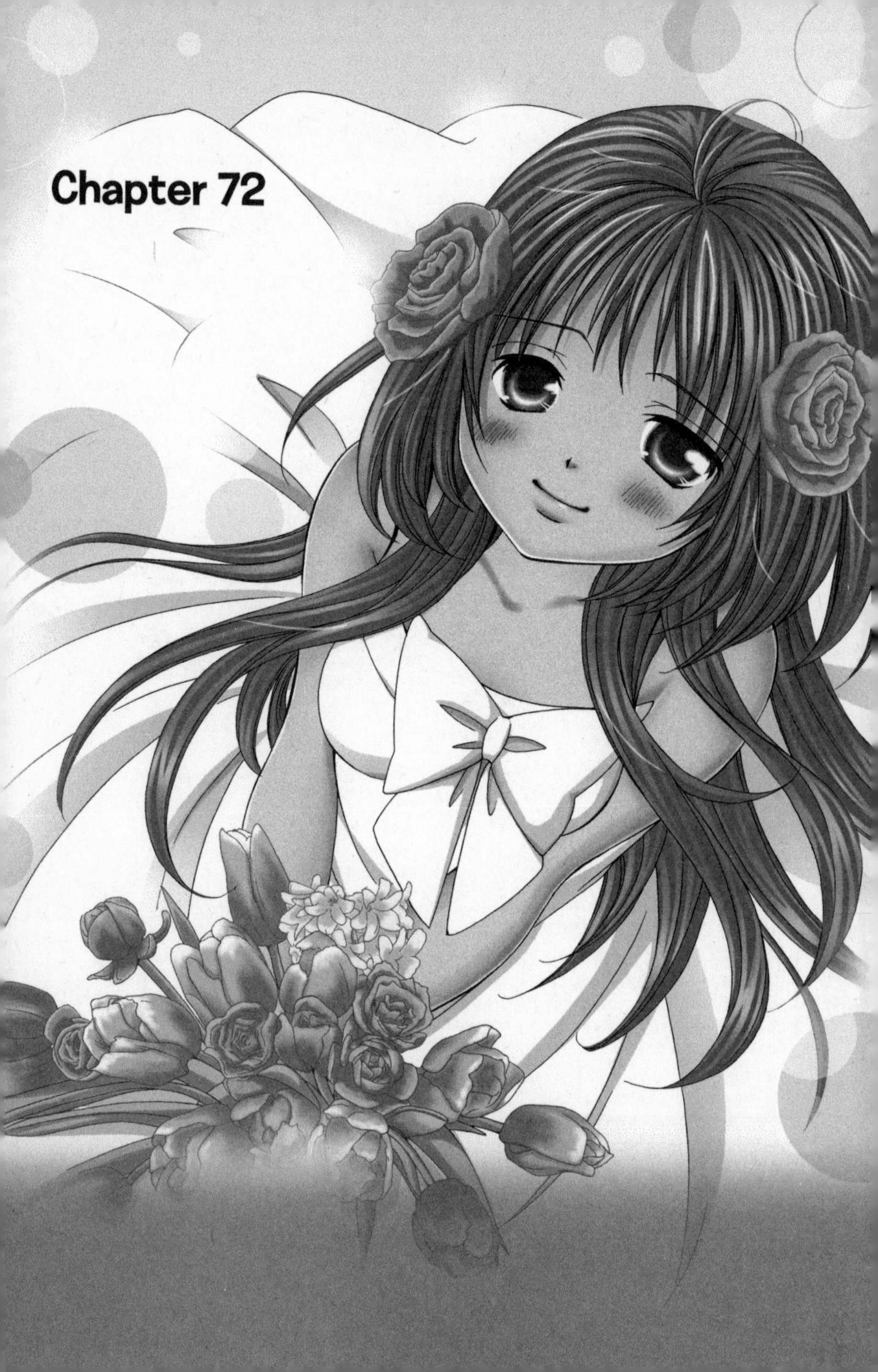

So Cute It Hurts!! ⁽ᵔ‿ᵔ⁾

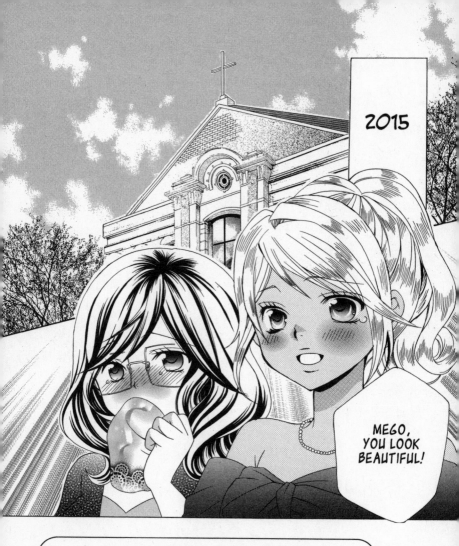

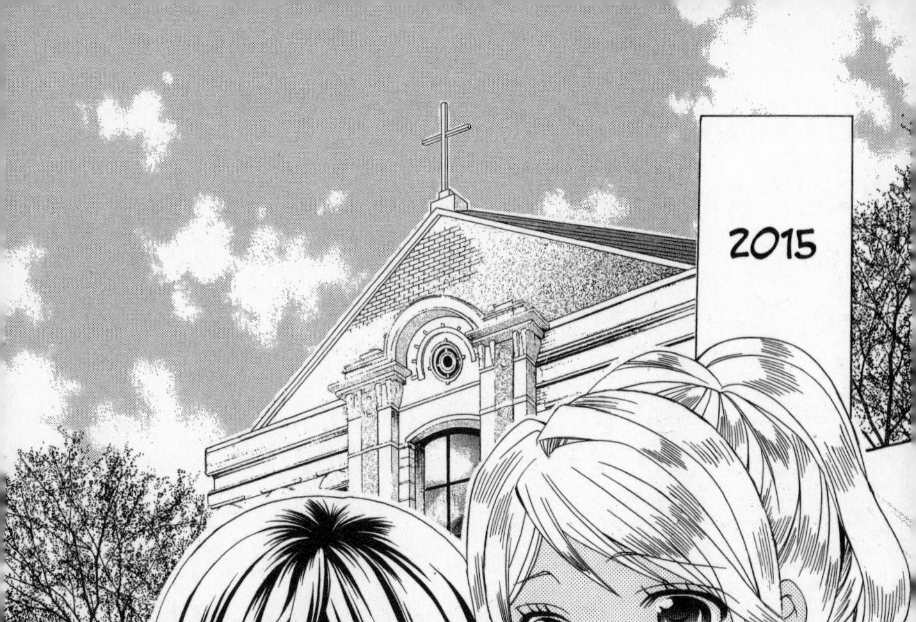
2015
MEGO, YOU LOOK BEAUTIFUL!

NICE TO MEET YOU AND HELLO. I'M GO IKEYAMADA.
THANK YOU FOR PICKING UP MY 58TH BOOK!!
THIS IS VOLUME 15, THE FINAL VOLUME OF *SO CUTE IT HURTS!!*
I'M GRATEFUL FOR ALL YOUR SUPPORT THESE LAST
THREE AND A HALF YEARS! I WAS ABLE TO DRAW THIS SERIES TO ITS
CONCLUSION BECAUSE EVERYONE GAVE ME THE STRENGTH TO DO SO.
IT'S 2016, A NEW YEAR. I'M VERY NERVOUS BECAUSE
THIS VOLUME WILL BE ON SALE (IN JAPAN)
AND MY NEW SERIES WILL BEGIN, BUT PLEASE DO KEEP READING!!

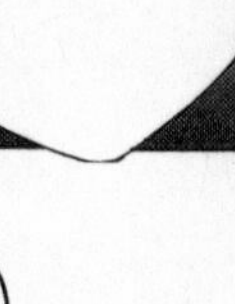

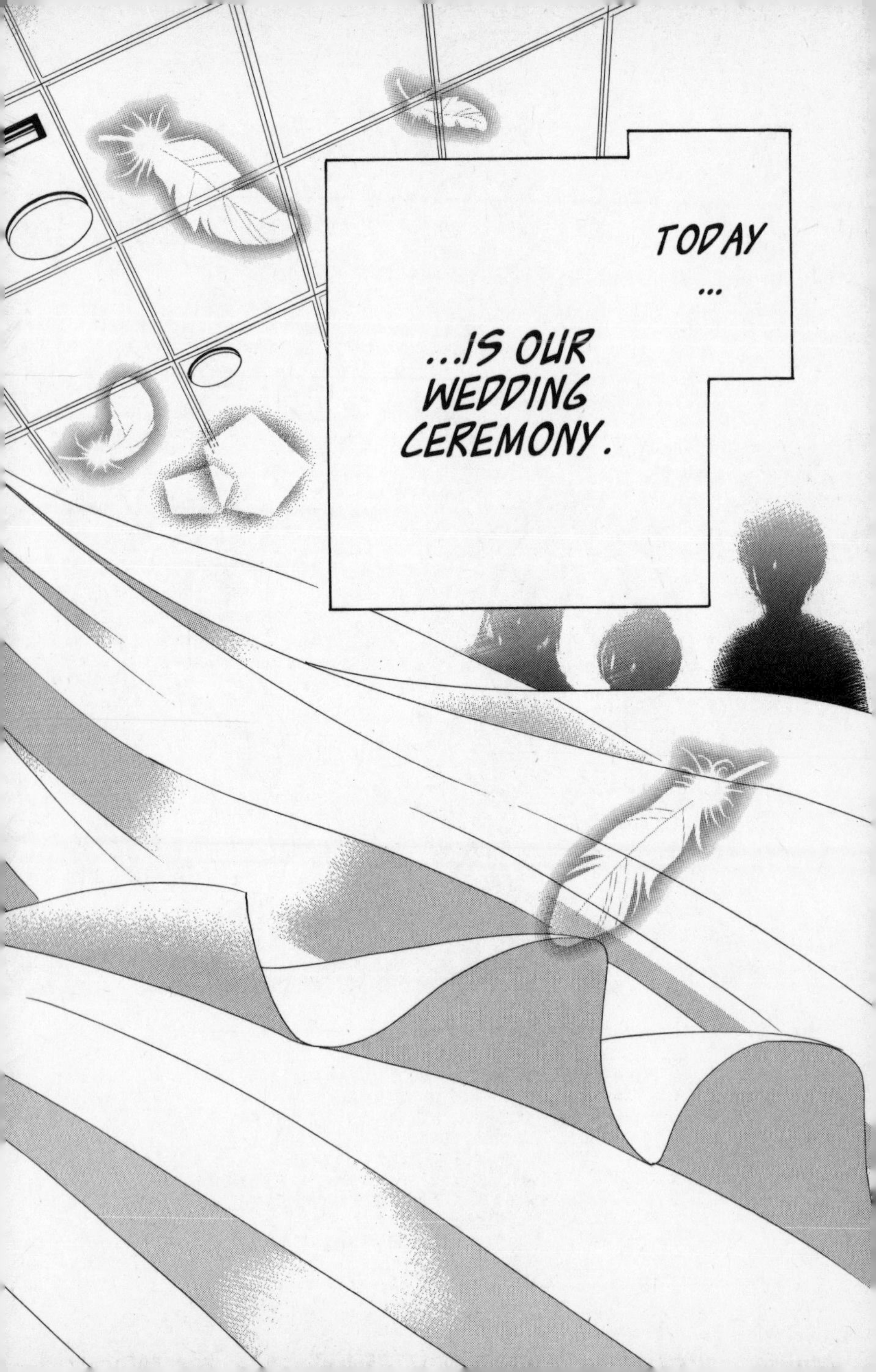
TODAY
...
...IS OUR WEDDING CEREMONY.

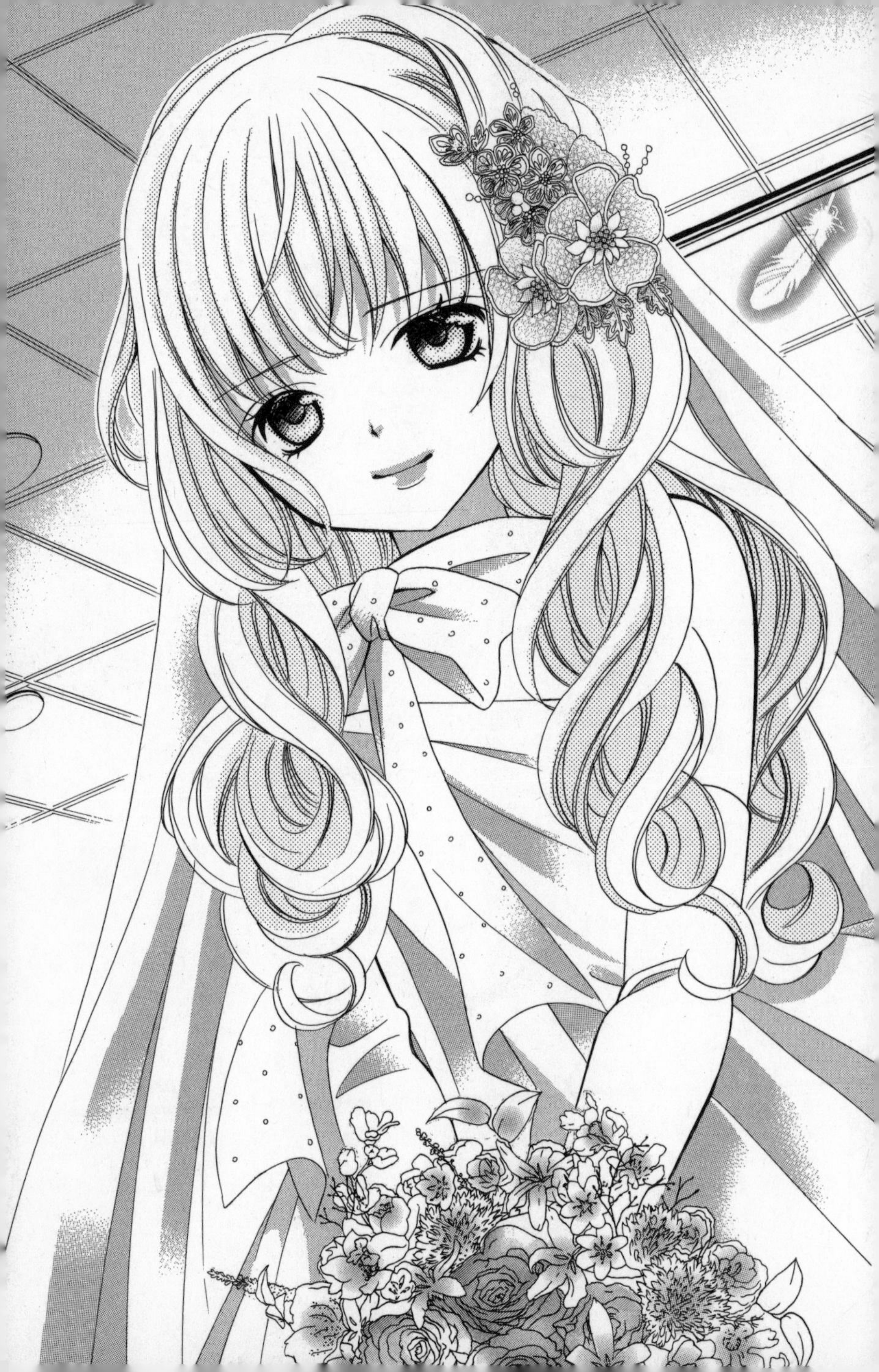

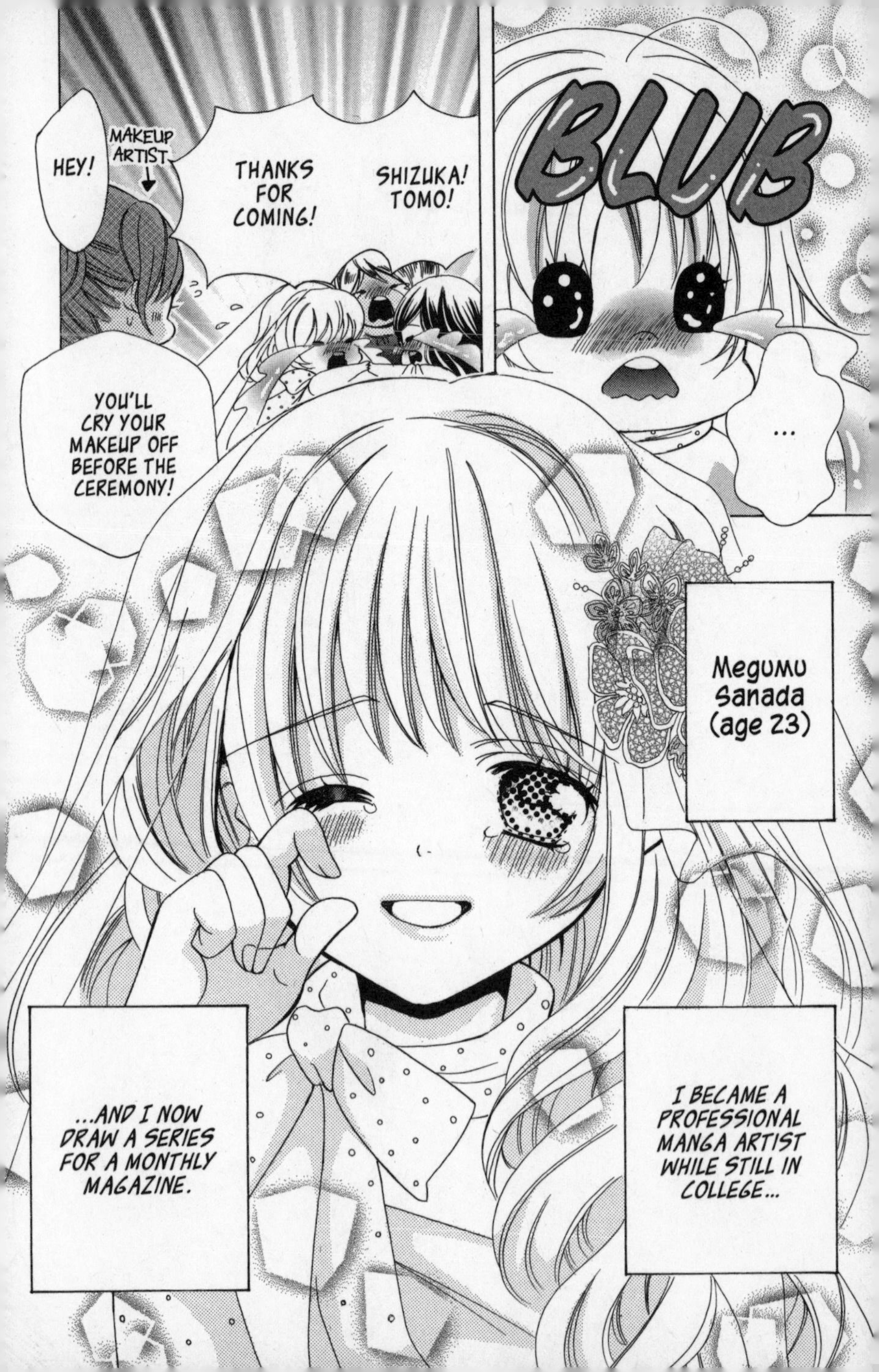
BLUB
...
SHIZUKA! TOMO!
THANKS FOR COMING!
MAKEUP ARTIST
HEY!
YOU'LL CRY YOUR MAKEUP OFF BEFORE THE CEREMONY!
Megumu Sanada (age 23)
I BECAME A PROFESSIONAL MANGA ARTIST WHILE STILL IN COLLEGE...
...AND I NOW DRAW A SERIES FOR A MONTHLY MAGAZINE.

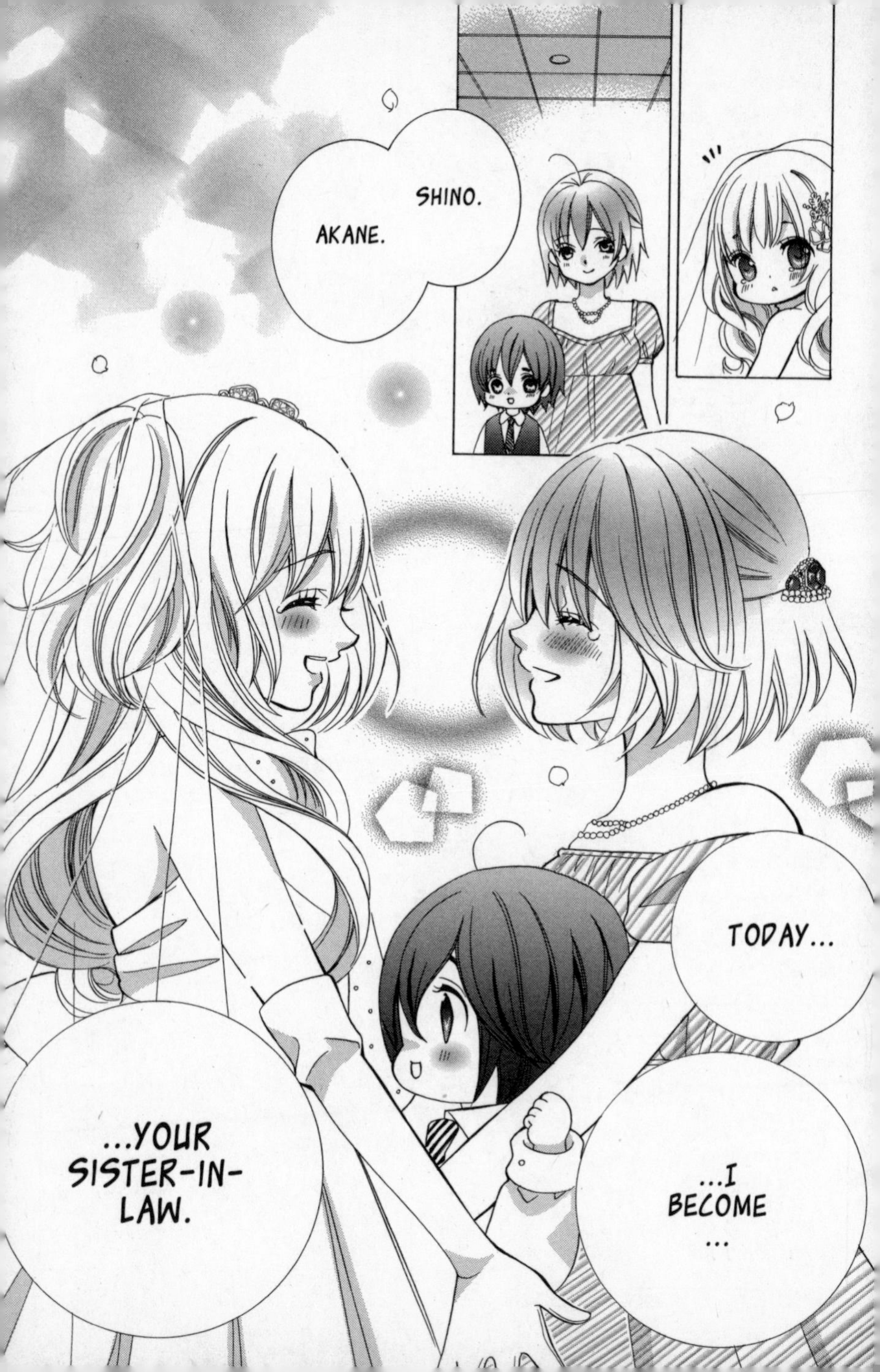
SHINO.
AKANE.
TODAY...
...I BECOME ...
...YOUR SISTER-IN-LAW.

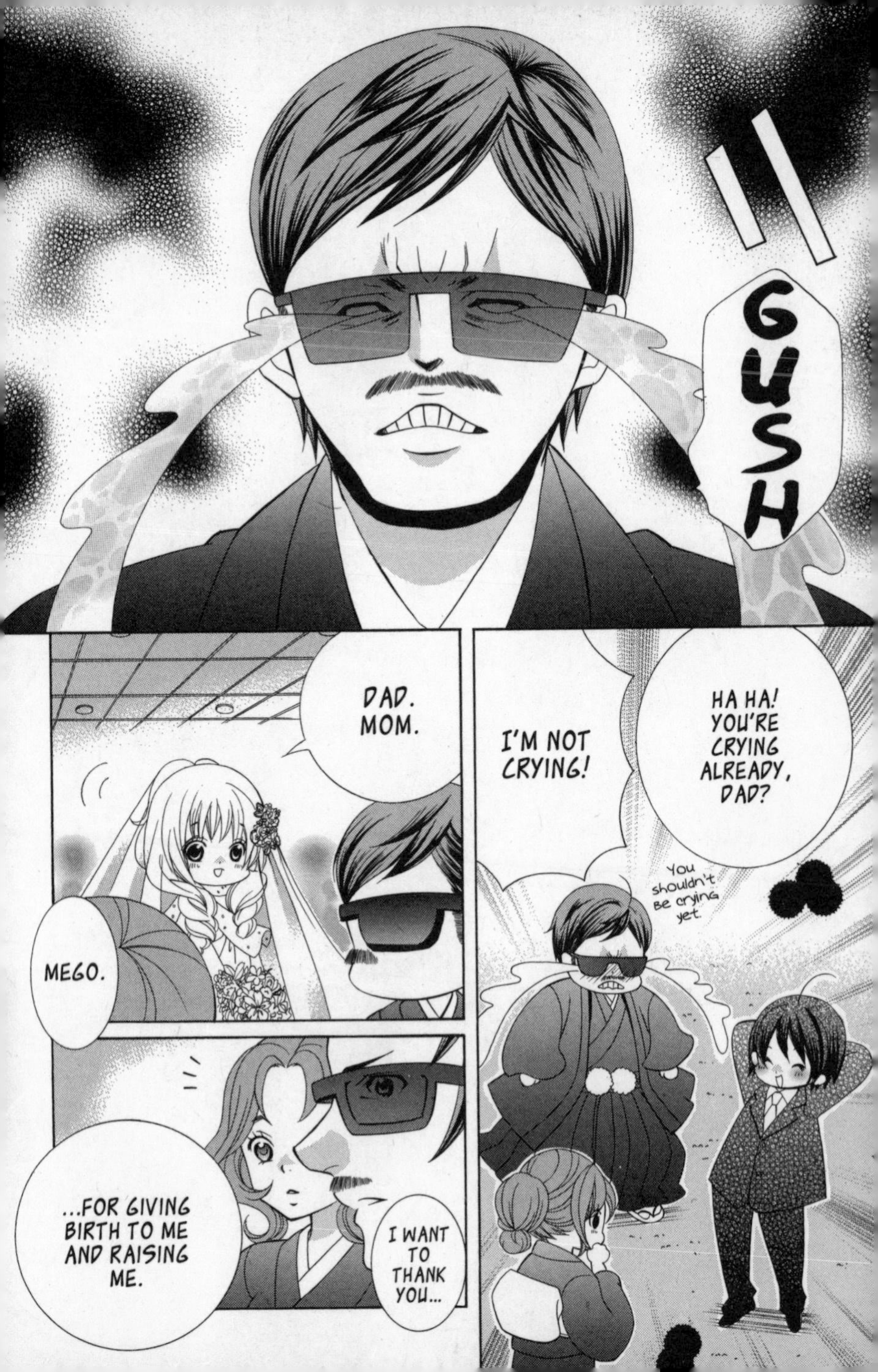
GUSH
HA HA! YOU'RE CRYING ALREADY, DAD?
I'M NOT CRYING!
You shouldn't be crying yet.
DAD. MOM.
MEGO.
I WANT TO THANK YOU...
...FOR GIVING BIRTH TO ME AND RAISING ME.

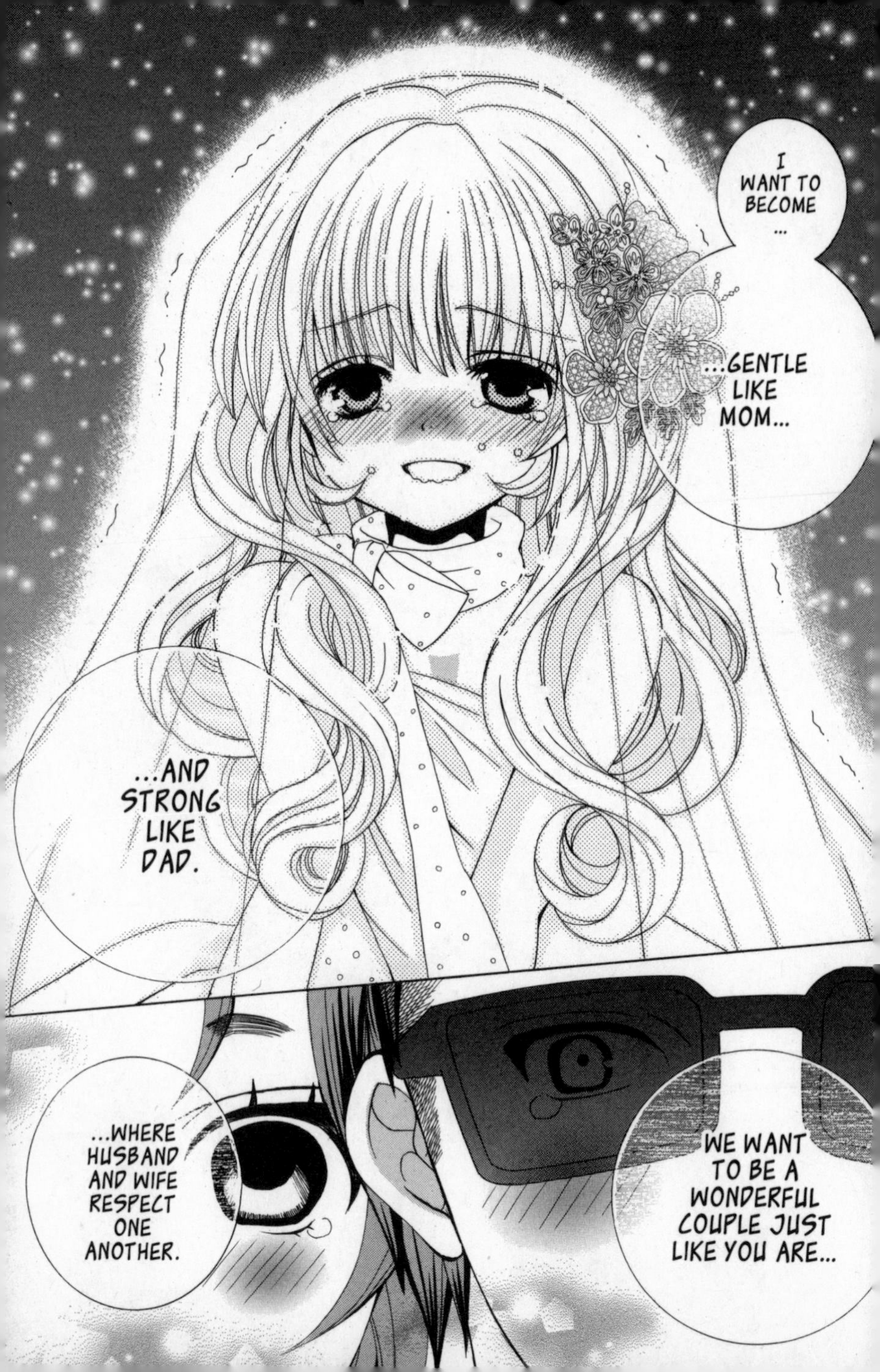
I WANT TO BECOME ...
...GENTLE LIKE MOM...
...AND STRONG LIKE DAD.
WE WANT TO BE A WONDERFUL COUPLE JUST LIKE YOU ARE...
...WHERE HUSBAND AND WIFE RESPECT ONE ANOTHER.

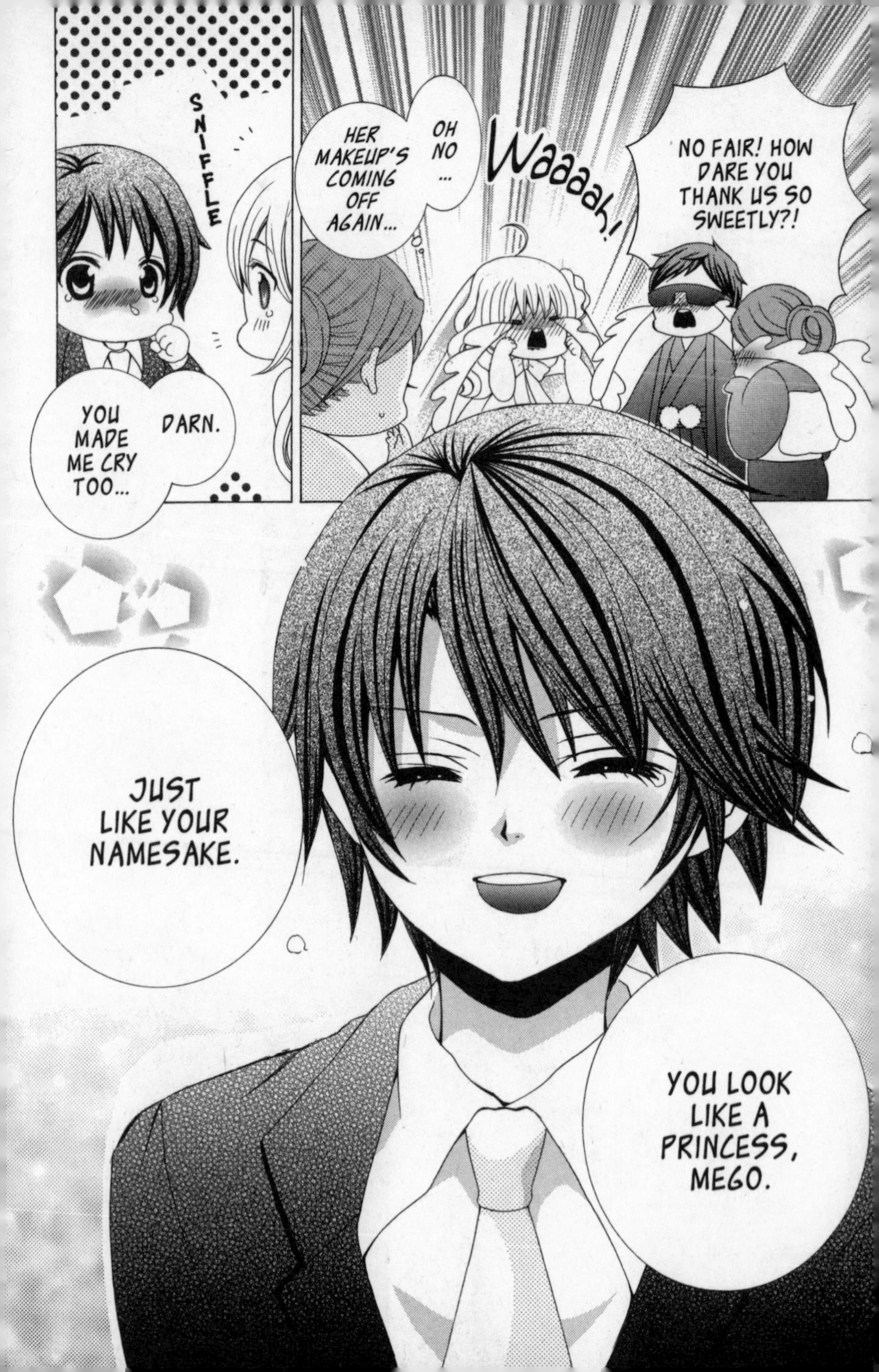
NO FAIR! HOW DARE YOU THANK US SO SWEETLY?!
Waaaah!
OH NO ...
HER MAKEUP'S COMING OFF AGAIN...
SNIFFLE
DARN.
YOU MADE ME CRY TOO...
YOU LOOK LIKE A PRINCESS, MEGO.
JUST LIKE YOUR NAMESAKE.

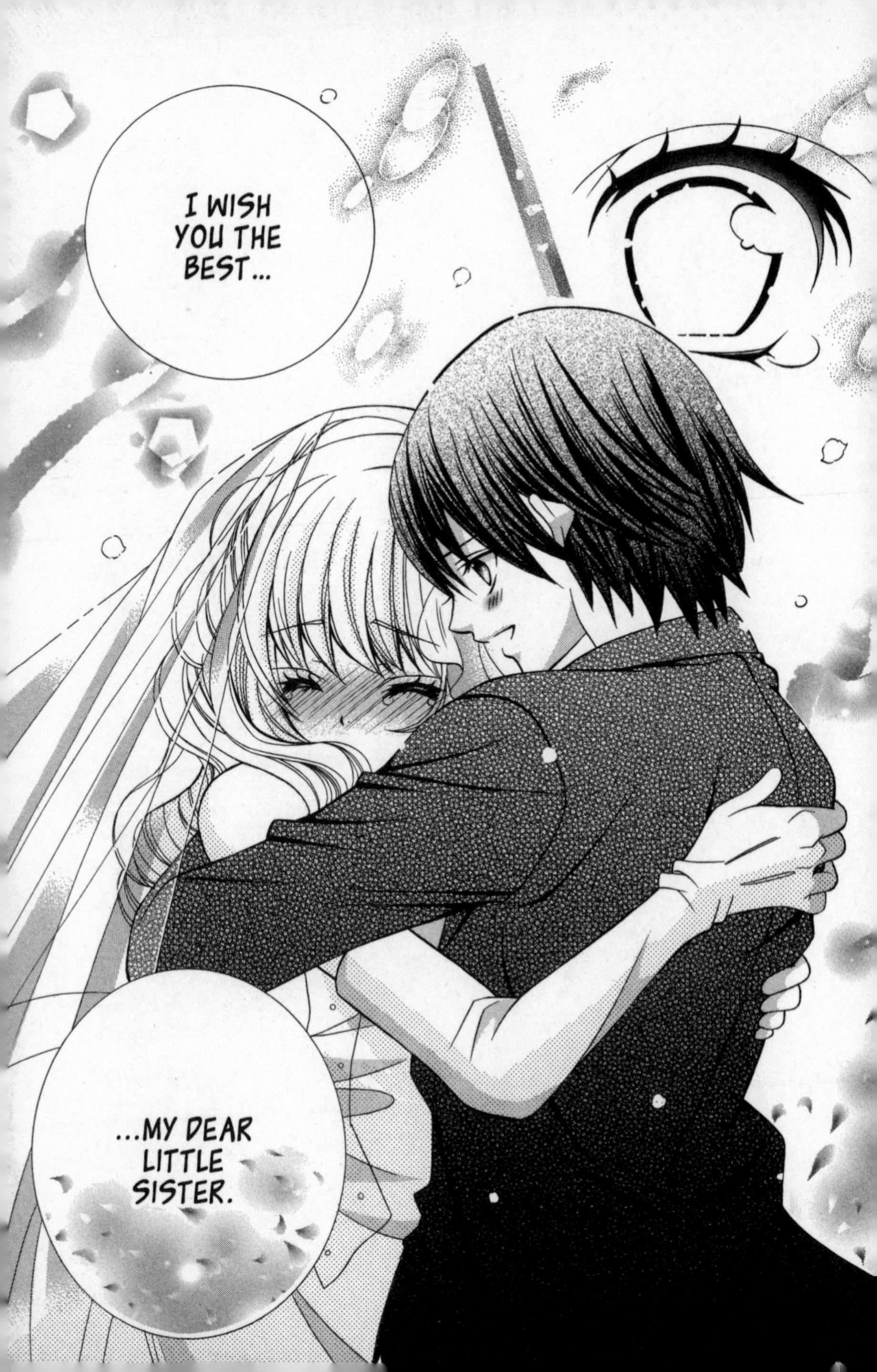
I WISH YOU THE BEST...
...MY DEAR LITTLE SISTER.

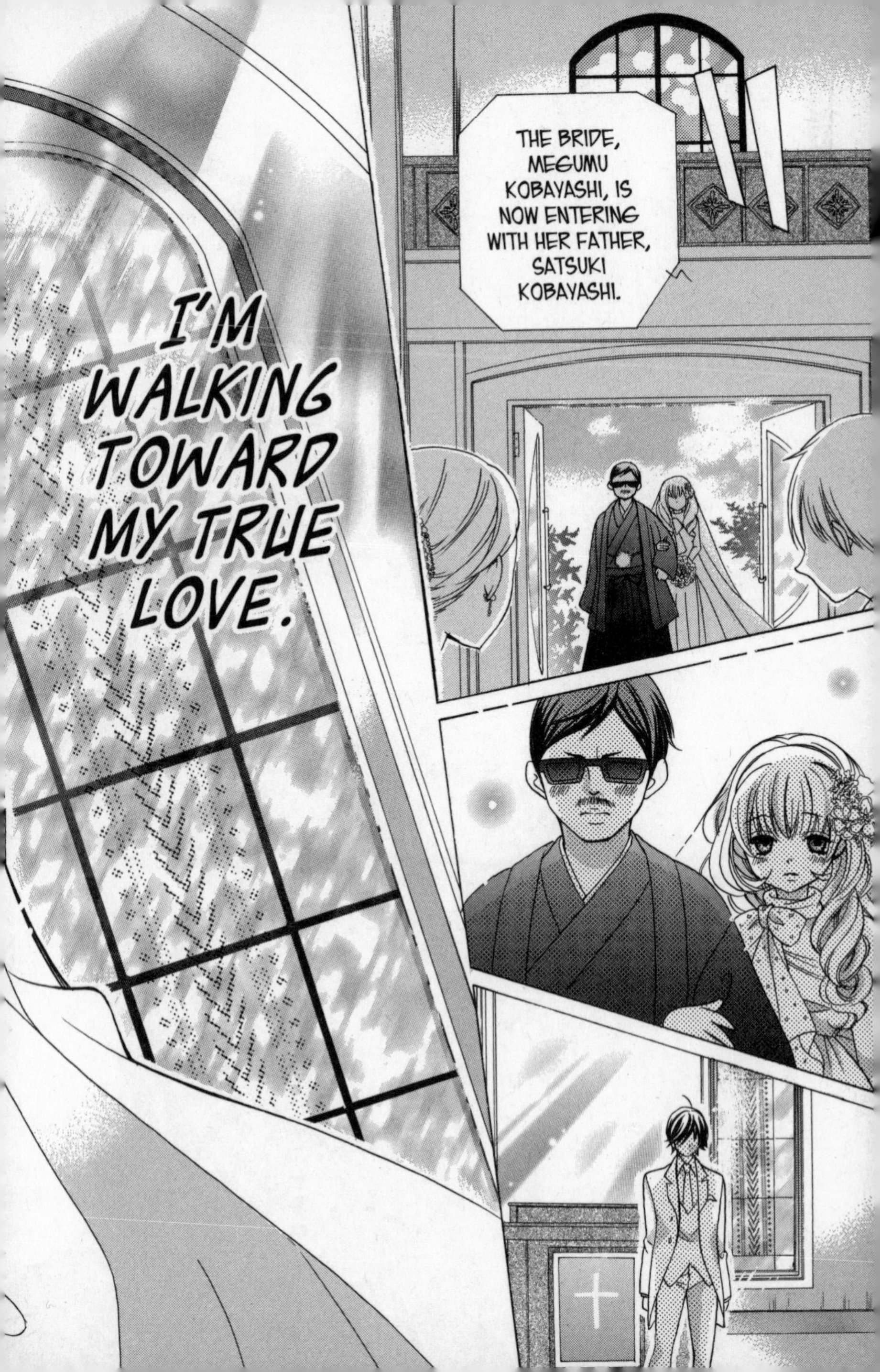
THE BRIDE, MEGUMU KOBAYASHI, IS NOW ENTERING WITH HER FATHER, SATSUKI KOBAYASHI.
I'M WALKING TOWARD MY TRUE LOVE.

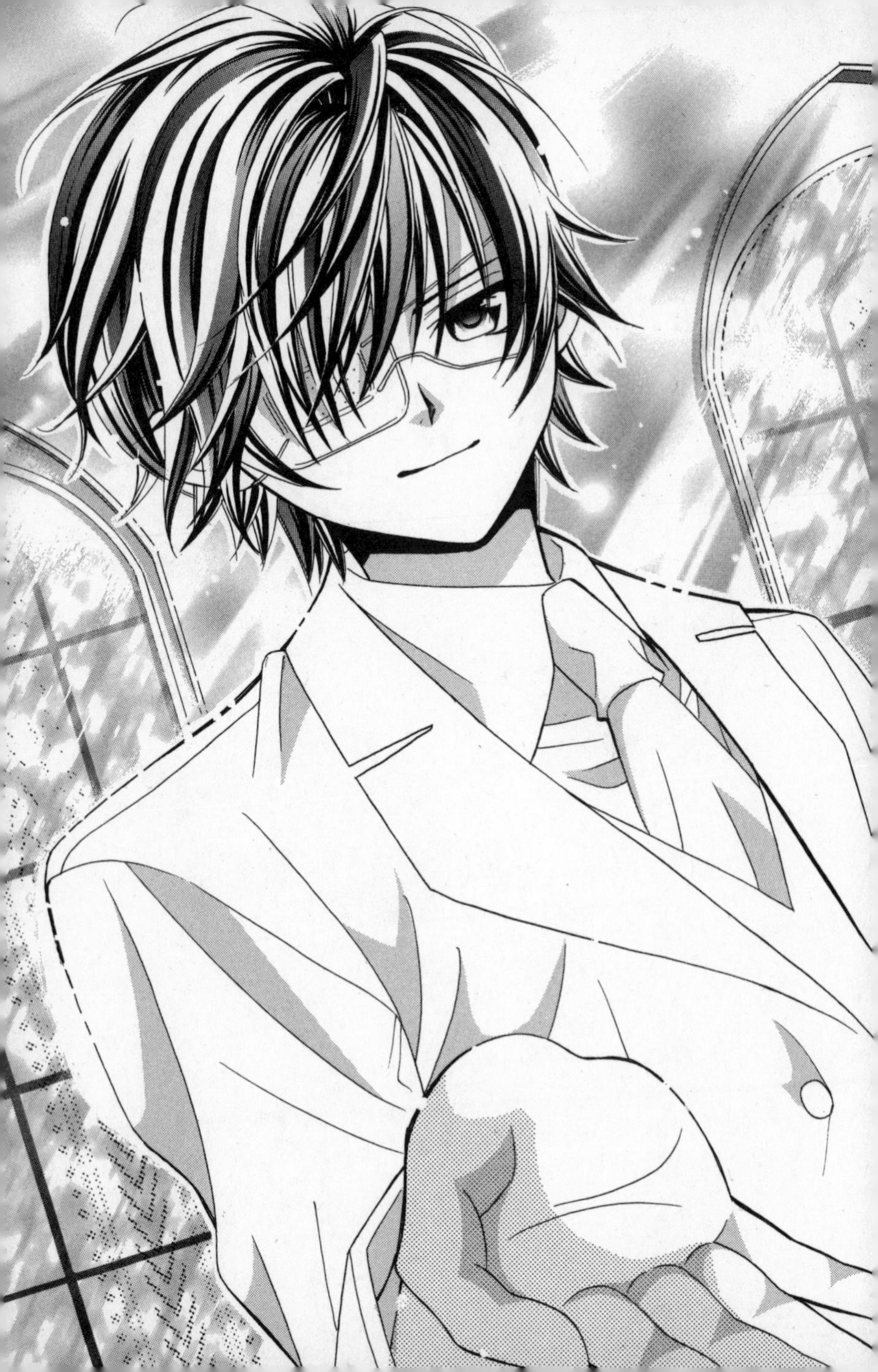

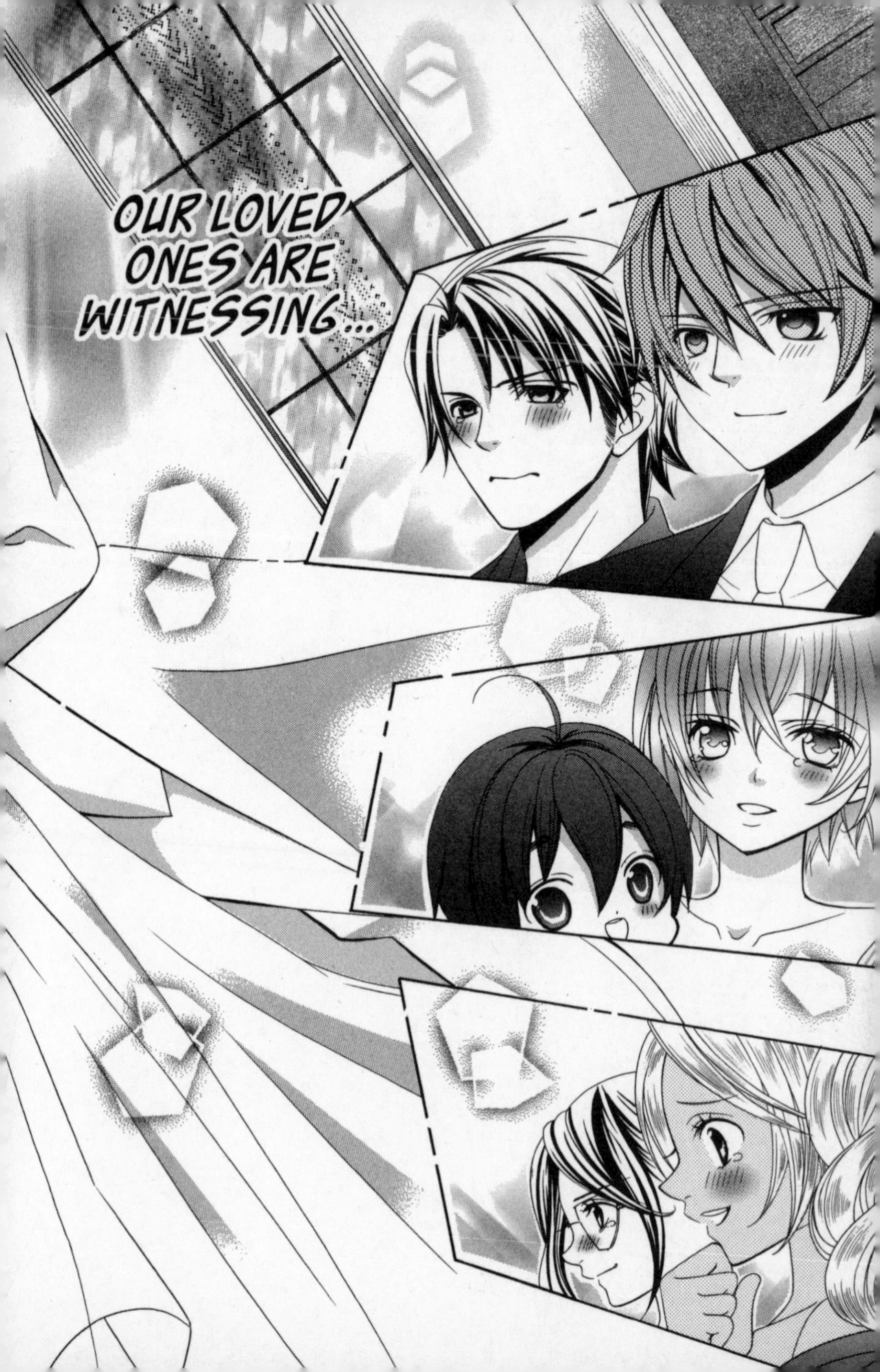
OUR LOVED ONES ARE WITNESSING...

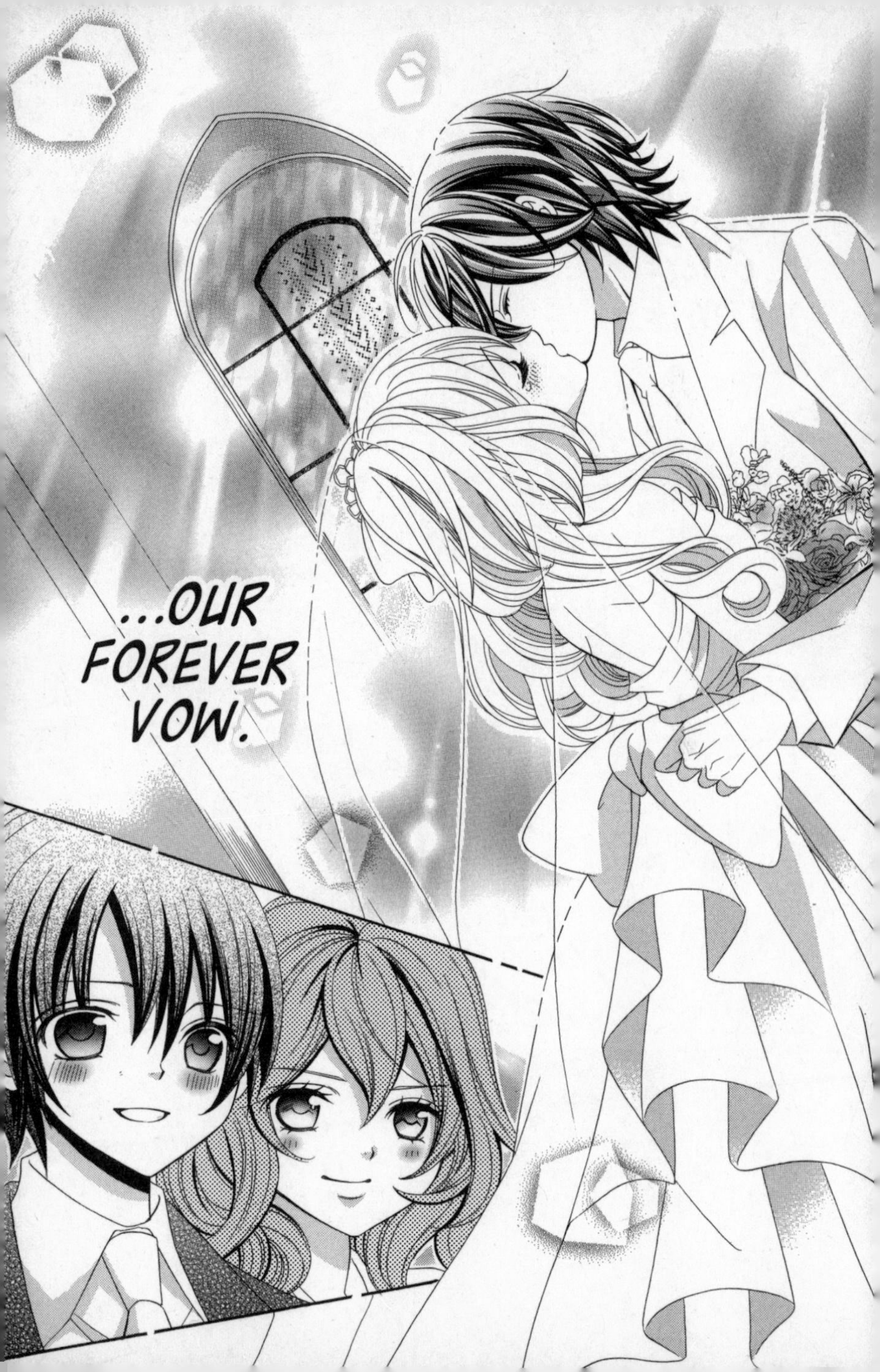
...OUR FOREVER VOW.

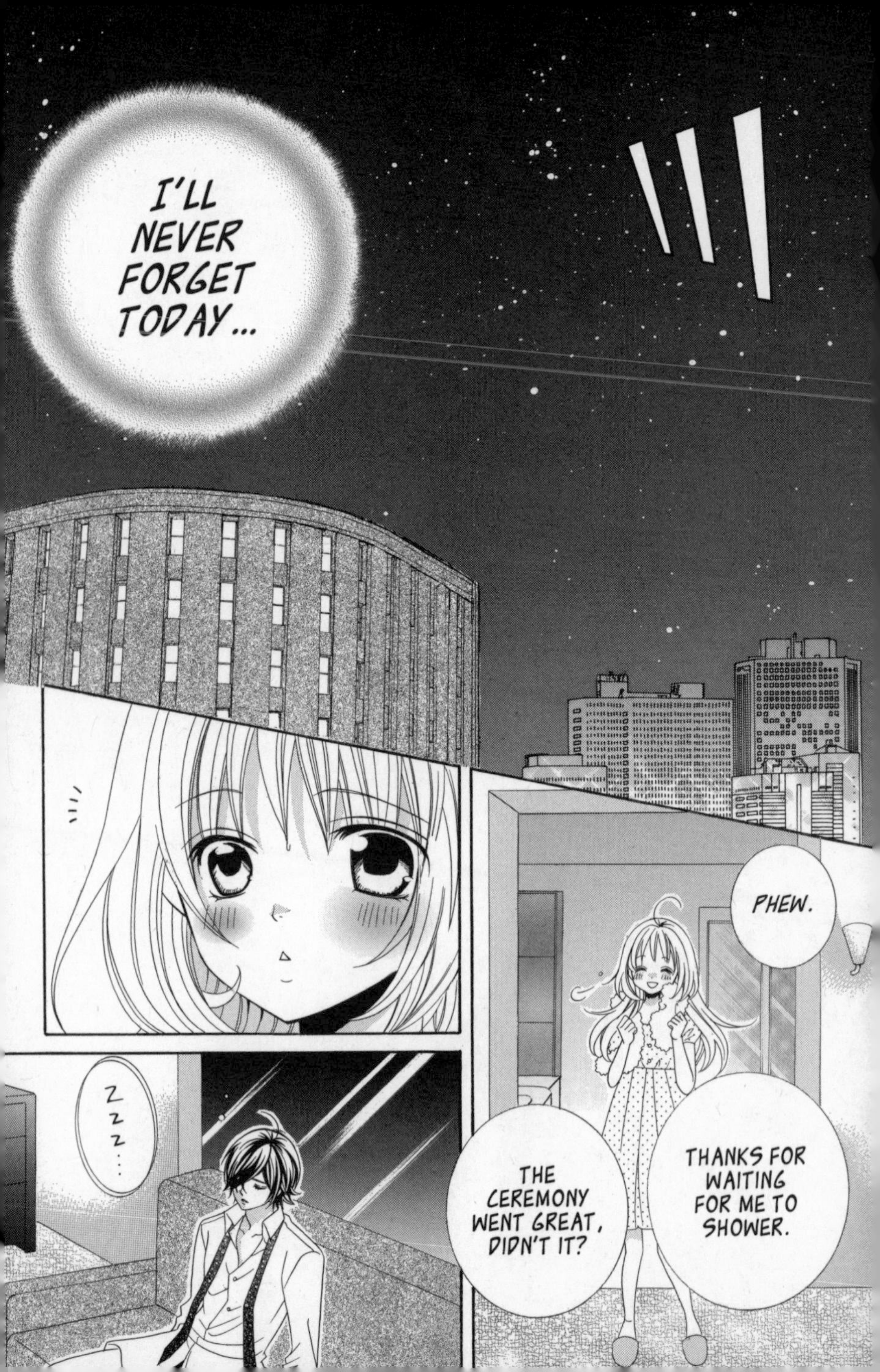
I'LL NEVER FORGET TODAY...
PHEW.
THANKS FOR WAITING FOR ME TO SHOWER.
THE CEREMONY WENT GREAT, DIDN'T IT?
ZZZ...

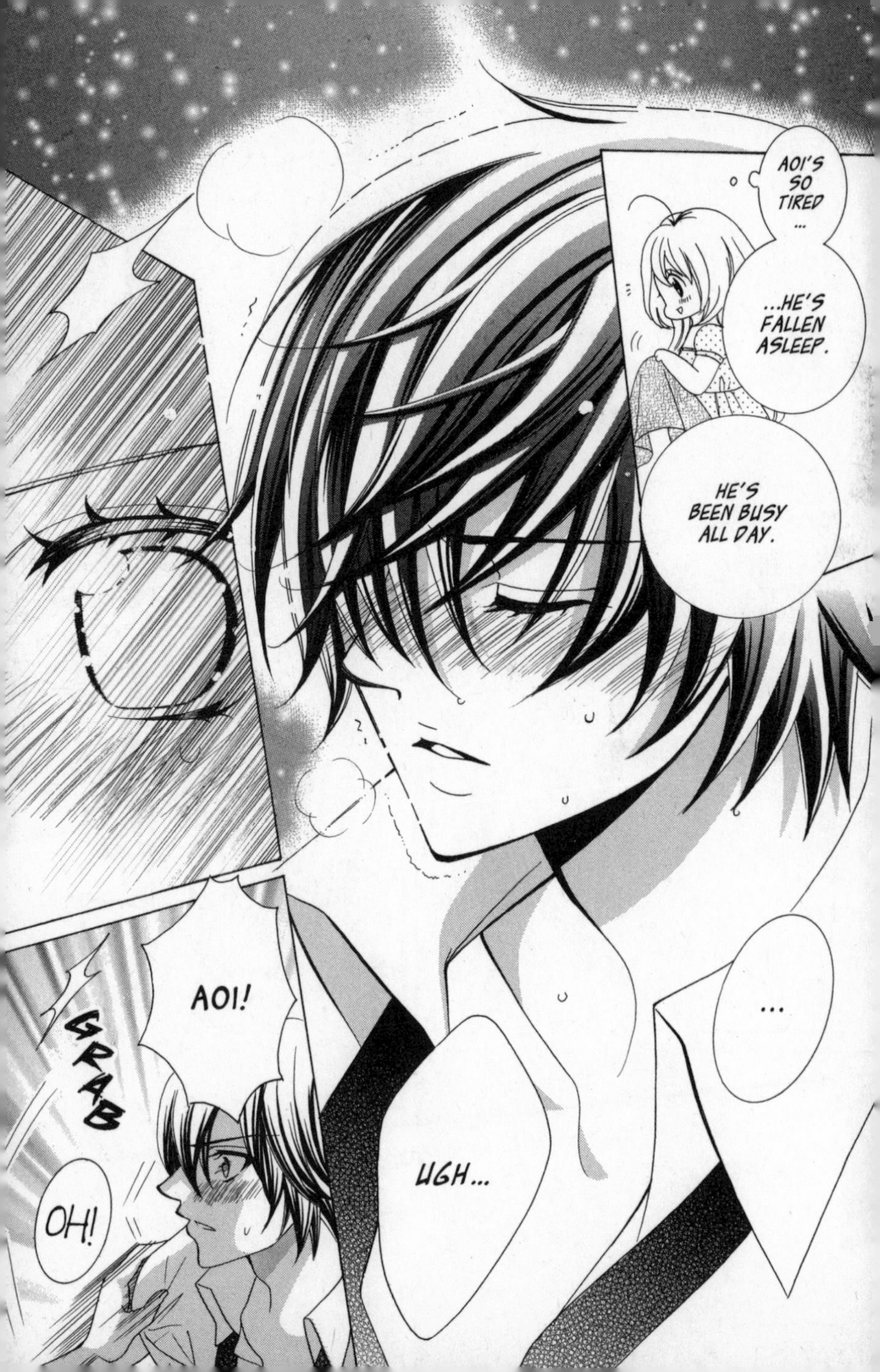
AOI'S SO TIRED...
...HE'S FALLEN ASLEEP.
HE'S BEEN BUSY ALL DAY.
...
UGH...
AOI!
GRAB
OH!

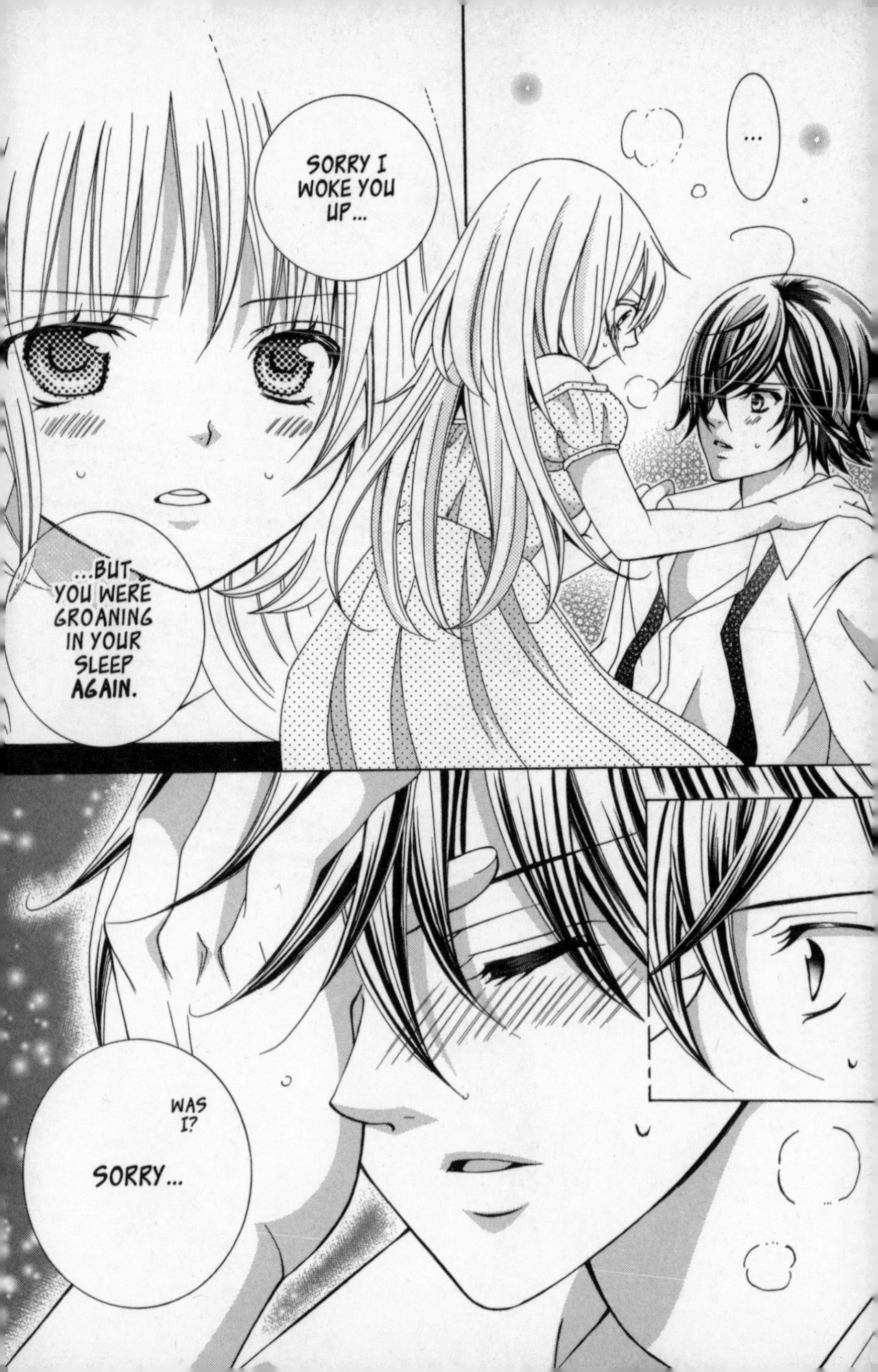
...
SORRY I WOKE YOU UP...
...BUT YOU WERE GROANING IN YOUR SLEEP AGAIN.
...
...
WAS I?
SORRY...

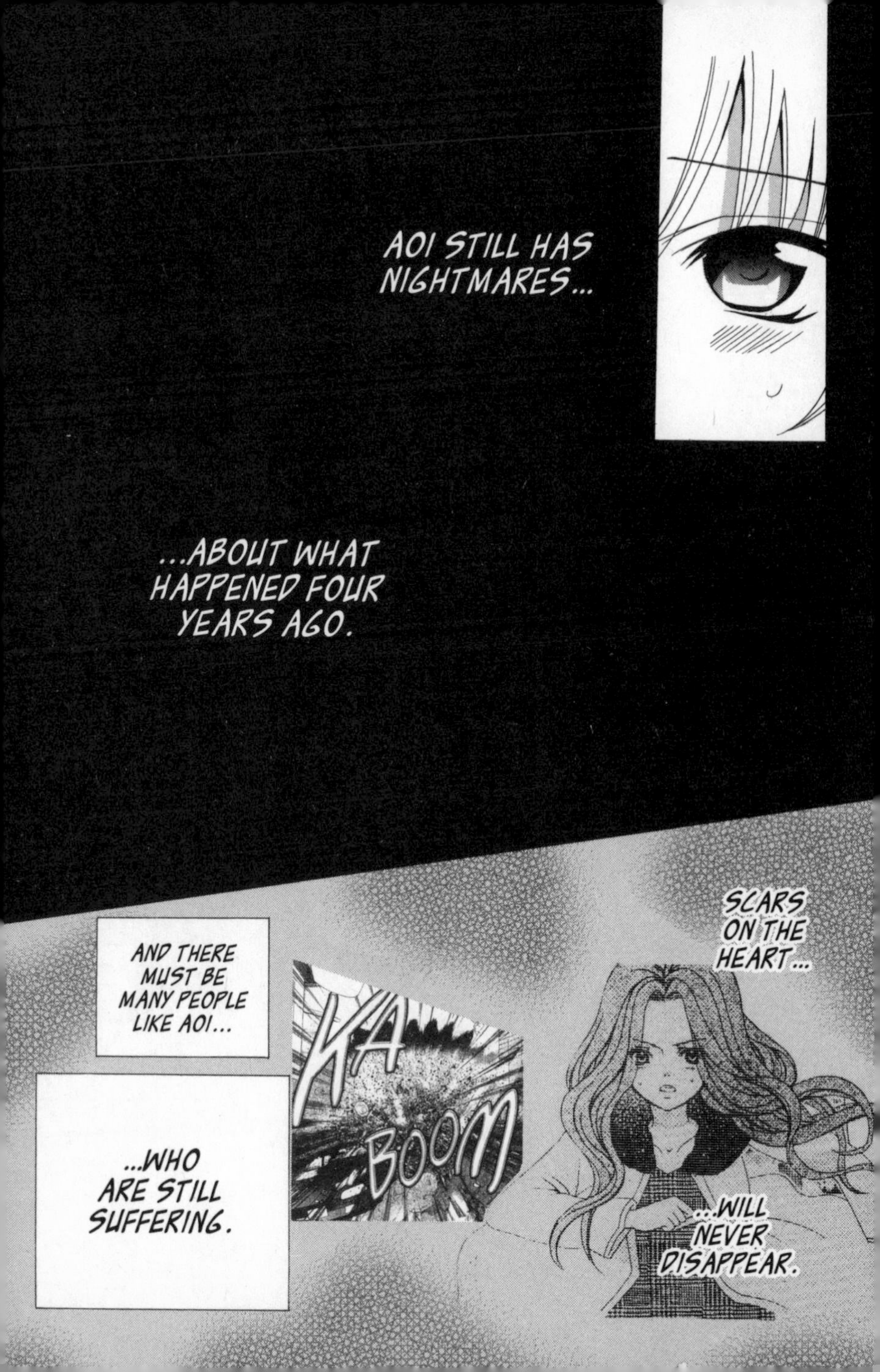
AOI STILL HAS NIGHTMARES...
...ABOUT WHAT HAPPENED FOUR YEARS AGO.
SCARS ON THE HEART...
...WILL NEVER DISAPPEAR.
KA BOOM
AND THERE MUST BE MANY PEOPLE LIKE AOI...
...WHO ARE STILL SUFFERING.

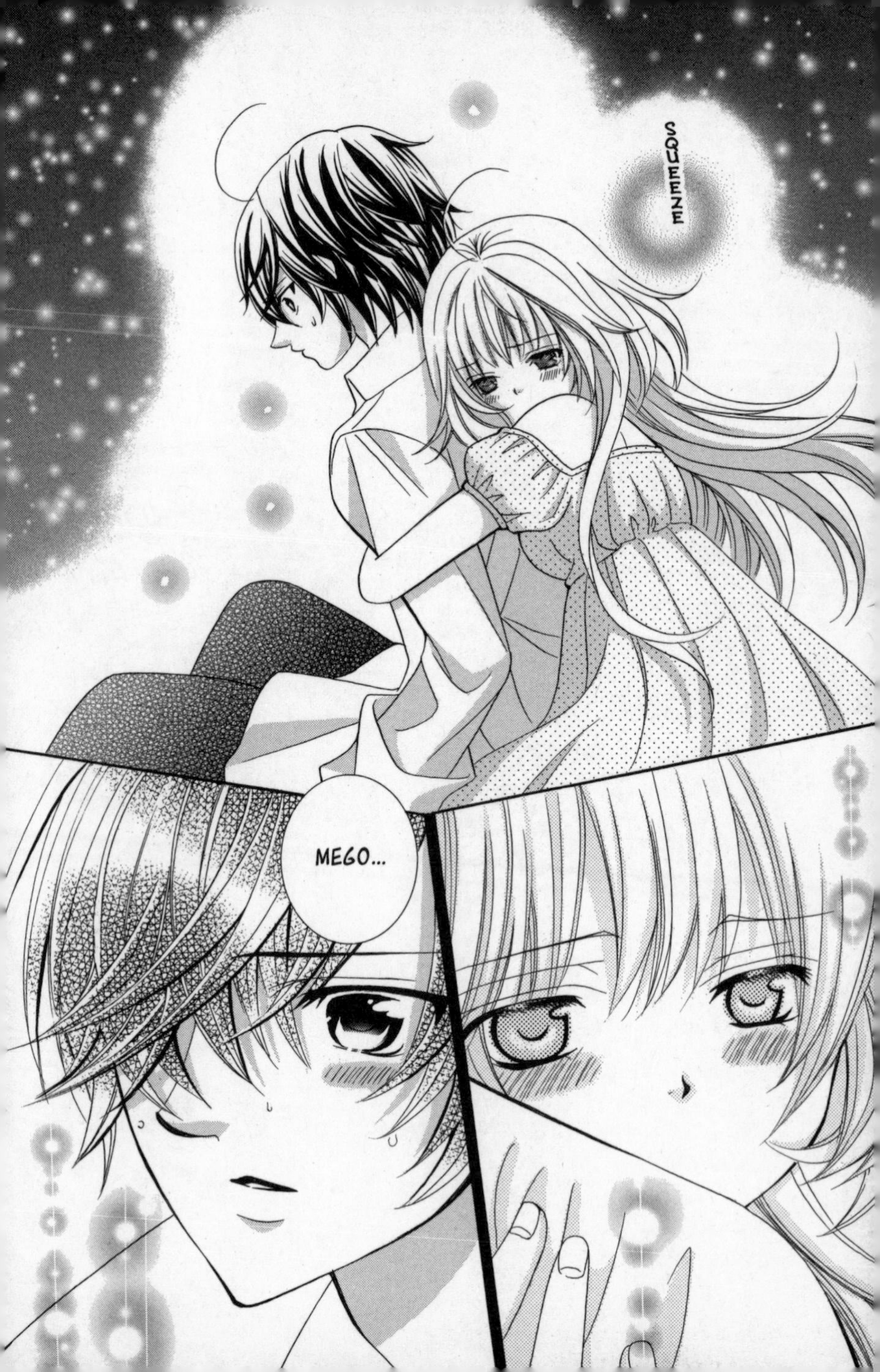
SQUEEZE
MEGO...

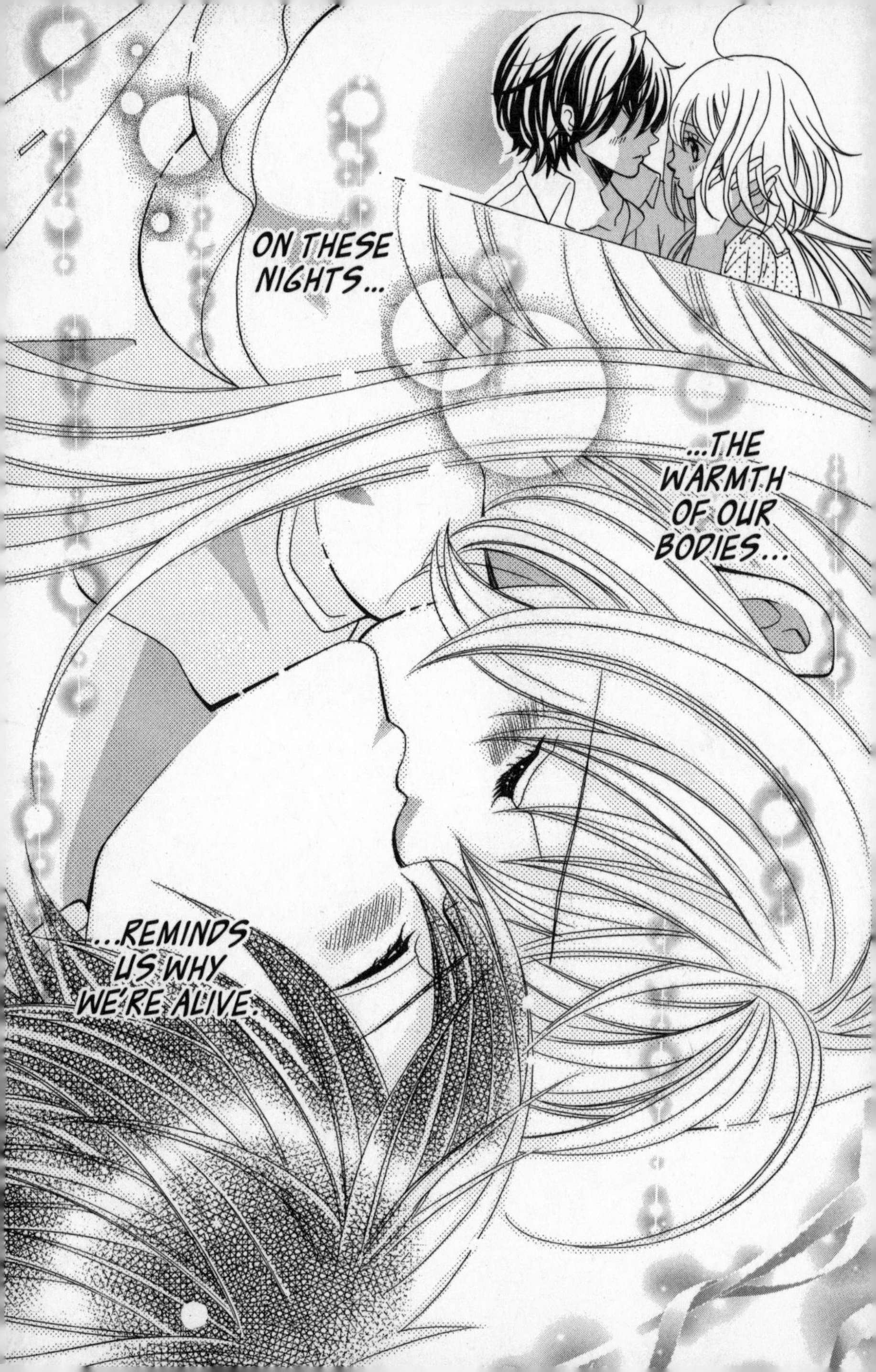
ON THESE NIGHTS...
...THE WARMTH OF OUR BODIES...
...REMINDS US WHY WE'RE ALIVE.

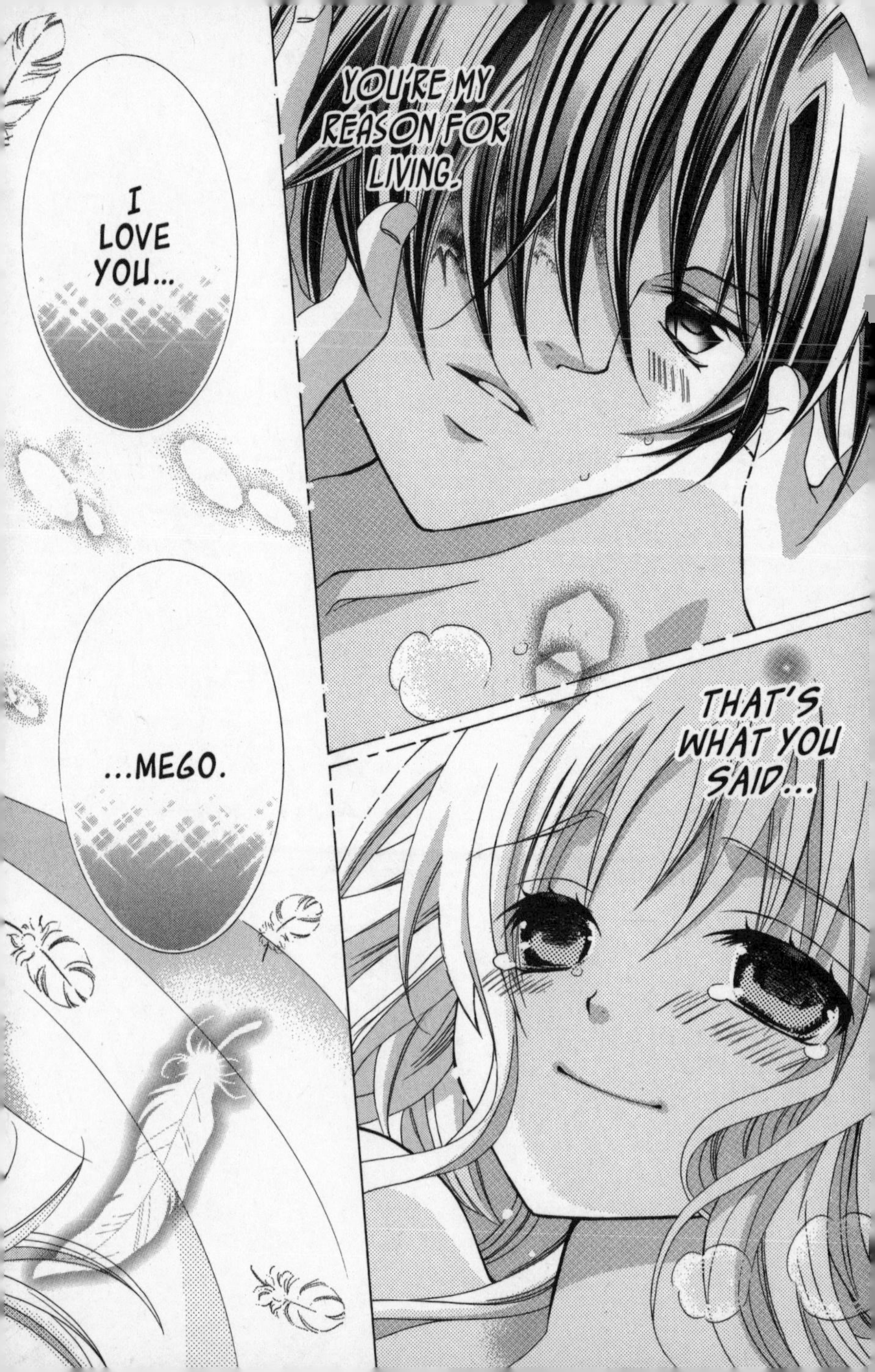
YOU'RE MY REASON FOR LIVING.
THAT'S WHAT YOU SAID...
I LOVE YOU...
...MEGO.

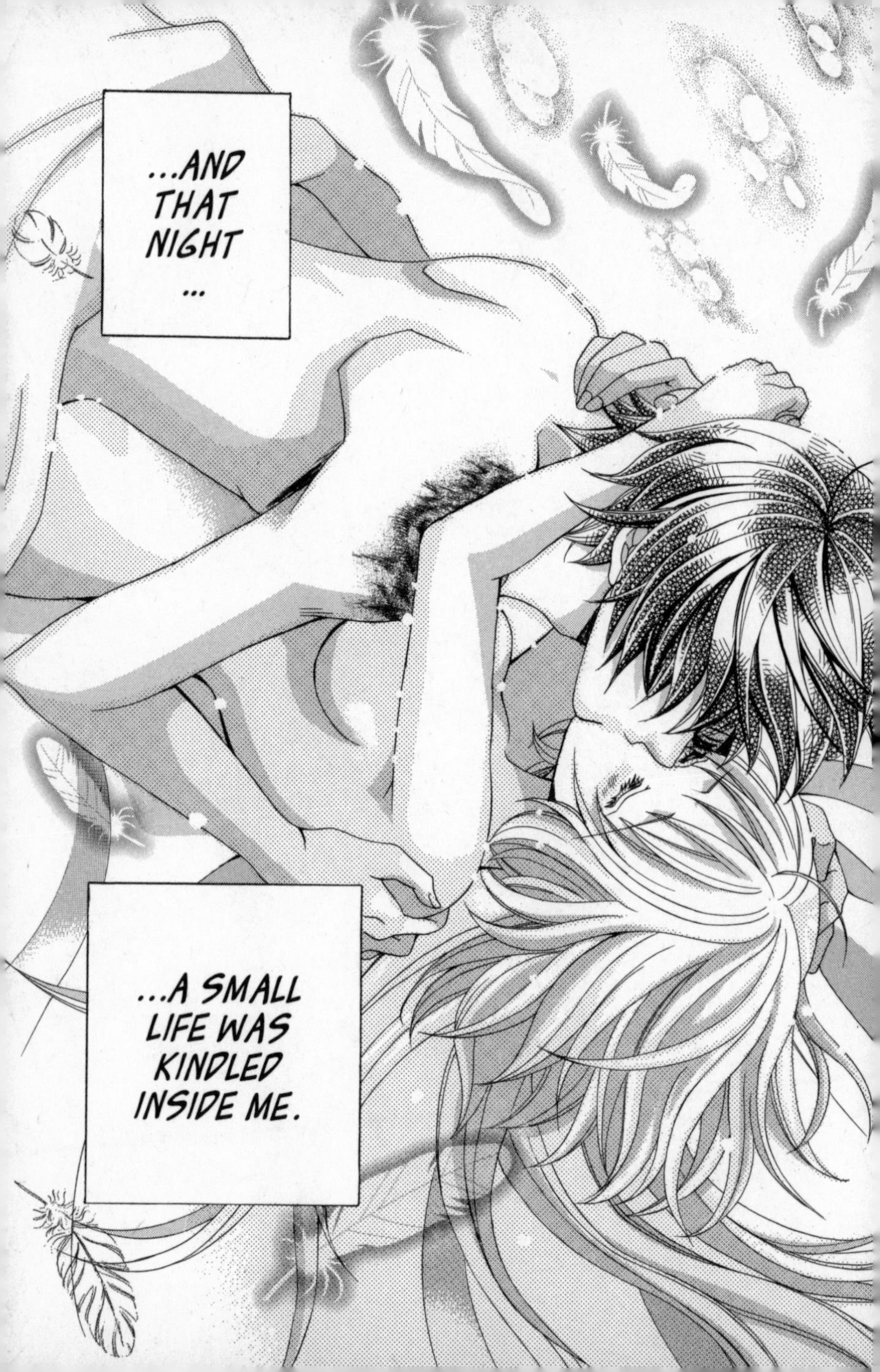
...AND THAT NIGHT ...
...A SMALL LIFE WAS KINDLED INSIDE ME.

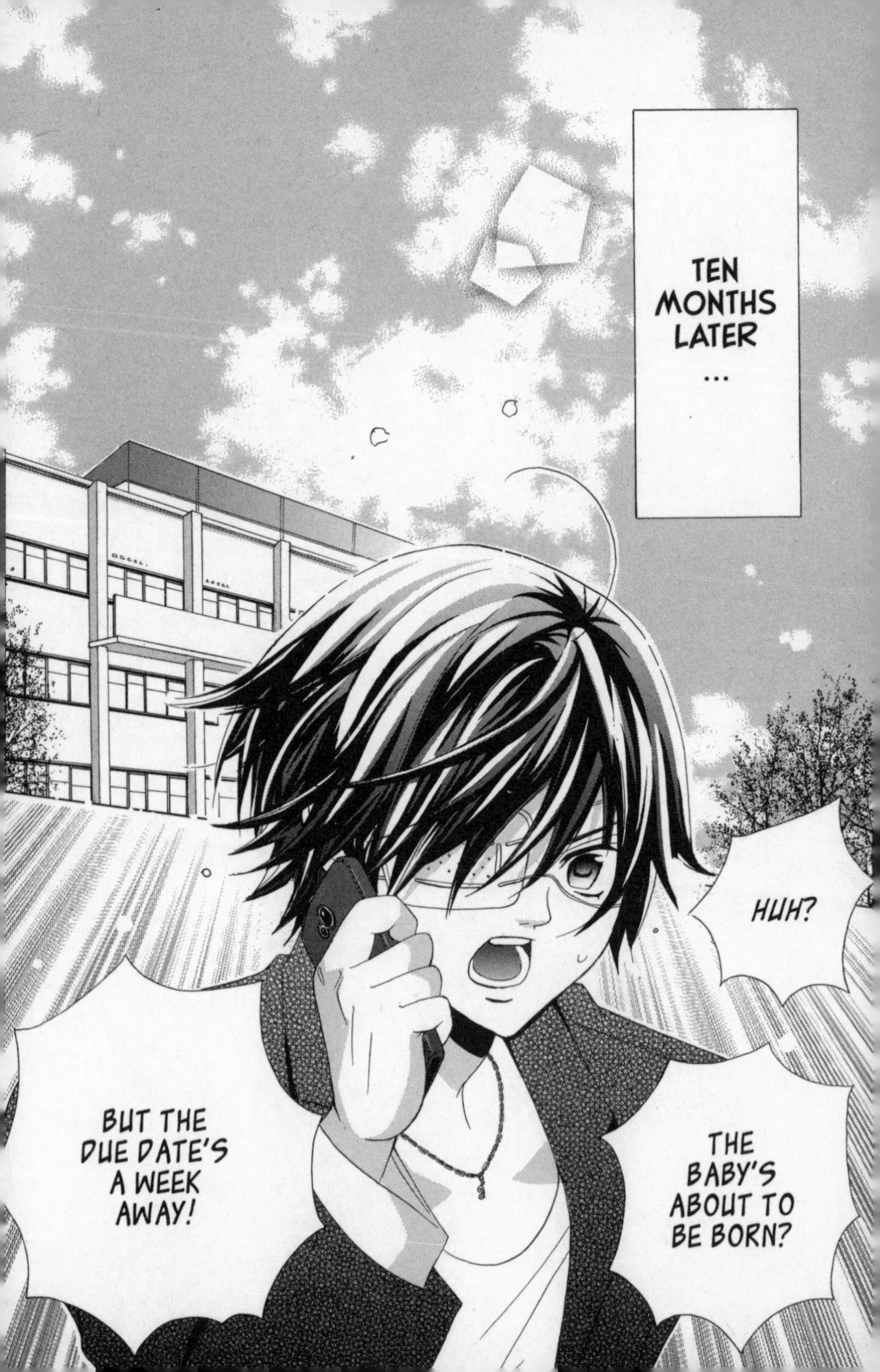
TEN MONTHS LATER ...
HUH?
THE BABY'S ABOUT TO BE BORN?
BUT THE DUE DATE'S A WEEK AWAY!

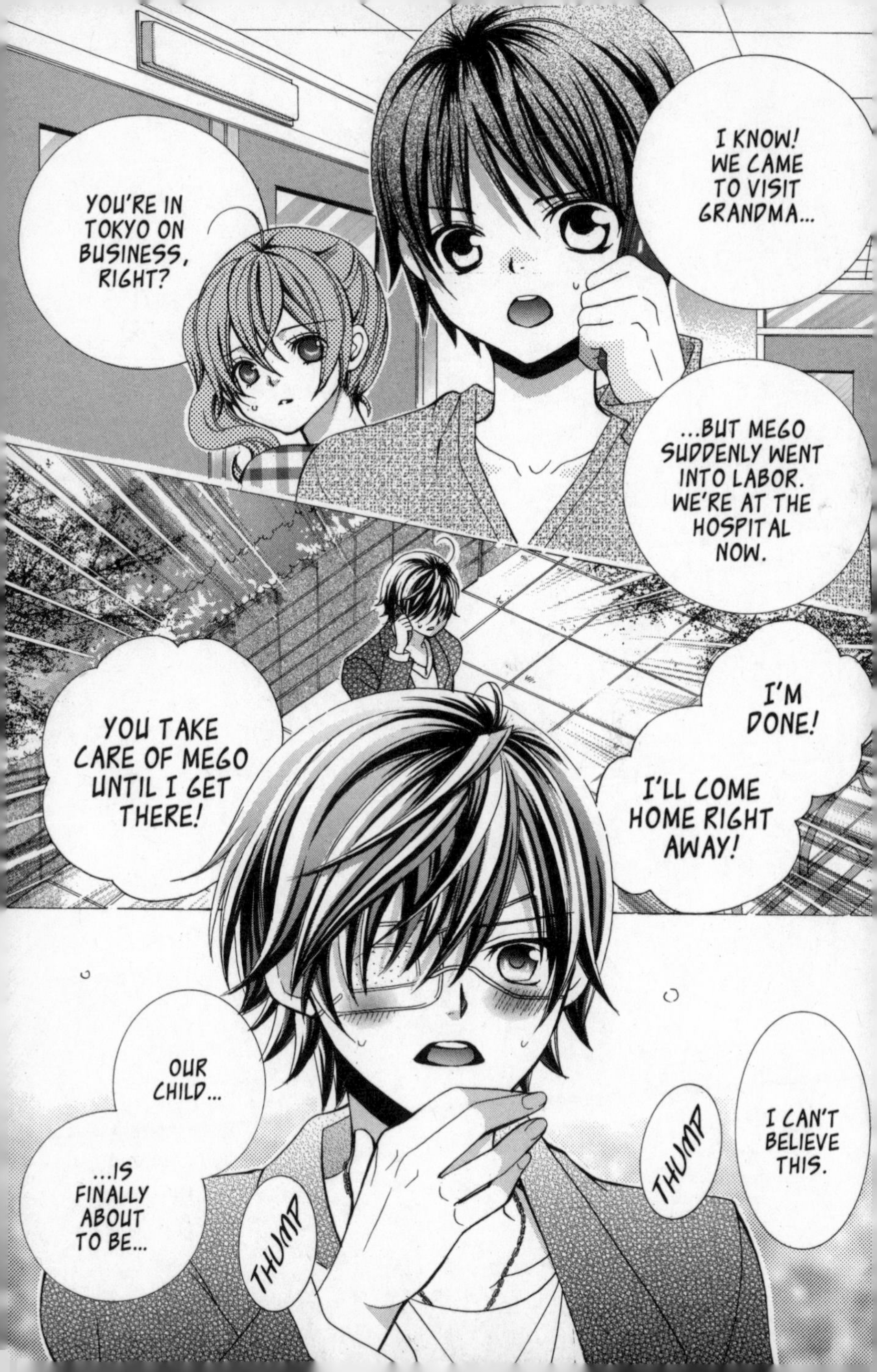
I KNOW! WE CAME TO VISIT GRANDMA...
YOU'RE IN TOKYO ON BUSINESS, RIGHT?
...BUT MEGO SUDDENLY WENT INTO LABOR. WE'RE AT THE HOSPITAL NOW.
I'M DONE!
I'LL COME HOME RIGHT AWAY!
YOU TAKE CARE OF MEGO UNTIL I GET THERE!
I CAN'T BELIEVE THIS.
THUMP
THUMP
OUR CHILD...
...IS FINALLY ABOUT TO BE...

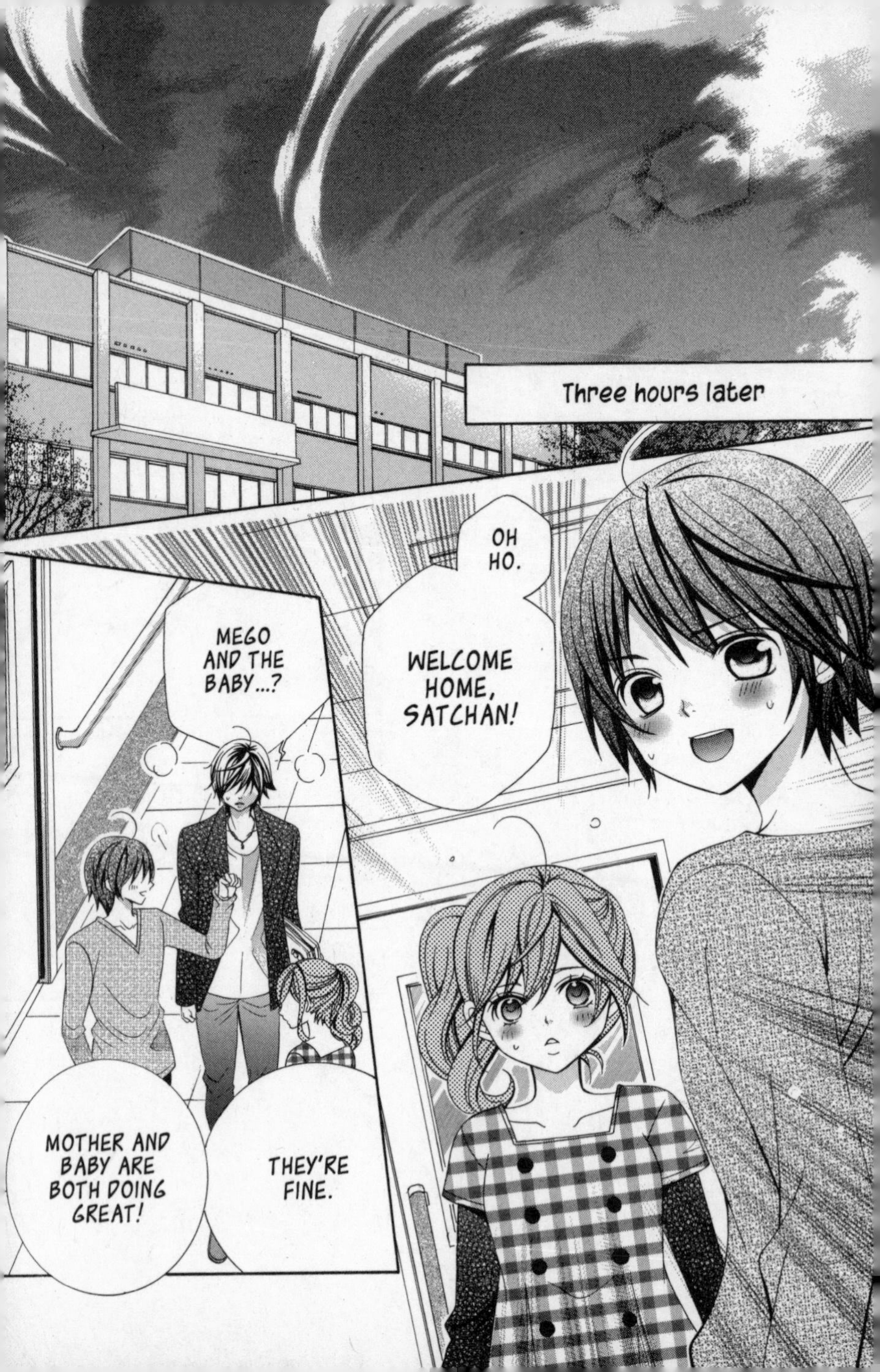
Three hours later
OH HO.
WELCOME HOME, SATCHAN!
MEGO AND THE BABY...?
THEY'RE FINE.
MOTHER AND BABY ARE BOTH DOING GREAT!

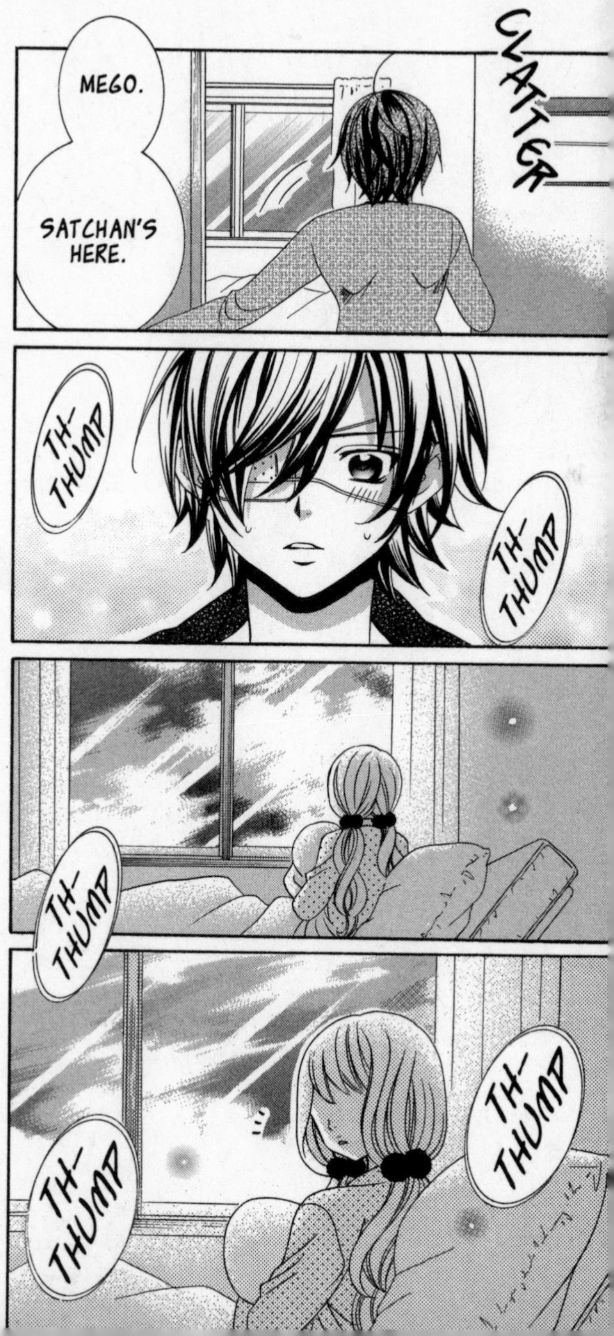
CLATTER
MEGO.
SATCHAN'S HERE.
TH-THUMP
TH-THUMP
TH-THUMP
TH-THUMP
TH-THUMP

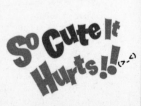

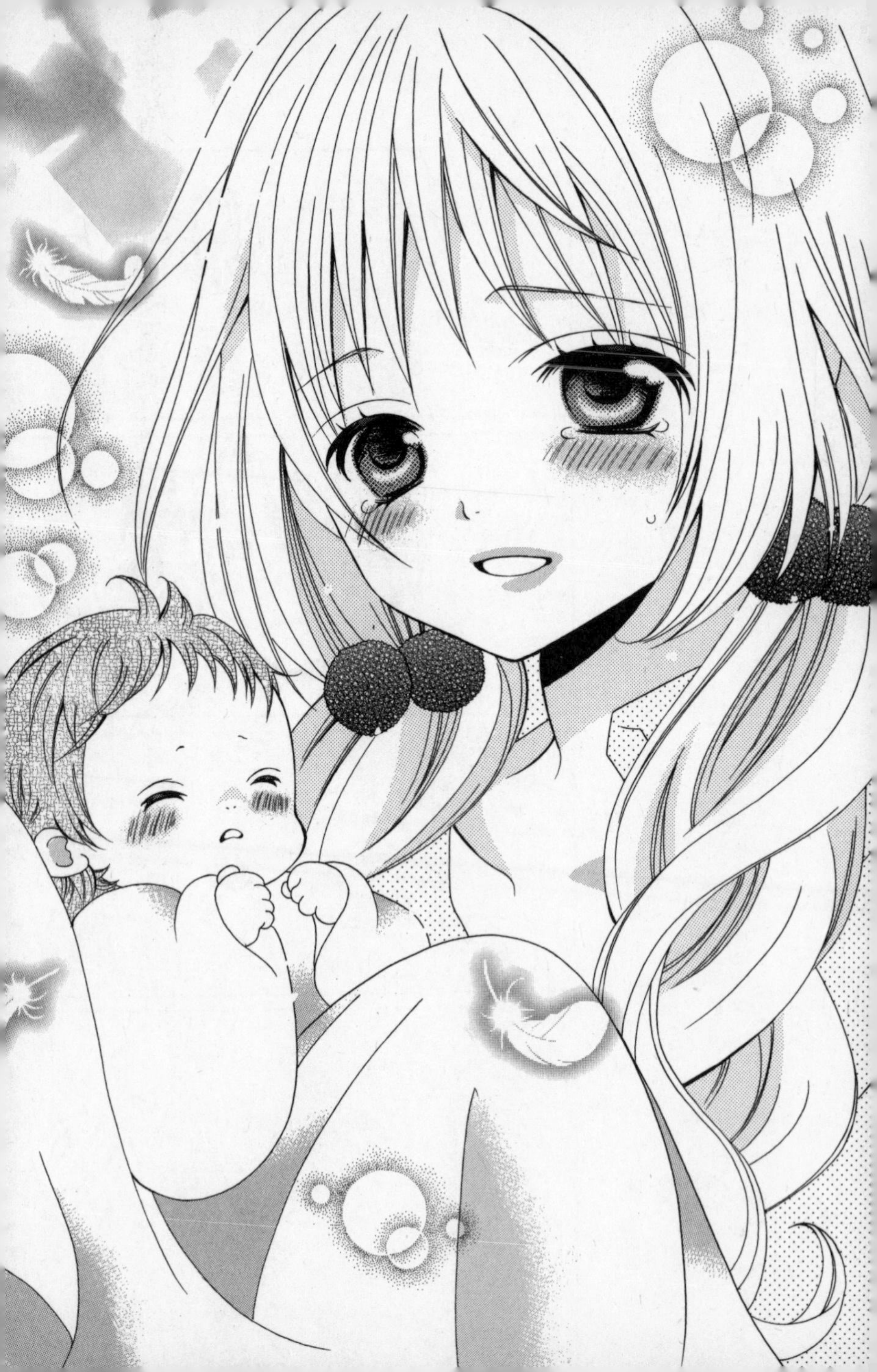

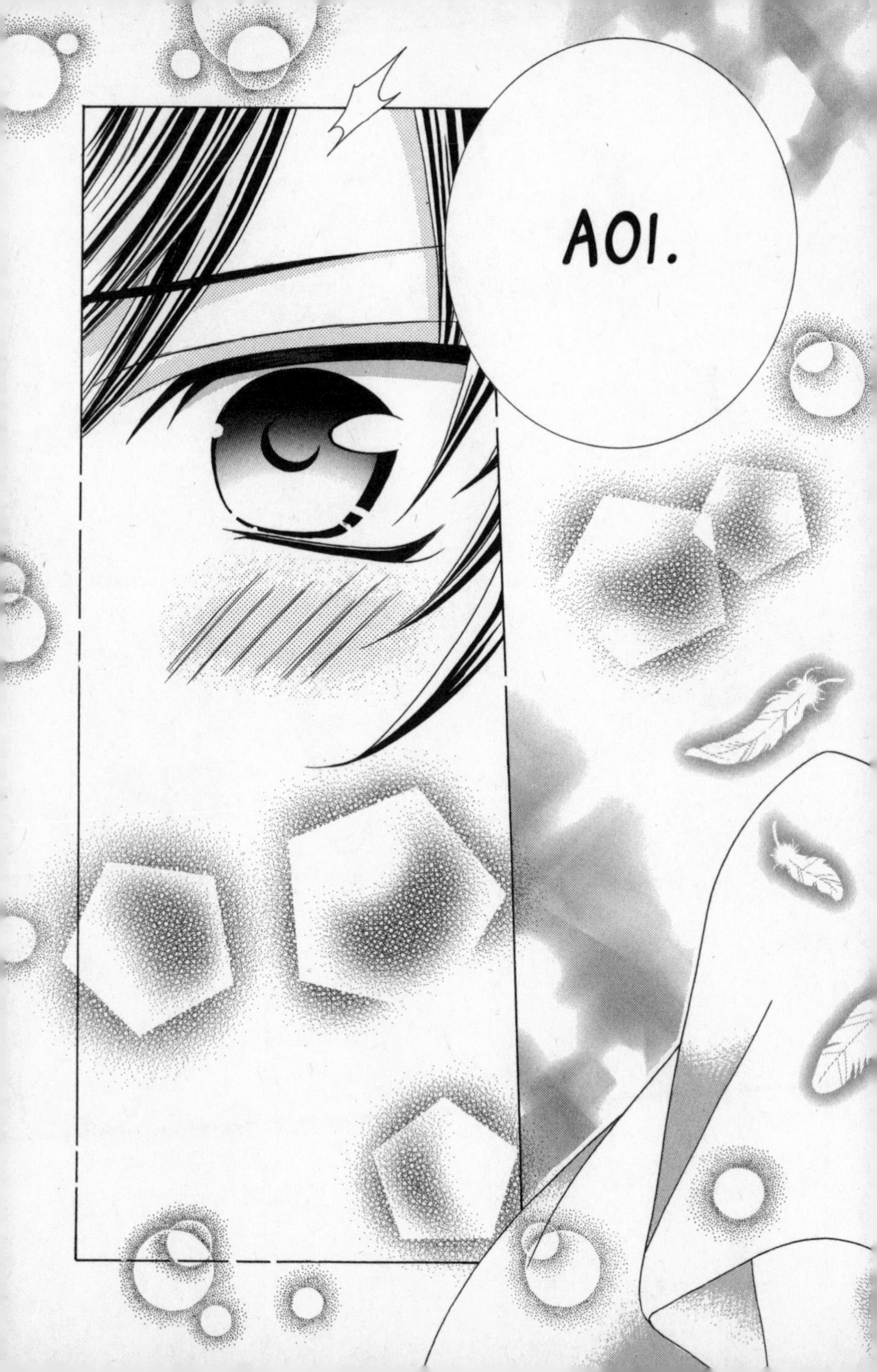
AOI.

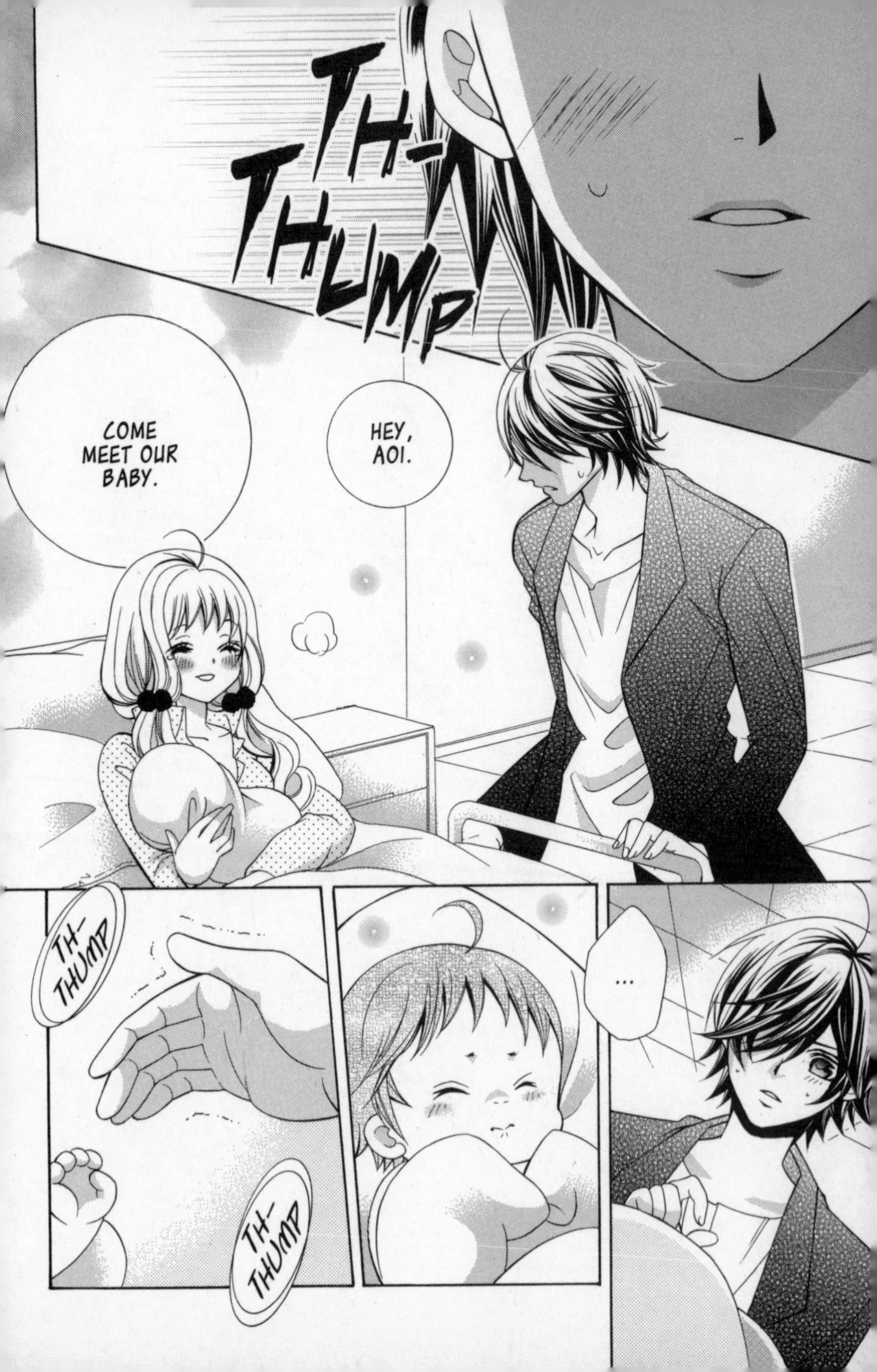
TH-THUMP
HEY, AOI.
COME MEET OUR BABY.
...
TH-THUMP
TH-THUMP

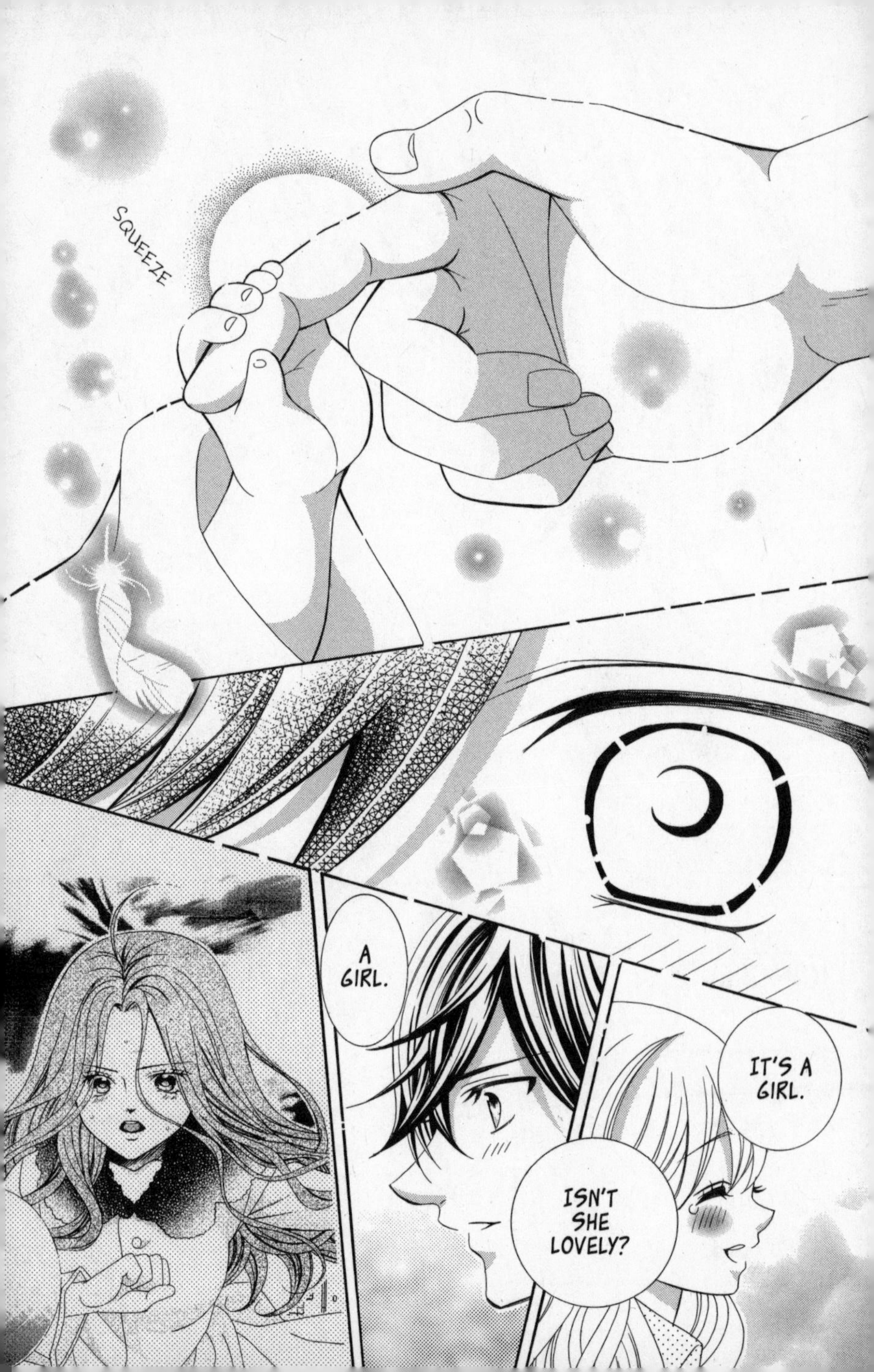
SQUEEZE
IT'S A GIRL.
ISN'T SHE LOVELY?
A GIRL.

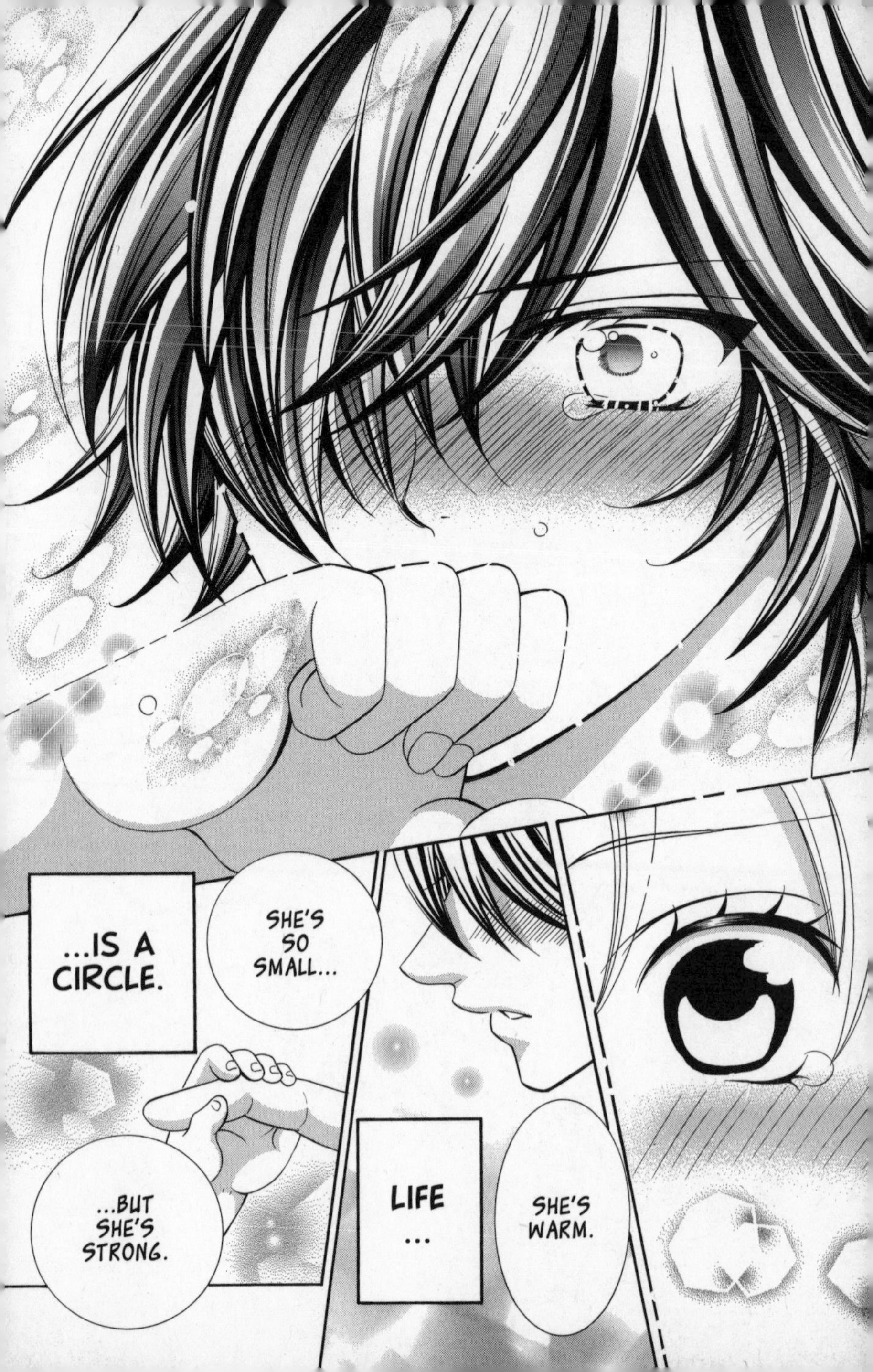
SHE'S WARM.
LIFE ...
SHE'S SO SMALL...
...IS A CIRCLE.
...BUT SHE'S STRONG.

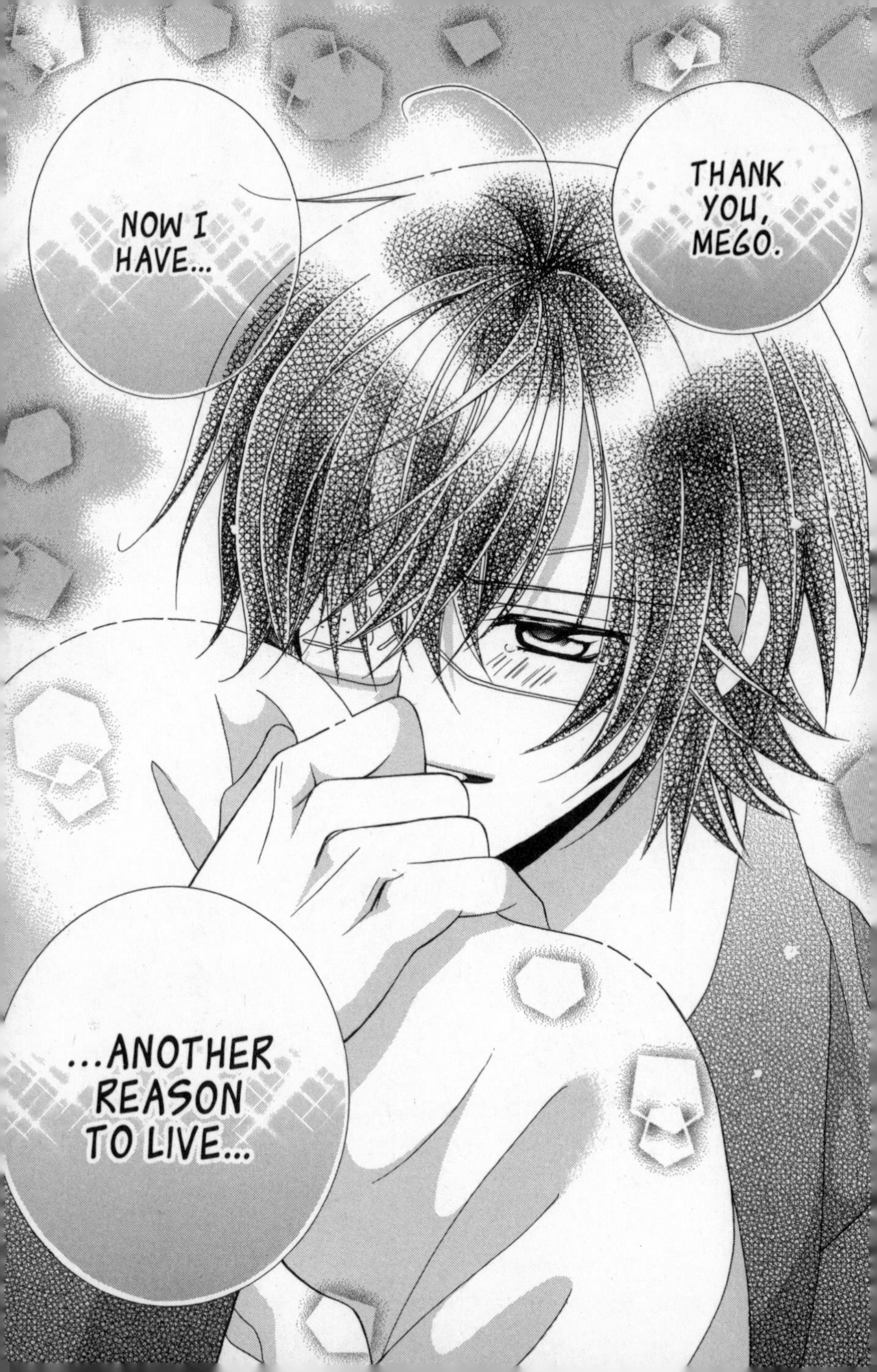
THANK YOU, MEGO.
NOW I HAVE...
...ANOTHER REASON TO LIVE...

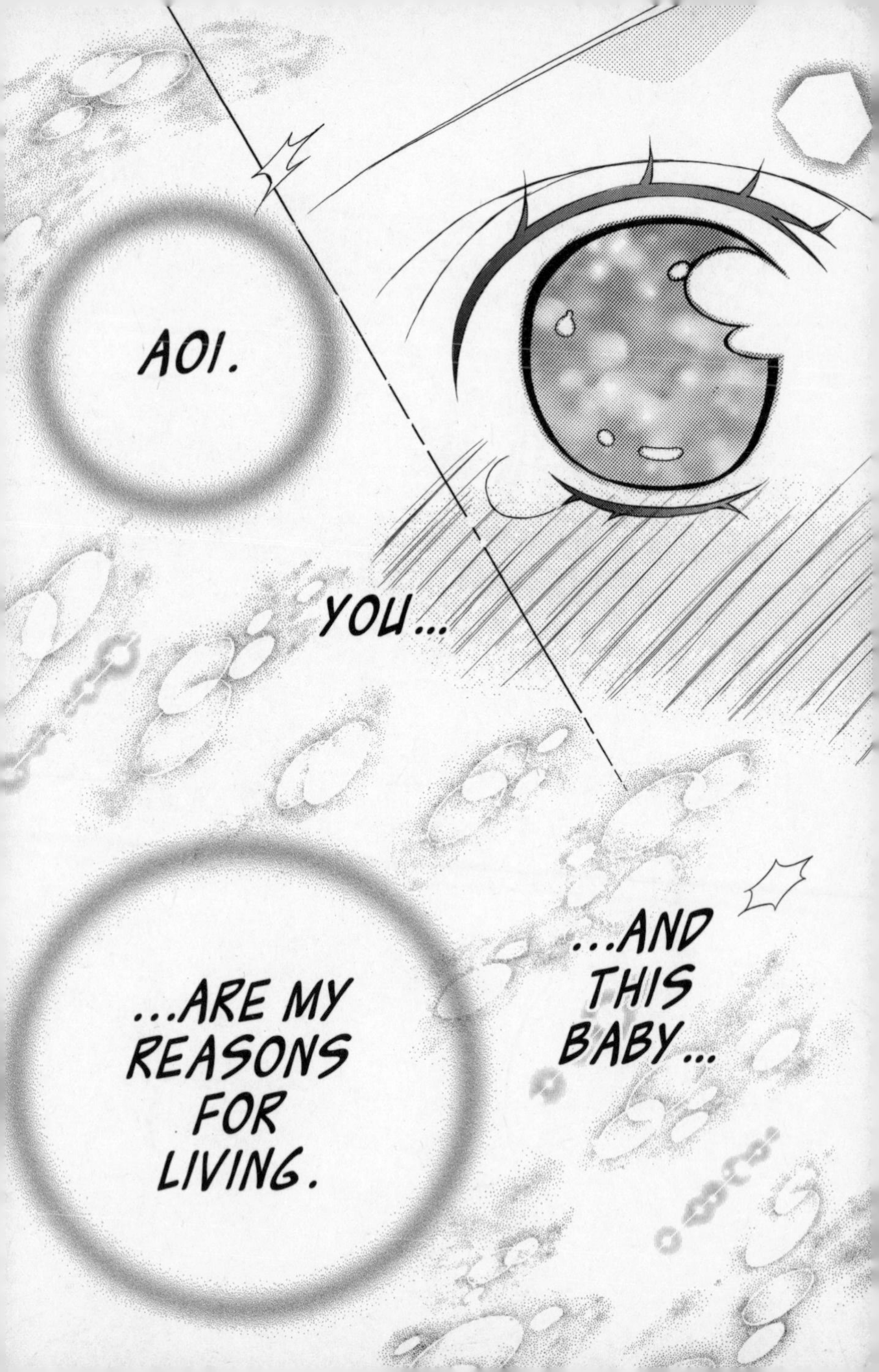
AOI.
YOU...
...AND THIS BABY...
...ARE MY REASONS FOR LIVING.

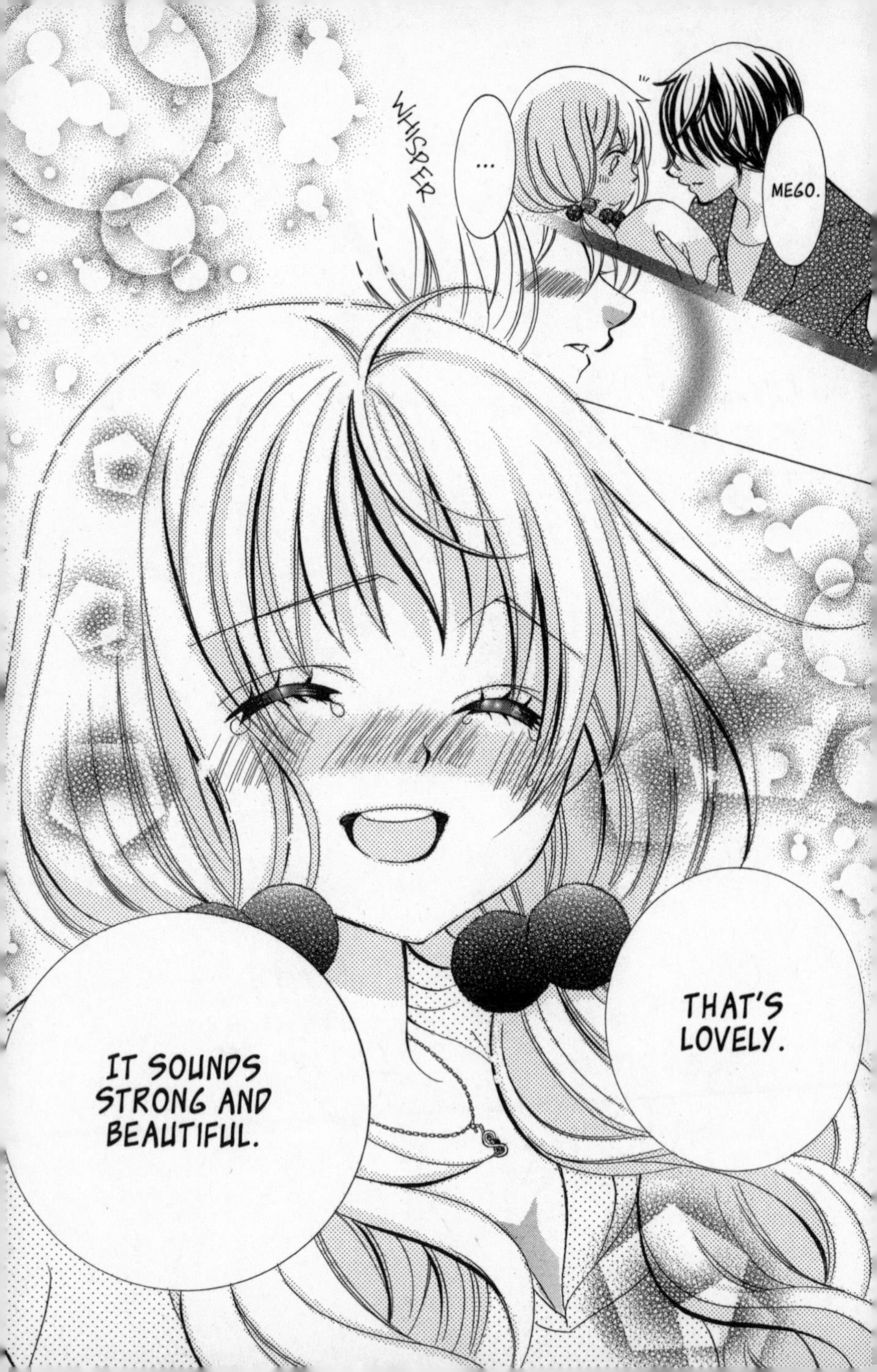
MEGO.
...
WHISPER
THAT'S LOVELY.
IT SOUNDS STRONG AND BEAUTIFUL.

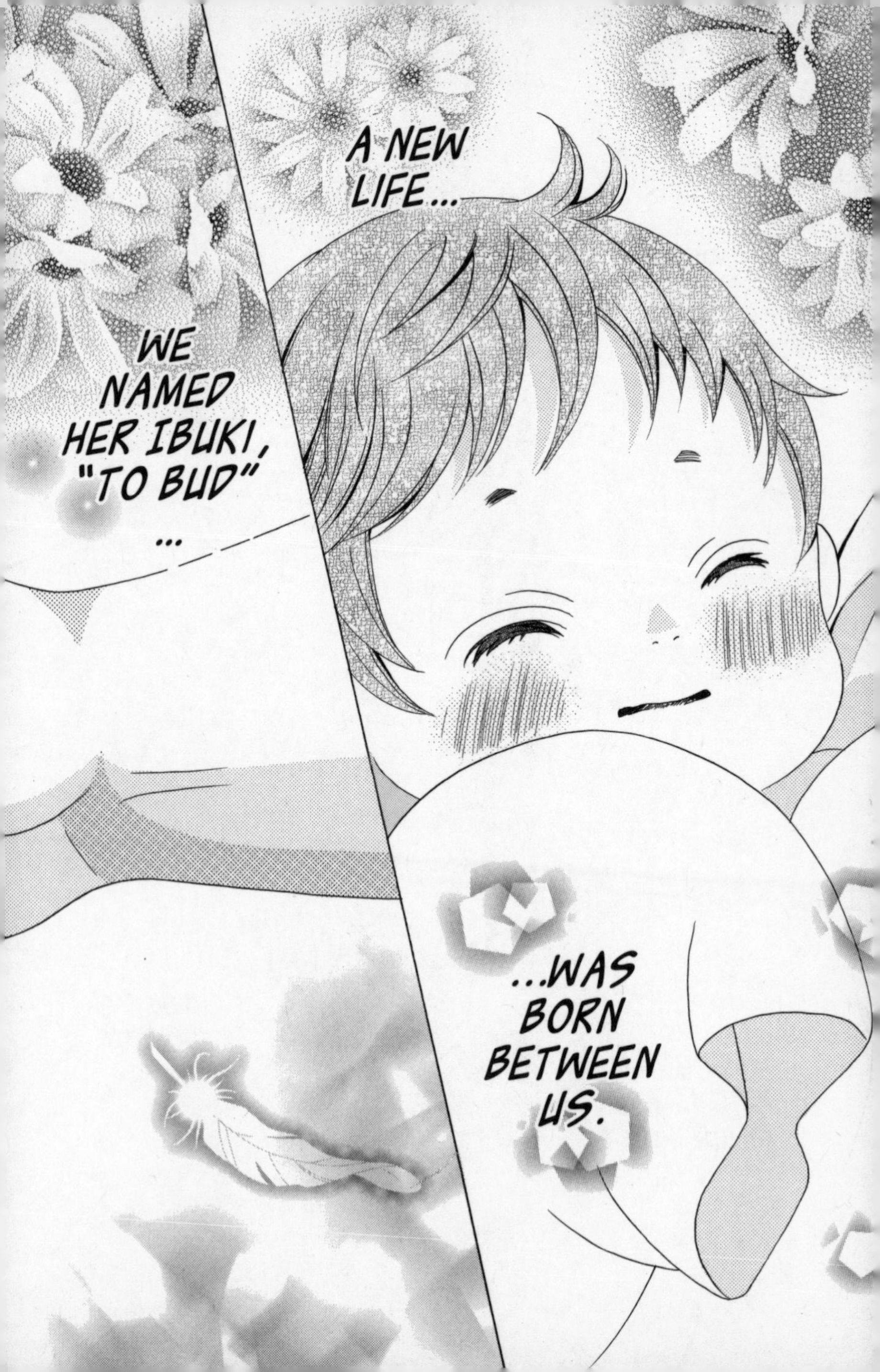
A NEW LIFE...
...WAS BORN BETWEEN US.
WE NAMED HER IBUKI, "TO BUD" ...

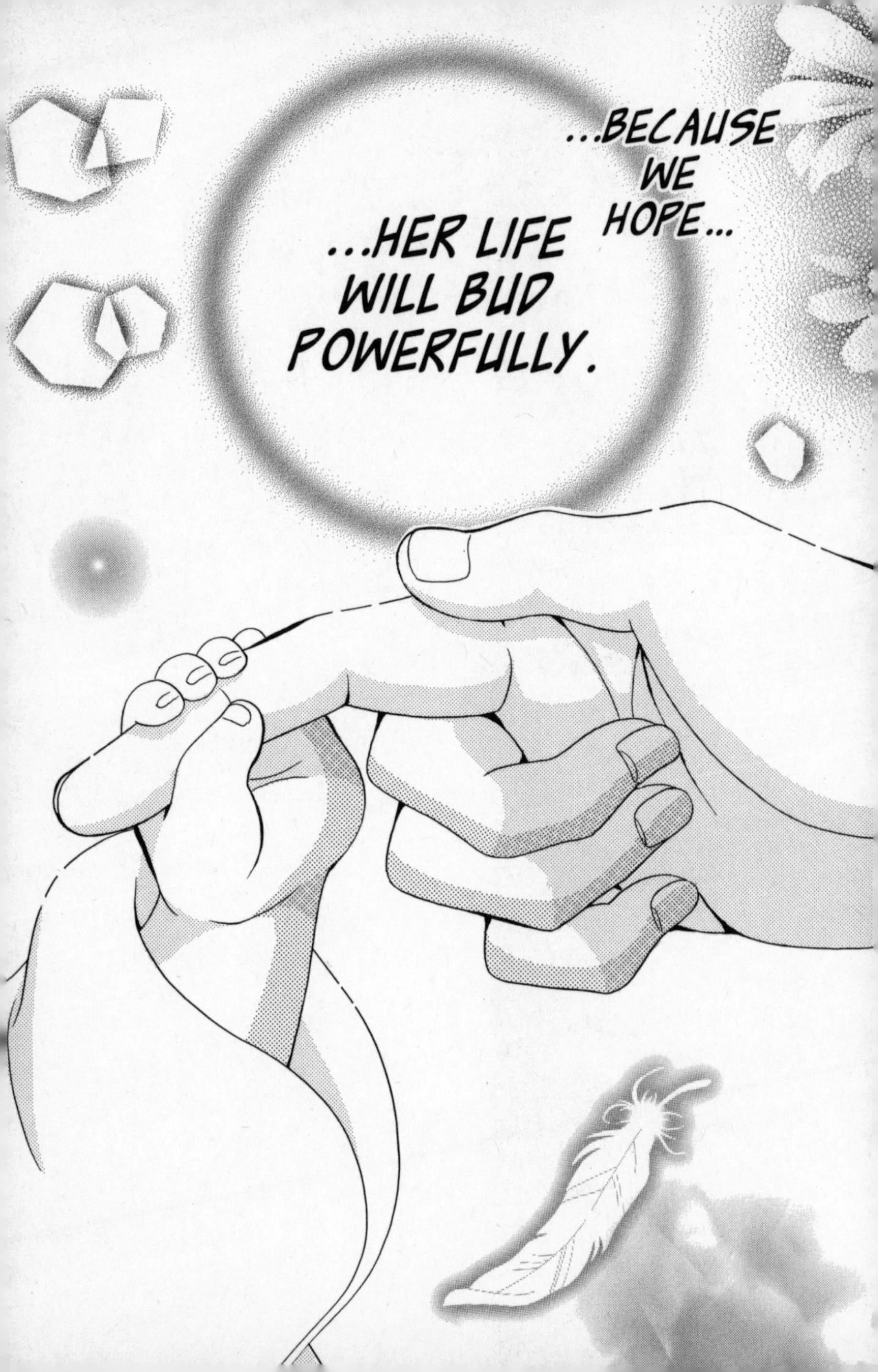
...BECAUSE WE HOPE...
...HER LIFE WILL BUD POWERFULLY.

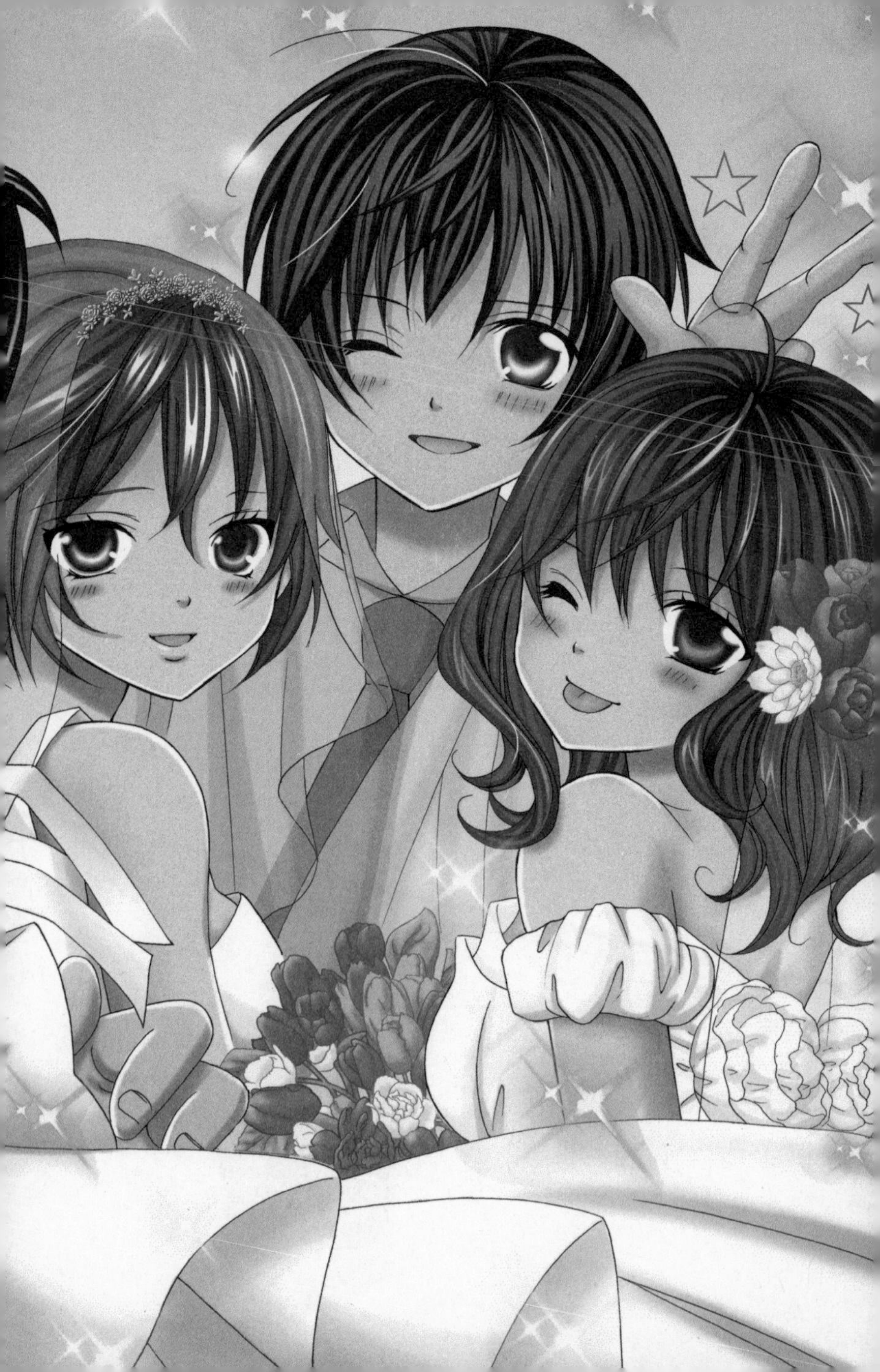

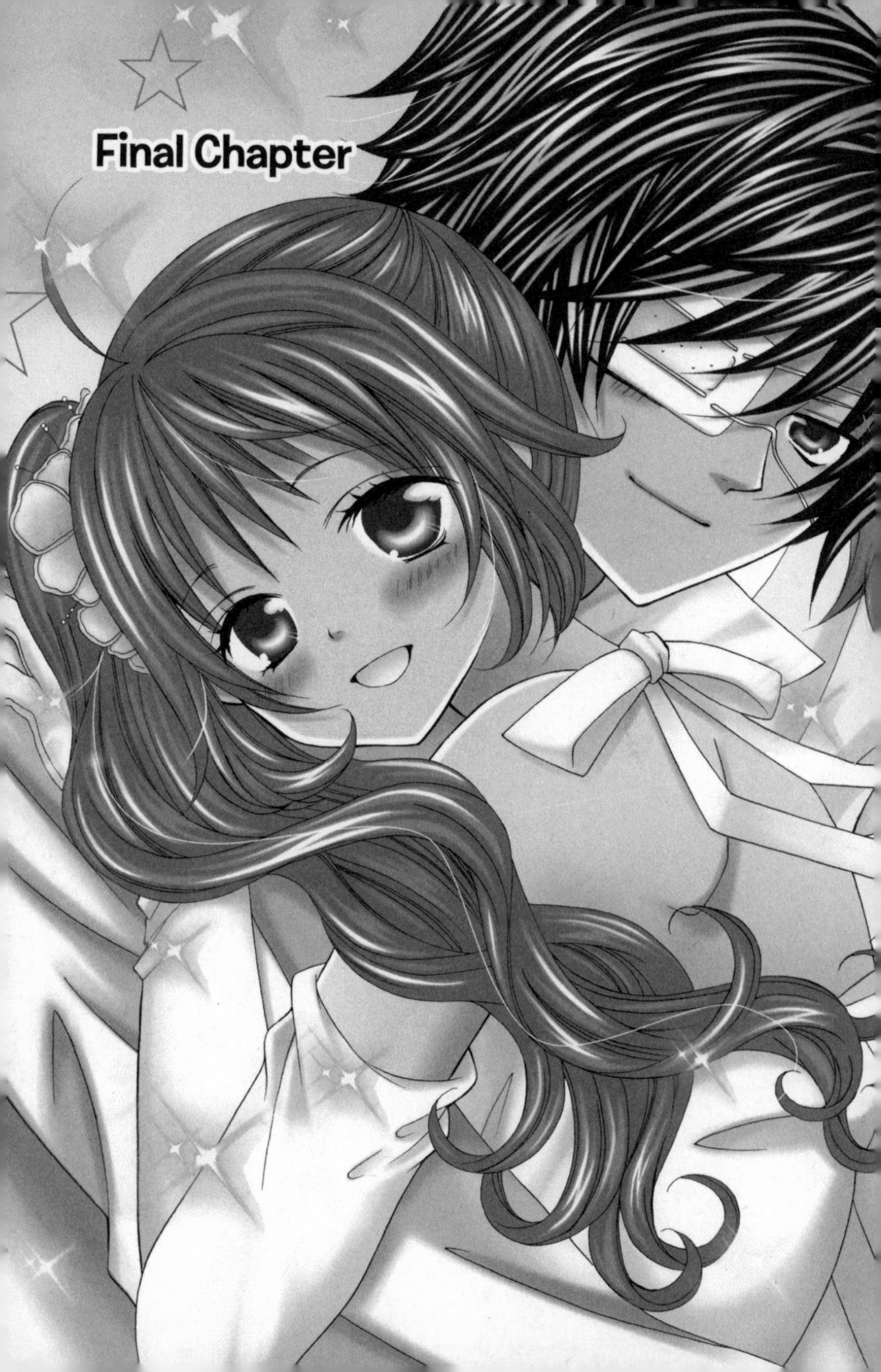
Final Chapter

So Cute! Fan Art Feature ♥

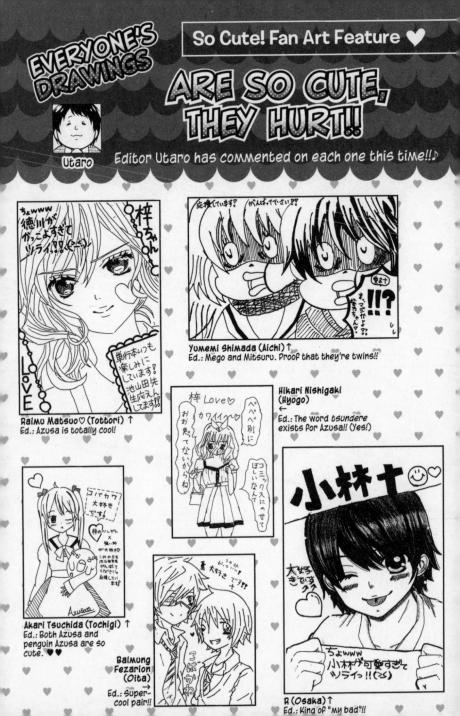

EVERYONE'S DRAWINGS ARE SO CUTE, THEY HURT!!

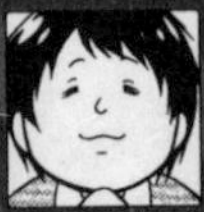

Utaro

Editor Utaro has commented on each one this time!!♪

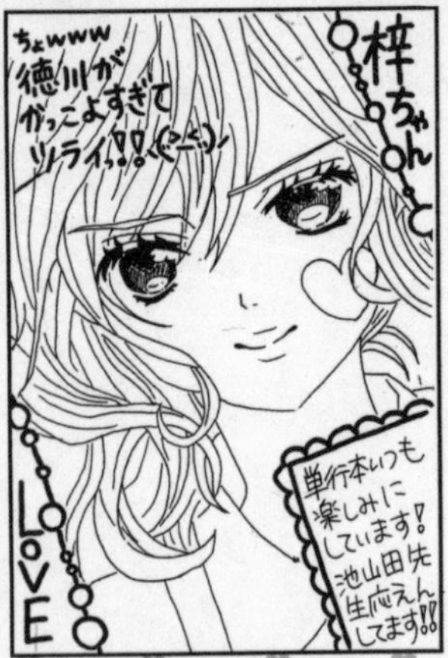
ちょwww
徳川がかっこよすぎてツライっ!!
梓ちゃん
LOVE
単行本いつも楽しみにしています! 池山田先生応えんしてます!!

Raimu Matsuo♡ (Tottori) ↑
Ed.: Azusa is totally cool!

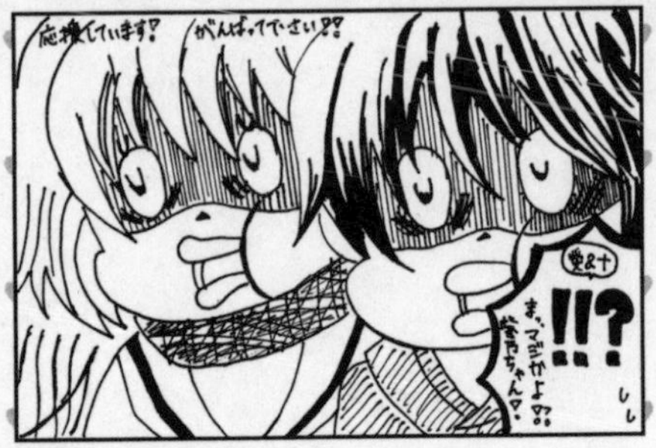
!!?

Yumemi Shimada (Aichi) ↑
Ed.: Mego and Mitsuru. Proof that they're twins!!

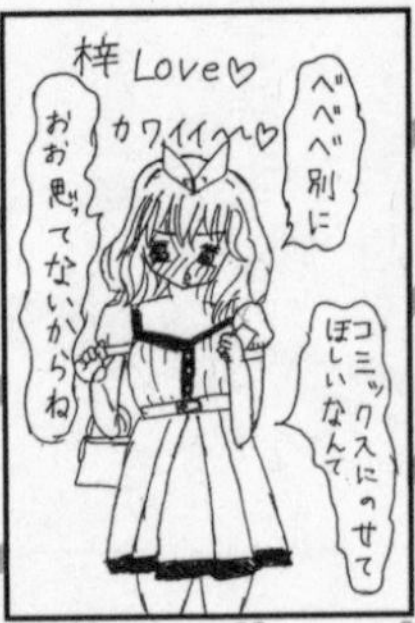
梓 Love♡
カワイイ〜♡
べべべ別に
おお思ってないからね
コミックスにのせてほしいなんて

Hikari Nishigaki (Hyogo) ←
Ed.: The word *tsundere* exists for Azusa!! (Yes!)

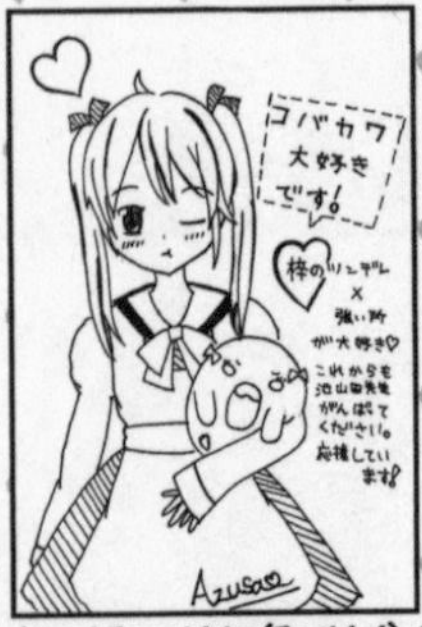
コバカワ大好きです!
Azusa

Akari Tsuchida (Tochigi) ↑
Ed.: Both Azusa and penguin Azusa are so cute. ♥♥

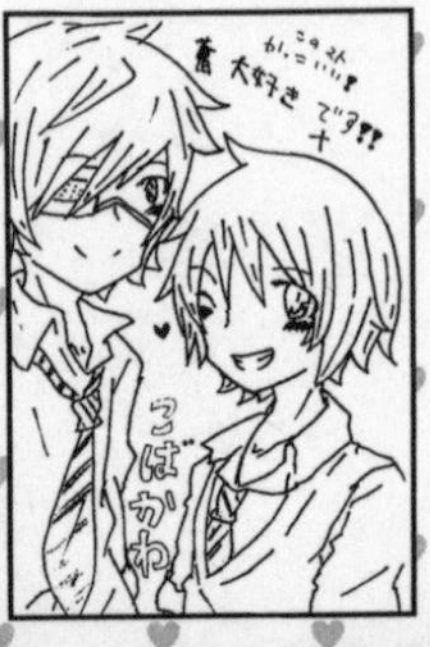
蒼 大好きです!!
こばかわ

Balmung Fezarion (Oita) →
Ed.: Super-cool pair!!

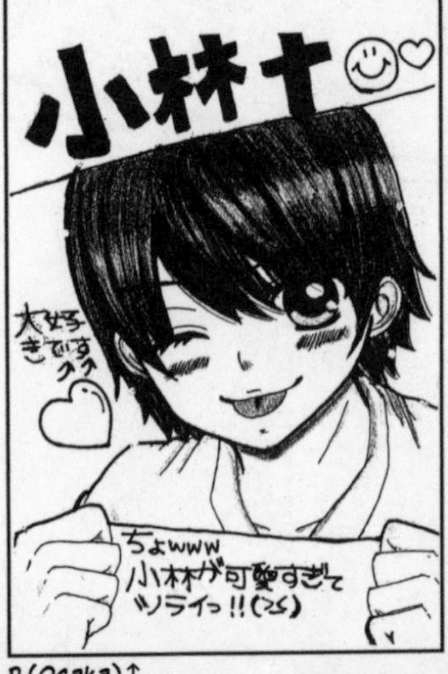
小林十
大好きです
ちょwww
小林が可愛すぎてツライっ!!

R (Osaka) ↑
Ed.: King of "my bad"!!

TEN
MONTHS
OLD.

IBUKI
SANADA.

THANK YOU FOR ALWAYS SENDING ME
LOVELY LETTERS AND DRAWINGS.

I RECEIVED MANY LETTERS WHERE READERS WROTE THEIR
SERIOUS AND SINCERE THOUGHTS ABOUT VOLUMES 13 AND
14. THESE LETTERS REALLY GAVE ME LOTS OF COURAGE.
I HOPE YOU SEND YOUR THOUGHTS ABOUT THIS SERIES
AFTER READING VOLUME 15.

GO IKEYAMADA
C/O SHOJO BEAT
VIZ MEDIA, LLC
P.O. BOX 77010
SAN FRANCISCO, CA
94107

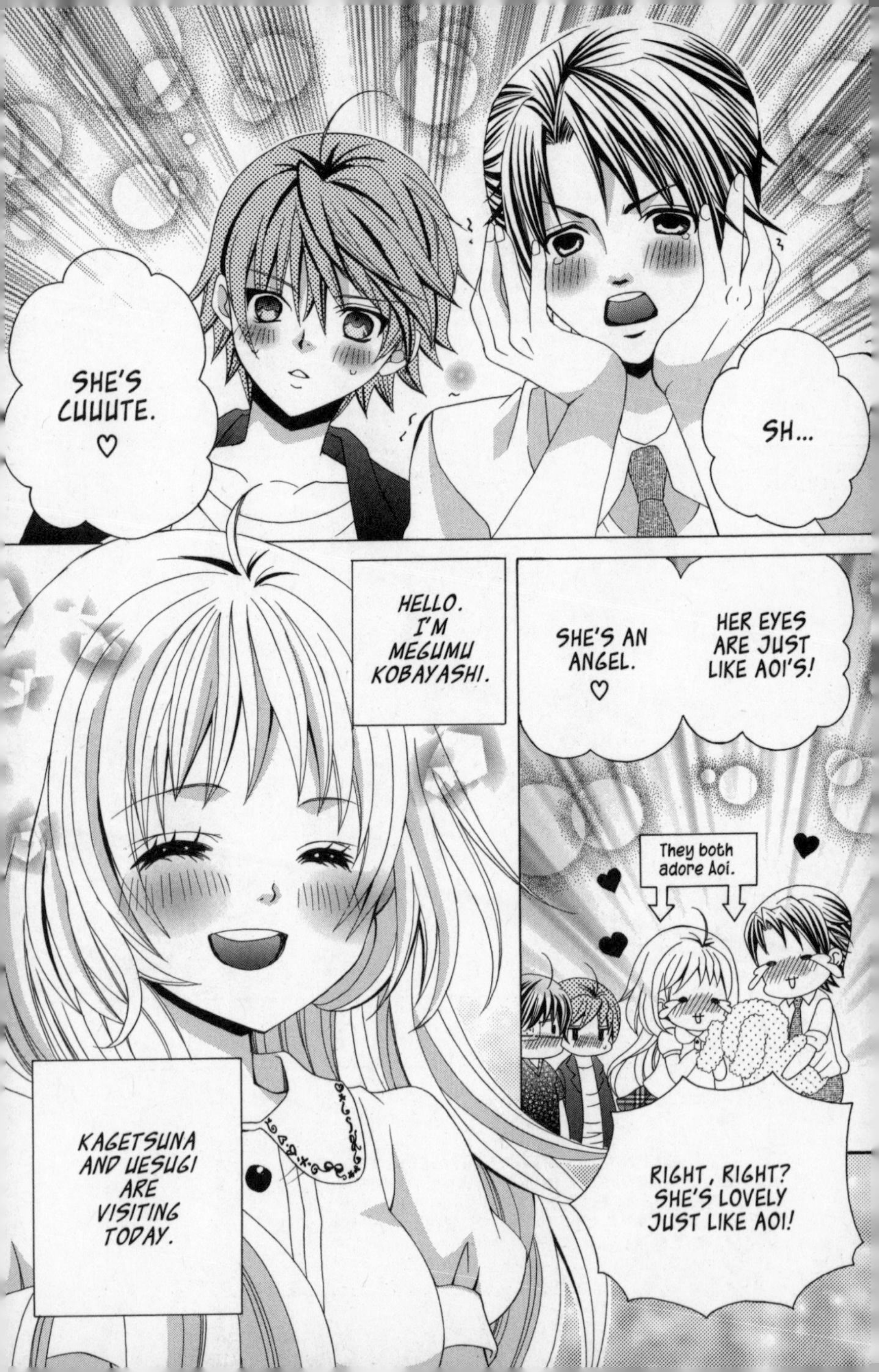
SH...
SHE'S CUUUTE. ♡
HER EYES ARE JUST LIKE AOI'S!
SHE'S AN ANGEL. ♡
They both adore Aoi.
RIGHT, RIGHT? SHE'S LOVELY JUST LIKE AOI!
HELLO. I'M MEGUMU KOBAYASHI.
KAGETSUNA AND UESUGI ARE VISITING TODAY.

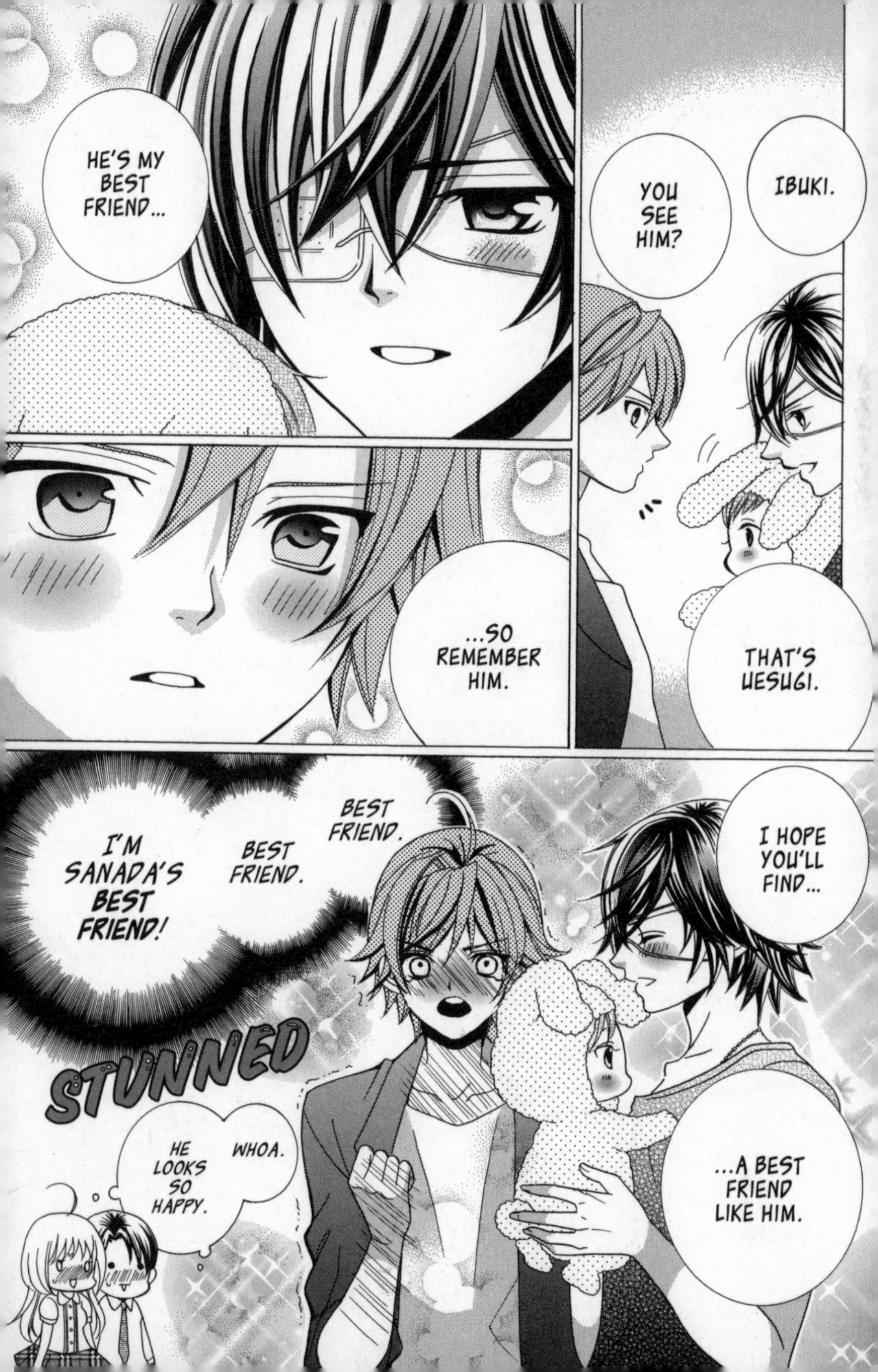
IBUKI.
YOU SEE HIM?
THAT'S UESUGI.
HE'S MY BEST FRIEND...
...SO REMEMBER HIM.
I HOPE YOU'LL FIND...
BEST FRIEND.
BEST FRIEND.
I'M SANADA'S BEST FRIEND!
...A BEST FRIEND LIKE HIM.
STUNNED
WHOA.
HE LOOKS SO HAPPY.

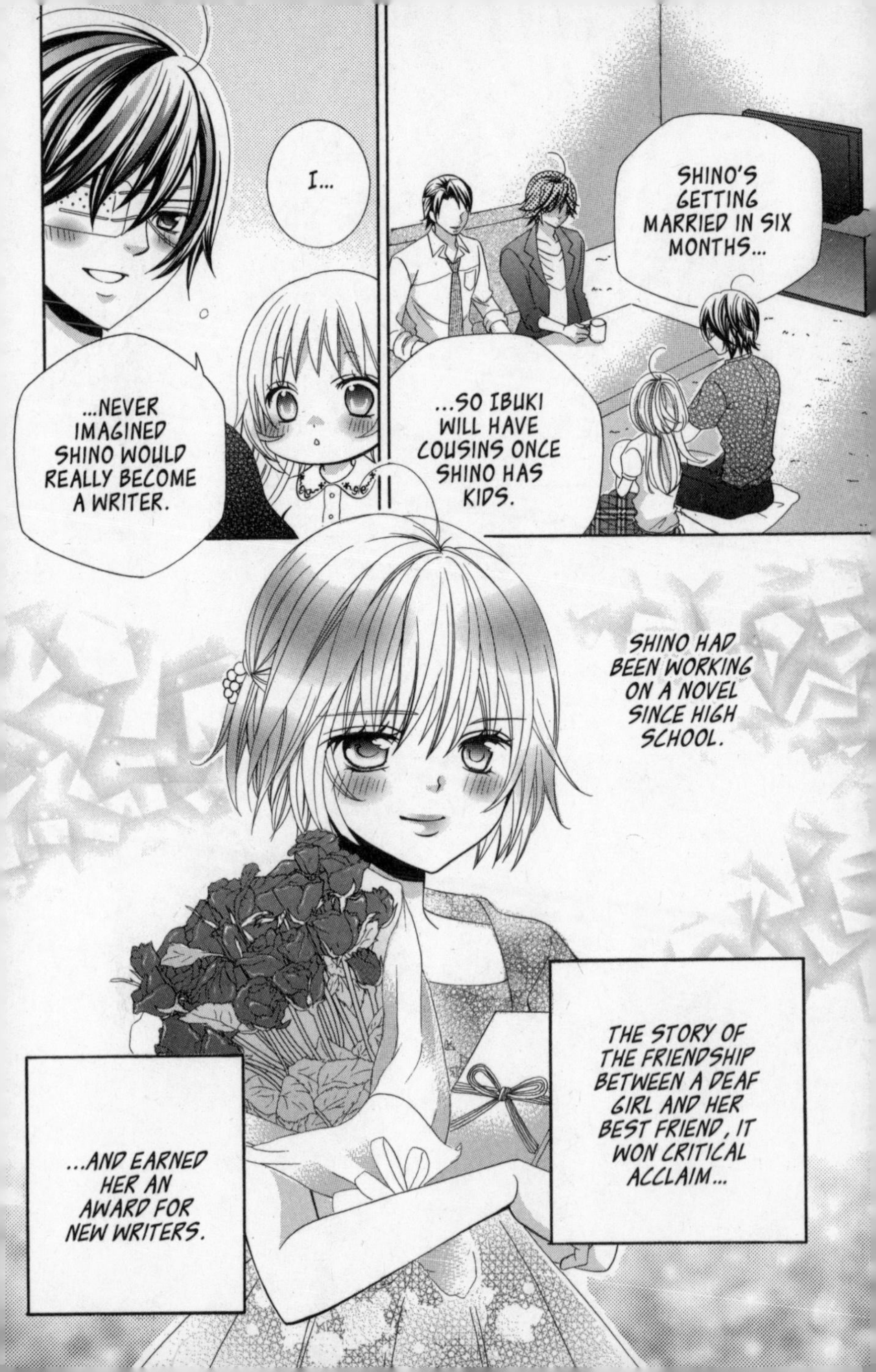
SHINO'S GETTING MARRIED IN SIX MONTHS...
...SO IBUKI WILL HAVE COUSINS ONCE SHINO HAS KIDS.
I...
...NEVER IMAGINED SHINO WOULD REALLY BECOME A WRITER.
SHINO HAD BEEN WORKING ON A NOVEL SINCE HIGH SCHOOL.
THE STORY OF THE FRIENDSHIP BETWEEN A DEAF GIRL AND HER BEST FRIEND, IT WON CRITICAL ACCLAIM...
...AND EARNED HER AN AWARD FOR NEW WRITERS.

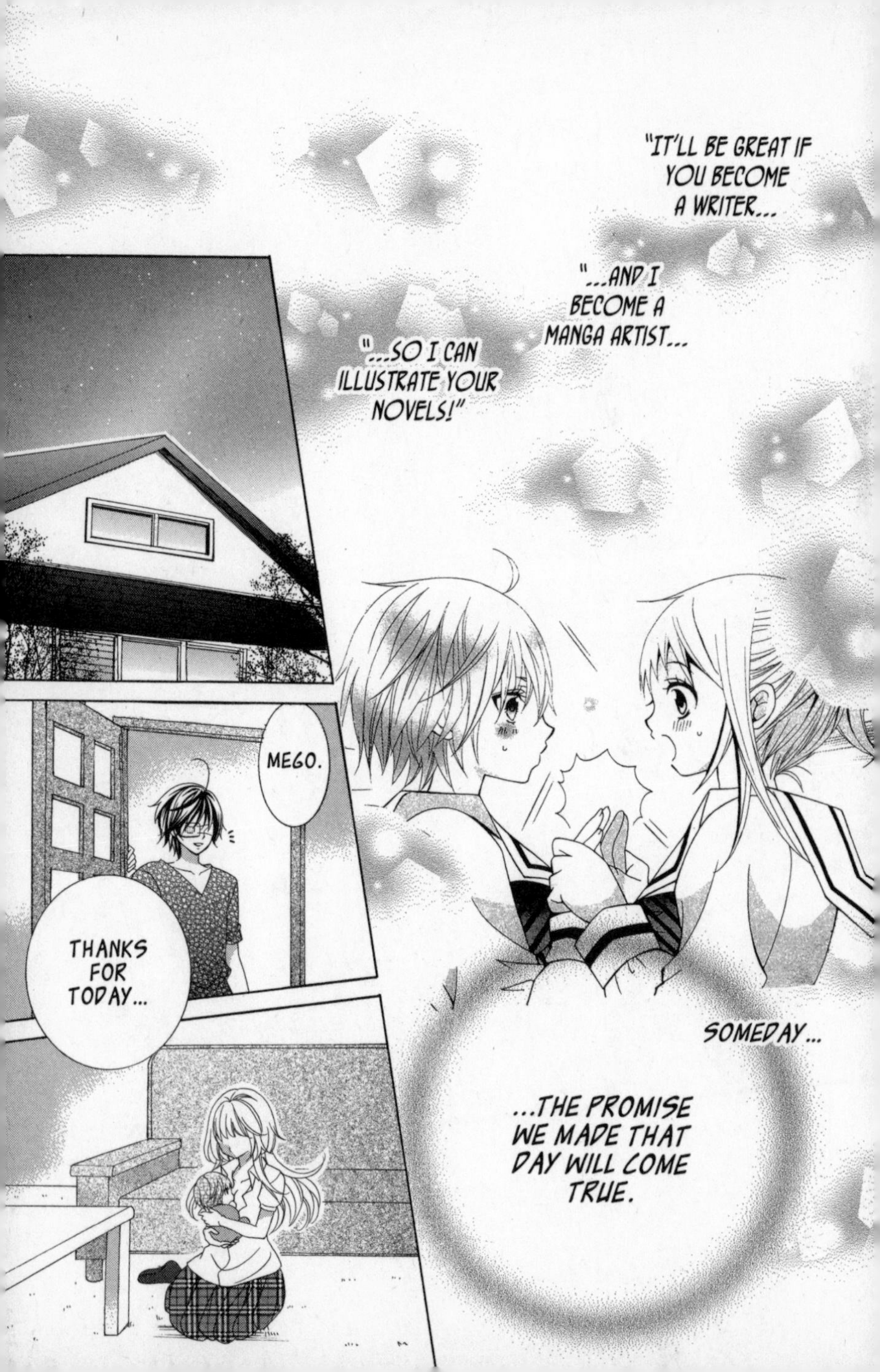
"IT'LL BE GREAT IF YOU BECOME A WRITER...
"...AND I BECOME A MANGA ARTIST...
"...SO I CAN ILLUSTRATE YOUR NOVELS!"
SOMEDAY...
...THE PROMISE WE MADE THAT DAY WILL COME TRUE.
MEGO.
THANKS FOR TODAY...

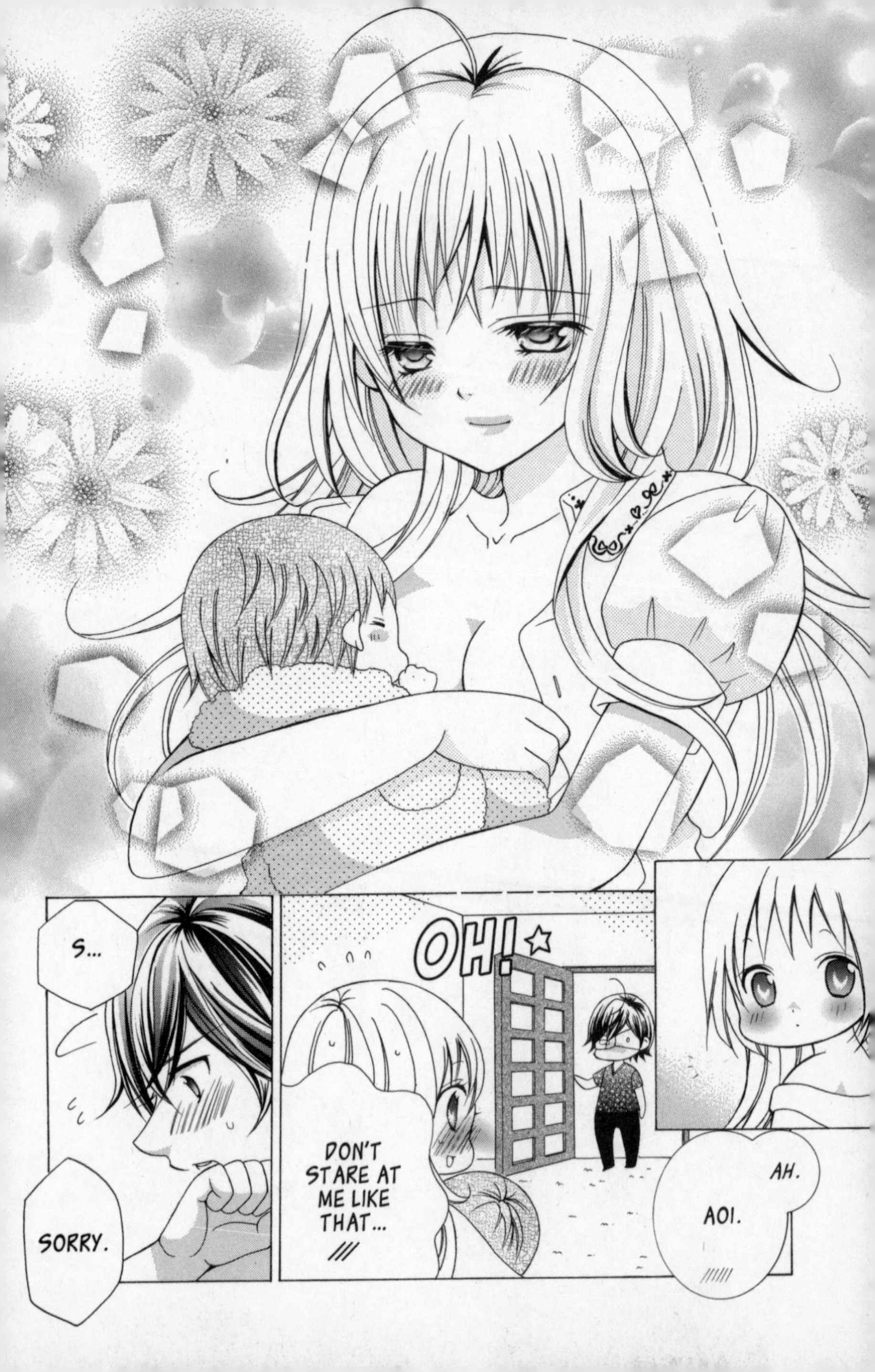
AH.
AOI.
OH!
DON'T STARE AT ME LIKE THAT...
S...
SORRY.

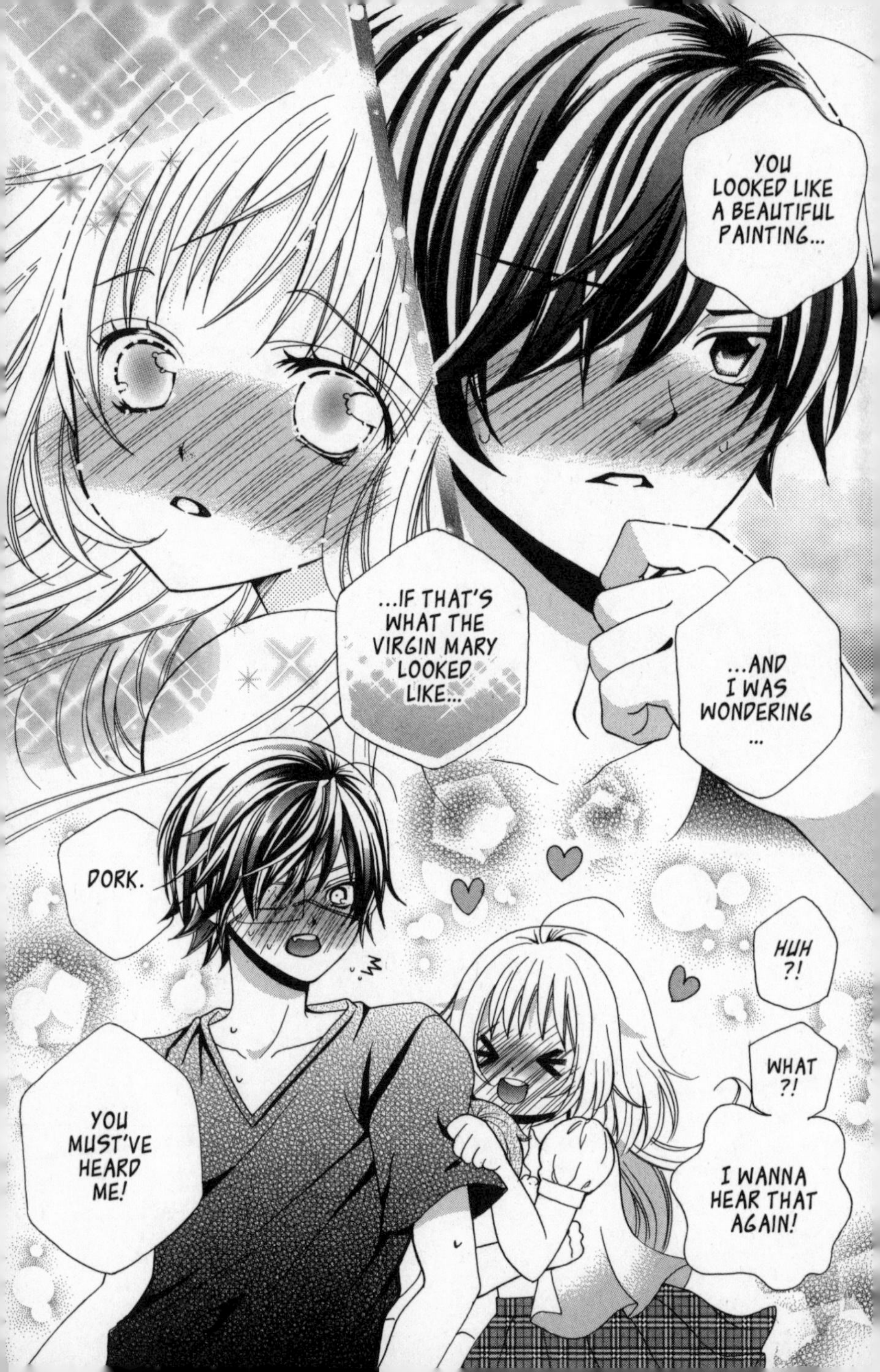
YOU LOOKED LIKE A BEAUTIFUL PAINTING...
...AND I WAS WONDERING...
...IF THAT'S WHAT THE VIRGIN MARY LOOKED LIKE...
DORK.
HUH?!
WHAT?!
I WANNA HEAR THAT AGAIN!
YOU MUST'VE HEARD ME!

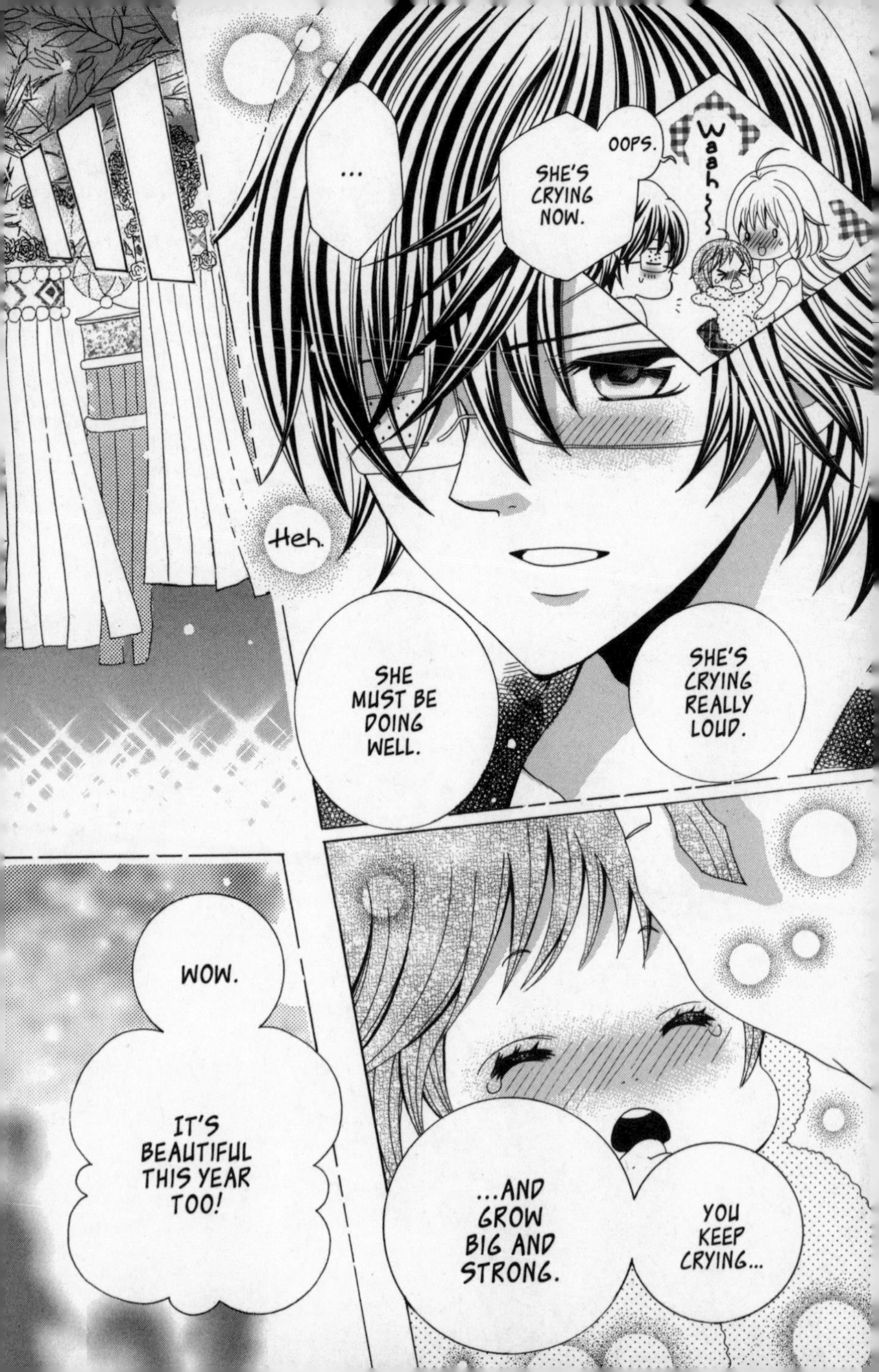
Waah~~~
OOPS.
SHE'S CRYING NOW.
...
Heh.
SHE'S CRYING REALLY LOUD.
SHE MUST BE DOING WELL.
YOU KEEP CRYING...
...AND GROW BIG AND STRONG.
WOW.
IT'S BEAUTIFUL THIS YEAR TOO!

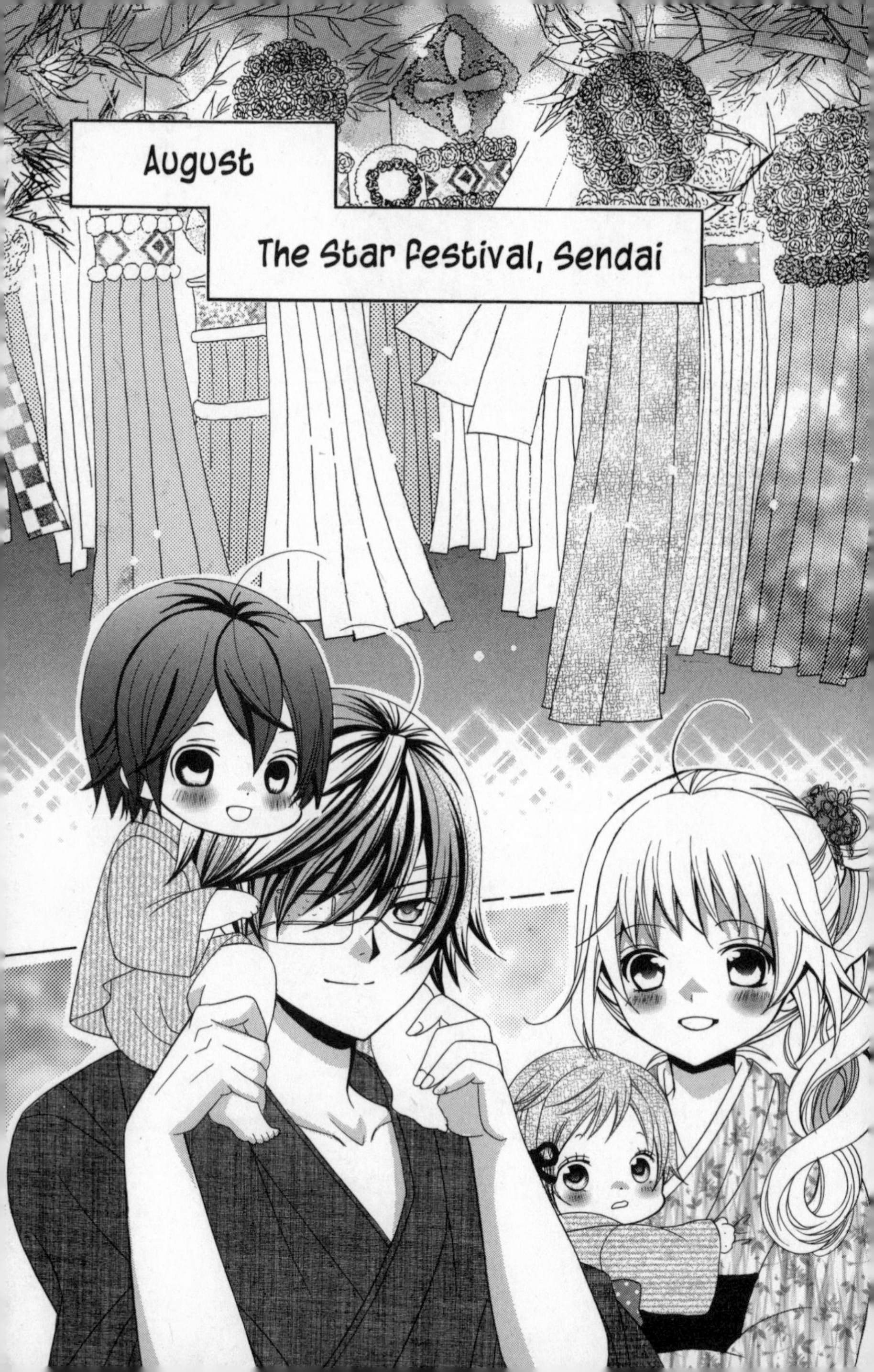
August
The Star Festival, Sendai

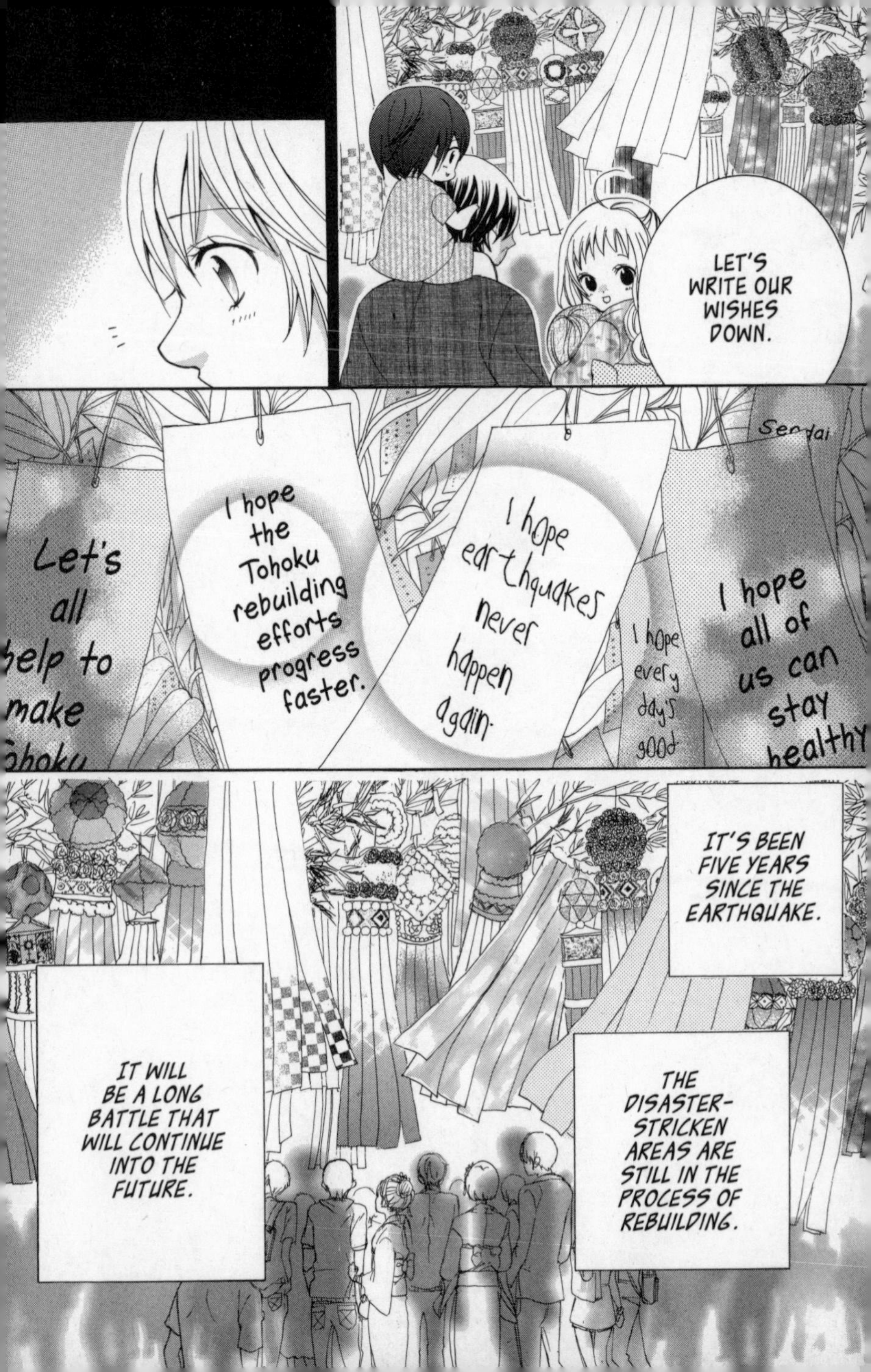
LET'S WRITE OUR WISHES DOWN.
Sendai
I hope all of us can stay healthy
I hope every day's good
I hope earthquakes never happen again.
I hope the Tohoku rebuilding efforts progress faster.
Let's all
IT'S BEEN FIVE YEARS SINCE THE EARTHQUAKE.
THE DISASTER-STRICKEN AREAS ARE STILL IN THE PROCESS OF REBUILDING.
IT WILL BE A LONG BATTLE THAT WILL CONTINUE INTO THE FUTURE.

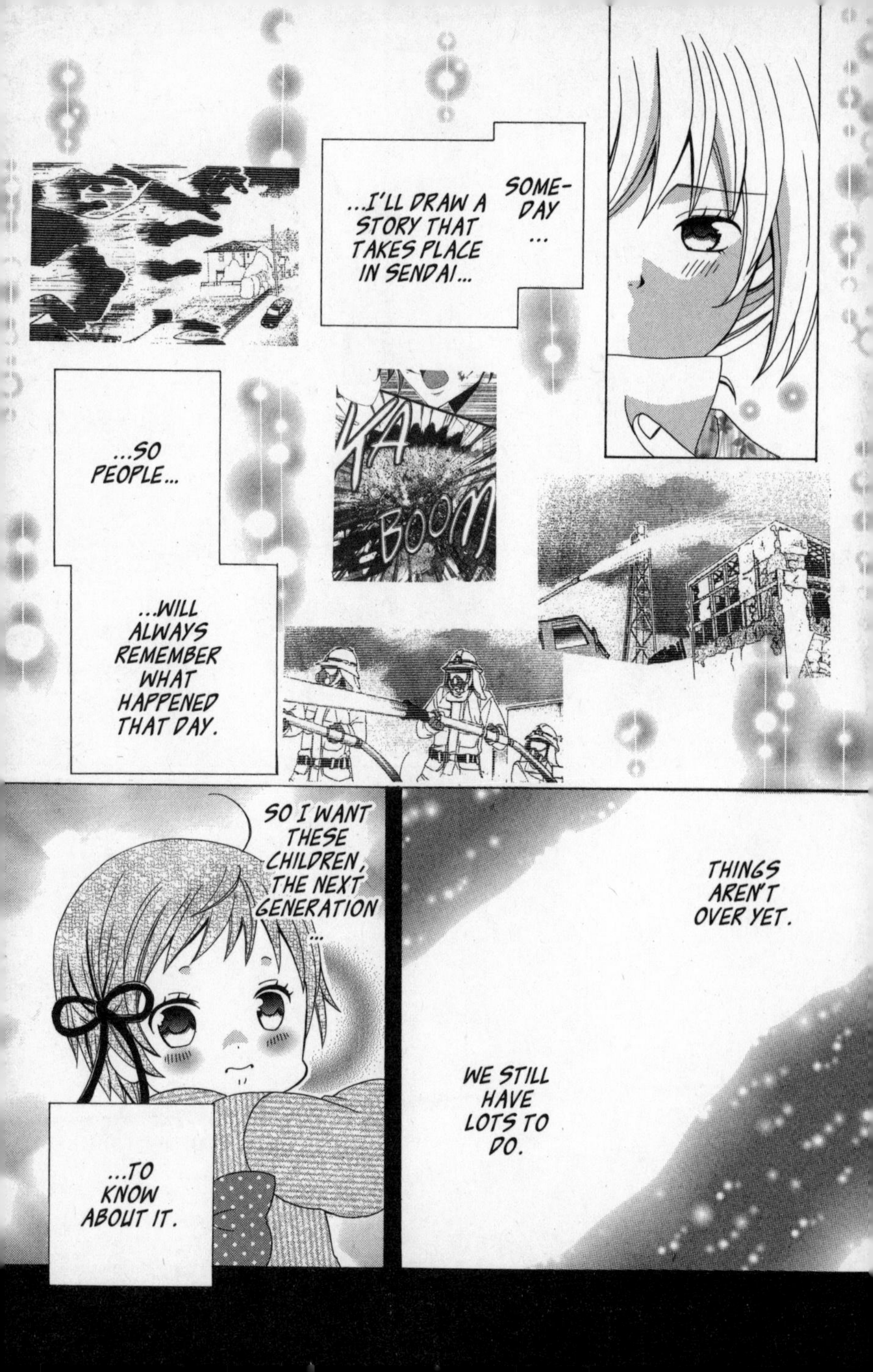
SOME-DAY...
...I'LL DRAW A STORY THAT TAKES PLACE IN SENDAI...
KA BOOM
...SO PEOPLE...
...WILL ALWAYS REMEMBER WHAT HAPPENED THAT DAY.
THINGS AREN'T OVER YET.
WE STILL HAVE LOTS TO DO.
SO I WANT THESE CHILDREN, THE NEXT GENERATION...
...TO KNOW ABOUT IT.

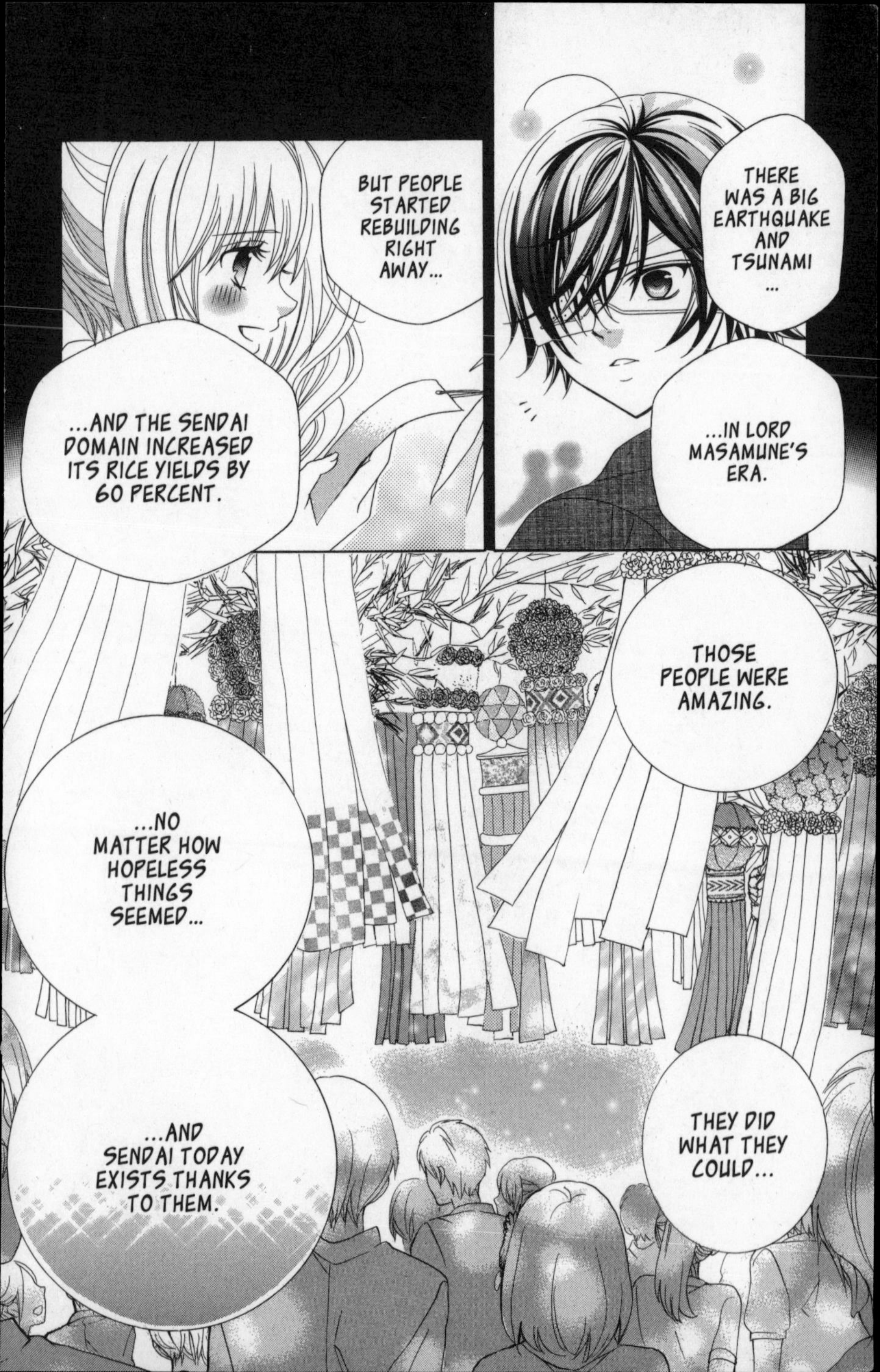
THERE WAS A BIG EARTHQUAKE AND TSUNAMI ...
...IN LORD MASAMUNE'S ERA.
BUT PEOPLE STARTED REBUILDING RIGHT AWAY...
...AND THE SENDAI DOMAIN INCREASED ITS RICE YIELDS BY 60 PERCENT.
THOSE PEOPLE WERE AMAZING.
THEY DID WHAT THEY COULD...
...NO MATTER HOW HOPELESS THINGS SEEMED...
...AND SENDAI TODAY EXISTS THANKS TO THEM.

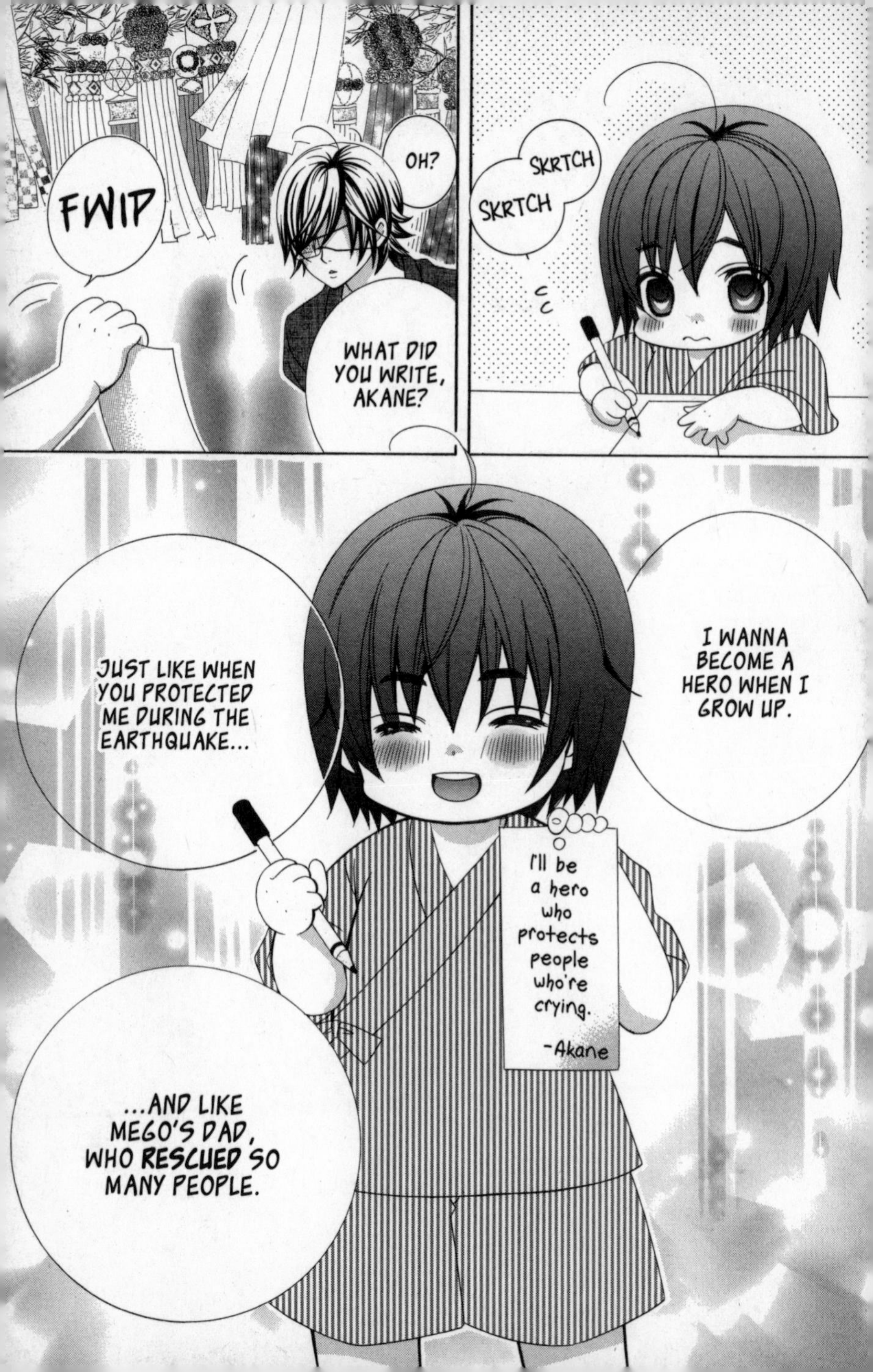
SKRTCH
SKRTCH
OH?
FWIP
WHAT DID YOU WRITE, AKANE?
I WANNA BECOME A HERO WHEN I GROW UP.
I'll be a hero who protects people who're crying. -Akane
JUST LIKE WHEN YOU PROTECTED ME DURING THE EARTHQUAKE...
...AND LIKE MEGO'S DAD, WHO **RESCUED** SO MANY PEOPLE.

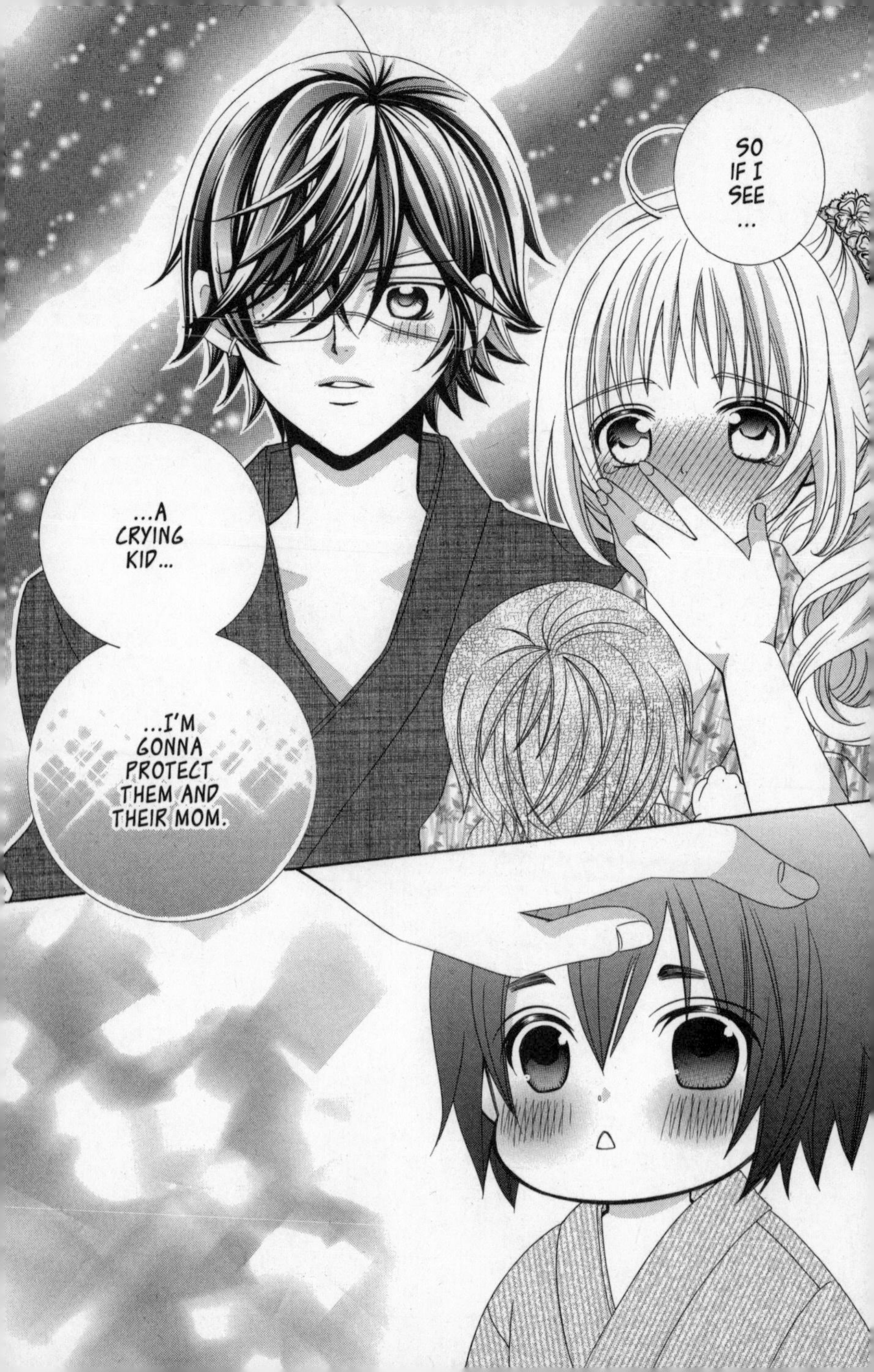
SO IF I SEE ...
...A CRYING KID...
...I'M GONNA PROTECT THEM AND THEIR MOM.

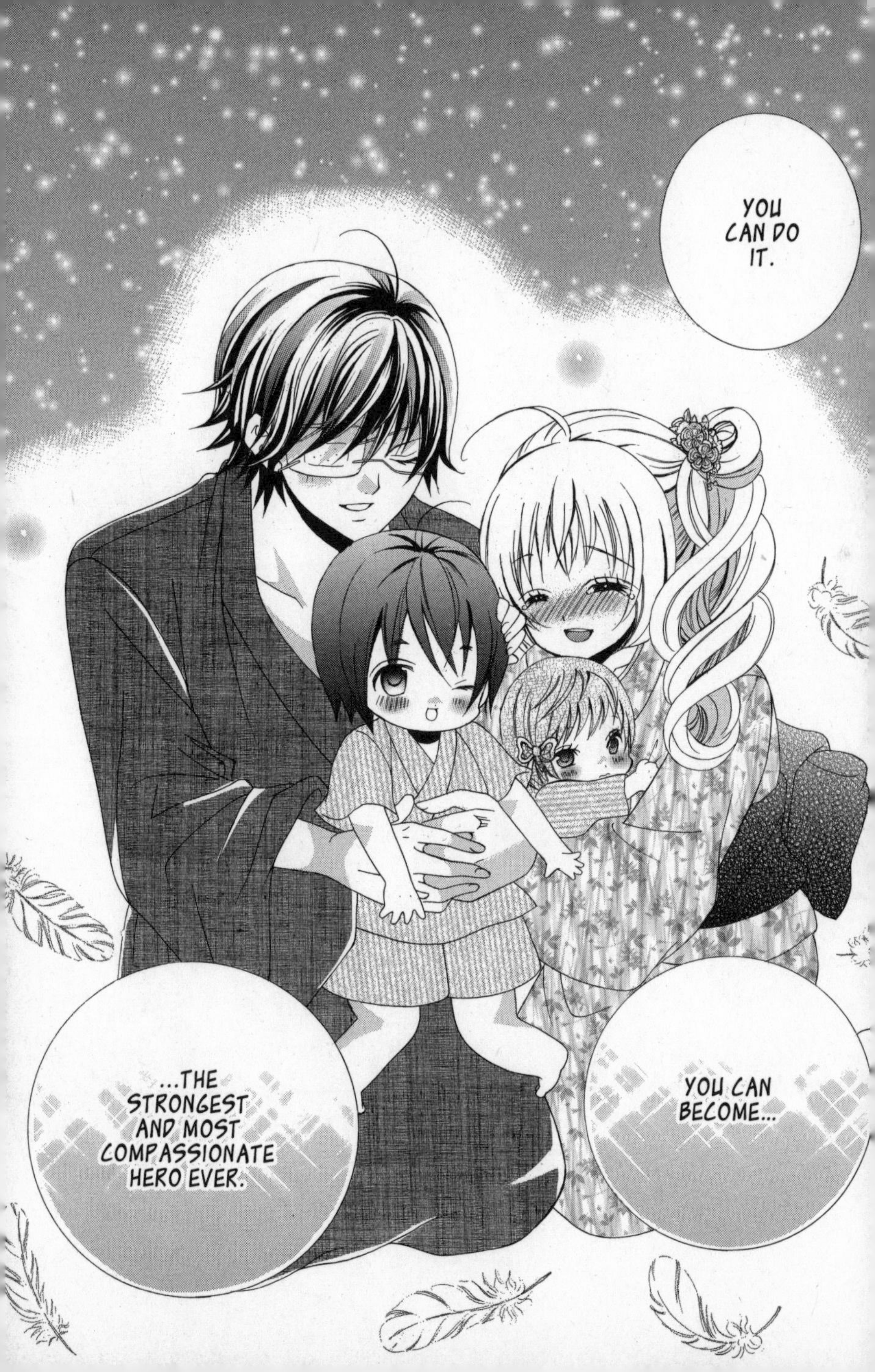
YOU CAN DO IT.
YOU CAN BECOME...
...THE STRONGEST AND MOST COMPASSIONATE HERO EVER.

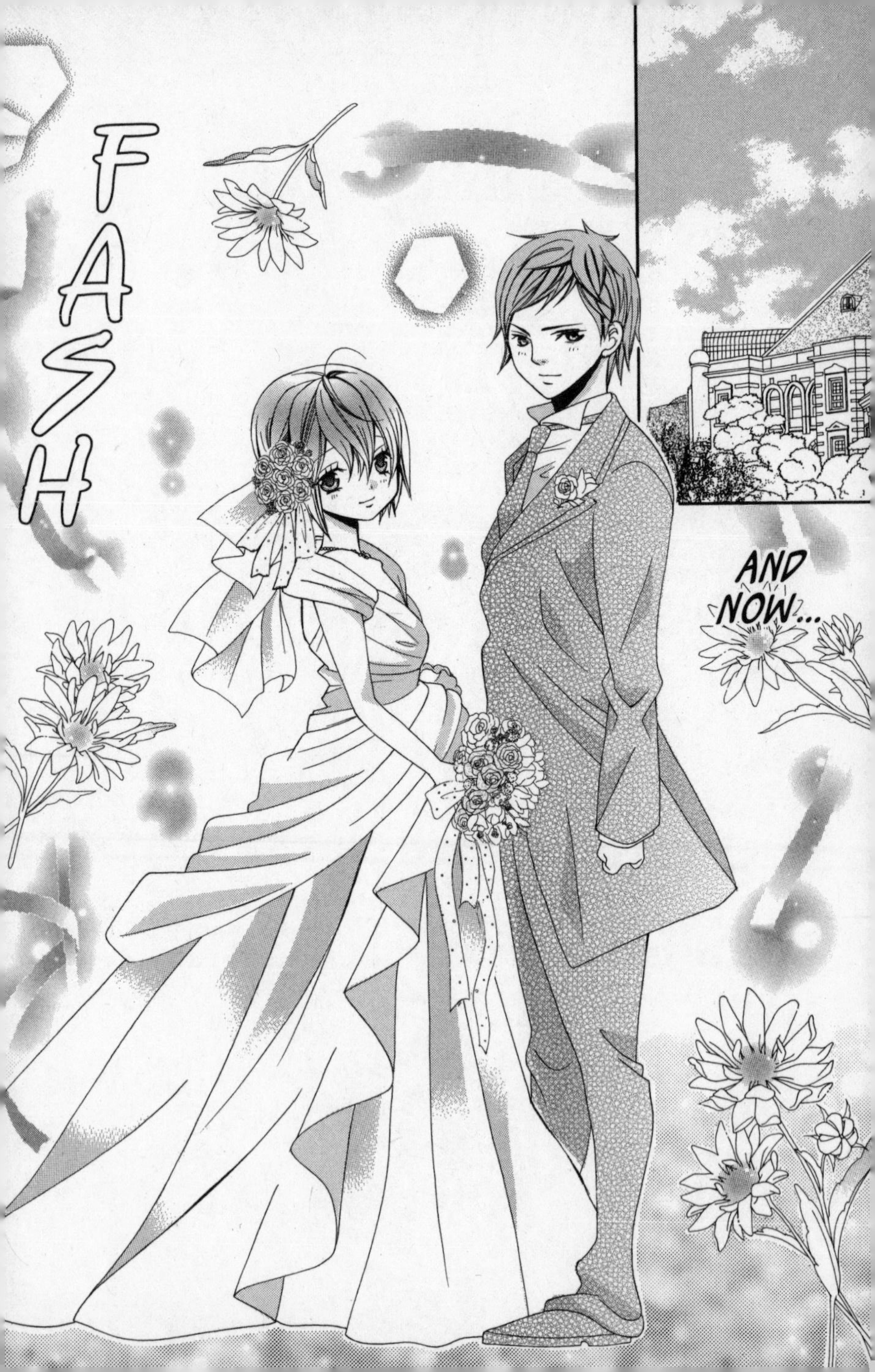
FASH
AND NOW...

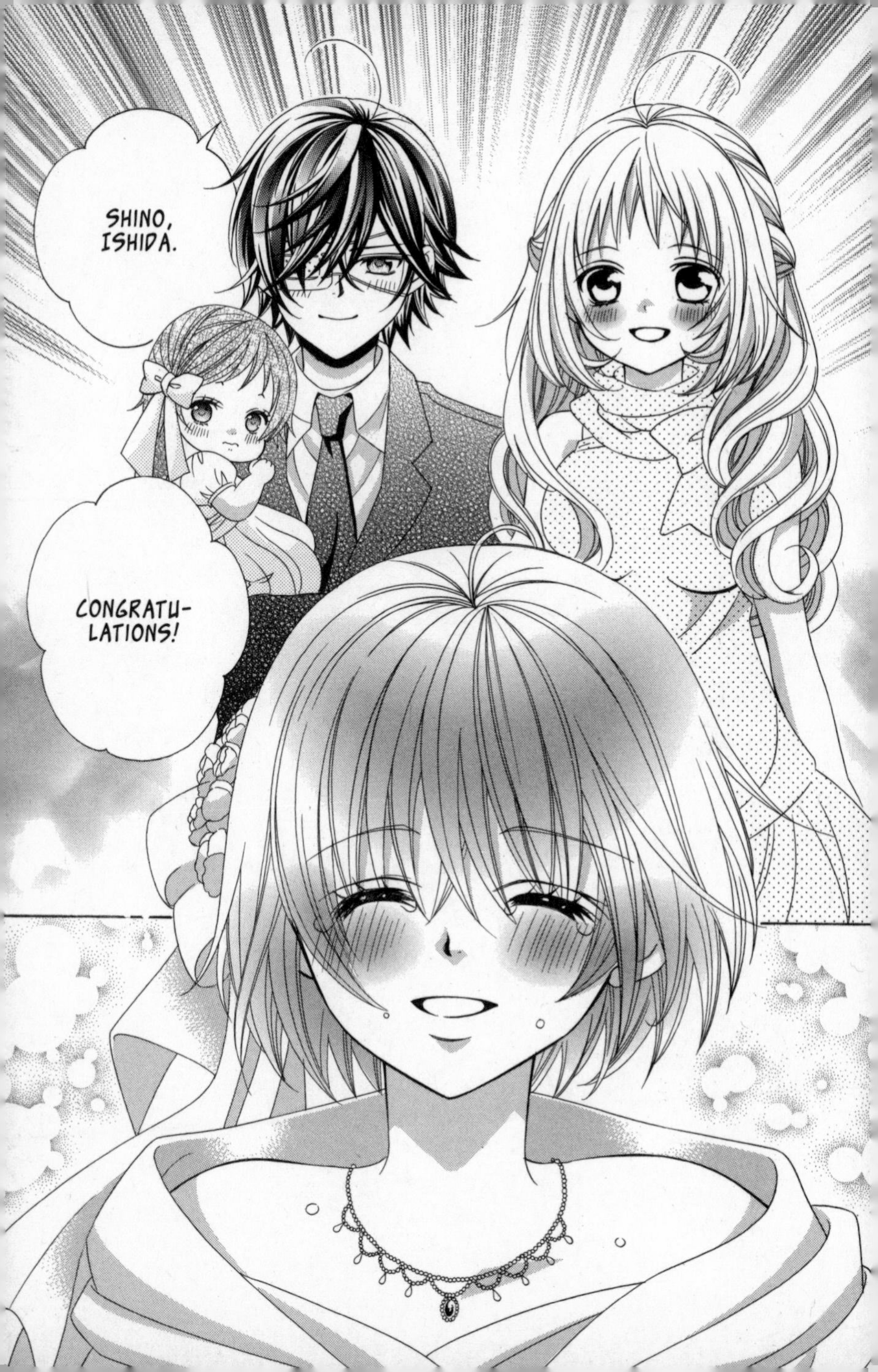
SHINO, ISHIDA.
CONGRATU-LATIONS!

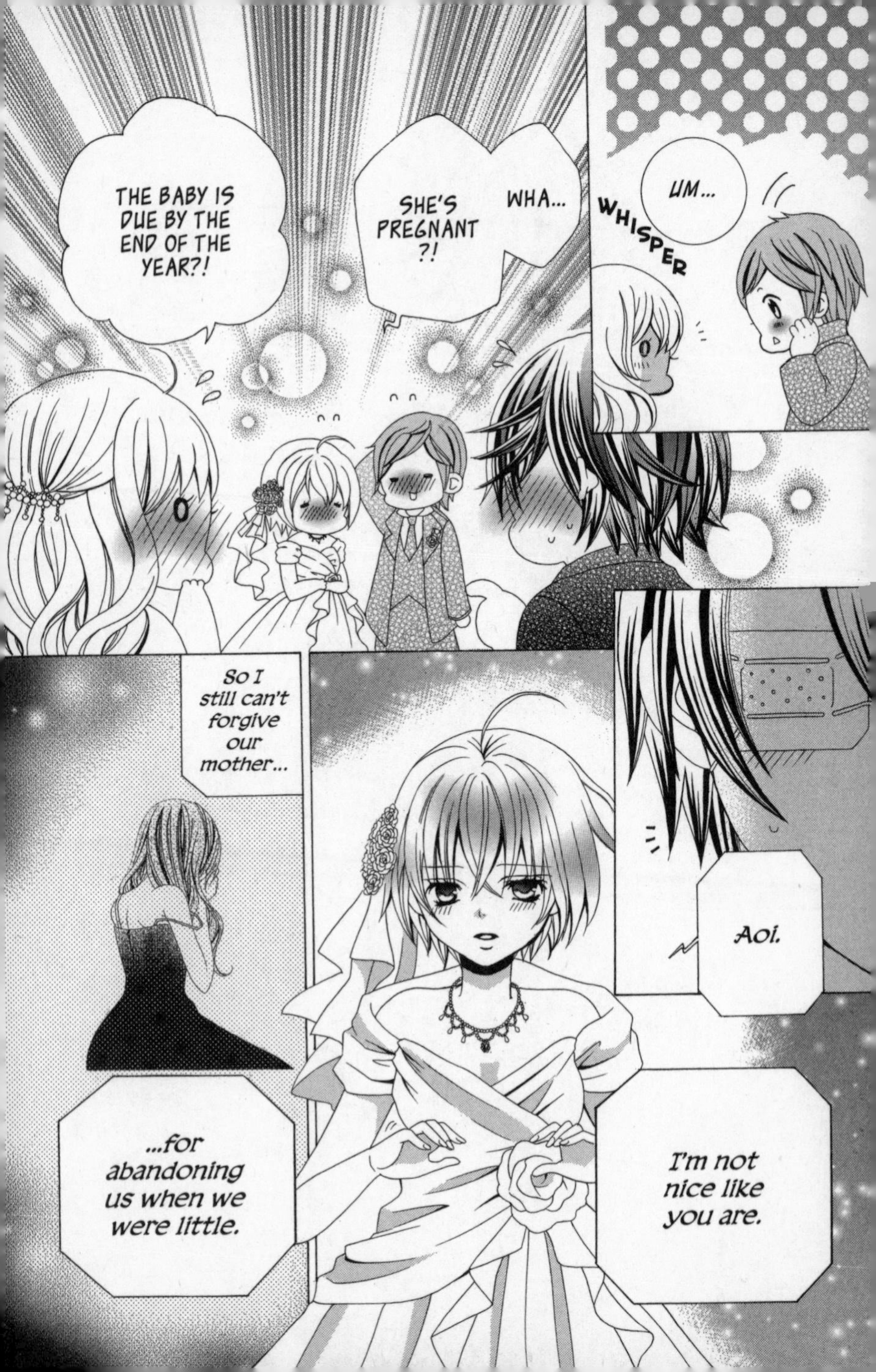
UM...
WHISPER
WHA...
SHE'S PREGNANT?!
THE BABY IS DUE BY THE END OF THE YEAR?!
Aoi.
I'm not nice like you are.
So I still can't forgive our mother...
...for abandoning us when we were little.

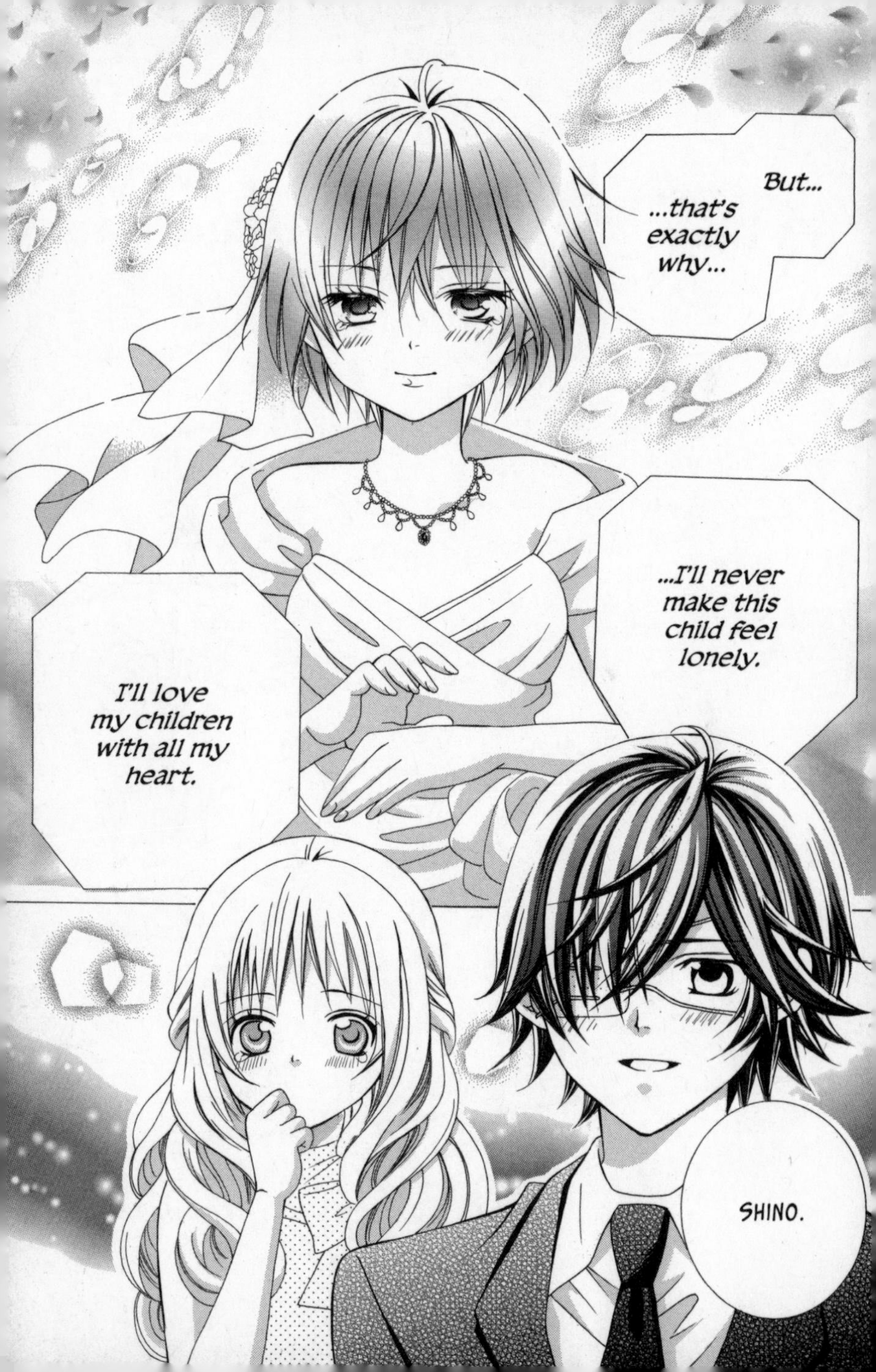
But... ...that's exactly why...
...I'll never make this child feel lonely.
I'll love my children with all my heart.
SHINO.

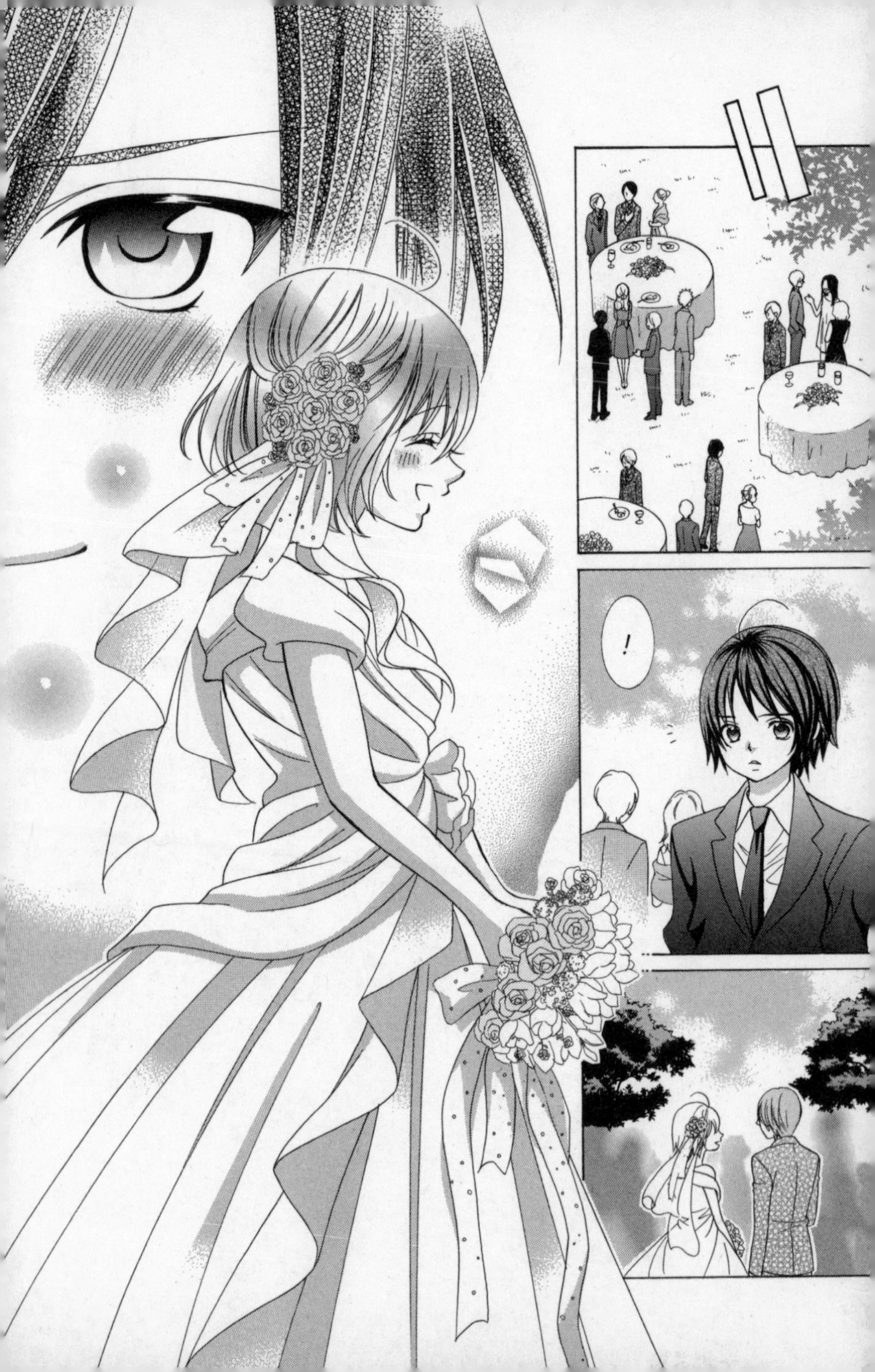
!

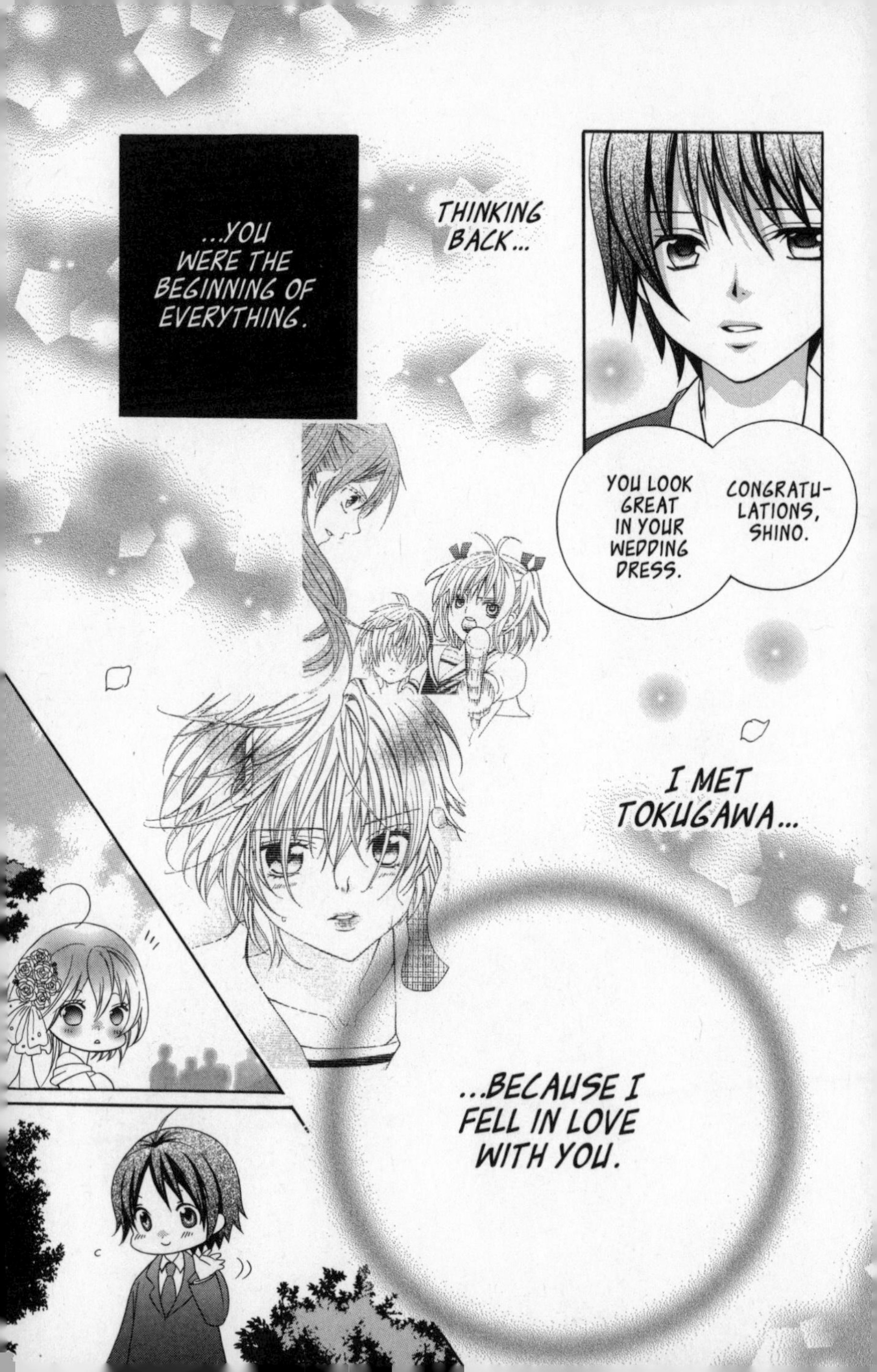
CONGRATU-LATIONS, SHINO.
YOU LOOK GREAT IN YOUR WEDDING DRESS.
THINKING BACK...
...YOU WERE THE BEGINNING OF EVERYTHING.
I MET TOKUGAWA...
...BECAUSE I FELL IN LOVE WITH YOU.

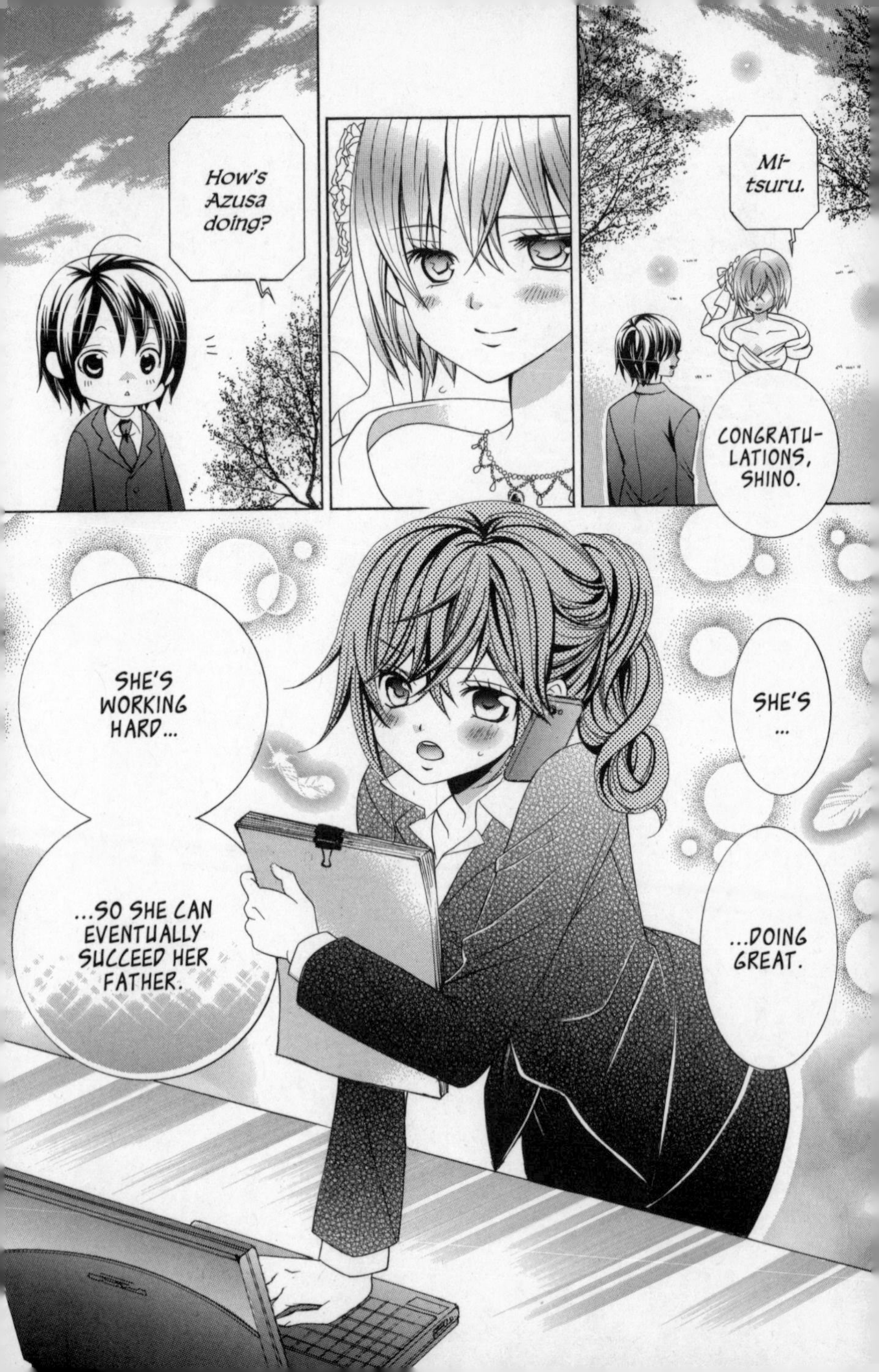
Mi-tsuru.
CONGRATULATIONS, SHINO.
How's Azusa doing?
SHE'S...
...DOING GREAT.
SHE'S WORKING HARD...
...SO SHE CAN EVENTUALLY SUCCEED HER FATHER.

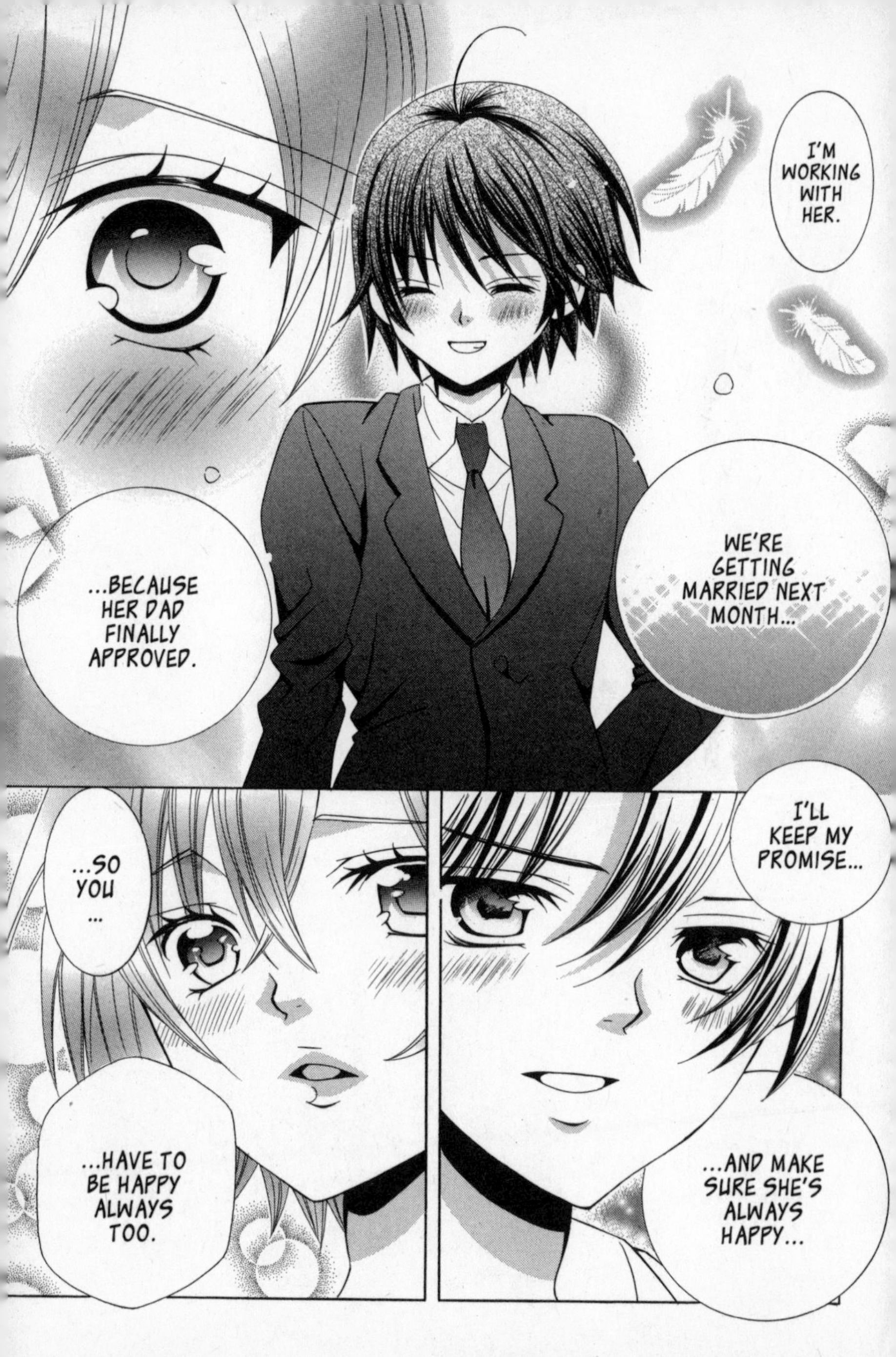
I'M WORKING WITH HER.
WE'RE GETTING MARRIED NEXT MONTH...
...BECAUSE HER DAD FINALLY APPROVED.
I'LL KEEP MY PROMISE...
...AND MAKE SURE SHE'S ALWAYS HAPPY...
...SO YOU ...
...HAVE TO BE HAPPY ALWAYS TOO.

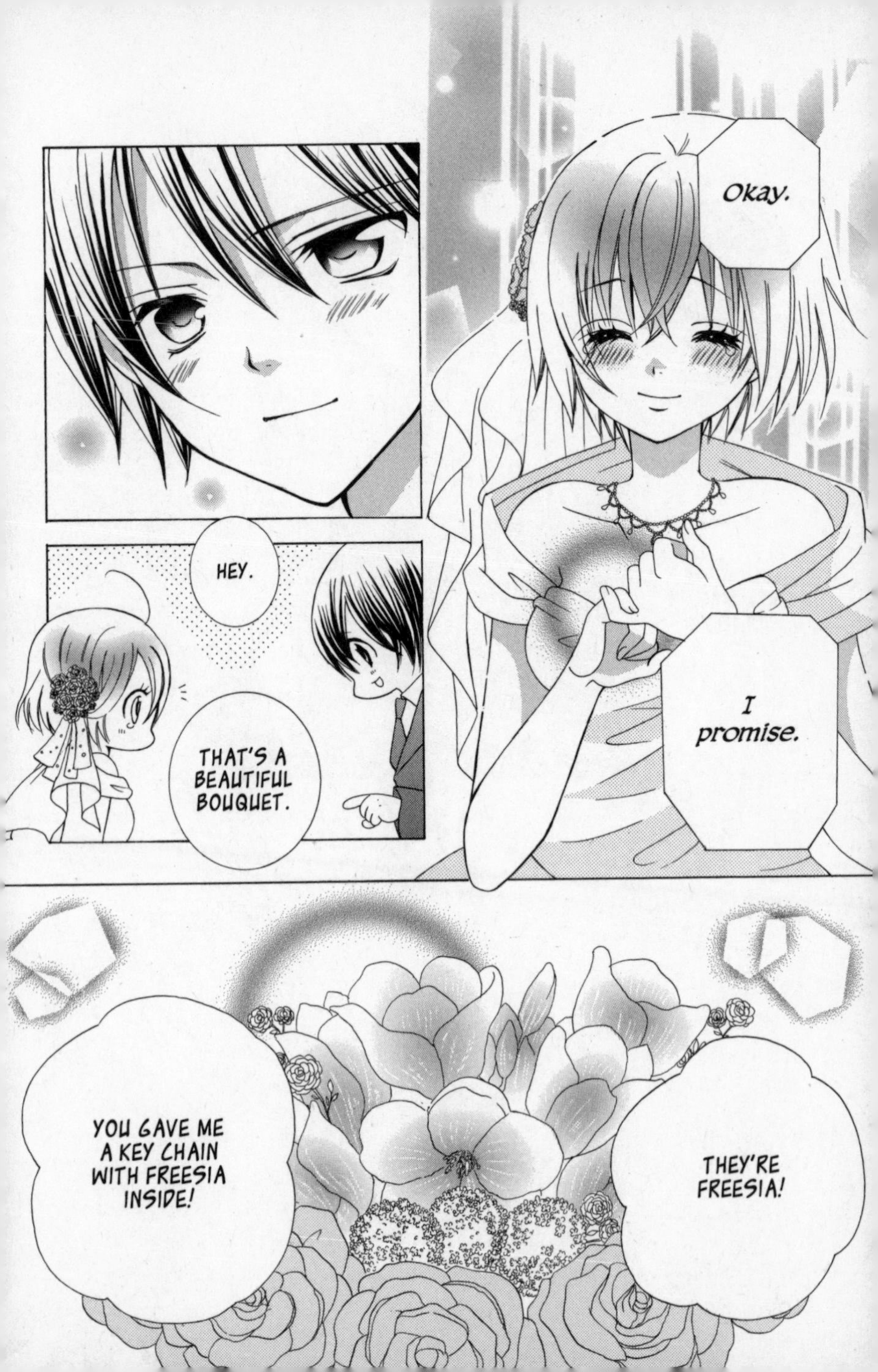
Okay.
I promise.
HEY.
THAT'S A BEAUTIFUL BOUQUET.
THEY'RE FREESIA!
YOU GAVE ME A KEY CHAIN WITH FREESIA INSIDE!

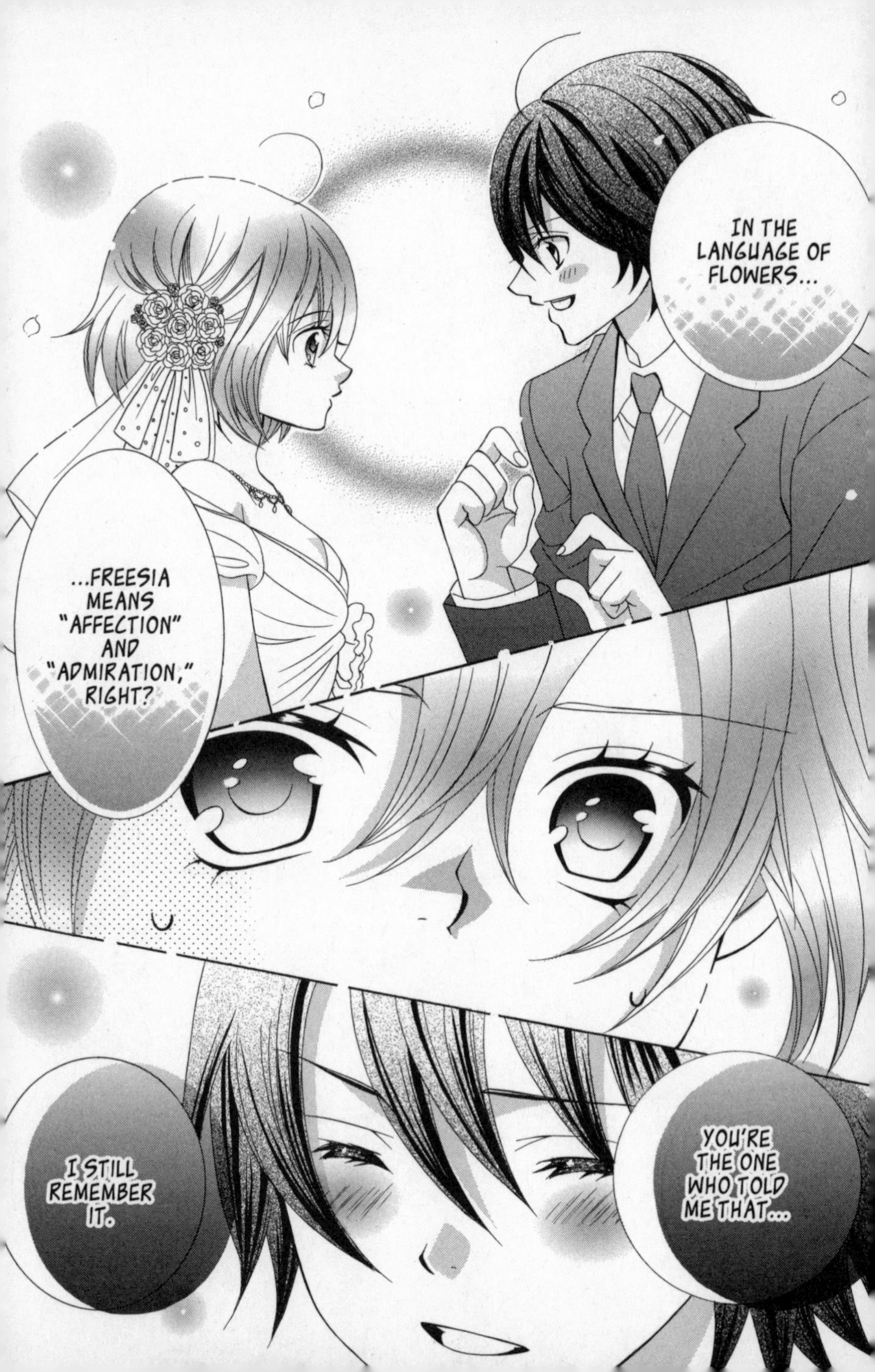
IN THE LANGUAGE OF FLOWERS...
...FREESIA MEANS "AFFECTION" AND "ADMIRATION," RIGHT?
YOU'RE THE ONE WHO TOLD ME THAT...
I STILL REMEMBER IT.

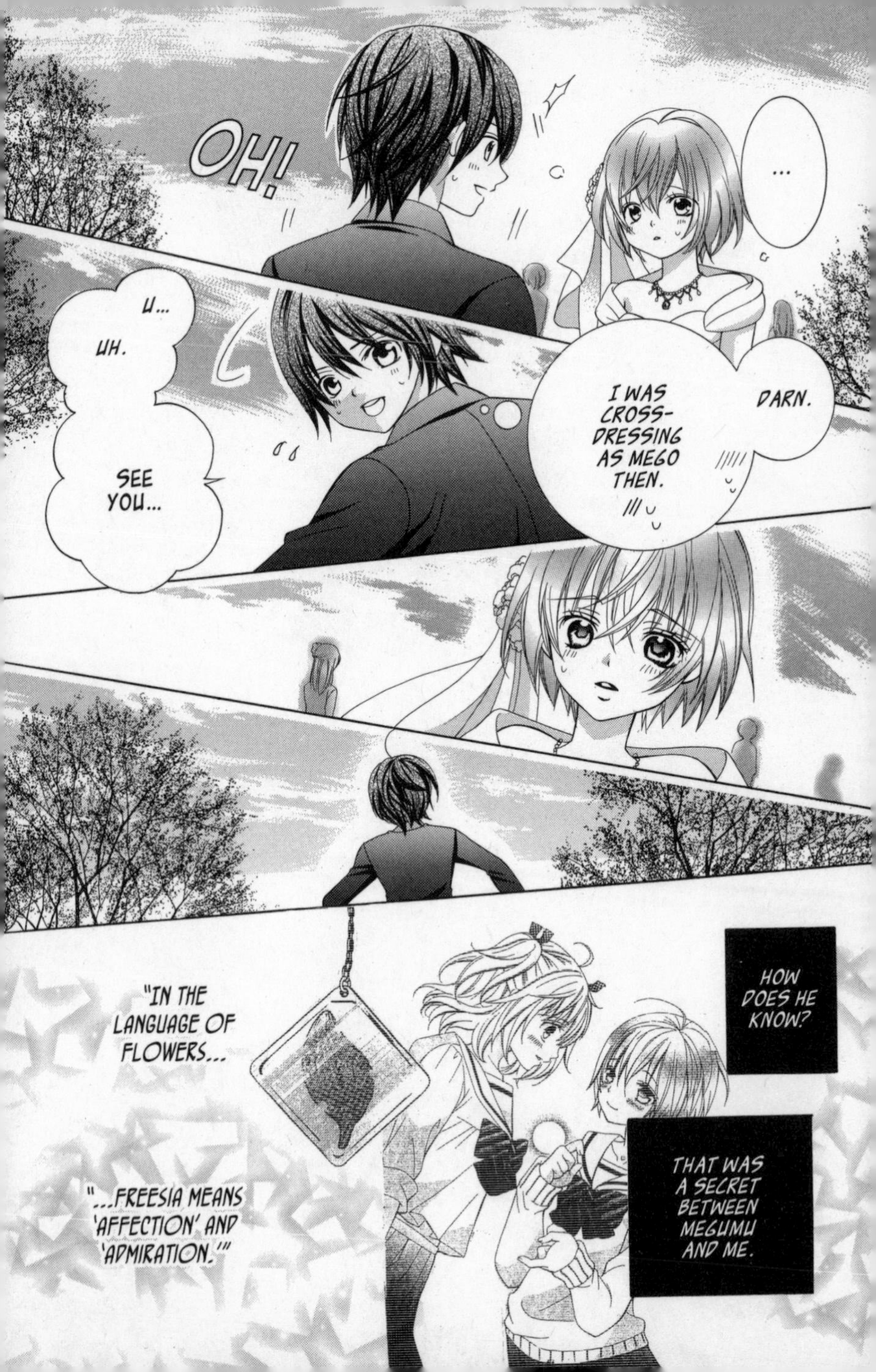
...
OH!
DARN.
I WAS CROSS-DRESSING AS MEGO THEN.
U... UH. SEE YOU...
HOW DOES HE KNOW?
THAT WAS A SECRET BETWEEN MEGUMU AND ME.
"IN THE LANGUAGE OF FLOWERS...
"...FREESIA MEANS 'AFFECTION' AND 'ADMIRATION.'"

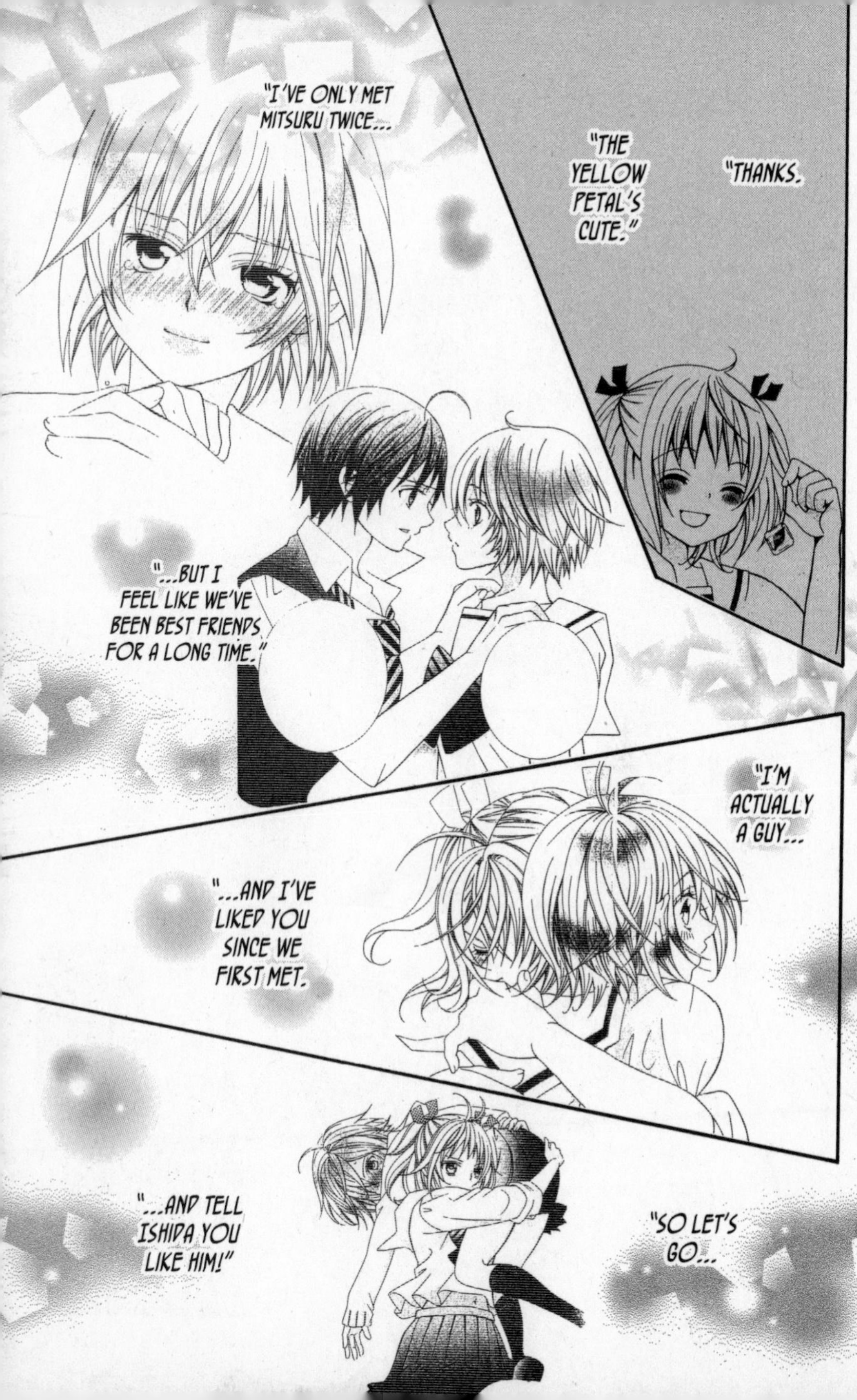
"THANKS.
"THE YELLOW PETAL'S CUTE."
"I'VE ONLY MET MITSURU TWICE...
"...BUT I FEEL LIKE WE'VE BEEN BEST FRIENDS FOR A LONG TIME."
"I'M ACTUALLY A GUY...
"...AND I'VE LIKED YOU SINCE WE FIRST MET.
"SO LET'S GO...
"...AND TELL ISHIDA YOU LIKE HIM!"

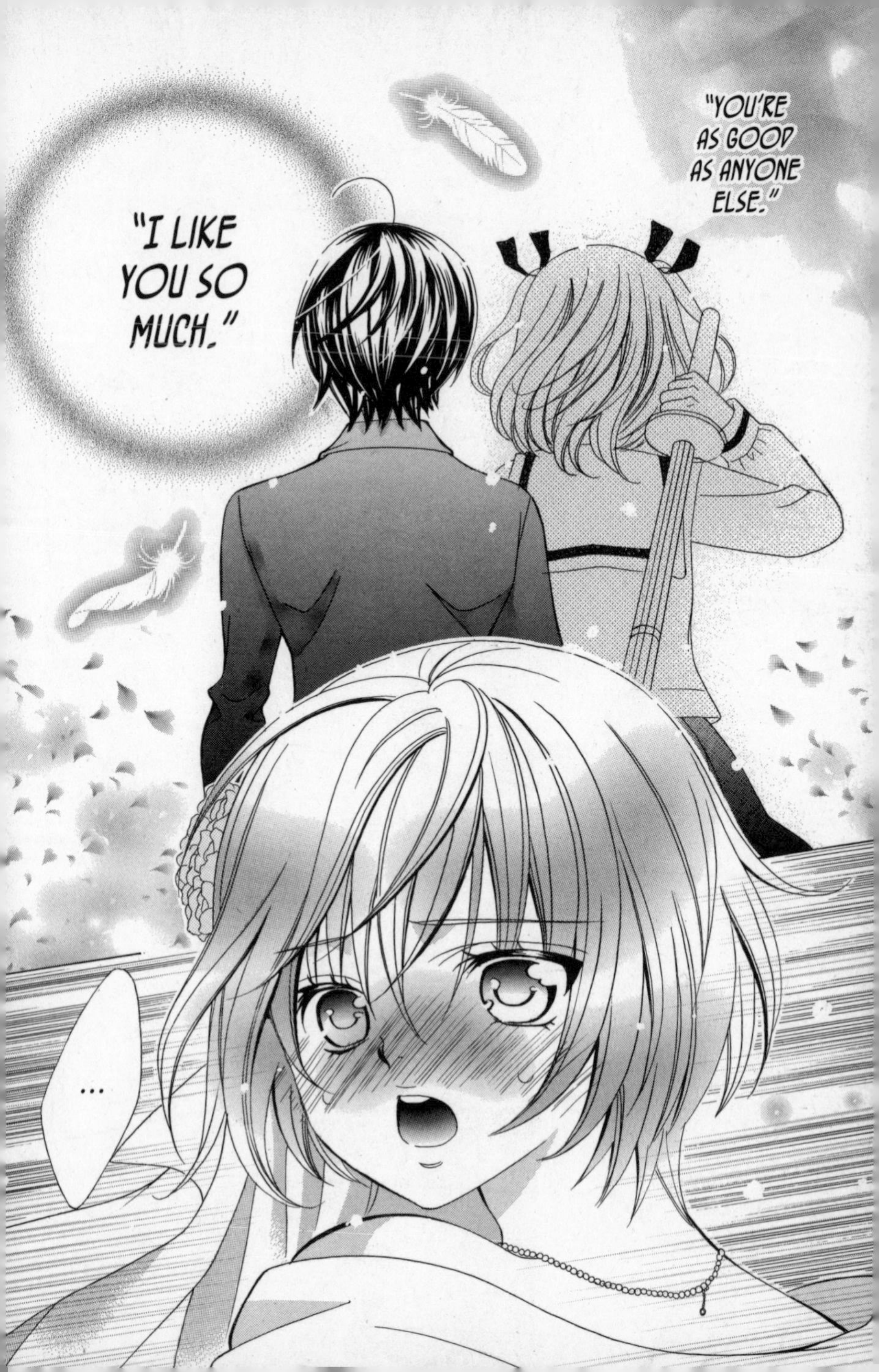
"YOU'RE AS GOOD AS ANYONE ELSE."
"I LIKE YOU SO MUCH."
...

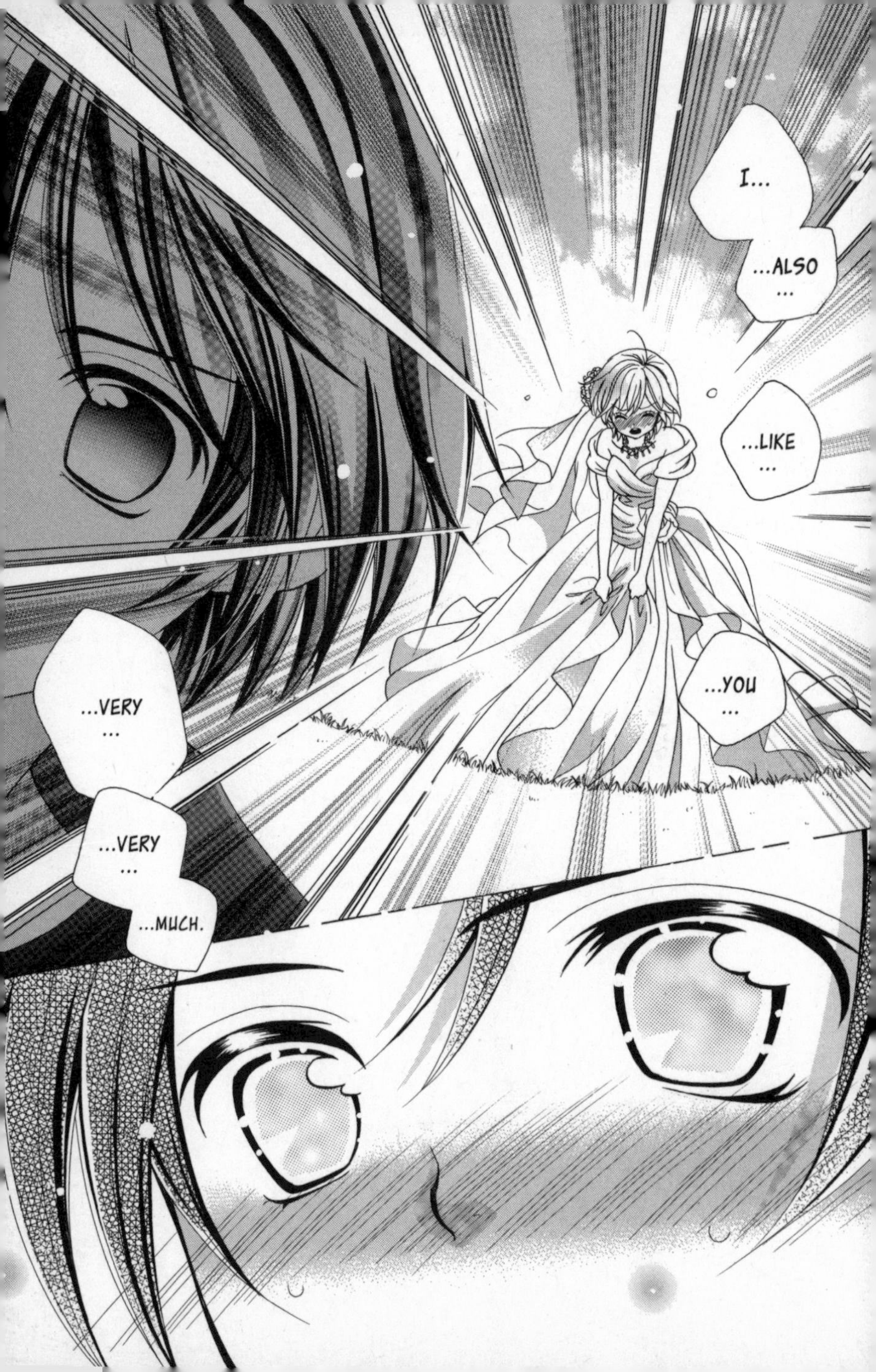
I...
...ALSO ...
...LIKE ...
...YOU ...
...VERY ...
...VERY ...
...MUCH.

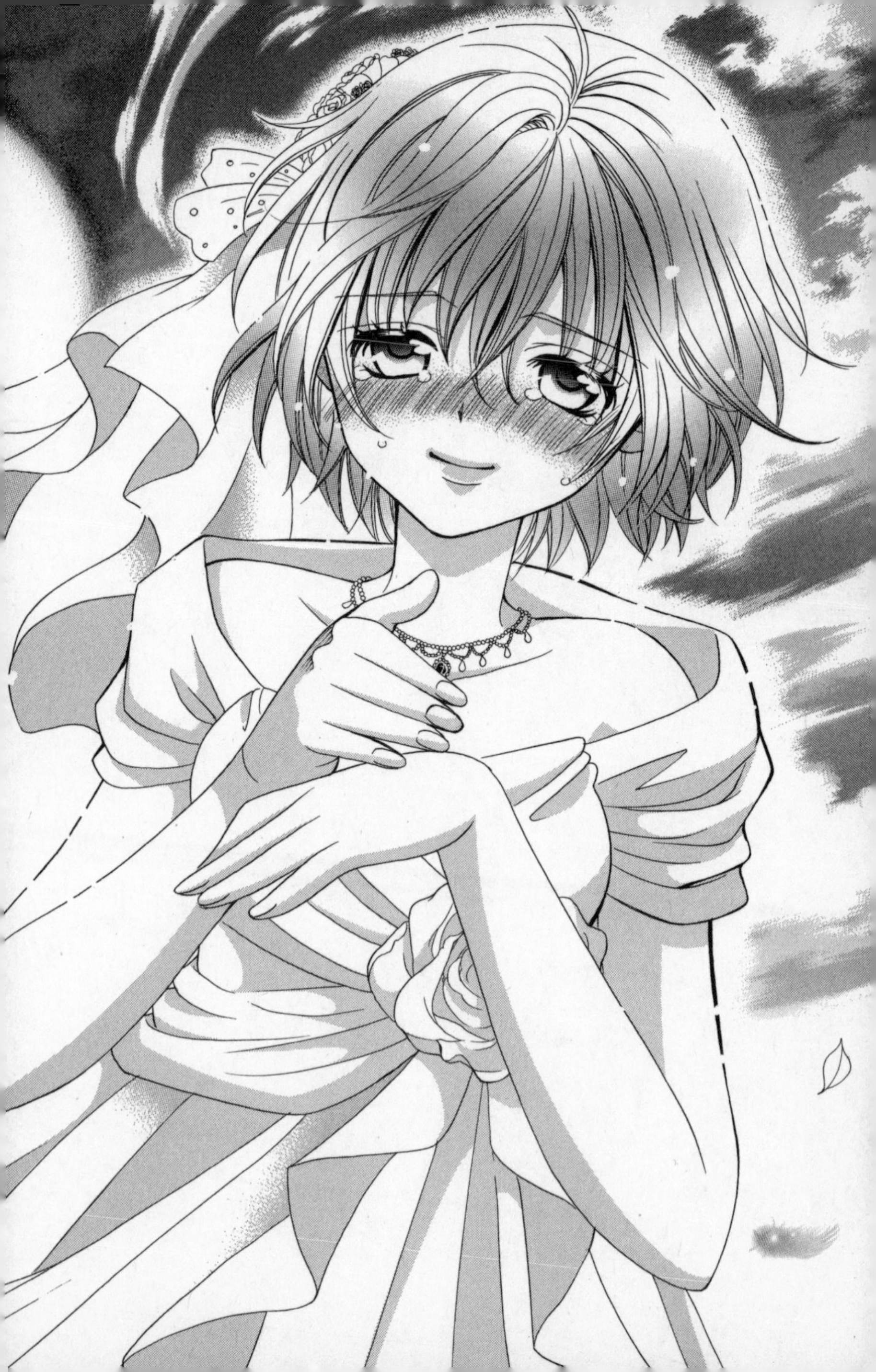

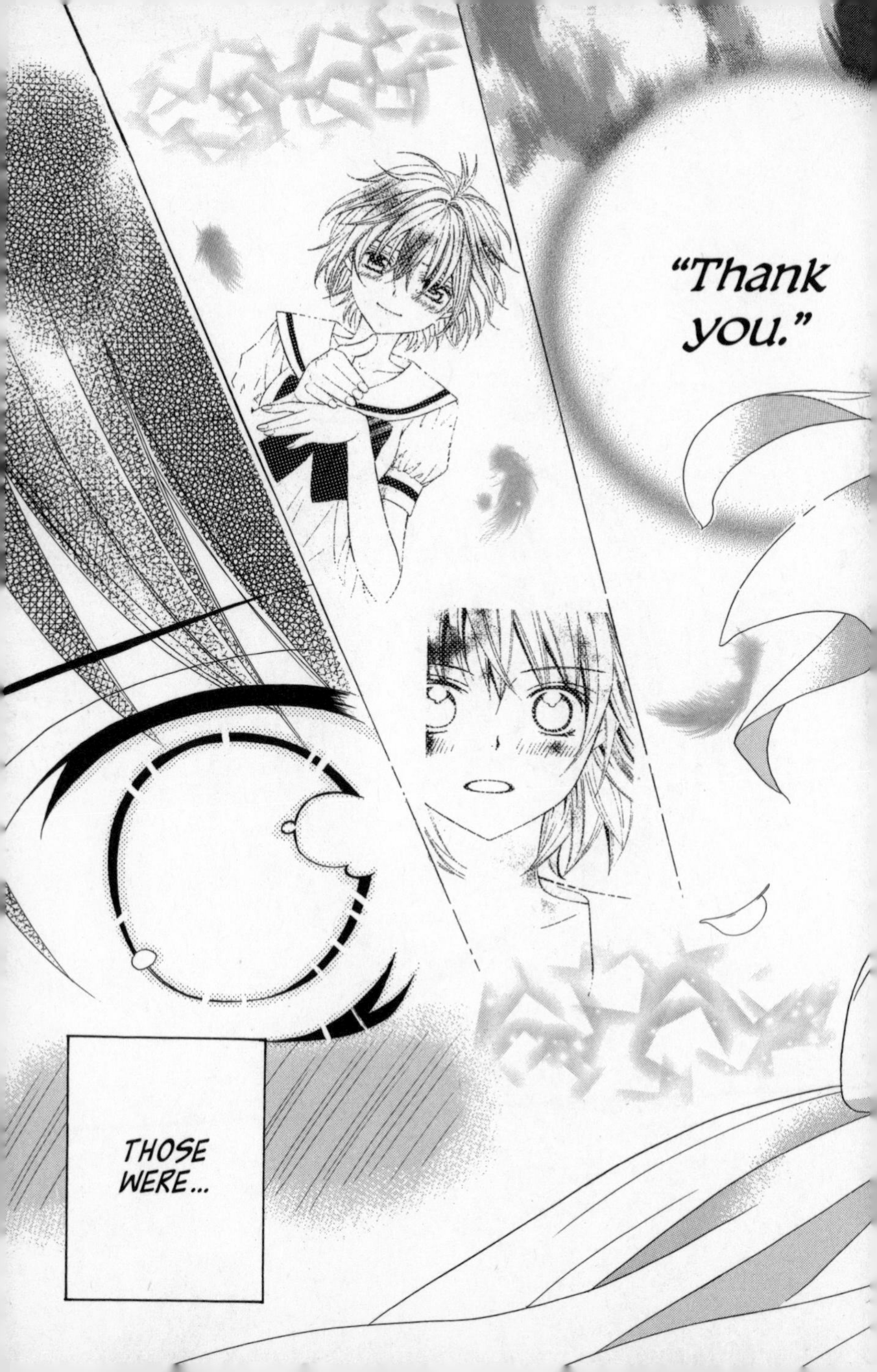
"Thank you."
THOSE WERE...

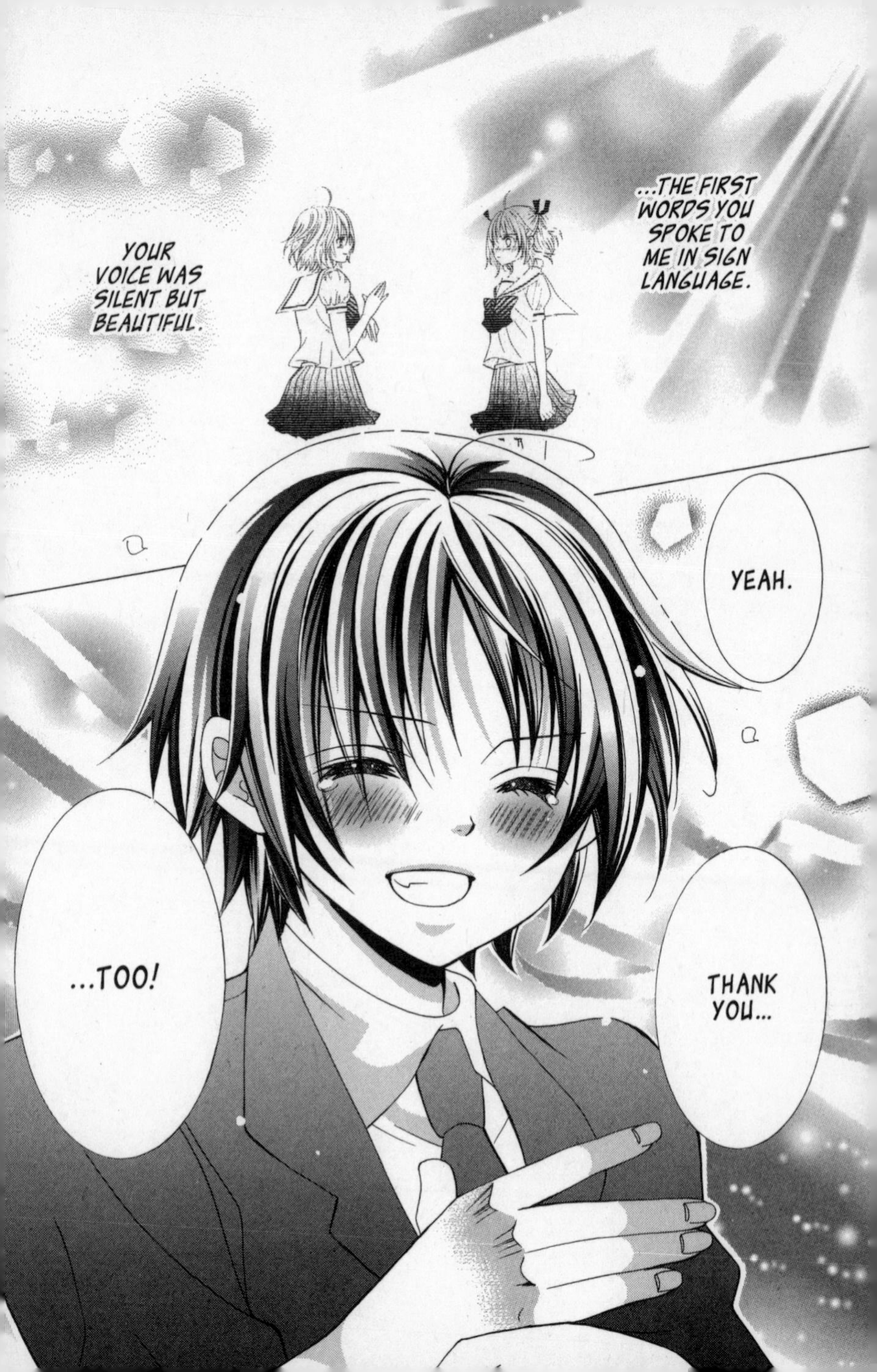
...THE FIRST WORDS YOU SPOKE TO ME IN SIGN LANGUAGE.
YOUR VOICE WAS SILENT BUT BEAUTIFUL.
YEAH.
THANK YOU...
...TOO!

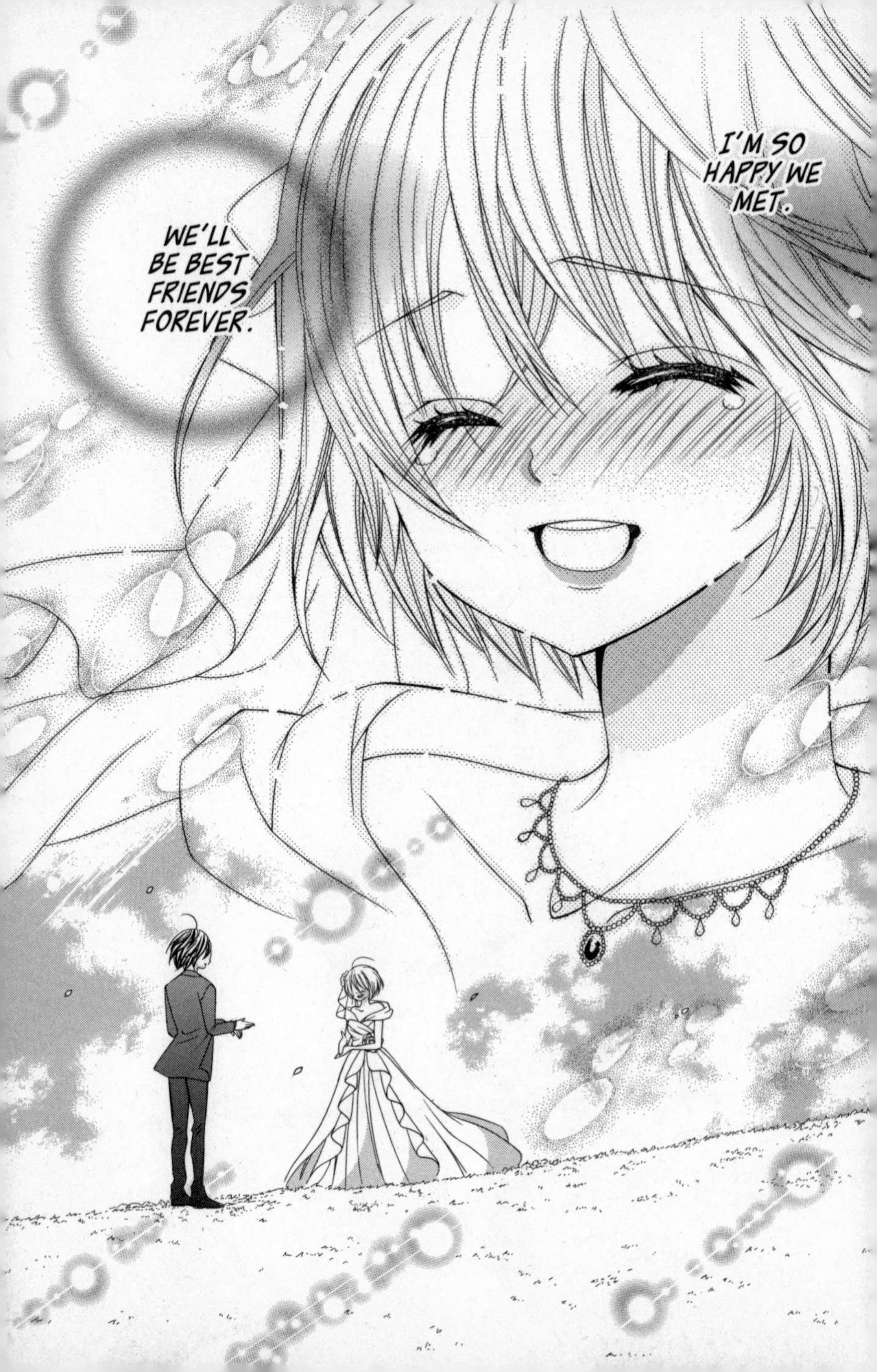
I'M SO HAPPY WE MET.
WE'LL BE BEST FRIENDS FOREVER.

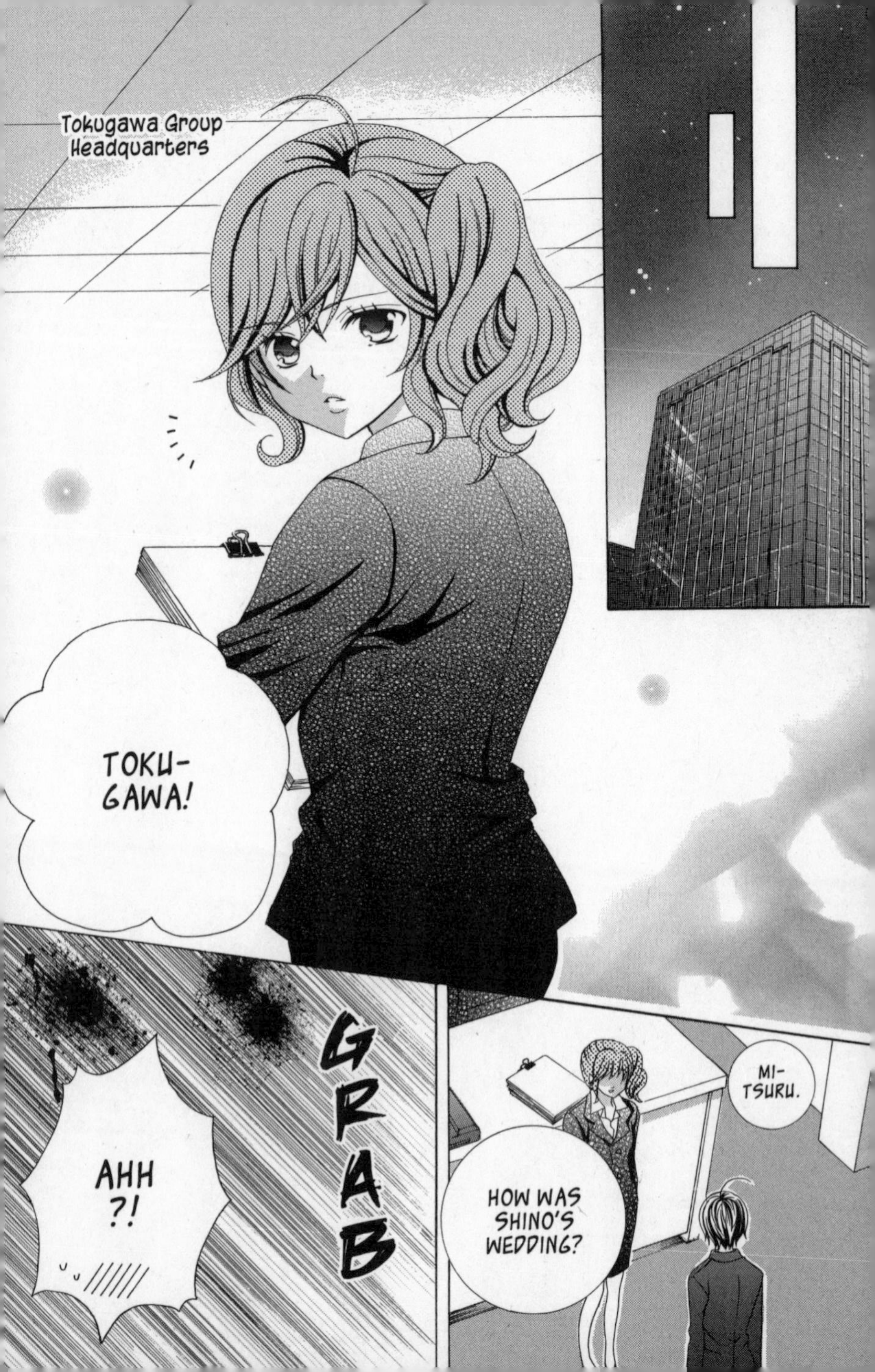
Tokugawa Group Headquarters
TOKU-GAWA!
MI-TSURU.
HOW WAS SHINO'S WEDDING?
GRAB
AHH ?!

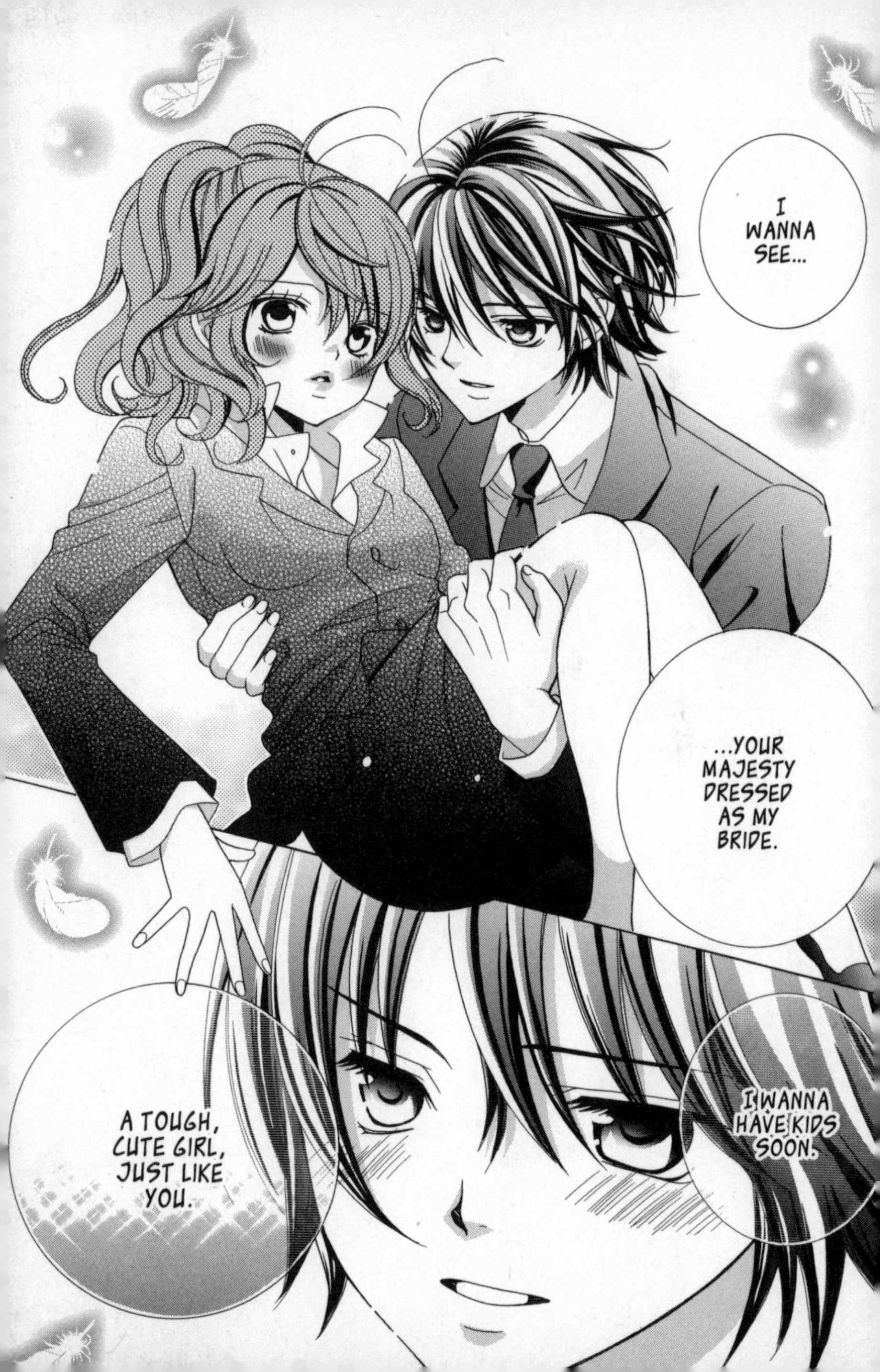
I WANNA SEE...
...YOUR MAJESTY DRESSED AS MY BRIDE.
I WANNA HAVE KIDS SOON.
A TOUGH, CUTE GIRL, JUST LIKE YOU.

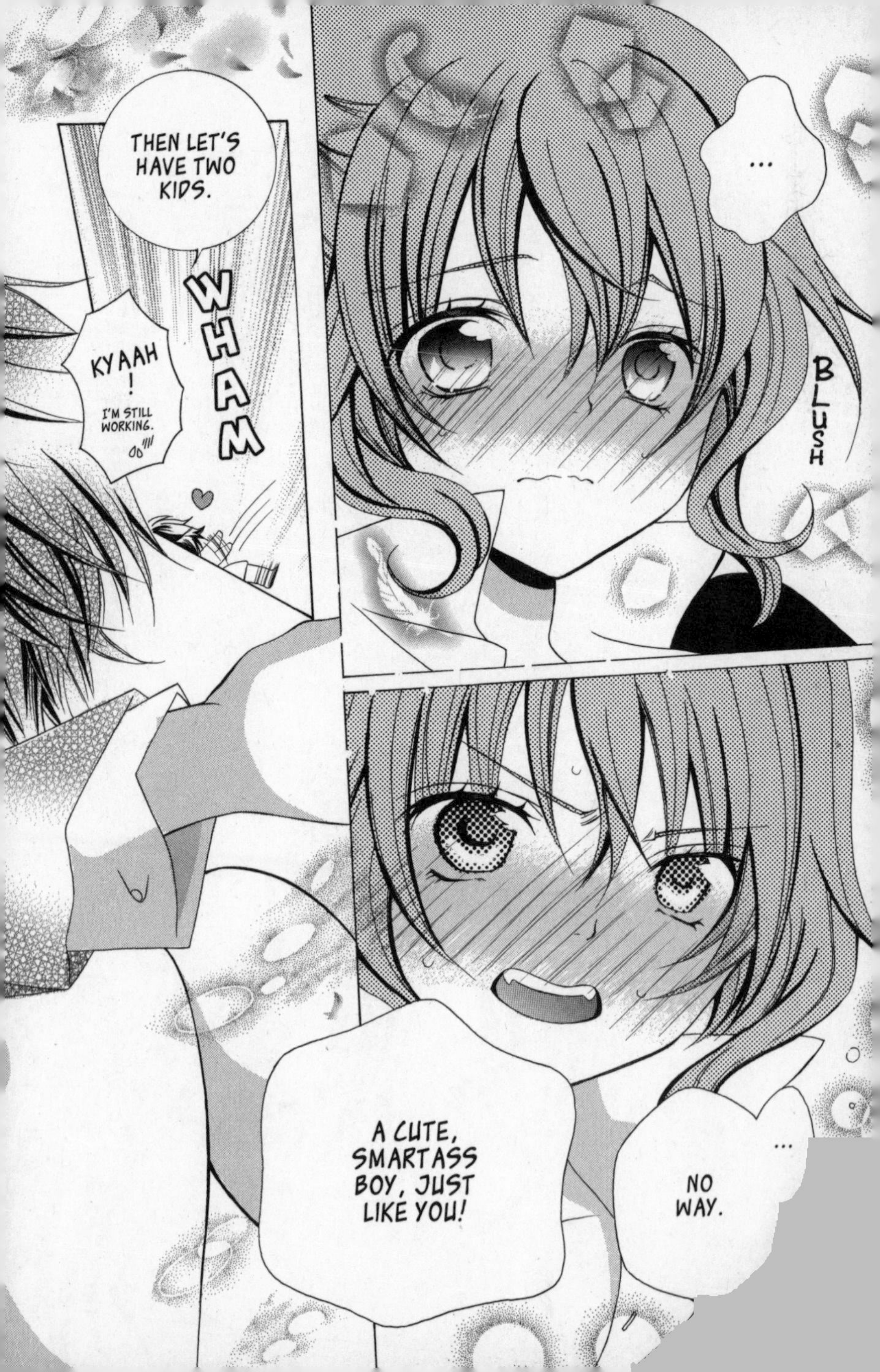
...
BLUSH
THEN LET'S HAVE TWO KIDS.
WHAM
KYAAH!
I'M STILL WORKING.
A CUTE, SMARTASS BOY, JUST LIKE YOU!
... NO WAY.

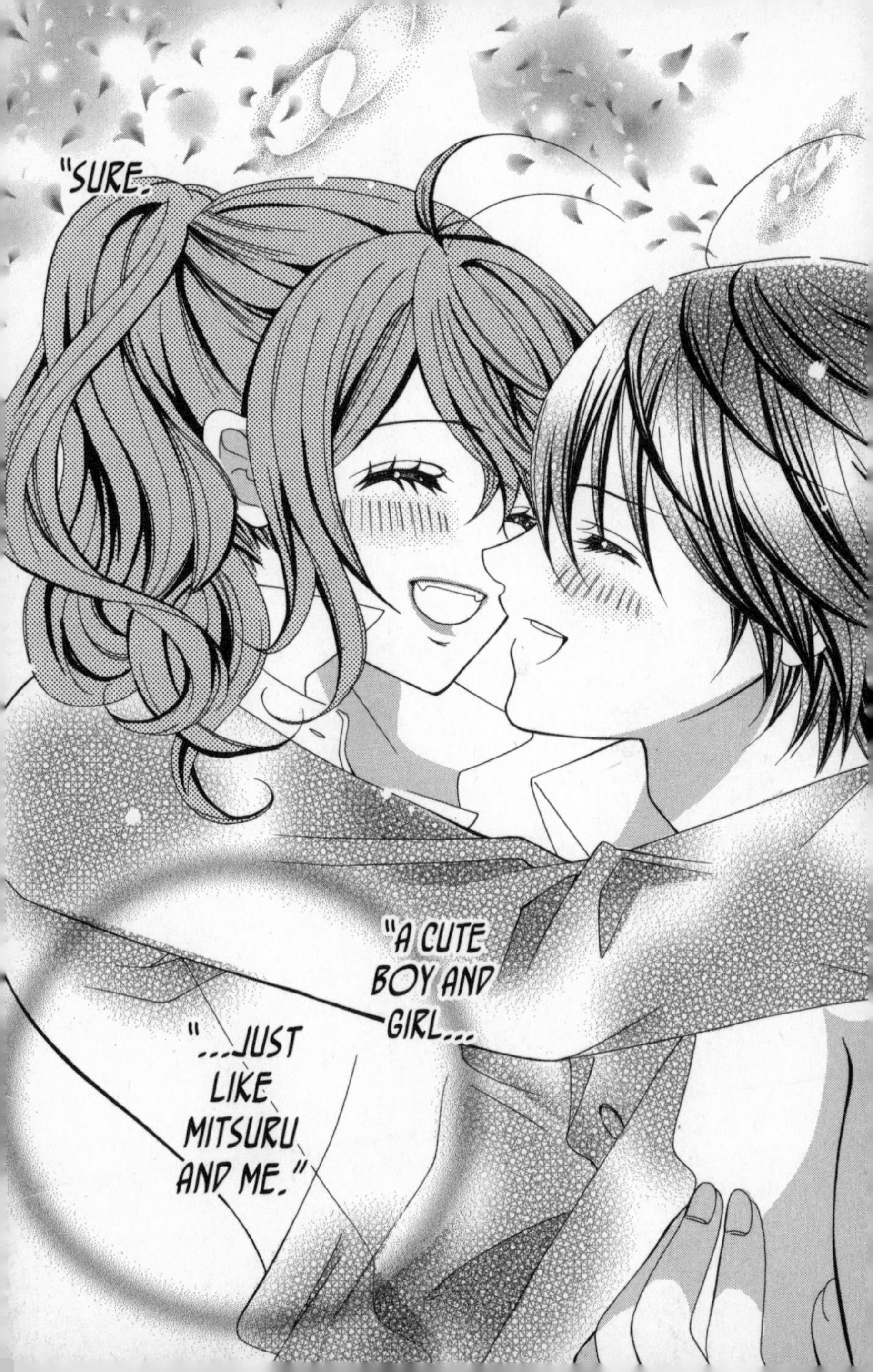
"SURE.
"A CUTE BOY AND GIRL...
"...JUST LIKE MITSURU AND ME."

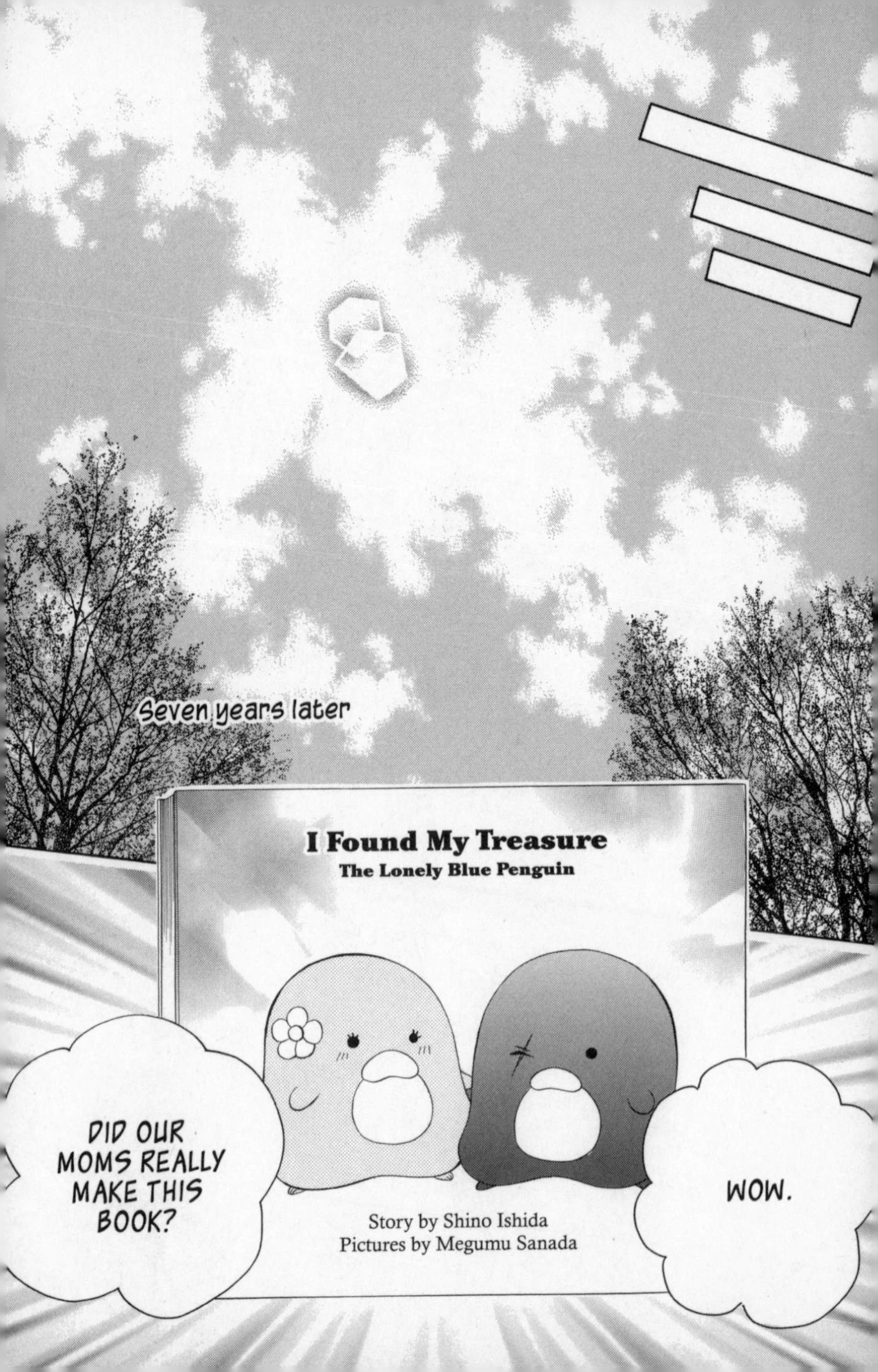
Seven years later
I Found My Treasure
The Lonely Blue Penguin
Story by Shino Ishida
Pictures by Megumu Sanada
WOW.
DID OUR MOMS REALLY MAKE THIS BOOK?

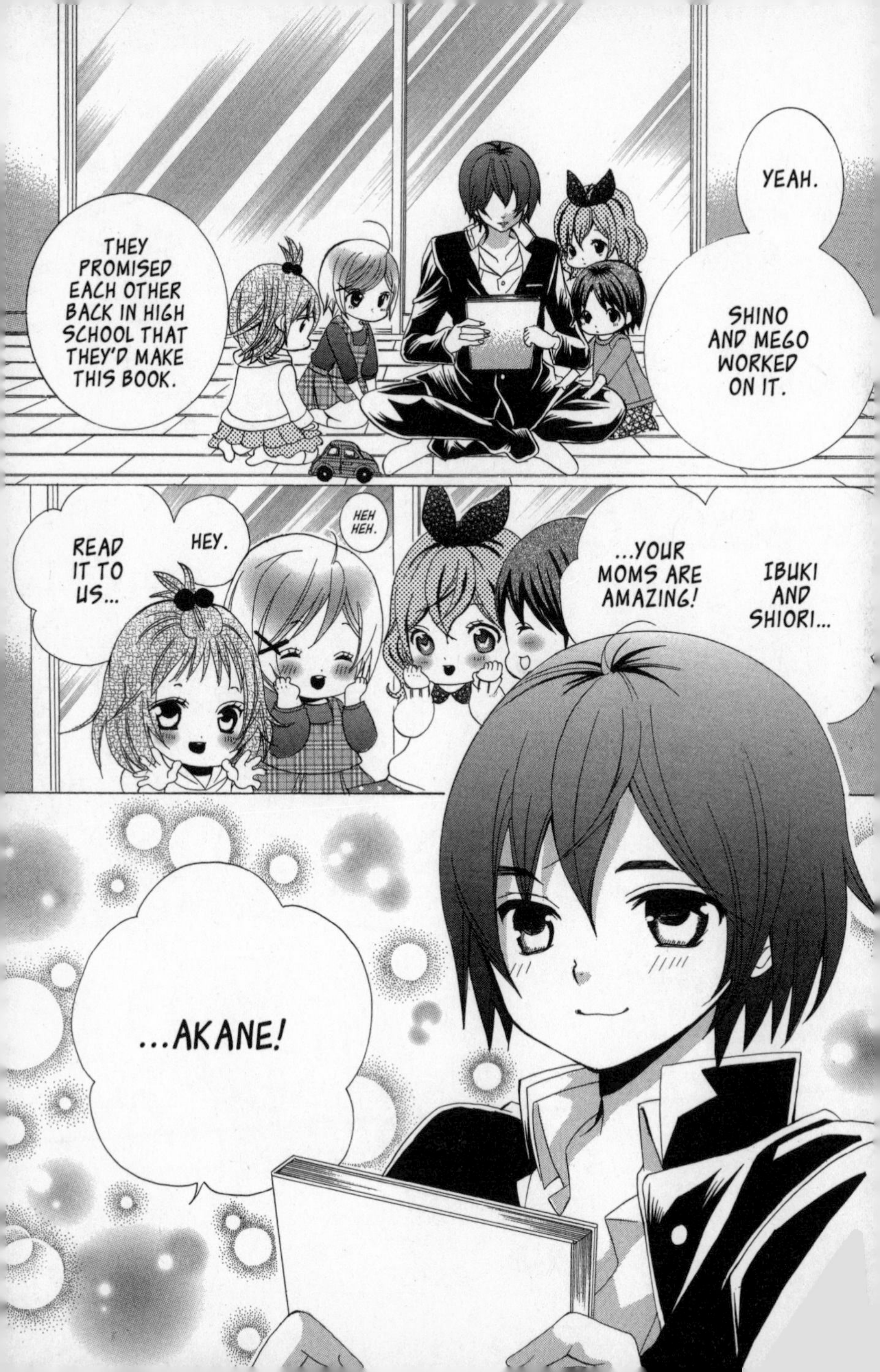
YEAH.
SHINO AND MEGO WORKED ON IT.
THEY PROMISED EACH OTHER BACK IN HIGH SCHOOL THAT THEY'D MAKE THIS BOOK.
IBUKI AND SHIORI...
...YOUR MOMS ARE AMAZING!
HEH HEH.
HEY.
READ IT TO US...
...AKANE!

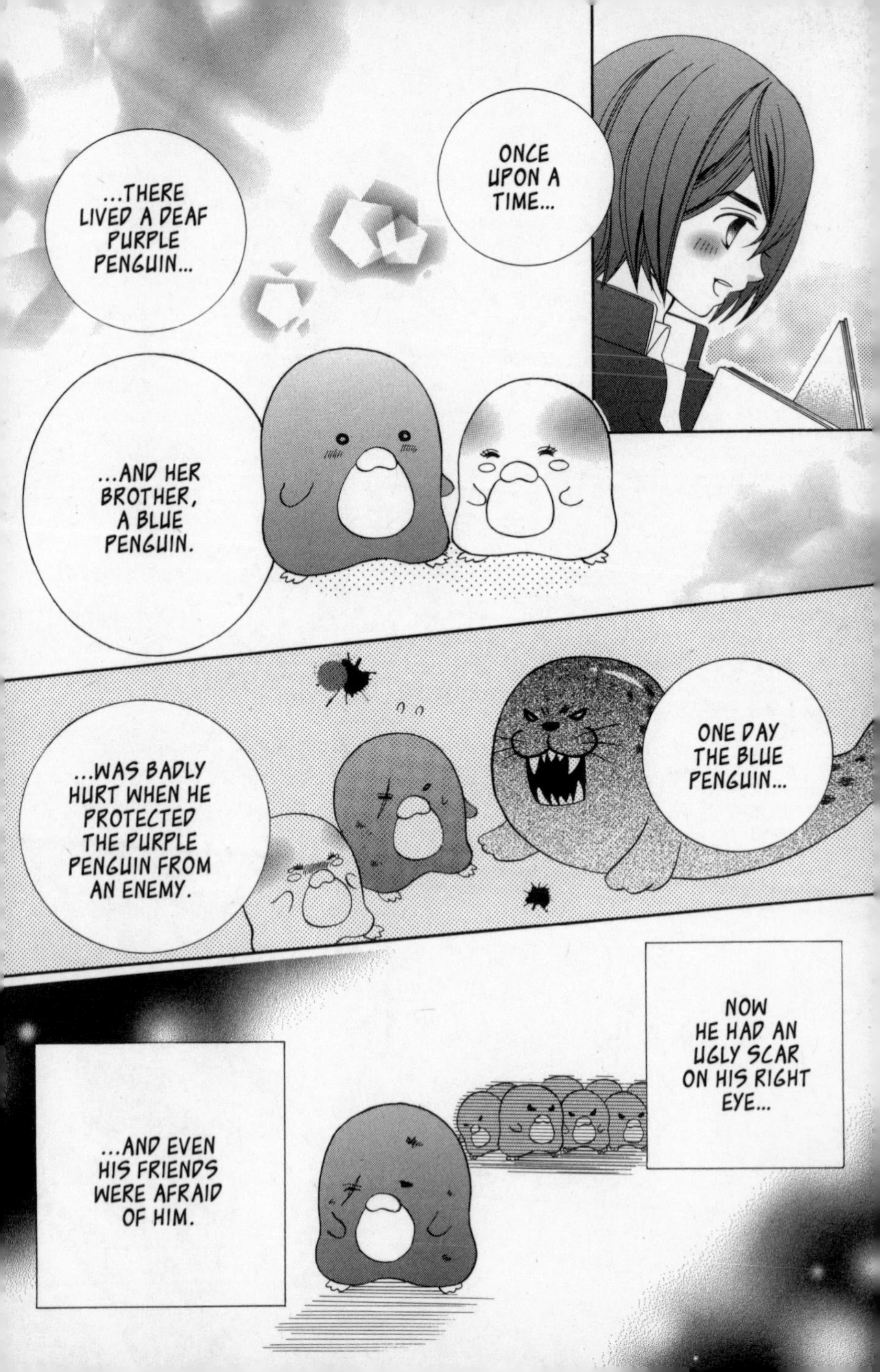
ONCE UPON A TIME...
...THERE LIVED A DEAF PURPLE PENGUIN...
...AND HER BROTHER, A BLUE PENGUIN.
ONE DAY THE BLUE PENGUIN...
...WAS BADLY HURT WHEN HE PROTECTED THE PURPLE PENGUIN FROM AN ENEMY.
NOW HE HAD AN UGLY SCAR ON HIS RIGHT EYE...
...AND EVEN HIS FRIENDS WERE AFRAID OF HIM.

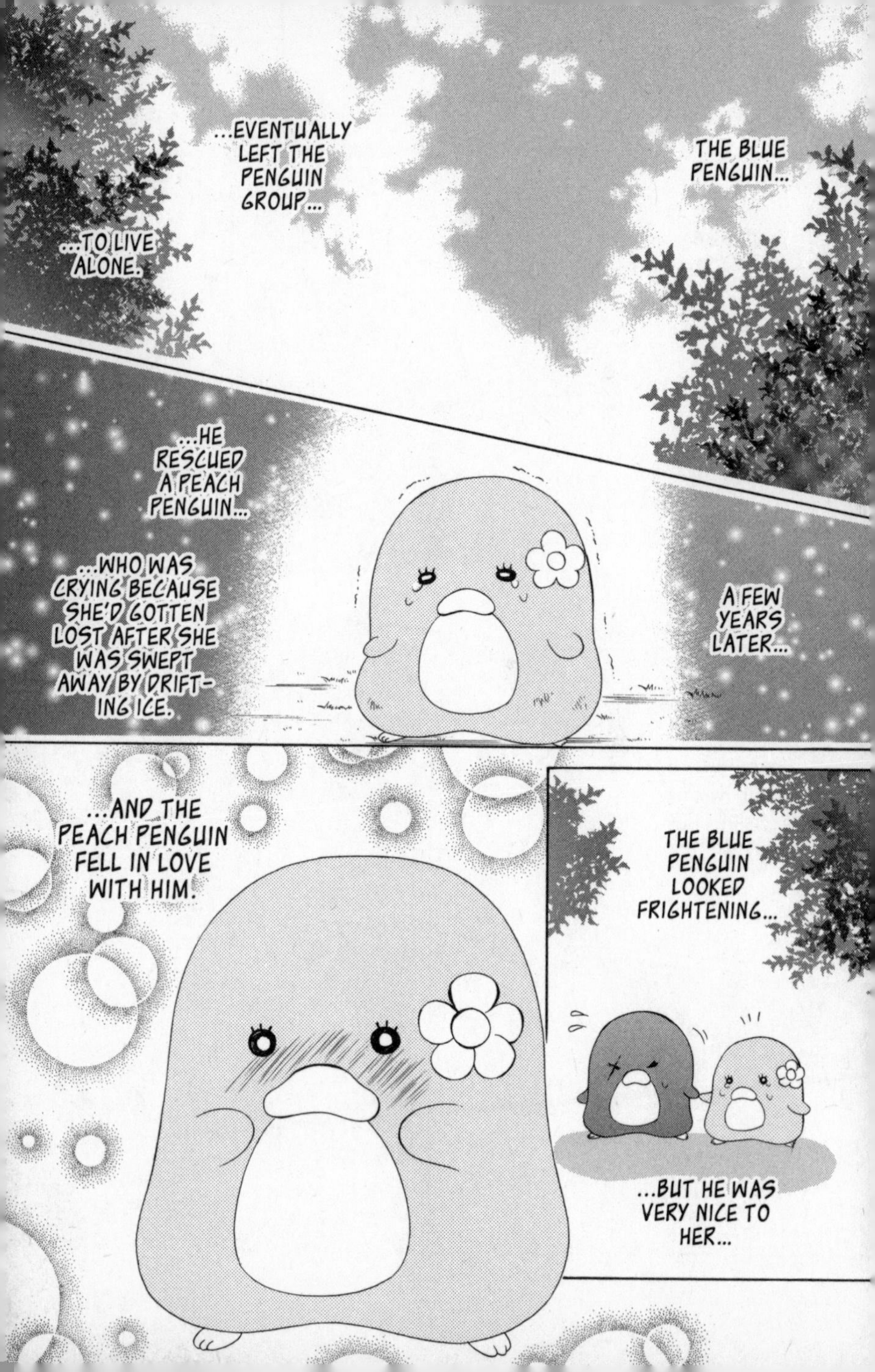
THE BLUE PENGUIN...
...EVENTUALLY LEFT THE PENGUIN GROUP...
...TO LIVE ALONE.
A FEW YEARS LATER...
...HE RESCUED A PEACH PENGUIN...
...WHO WAS CRYING BECAUSE SHE'D GOTTEN LOST AFTER SHE WAS SWEPT AWAY BY DRIFT-ING ICE.
THE BLUE PENGUIN LOOKED FRIGHTENING...
...BUT HE WAS VERY NICE TO HER...
...AND THE PEACH PENGUIN FELL IN LOVE WITH HIM.

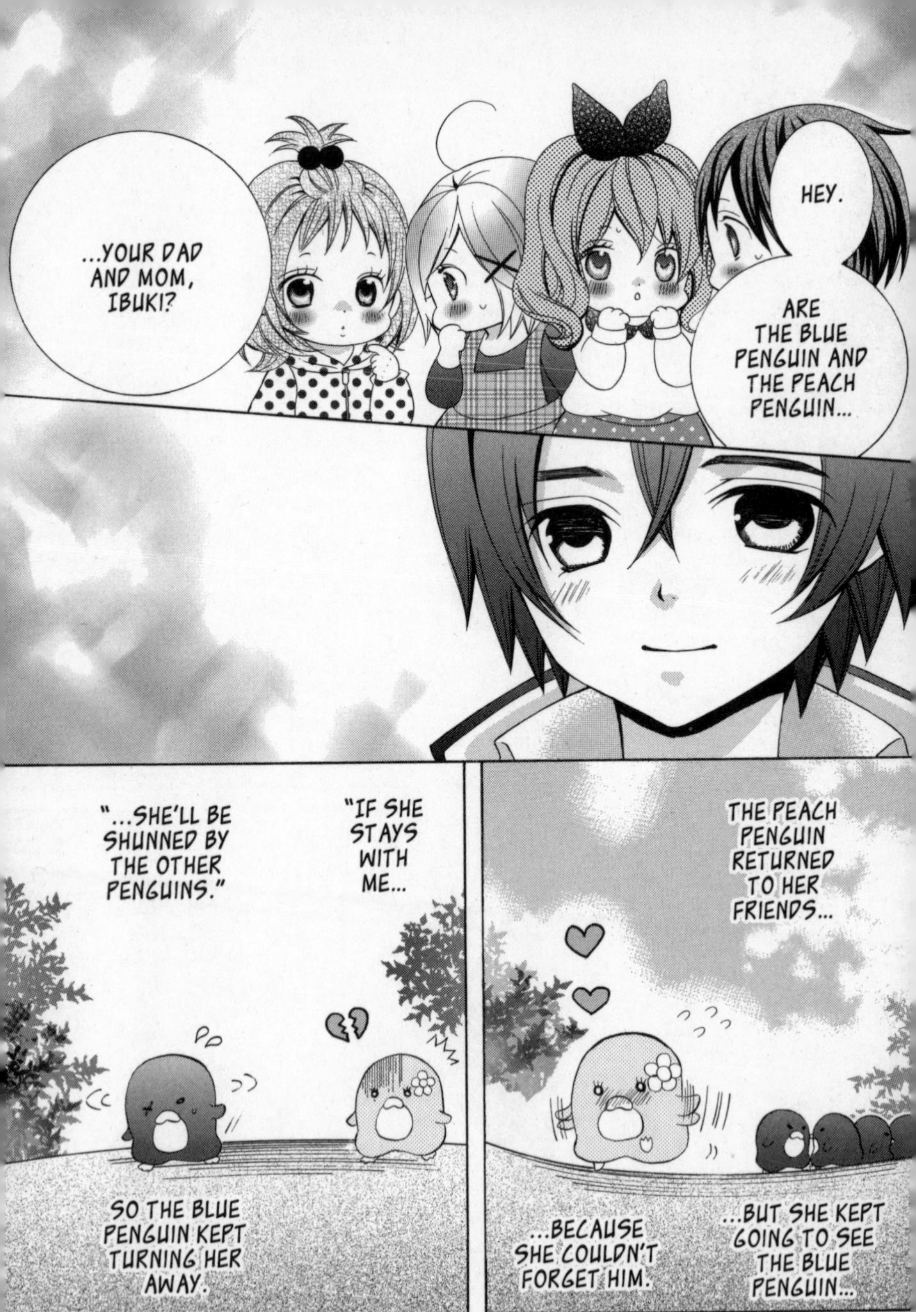
HEY.
ARE THE BLUE PENGUIN AND THE PEACH PENGUIN...
...YOUR DAD AND MOM, IBUKI?
THE PEACH PENGUIN RETURNED TO HER FRIENDS...
...BUT SHE KEPT GOING TO SEE THE BLUE PENGUIN...
...BECAUSE SHE COULDN'T FORGET HIM.
"IF SHE STAYS WITH ME...
"...SHE'LL BE SHUNNED BY THE OTHER PENGUINS."
SO THE BLUE PENGUIN KEPT TURNING HER AWAY.

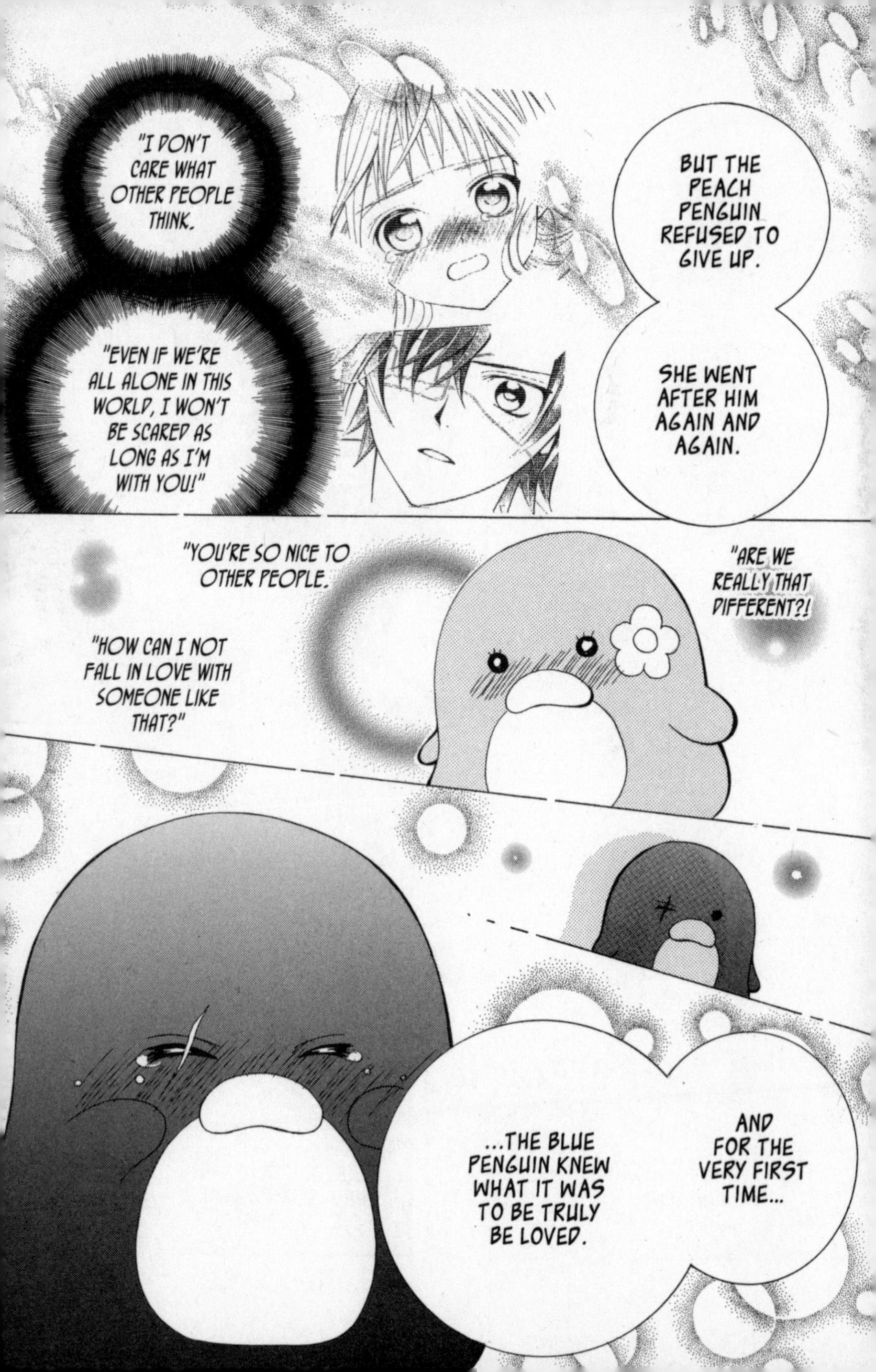
BUT THE PEACH PENGUIN REFUSED TO GIVE UP.
SHE WENT AFTER HIM AGAIN AND AGAIN.
"I DON'T CARE WHAT OTHER PEOPLE THINK.
"EVEN IF WE'RE ALL ALONE IN THIS WORLD, I WON'T BE SCARED AS LONG AS I'M WITH YOU!"
"ARE WE REALLY THAT DIFFERENT?!
"YOU'RE SO NICE TO OTHER PEOPLE.
"HOW CAN I NOT FALL IN LOVE WITH SOMEONE LIKE THAT?"
AND FOR THE VERY FIRST TIME...
...THE BLUE PENGUIN KNEW WHAT IT WAS TO BE TRULY BE LOVED.

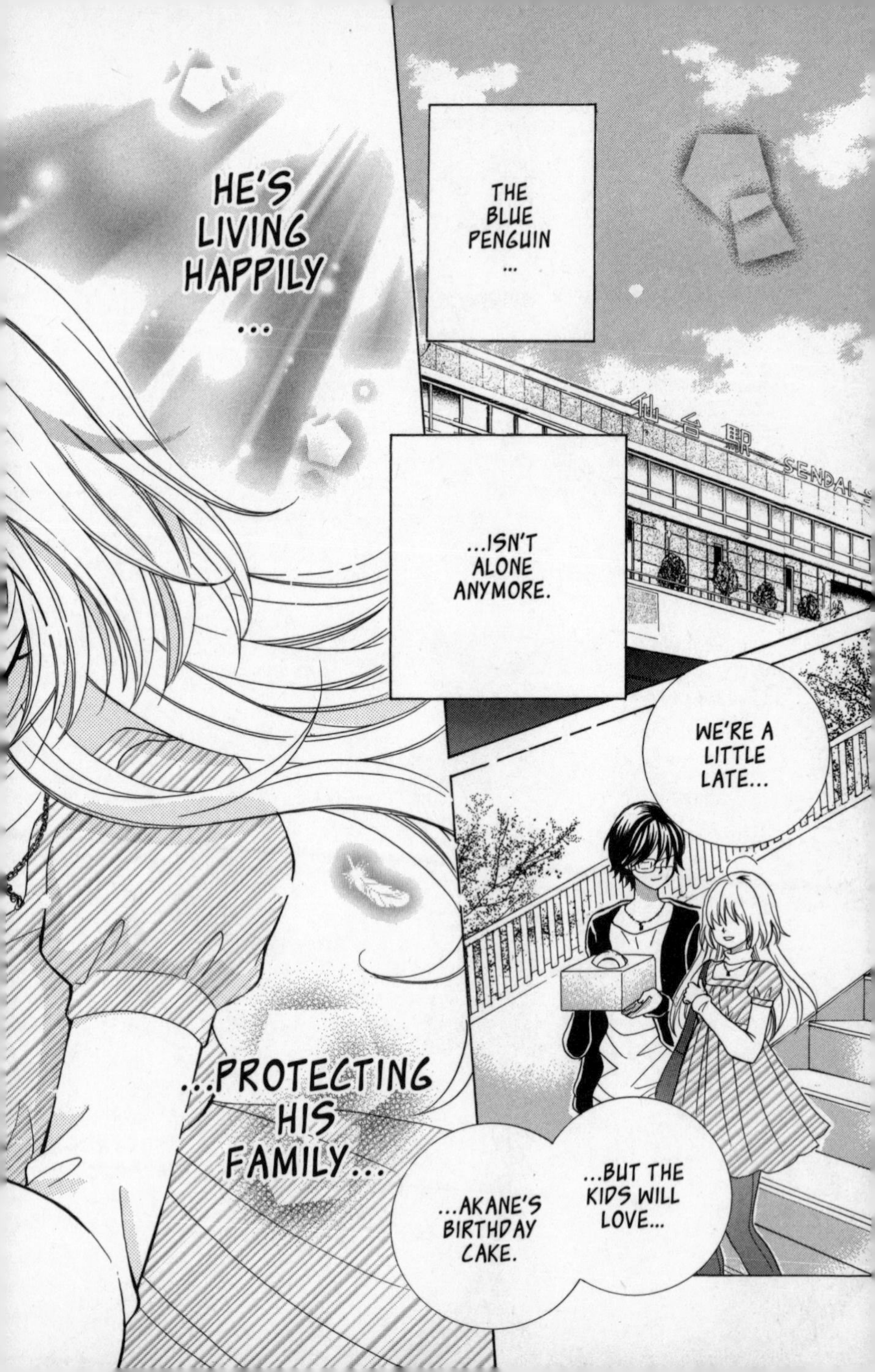
THE BLUE PENGUIN ...
仙台駅
SENDAI
...ISN'T ALONE ANYMORE.
WE'RE A LITTLE LATE...
...BUT THE KIDS WILL LOVE...
...AKANE'S BIRTHDAY CAKE.
HE'S LIVING HAPPILY ...
...PROTECTING HIS FAMILY...

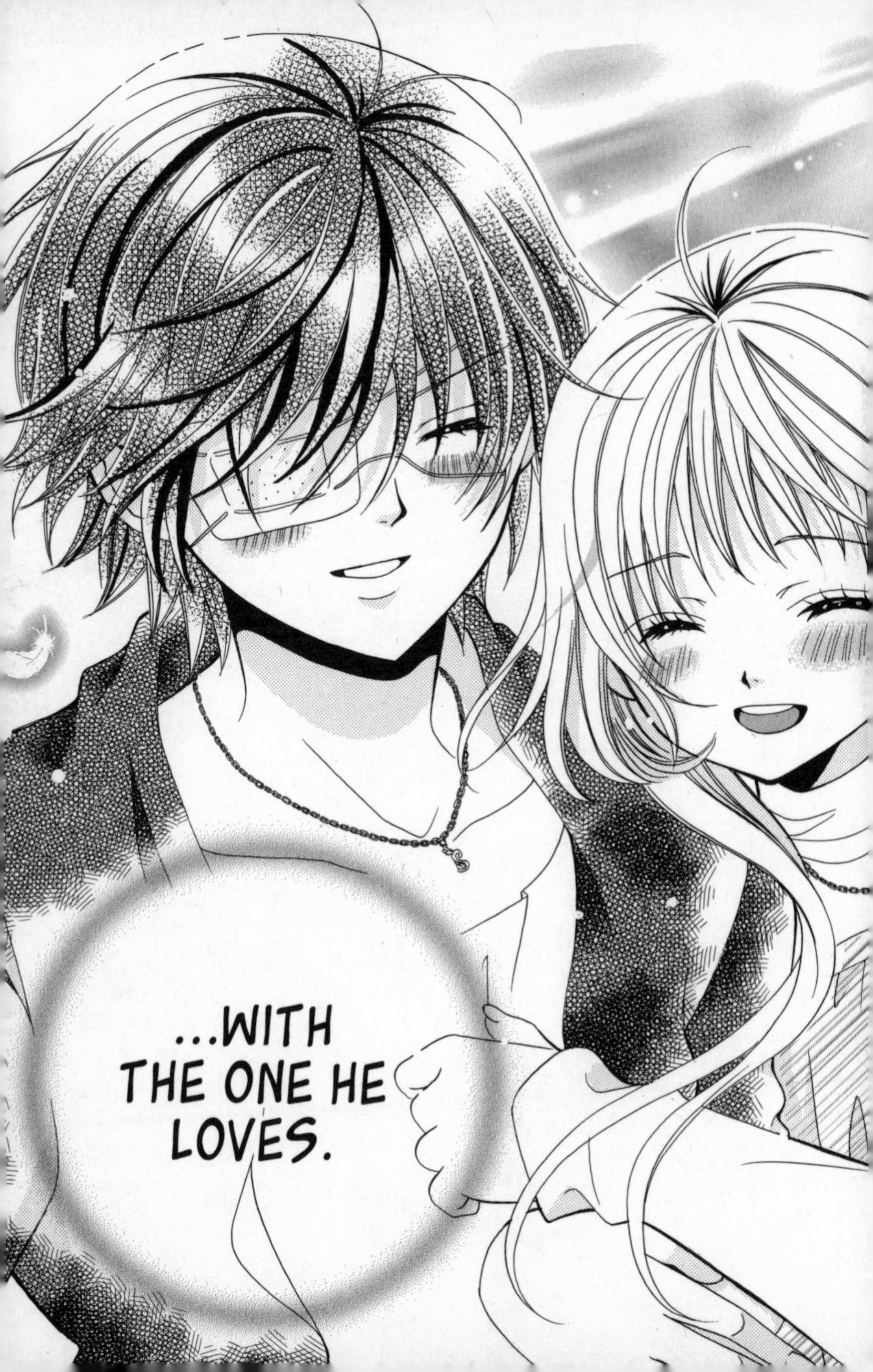
...WITH THE ONE HE LOVES.

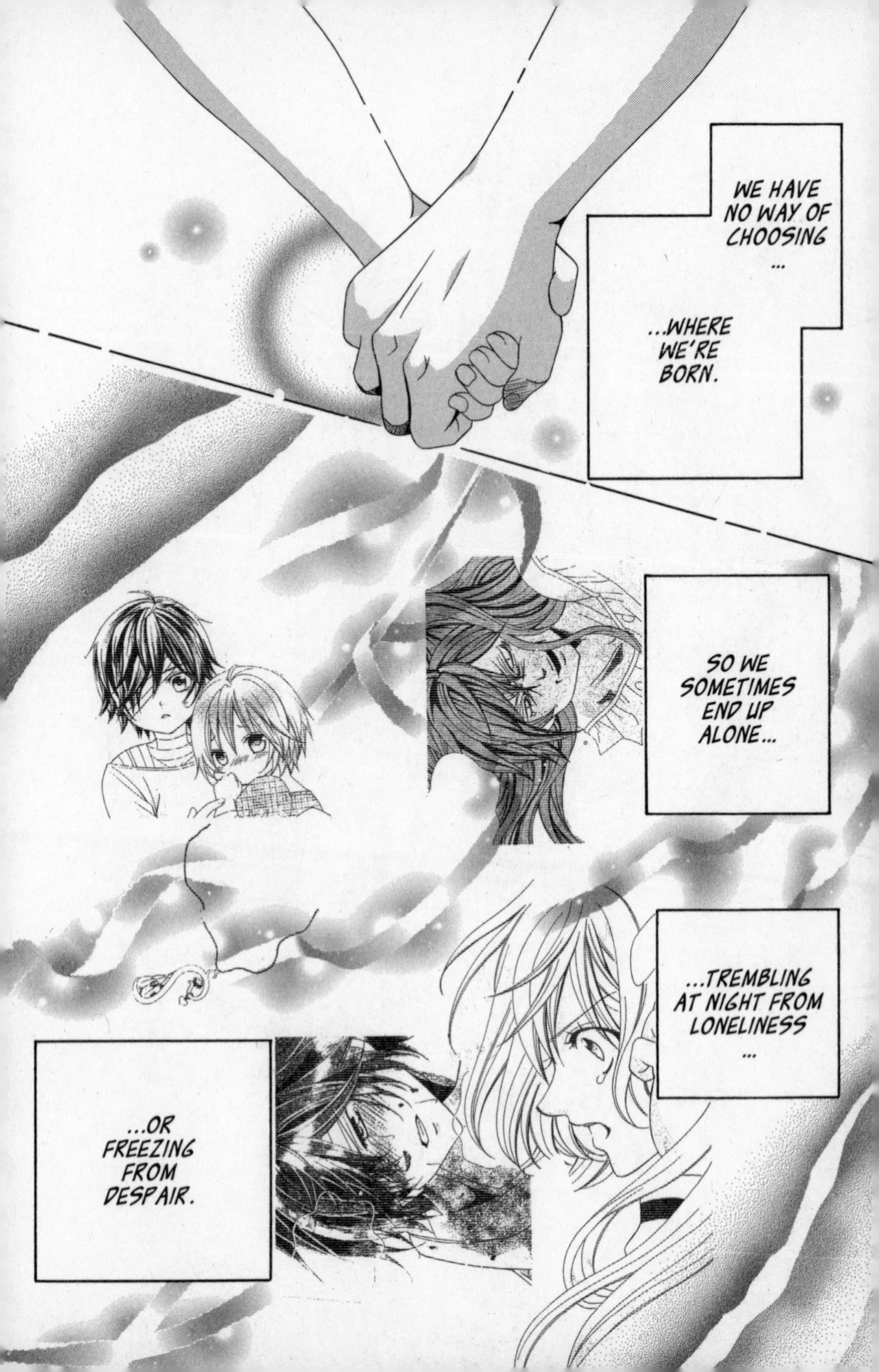
WE HAVE NO WAY OF CHOOSING ...
...WHERE WE'RE BORN.
SO WE SOMETIMES END UP ALONE...
...TREMBLING AT NIGHT FROM LONELINESS ...
...OR FREEZING FROM DESPAIR.

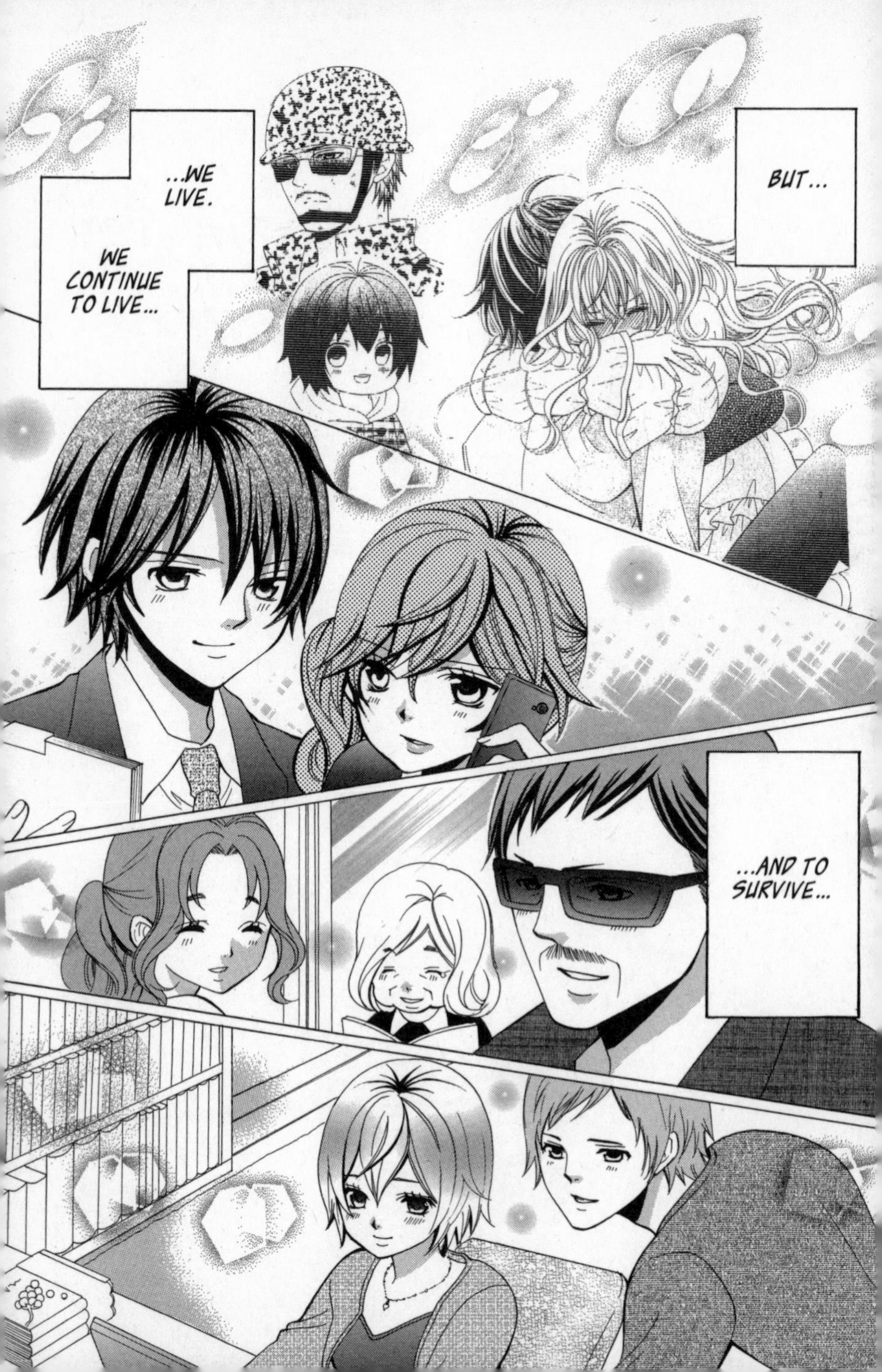
BUT...
...WE LIVE.
WE CONTINUE TO LIVE...
...AND TO SURVIVE...

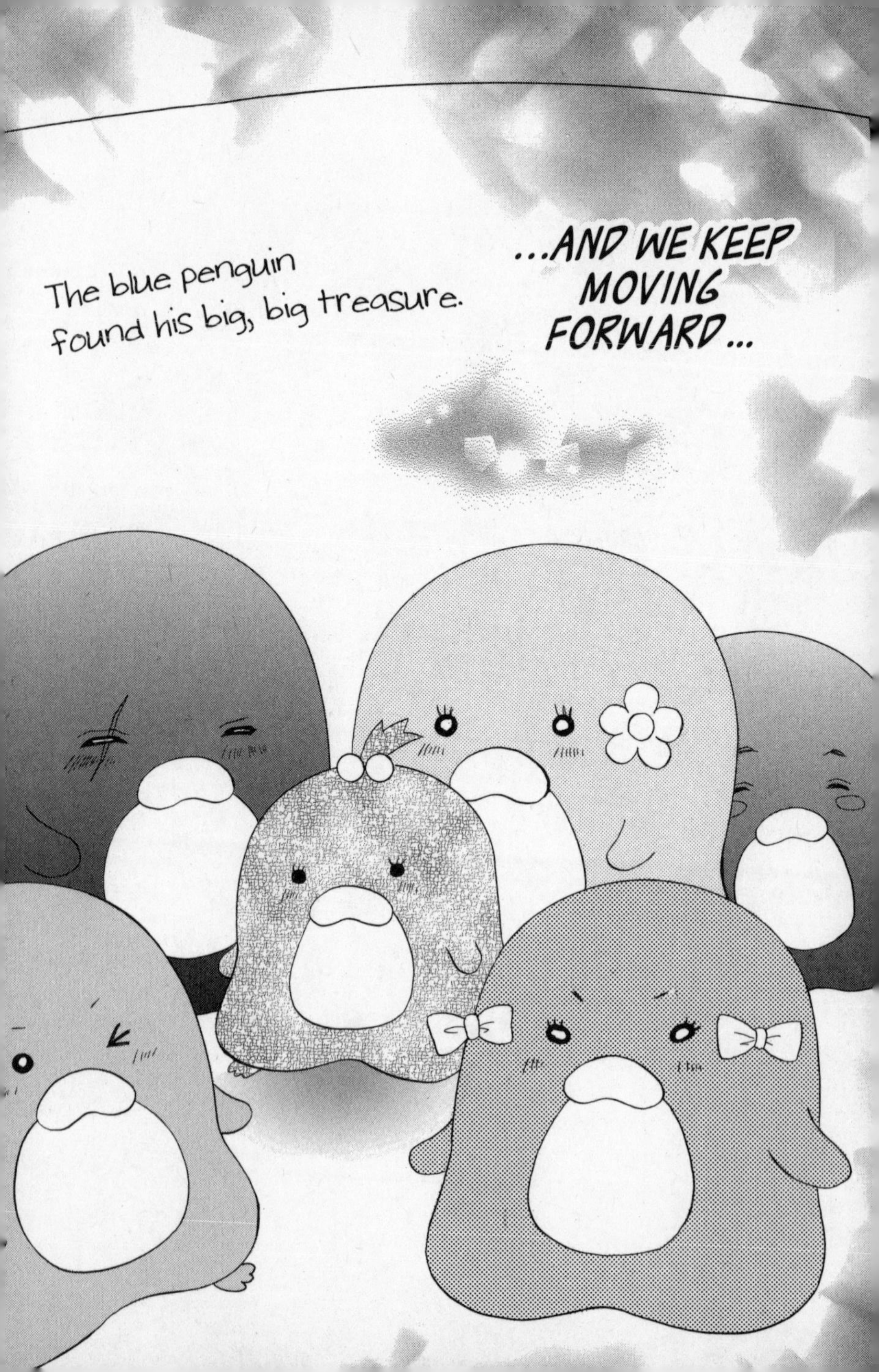
...AND WE KEEP MOVING FORWARD...
The blue penguin found his big, big treasure.

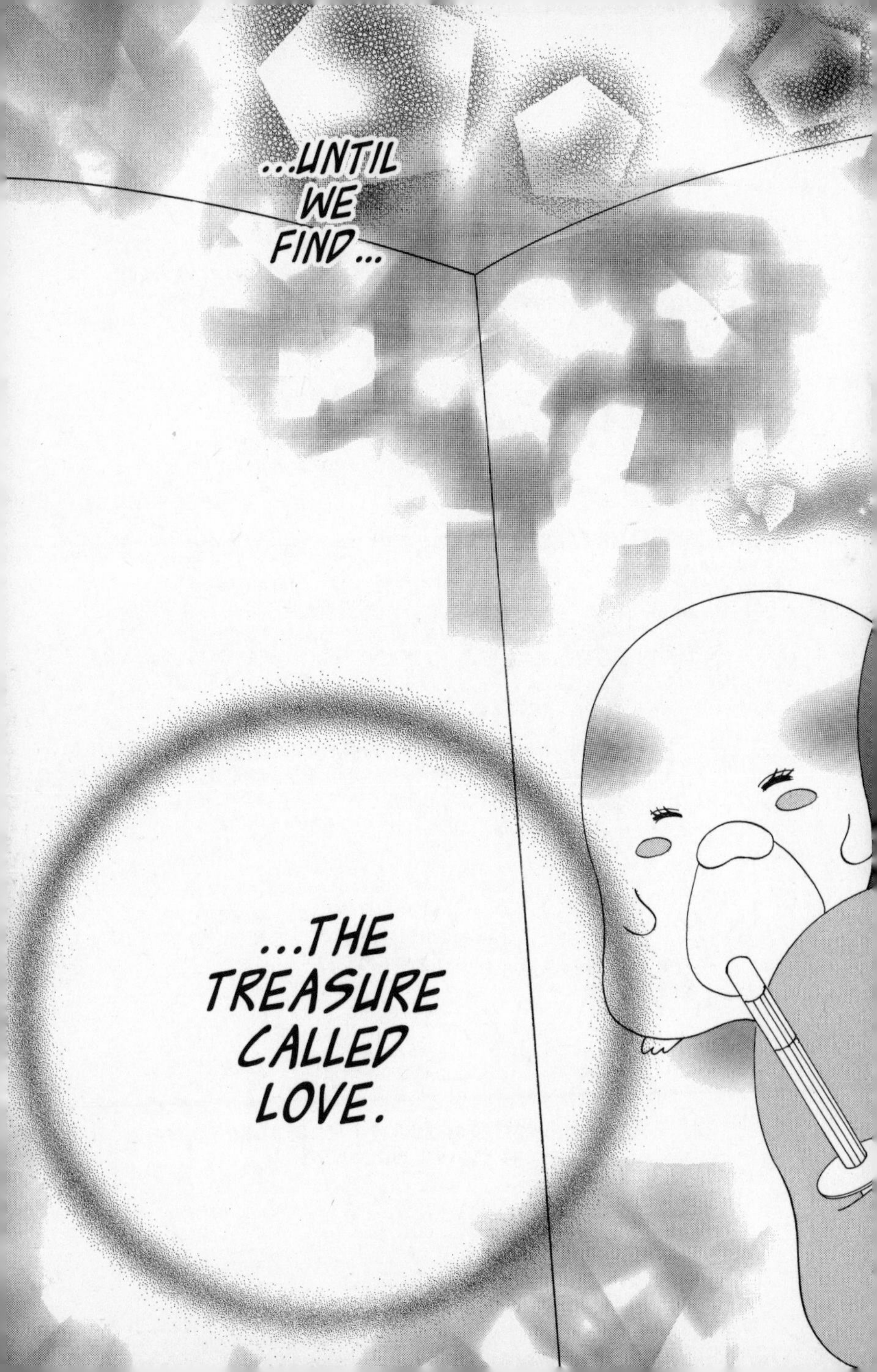
...UNTIL WE FIND...
...THE TREASURE CALLED LOVE.

SPECIAL THANKS!!

THANK YOU SO MUCH FOR SUPPORTING SO CUTE!

KAYOKO TAKAHASHI-SAMA, YUKAKO KAWASAKI-SAMA, NAGISA SATO SENSEI, MUMI MIMURA SENSEI, ARISU FUJISHIRO SENSEI, MASAYO NAGATA-SAMA, YUKO NEGISHI-SAMA, ERINA HOSHIKAWA-SAMA, ASUKA SAKURA-SAMA, NAO-CHAN-SAMA.

YUKA ITO-SAMA, RIEKO HIRAI-SAMA, REI NANASE SENSEI, MIEKO-SUGIMOTO-SAMA, AND MANY OTHERS.

HAPPINET-SAMA FOR THE GAME, AND SOFTGARAGE-SAMA FOR THE OVA.

DAISUKE ONO-SAMA (GAME/ANIME), AYUMI FUJIMURA-SAMA (ANIME), AYAHI TAKAGAKI-SAMA (GAME), TATSUO SUZUKI-SAMA (GAME), AZUMI ASAKURA-SAMA (ANIME), YU SERIZAWA-SAMA (GAME), EMI HIRAYAMA-SAMA (GAME), SHOUTA AOI-SAMA (GAME), DAIKI YAMASHITA-SAMA (GAME), YUKI WAKAI-SAMA (GAME), RICCA TACHIBANA-SAMA (GAME), KOUTARO NISHIYAMA-SAMA (GAME), ATSUSHI IMARUOKA-SAMA (GAME), YU KIMURA-SAMA (SO CUTE! GAME GOODWILL AMBASSADOR).

BOOKSTORE DAN KINSHICHO BRANCH, KINOKUNIYA SHINJUKU BRANCH, LIBRO IKEBUKURO BRANCH, KINOKUNIYA HANKYU 32-BANGAI BRANCH, SENDAI HACHIMONJIYA BOOKSTORE, BOOKS HOSHINO KINTETSU PASS'E BRANCH, ASAHIYA TENNNOJI MIO BRANCH, KURASHIKI KIKUYA BOOKSTORE.

PREVIOUS EDITOR: KOHEI SHOJI-SAMA
CURRENT EDITOR: YUTARO ITO-SAMA
SALESPEOPLE: HATA-SAMA, IINUMA-SAMA
CHIEKO KUROKAWA-SAMA, KAORU KUROKI-SAMA,
MISATO HONMA-SAMA

MY SINCEREST GRATITUDE TO ALL OF YOU!!
THANK YOU SO, SO MUCH!!

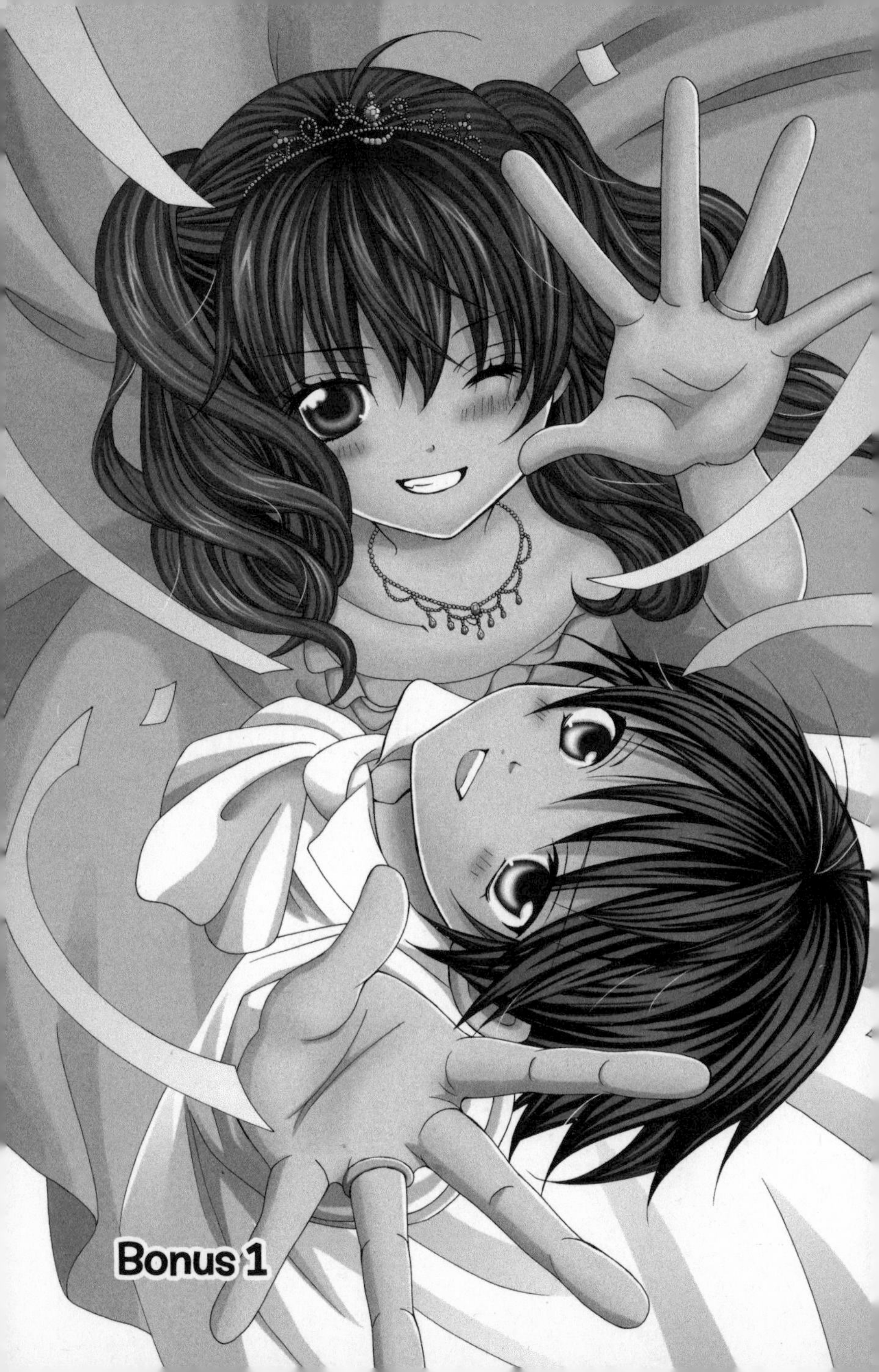
Bonus 1

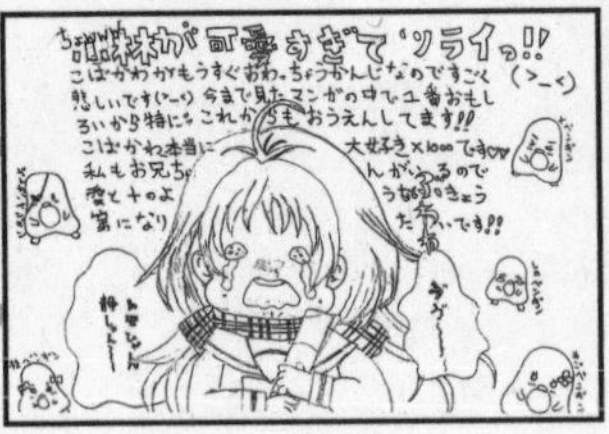
小林が可愛すぎてツライっ!!
(>_<)

Aina Kamisawa (Kanagawa) ←

Ed.: Mego's so adorably ugly it hurts!!

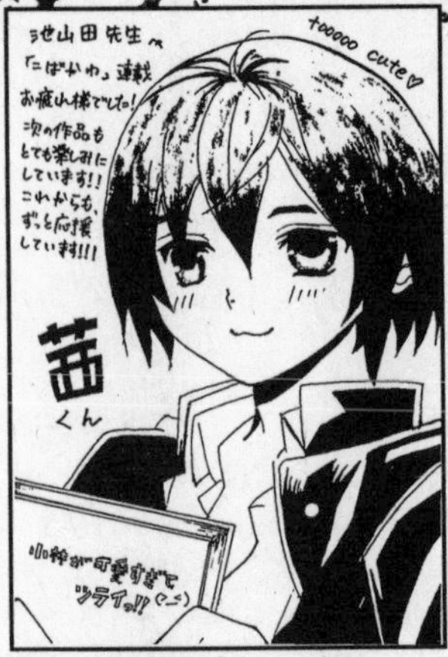
ミセ山田先生へ
「こばかわ」連載お疲れ様でした!
次の作品もとても楽しみにしています!!
これからも、ずっと応援しています!!!
tooooo cute♡
茜くん
小林が可愛すぎてツライっ!! (>_<)

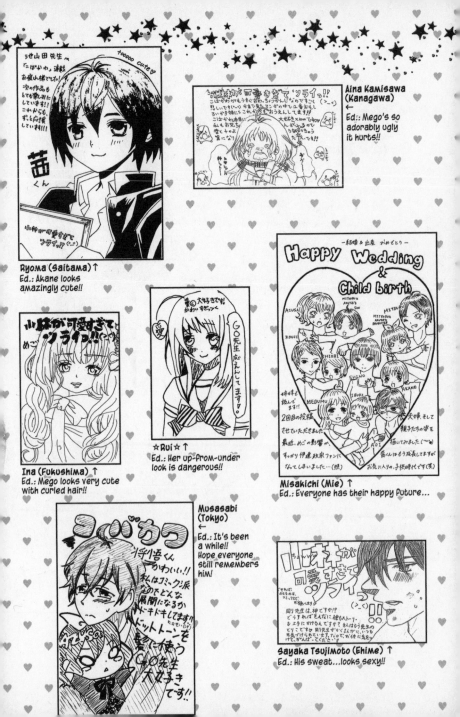

Ryoma (Saitama) ↑

Ed.: Akane looks amazingly cute!!

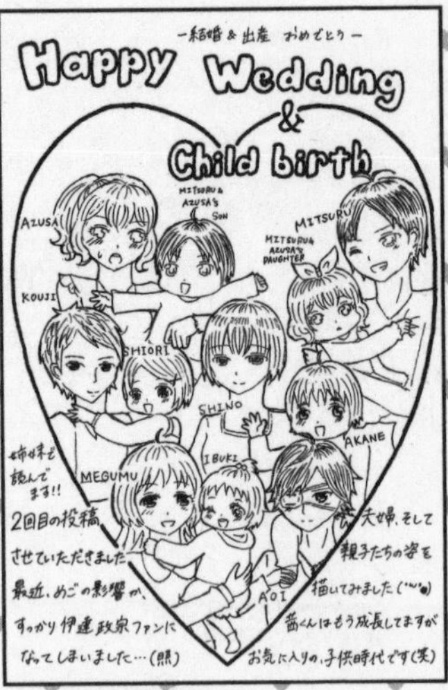
―結婚&出産 おめでとう―
Happy Wedding & Child birth
AZUSA
MITSURU & AZUSA'S SON
MITSURU
MITSURU & AZUSA'S DAUGHTER
KOUJI
SHIORI
SHINO
AKANE
MEGUMU
IBUKI
AOI
姉妹で読んでます!!
2回目の投稿させていただきました
最近、めごの影響か、すっかり伊達政宗ファンになってしまいました…(照)
夫婦、そして親子たちの姿を描いてみました
茜くんはもう成長してますがお気に入りの子供時代です(笑)

Misakichi (Mie) ↑

Ed.: Everyone has their happy future...

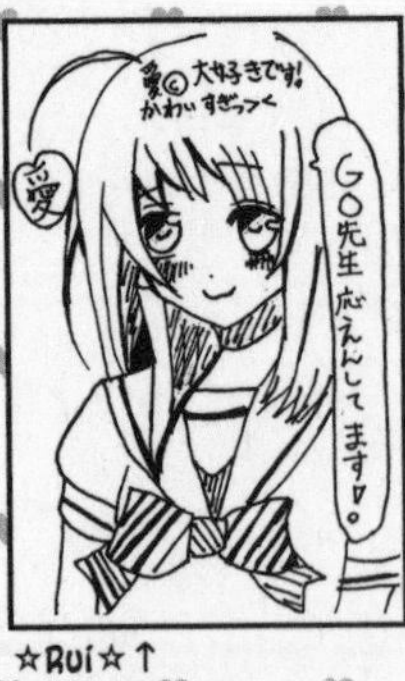
愛© 大好きです!
かわいすぎっっく
愛
GO先生応えんしてます♡。

☆Rui☆ ↑

Ed.: Her up-from-under look is dangerous!!

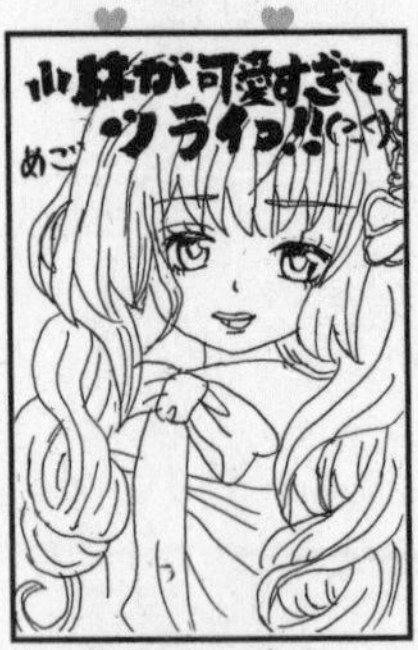
小林が可愛すぎてツライっ!! (>_<)
めご

Ina (Fukushima) ↑

Ed.: Mego looks very cute with curled hair!!

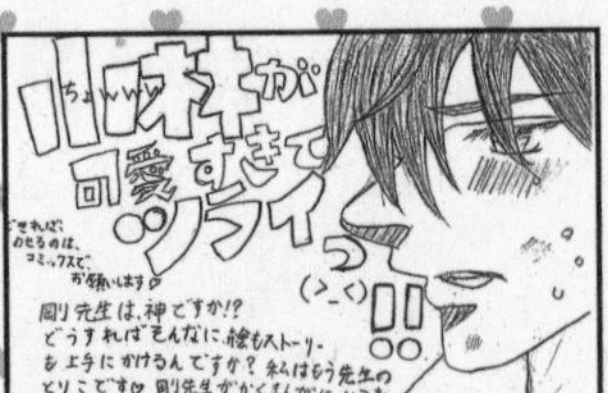
小林が可愛すぎてツライっ!!
(>_<)

Sayaka Tsujimoto (Ehime) ↑

Ed.: His sweat...looks sexy!!

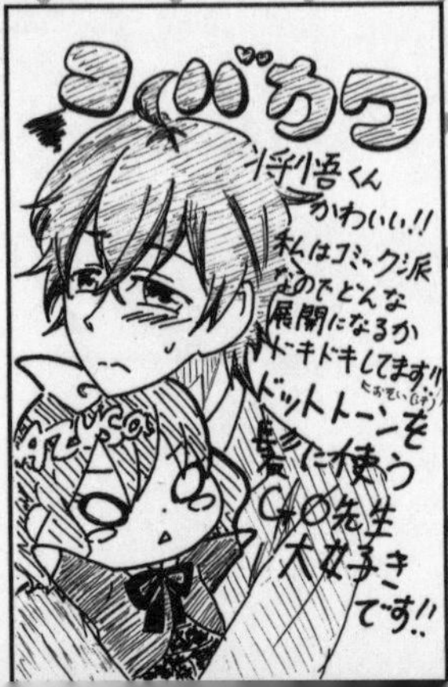
こばかわ
将悟くんかわいい!!
私はコミック派なのでどんな展開になるかドキドキしてます!!
ドットトーンを多用に使うGO先生大好きです!!

Musasabi (Tokyo) ←

Ed.: It's been a while!! Hope everyone still remembers him!

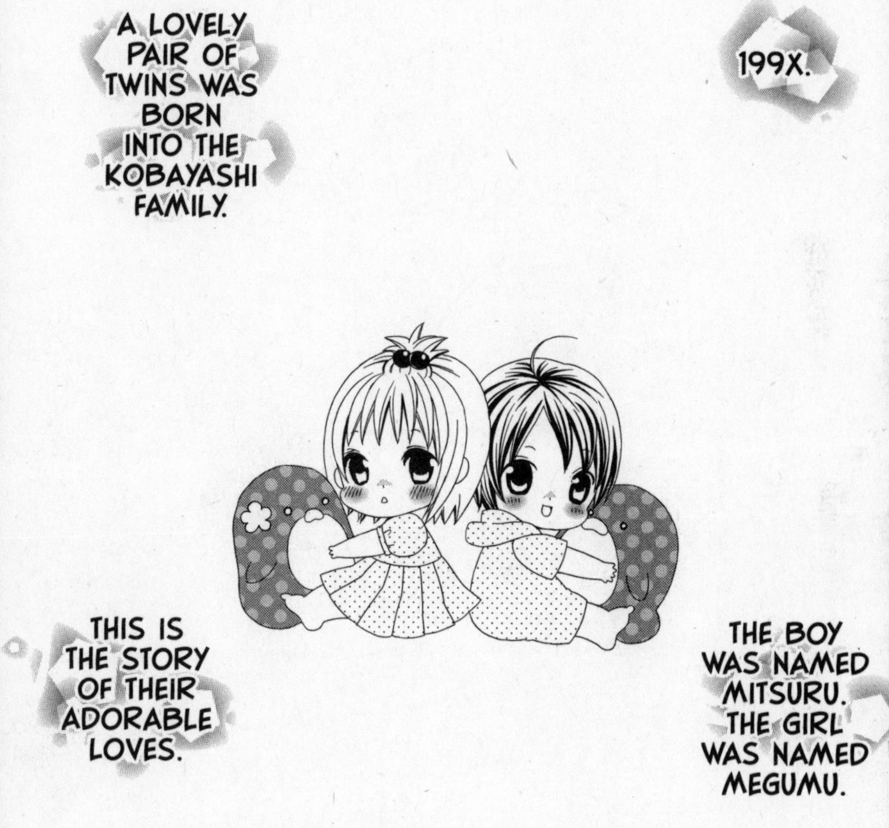
199X.
A LOVELY PAIR OF TWINS WAS BORN INTO THE KOBAYASHI FAMILY.
THE BOY WAS NAMED MITSURU. THE GIRL WAS NAMED MEGUMU.
THIS IS THE STORY OF THEIR ADORABLE LOVES.

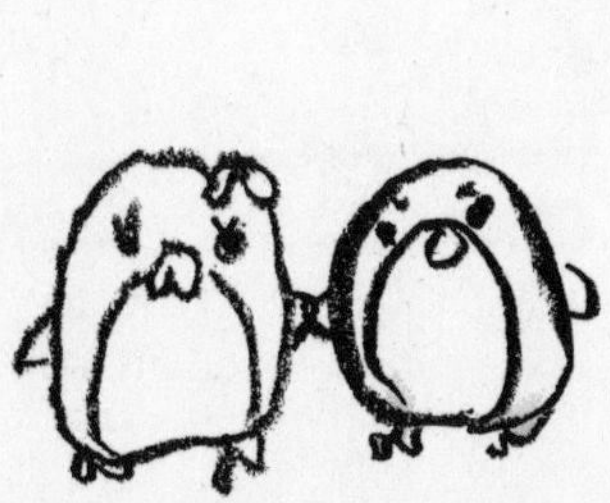

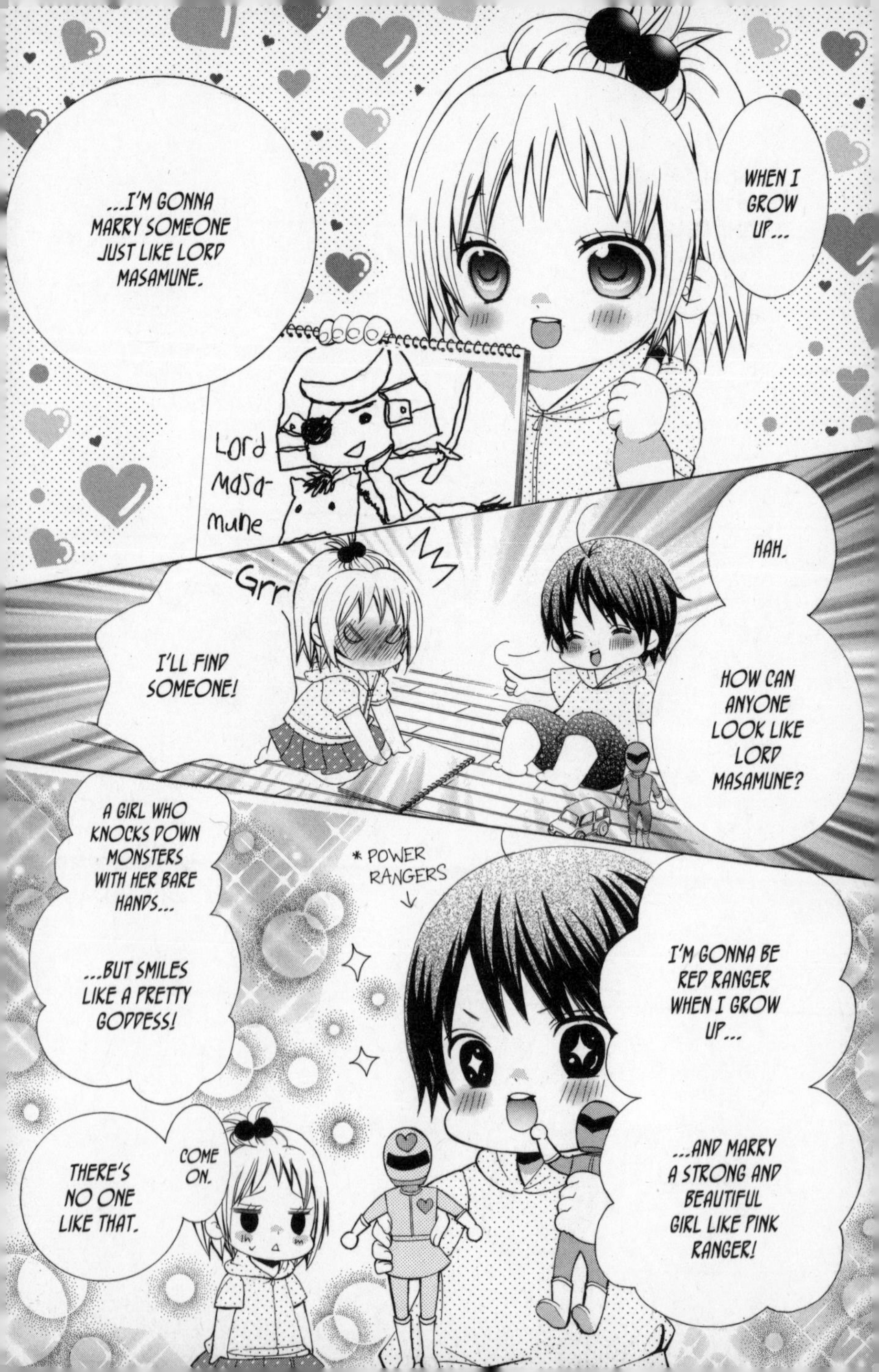
WHEN I GROW UP...
...I'M GONNA MARRY SOMEONE JUST LIKE LORD MASAMUNE.
Lord Masa-mune
HAH.
HOW CAN ANYONE LOOK LIKE LORD MASAMUNE?
Grr
I'LL FIND SOMEONE!
I'M GONNA BE RED RANGER WHEN I GROW UP...
...AND MARRY A STRONG AND BEAUTIFUL GIRL LIKE PINK RANGER!
* POWER RANGERS
A GIRL WHO KNOCKS DOWN MONSTERS WITH HER BARE HANDS...
...BUT SMILES LIKE A PRETTY GODDESS!
COME ON.
THERE'S NO ONE LIKE THAT.

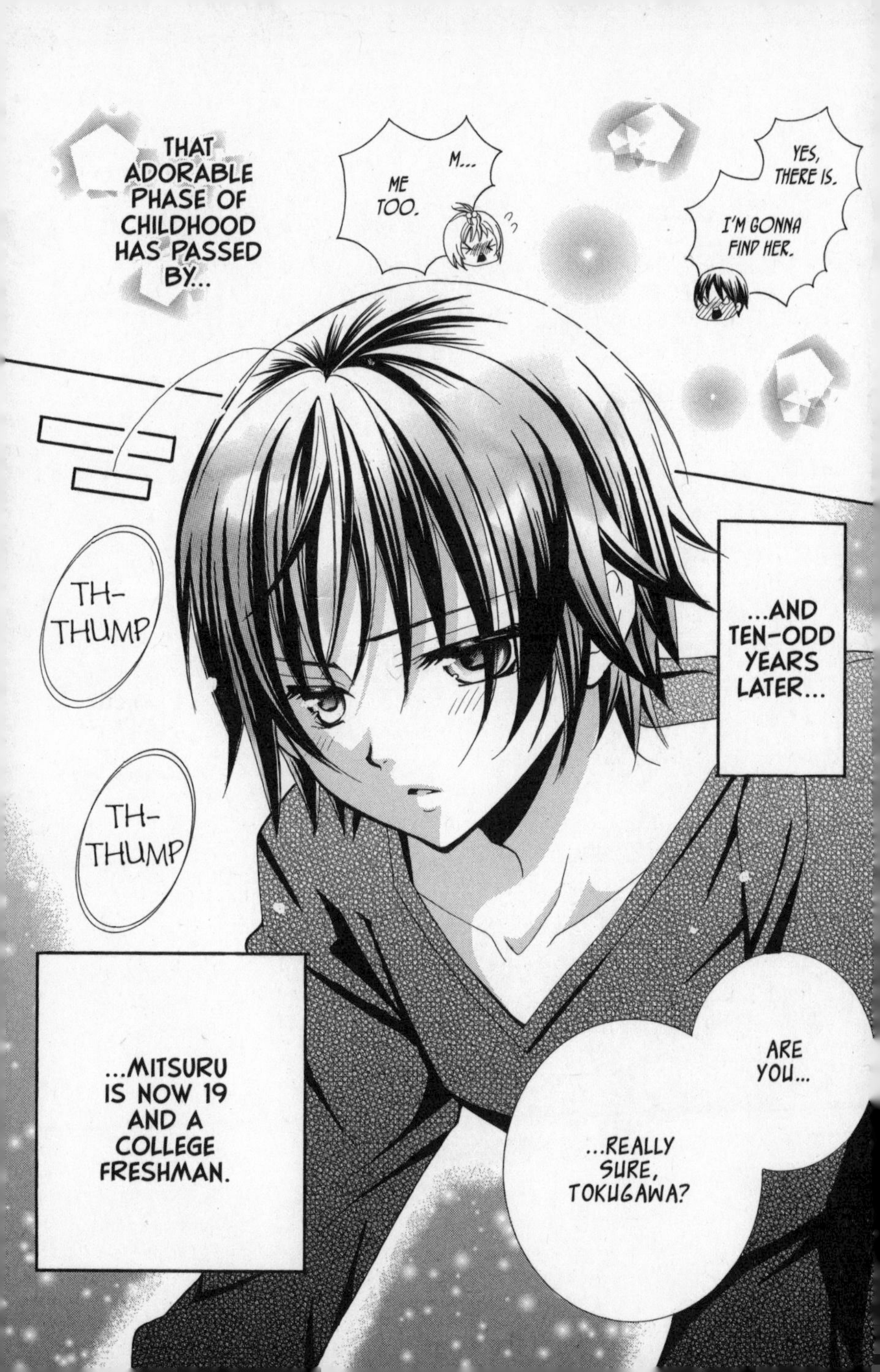
YES, THERE IS.
I'M GONNA FIND HER.
M...
ME TOO.
THAT ADORABLE PHASE OF CHILDHOOD HAS PASSED BY...
...AND TEN-ODD YEARS LATER...
TH-THUMP
TH-THUMP
ARE YOU...
...REALLY SURE, TOKUGAWA?
...MITSURU IS NOW 19 AND A COLLEGE FRESHMAN.

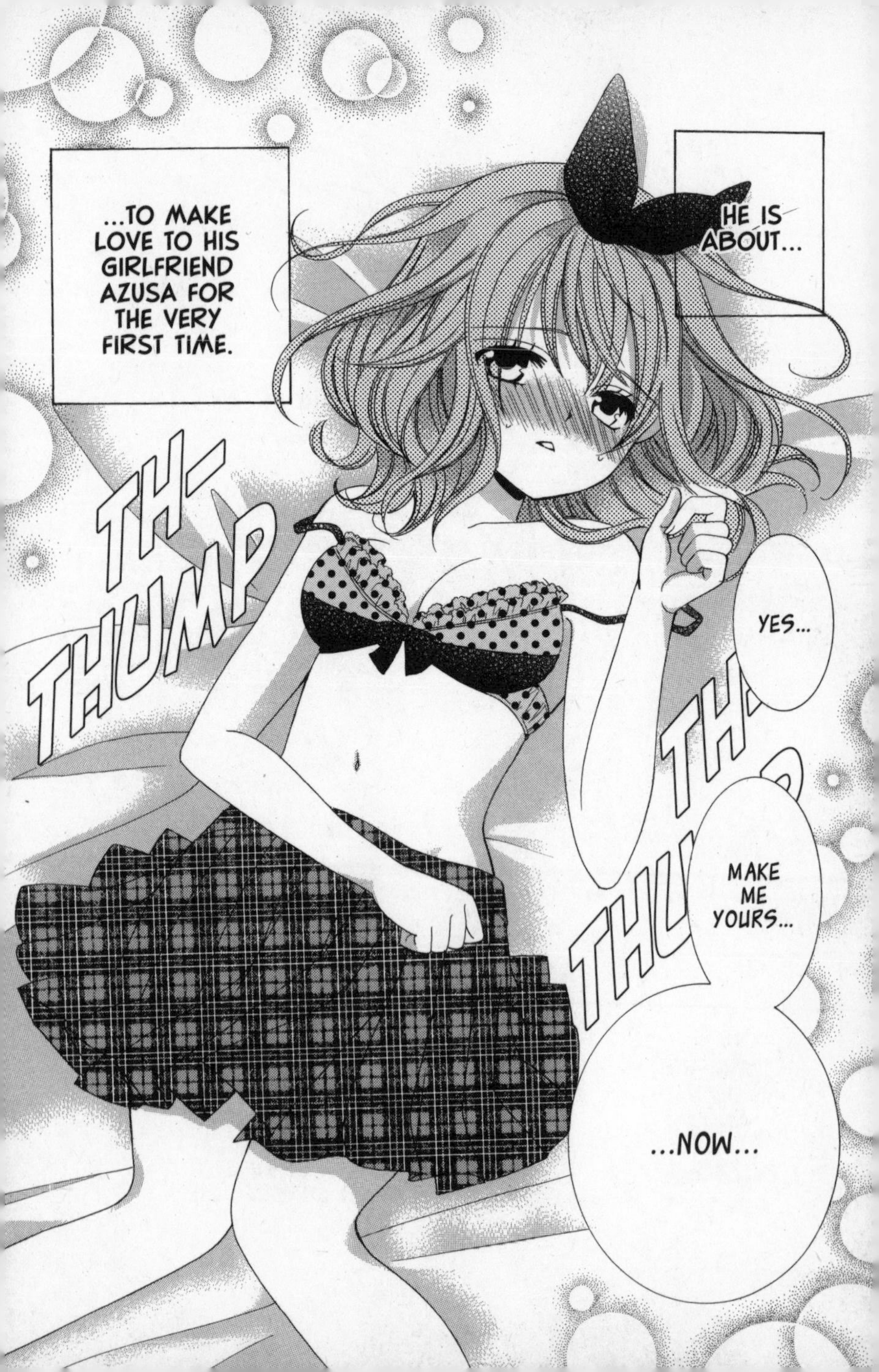
HE IS ABOUT...
...TO MAKE LOVE TO HIS GIRLFRIEND AZUSA FOR THE VERY FIRST TIME.
YES...
MAKE ME YOURS...
...NOW...
TH-THUMP

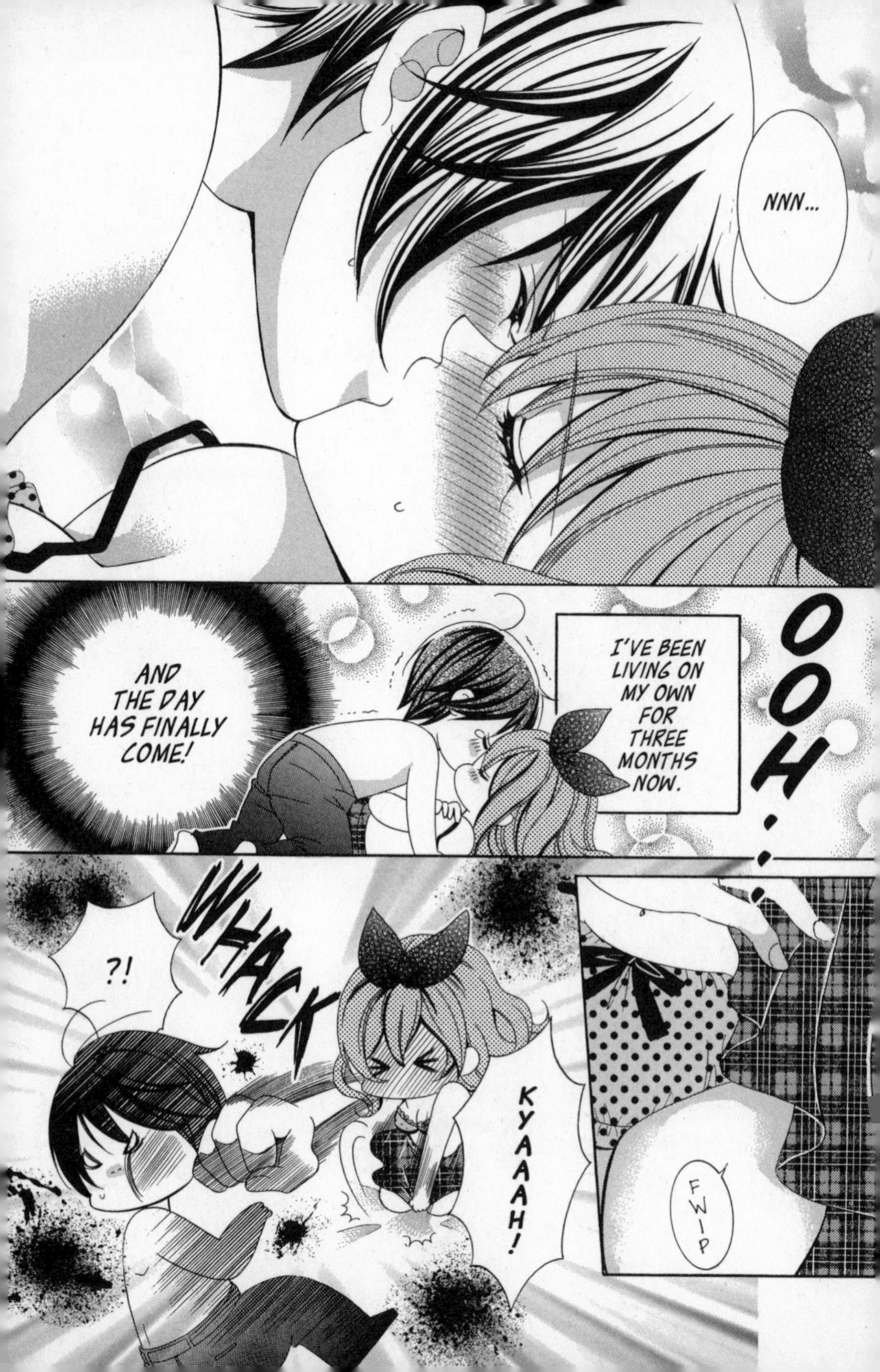
NNN...
OOOH...
I'VE BEEN LIVING ON MY OWN FOR THREE MONTHS NOW.
AND THE DAY HAS FINALLY COME!
FWIP
WHACK
?!
KYAAAAH!

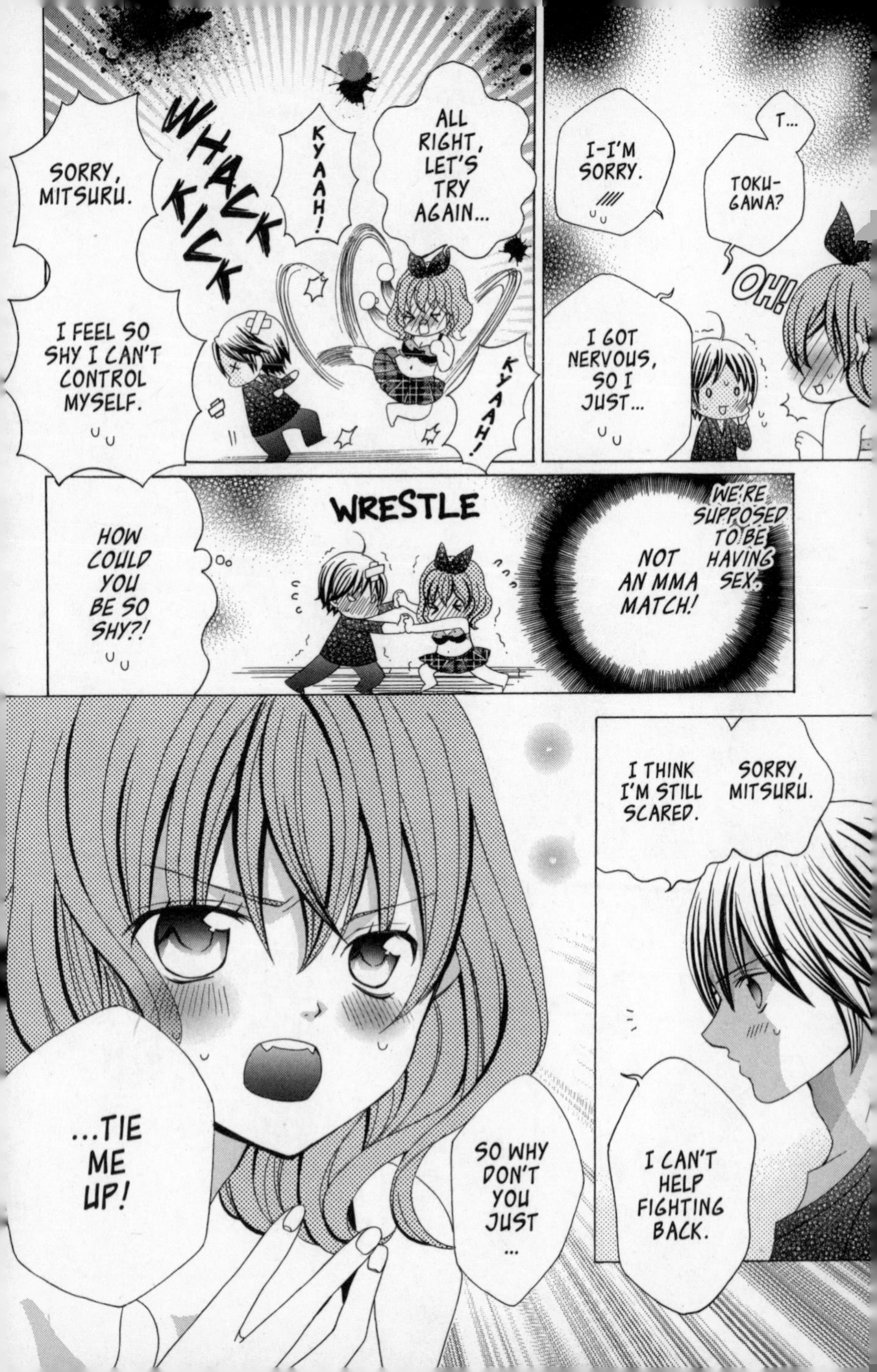
T...
TOKU-GAWA?
I-I'M SORRY.
OH!
I GOT NERVOUS, SO I JUST...
ALL RIGHT, LET'S TRY AGAIN...
KYAAAH!
KYAAAH!
WHACK
KICK
SORRY, MITSURU.
I FEEL SO SHY I CAN'T CONTROL MYSELF.
WE'RE SUPPOSED TO BE HAVING SEX,
NOT AN MMA MATCH!
WRESTLE
HOW COULD YOU BE SO SHY?!
SORRY, MITSURU.
I THINK I'M STILL SCARED.
I CAN'T HELP FIGHTING BACK.
SO WHY DON'T YOU JUST ...
...TIE ME UP!

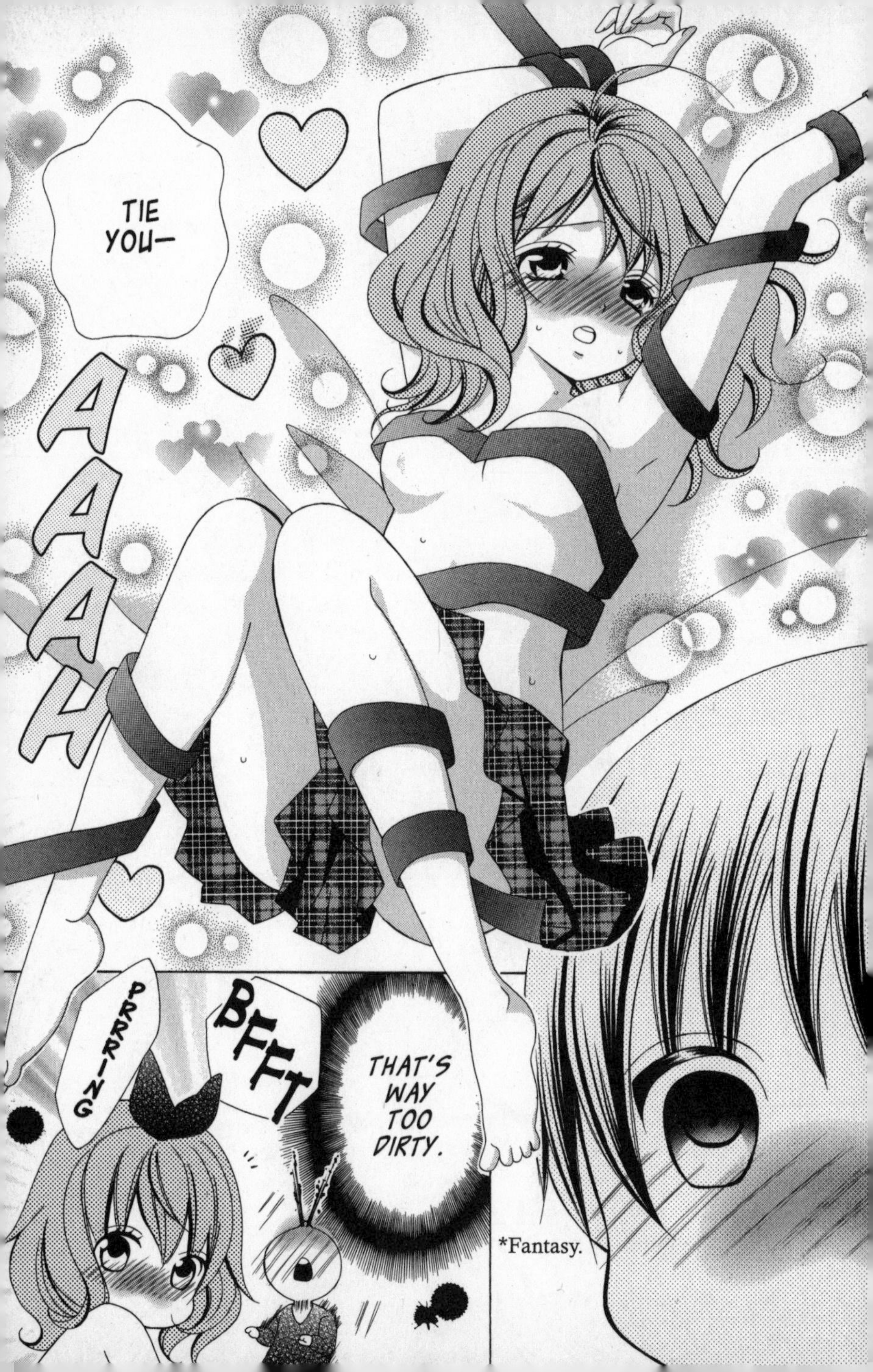
TIE YOU—
AAAAH
THAT'S WAY TOO DIRTY.
BFFT
PRRRING
*Fantasy.

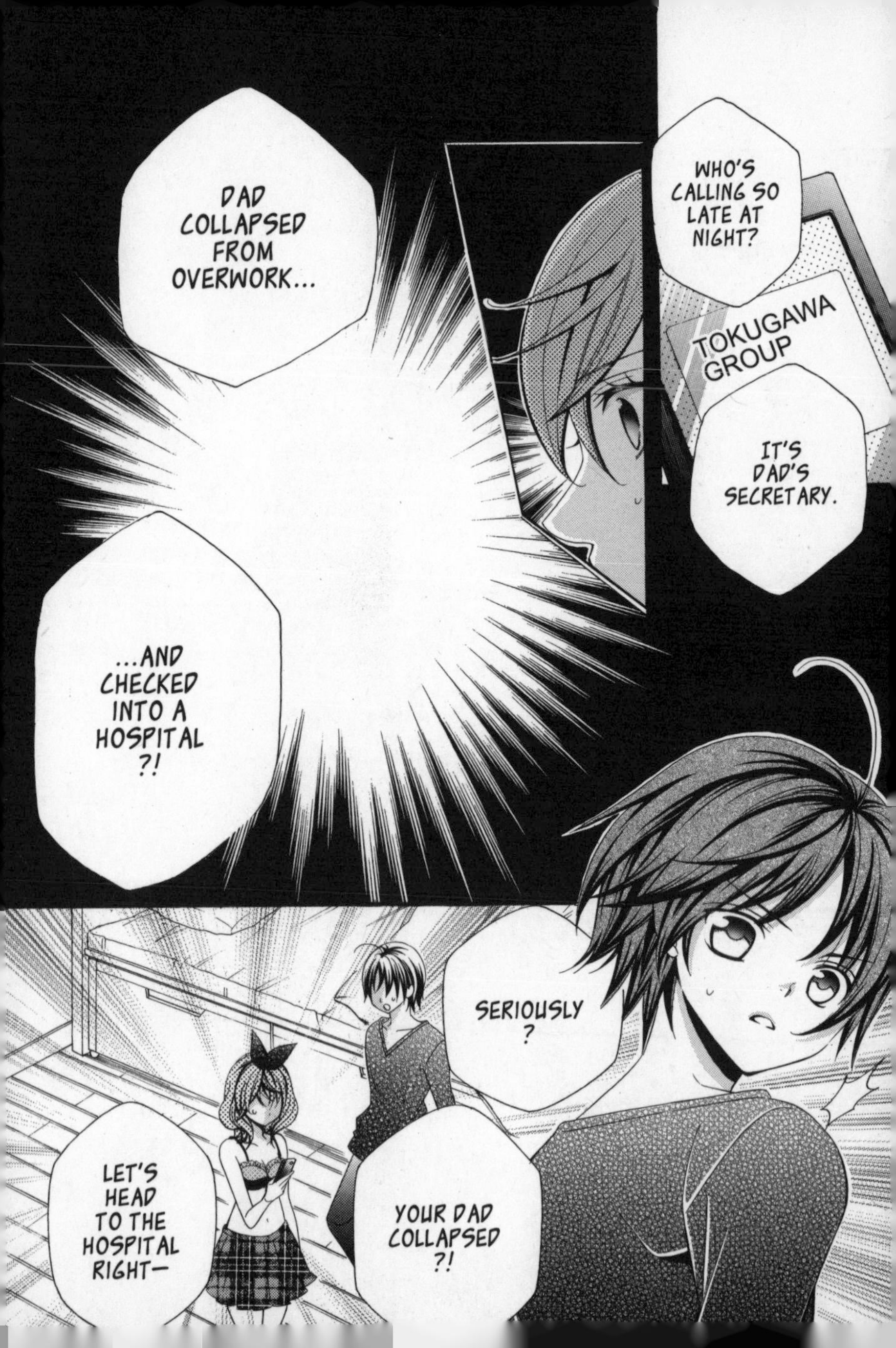
WHO'S CALLING SO LATE AT NIGHT?
TOKUGAWA GROUP
IT'S DAD'S SECRETARY.
DAD COLLAPSED FROM OVERWORK...
...AND CHECKED INTO A HOSPITAL?!
SERIOUSLY?
YOUR DAD COLLAPSED?!
LET'S HEAD TO THE HOSPITAL RIGHT—

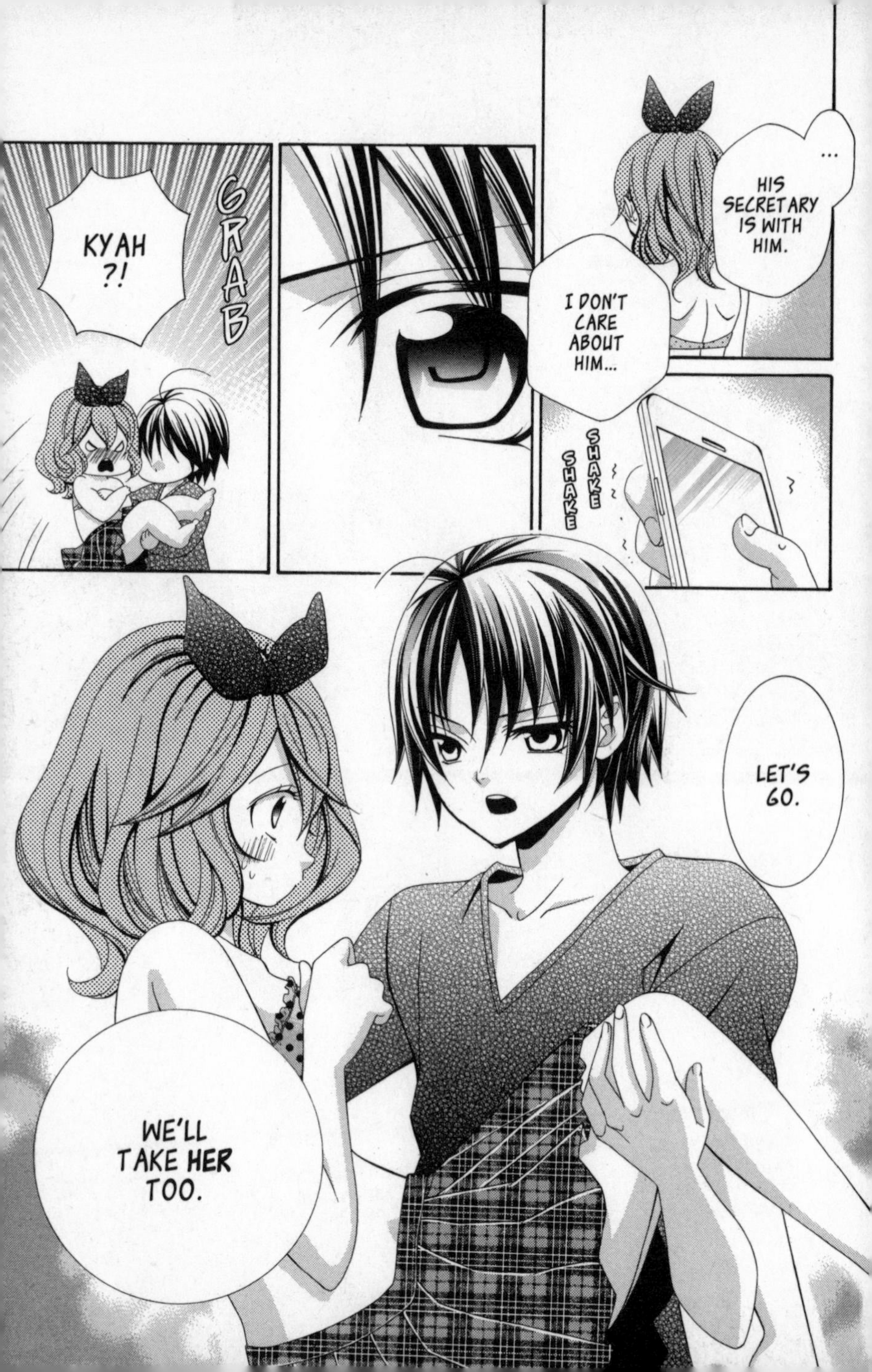
...
HIS SECRETARY IS WITH HIM.
SHAKE SHAKE
I DON'T CARE ABOUT HIM...
GRAB
KYAH ?!
LET'S GO.
WE'LL TAKE HER TOO.

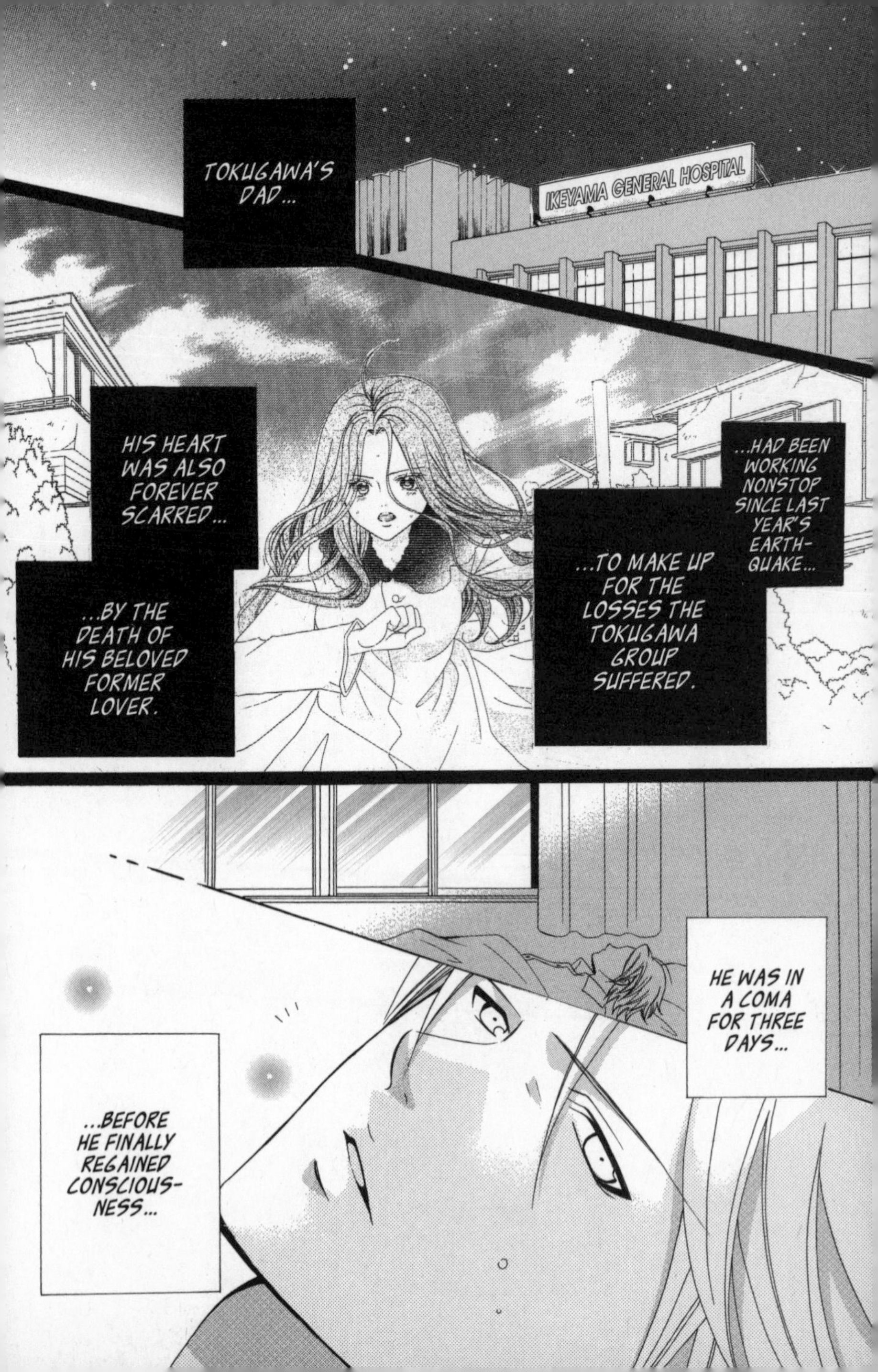
TOKUGAWA'S DAD...
IKEYAMA GENERAL HOSPITAL
...HAD BEEN WORKING NONSTOP SINCE LAST YEAR'S EARTHQUAKE...
...TO MAKE UP FOR THE LOSSES THE TOKUGAWA GROUP SUFFERED.
HIS HEART WAS ALSO FOREVER SCARRED...
...BY THE DEATH OF HIS BELOVED FORMER LOVER.
HE WAS IN A COMA FOR THREE DAYS...
...BEFORE HE FINALLY REGAINED CONSCIOUSNESS...

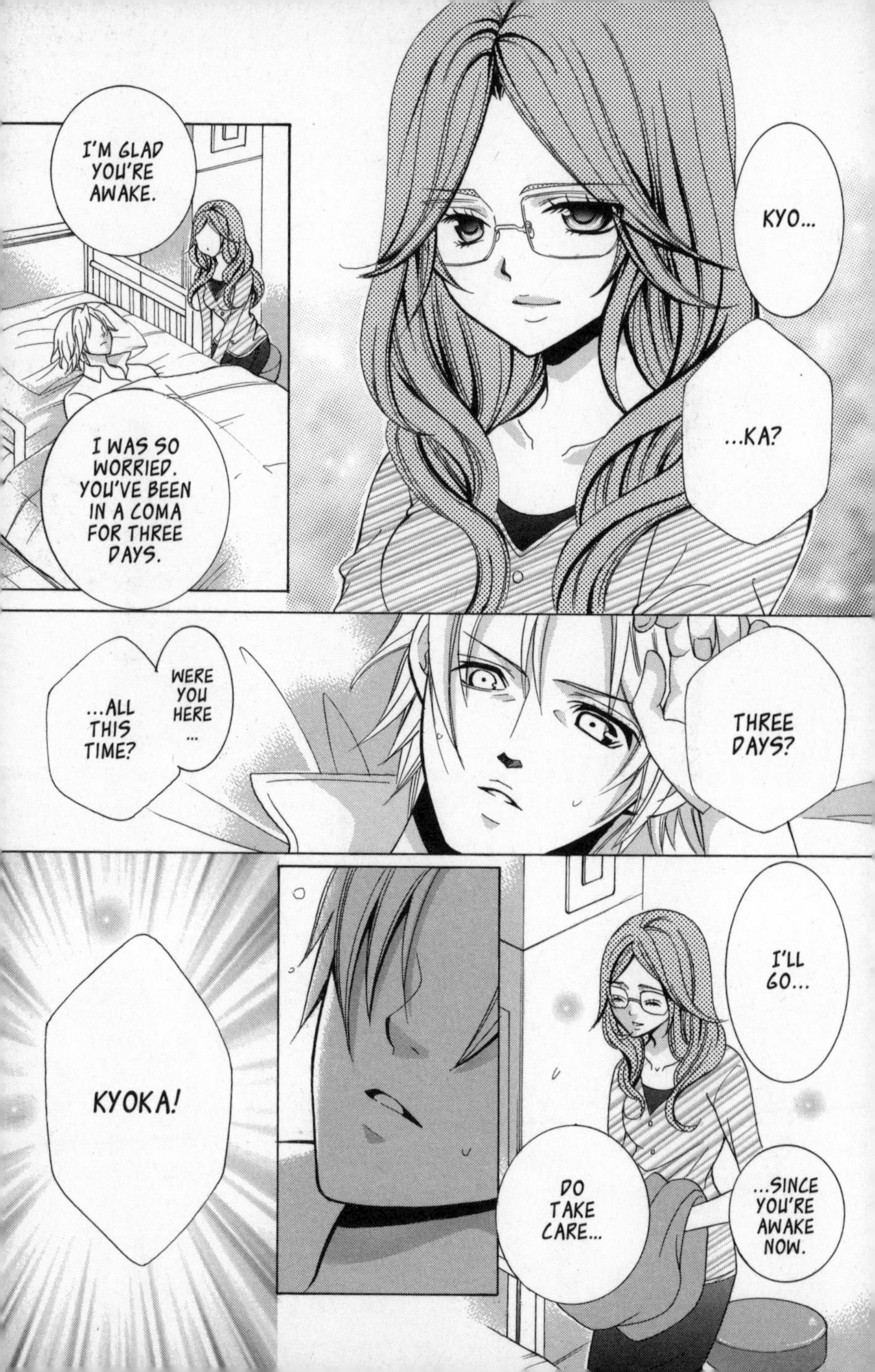
KYO...
...KA?
I'M GLAD YOU'RE AWAKE.
I WAS SO WORRIED. YOU'VE BEEN IN A COMA FOR THREE DAYS.
THREE DAYS?
WERE YOU HERE...
...ALL THIS TIME?
I'LL GO...
...SINCE YOU'RE AWAKE NOW.
DO TAKE CARE...
KYOKA!

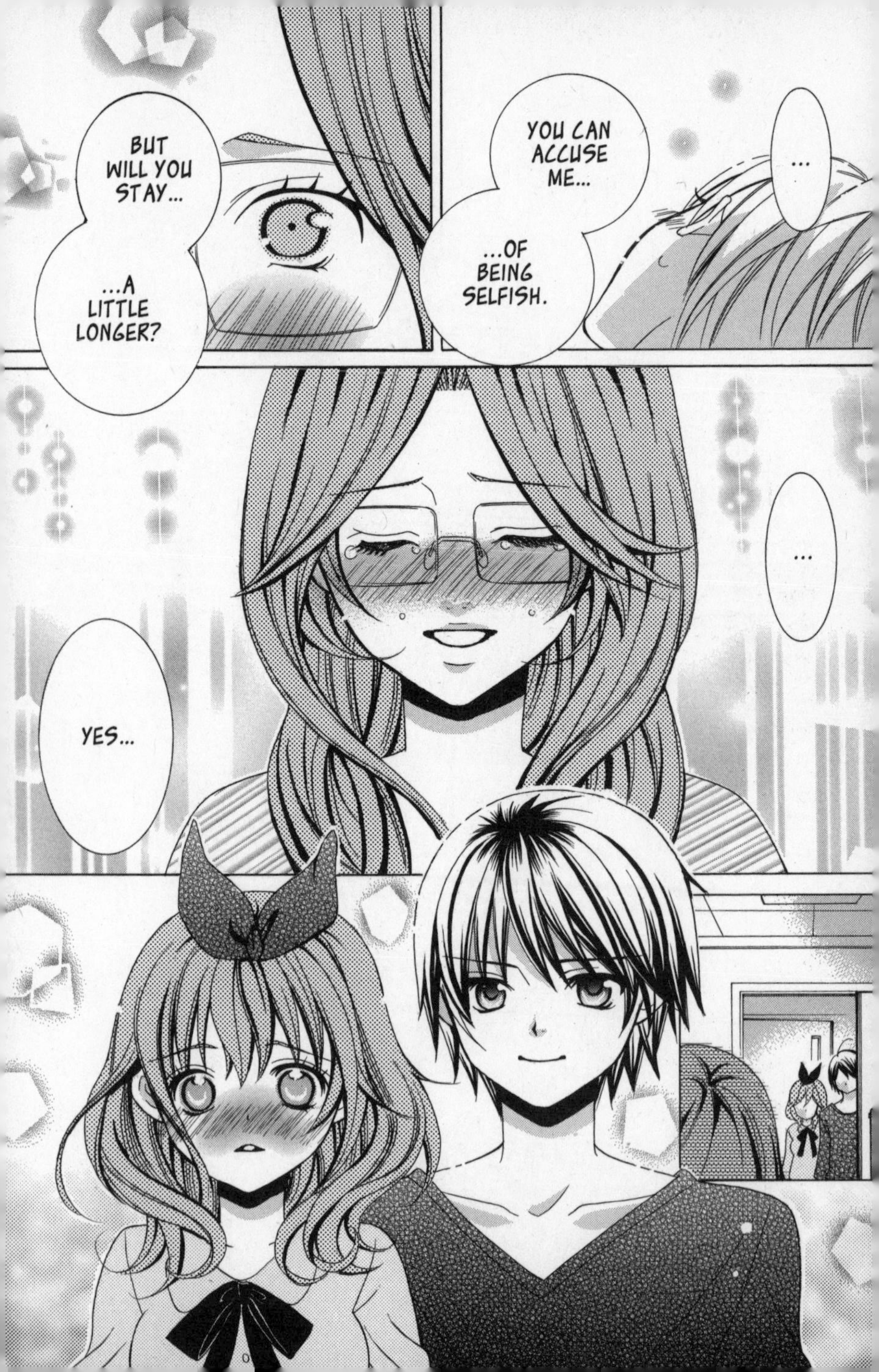
...
YOU CAN ACCUSE ME...
...OF BEING SELFISH.
BUT WILL YOU STAY...
...A LITTLE LONGER?
...
YES...

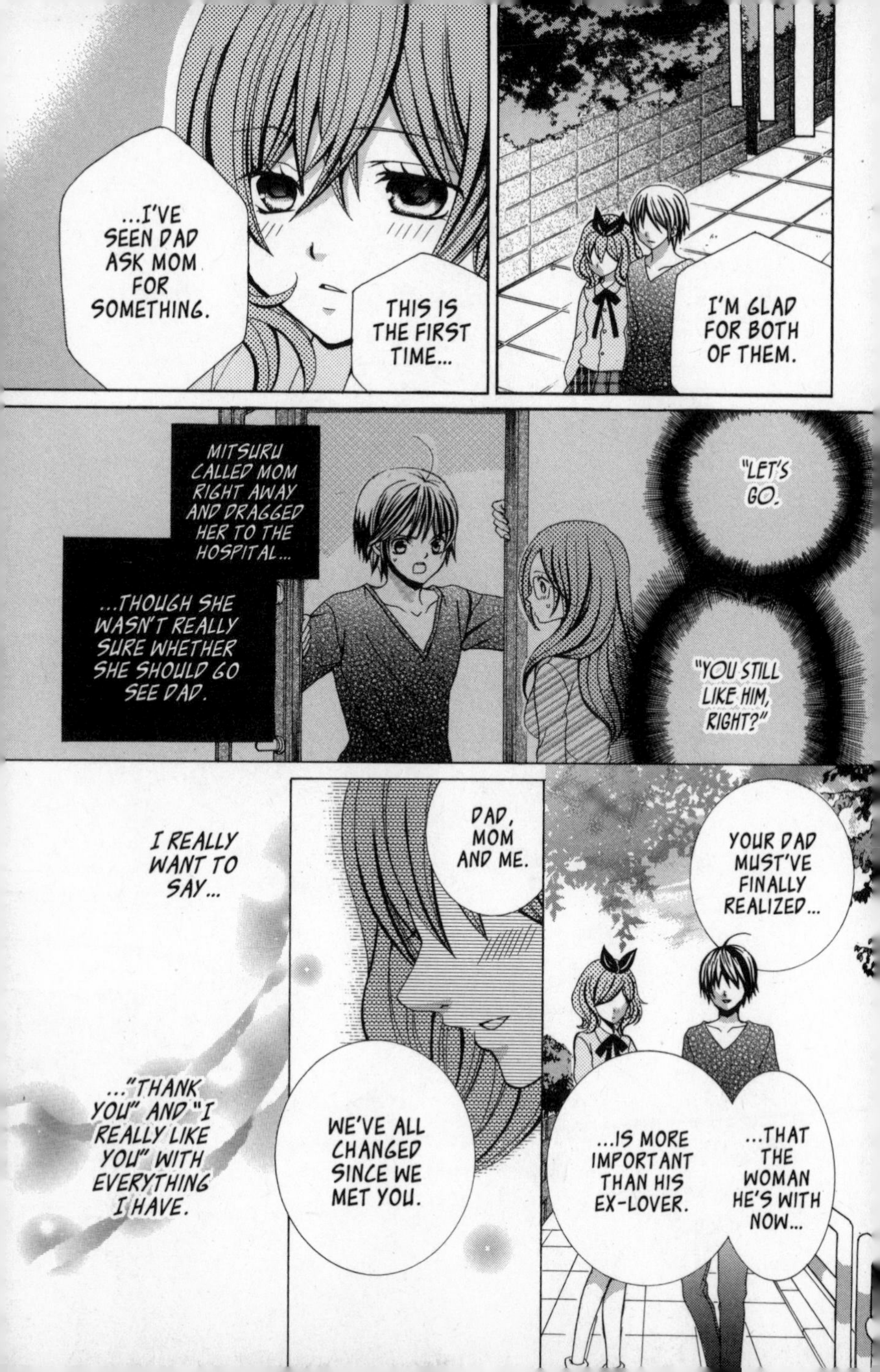
I'M GLAD FOR BOTH OF THEM.
THIS IS THE FIRST TIME...
...I'VE SEEN DAD ASK MOM FOR SOMETHING.
"LET'S GO.
"YOU STILL LIKE HIM, RIGHT?"
MITSURU CALLED MOM RIGHT AWAY AND DRAGGED HER TO THE HOSPITAL...
...THOUGH SHE WASN'T REALLY SURE WHETHER SHE SHOULD GO SEE DAD.
YOUR DAD MUST'VE FINALLY REALIZED...
...THAT THE WOMAN HE'S WITH NOW...
...IS MORE IMPORTANT THAN HIS EX-LOVER.
DAD, MOM AND ME.
WE'VE ALL CHANGED SINCE WE MET YOU.
I REALLY WANT TO SAY...
..."THANK YOU" AND "I REALLY LIKE YOU" WITH EVERYTHING I HAVE.

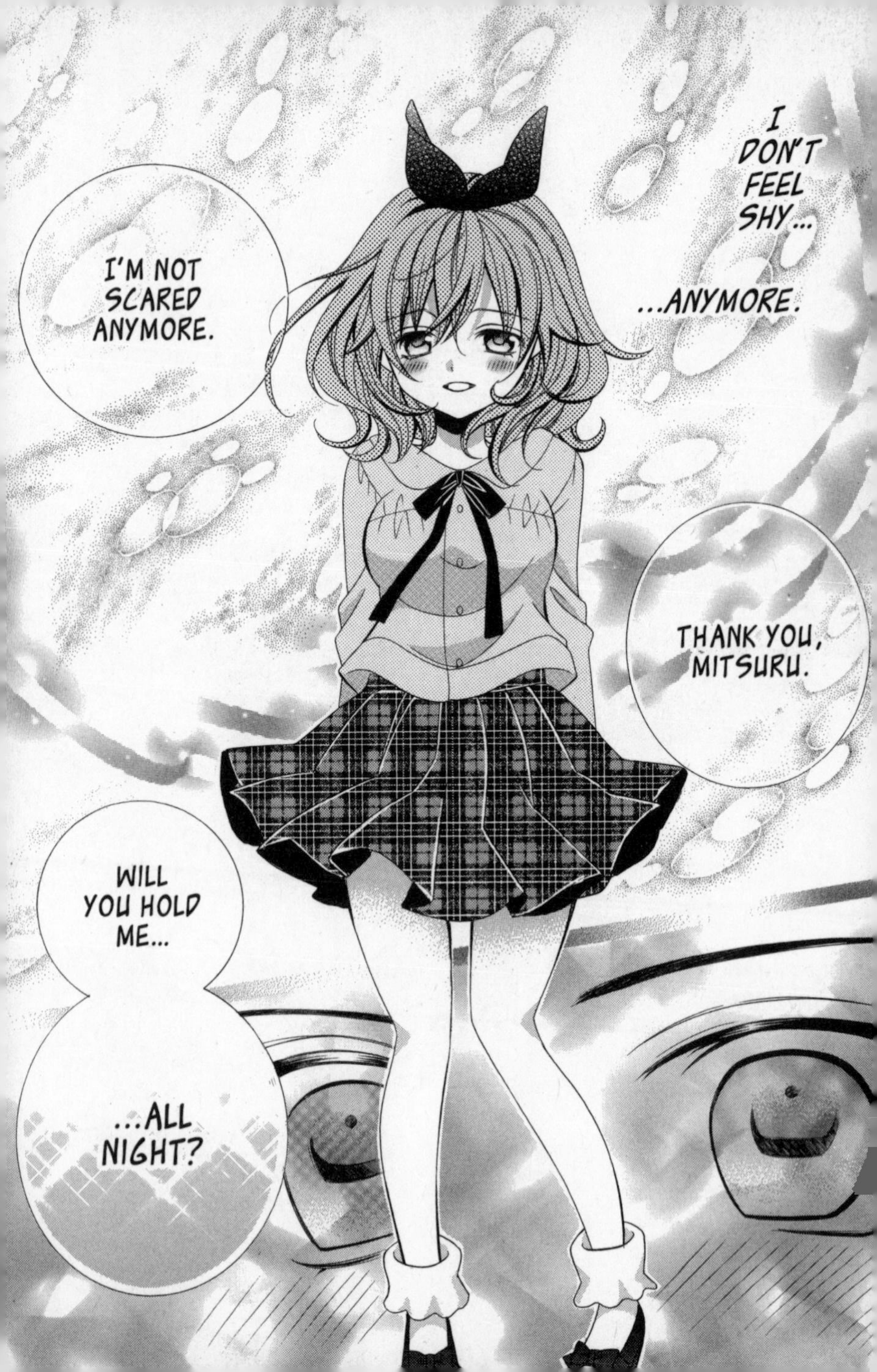
I DON'T FEEL SHY...
...ANYMORE.
I'M NOT SCARED ANYMORE.
THANK YOU, MITSURU.
WILL YOU HOLD ME...
...ALL NIGHT?

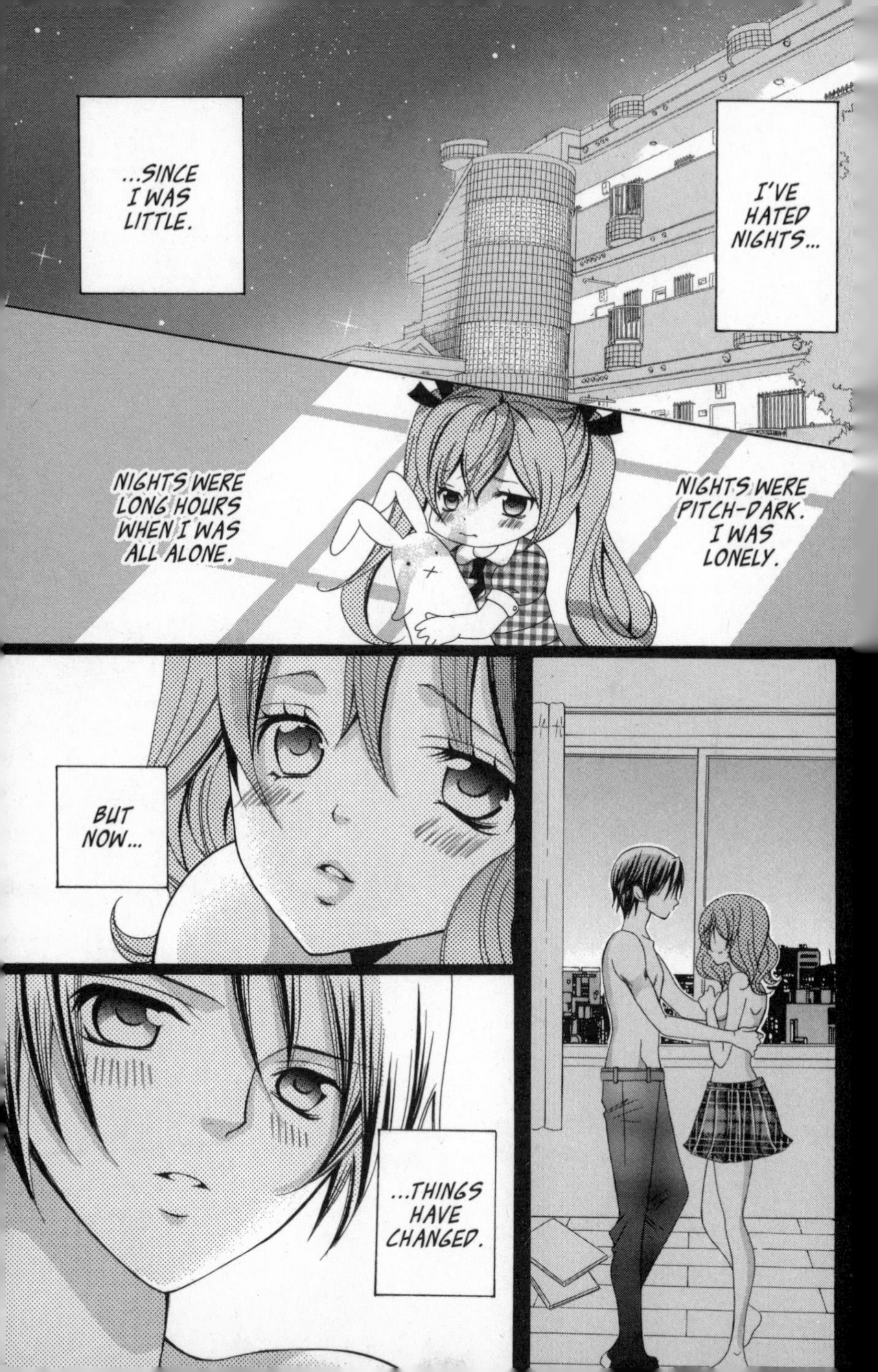
I'VE HATED NIGHTS...
...SINCE I WAS LITTLE.
NIGHTS WERE PITCH-DARK. I WAS LONELY.
NIGHTS WERE LONG HOURS WHEN I WAS ALL ALONE.
BUT NOW...
...THINGS HAVE CHANGED.

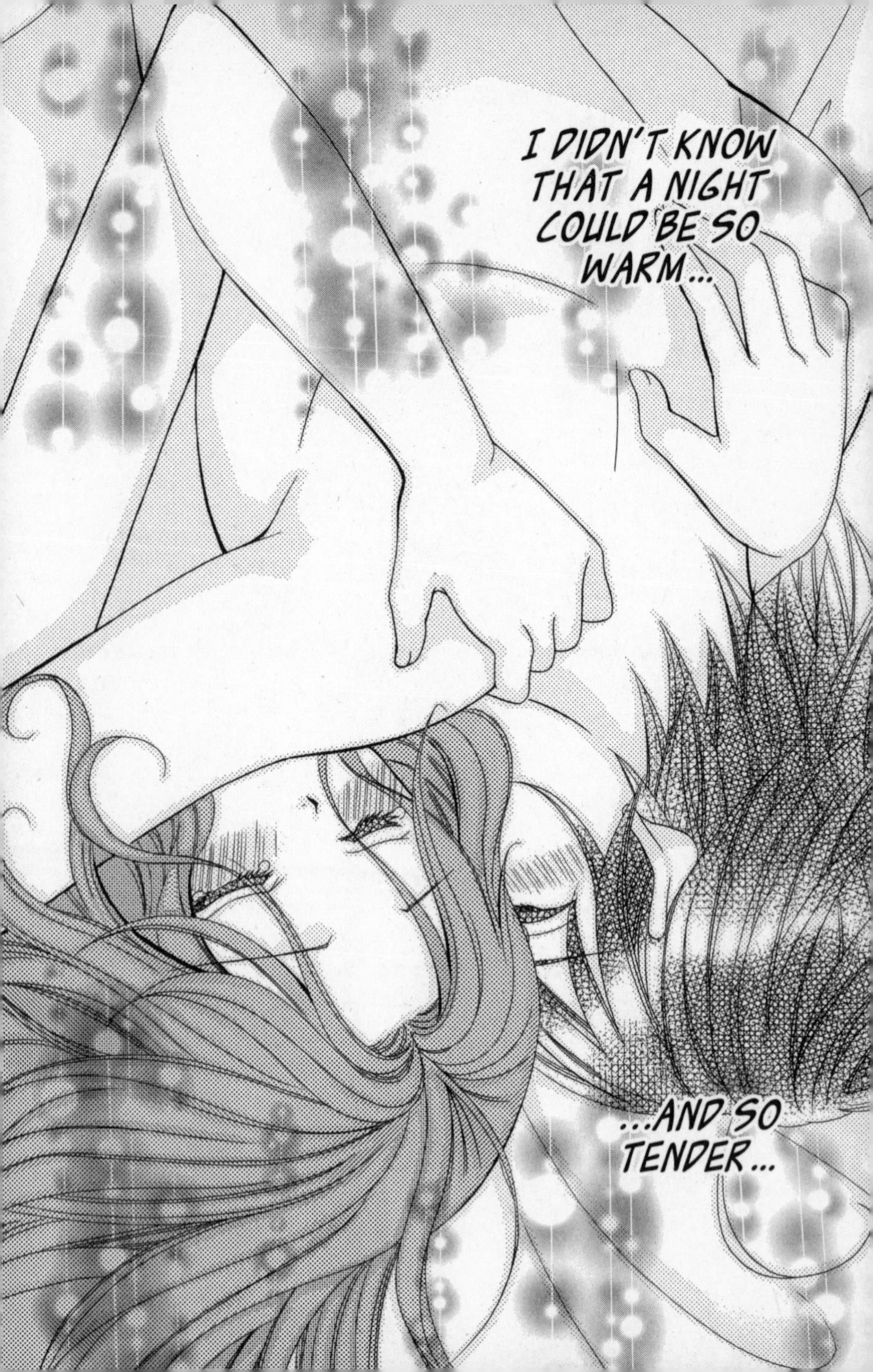
I DIDN'T KNOW THAT A NIGHT COULD BE SO WARM...
...AND SO TENDER...

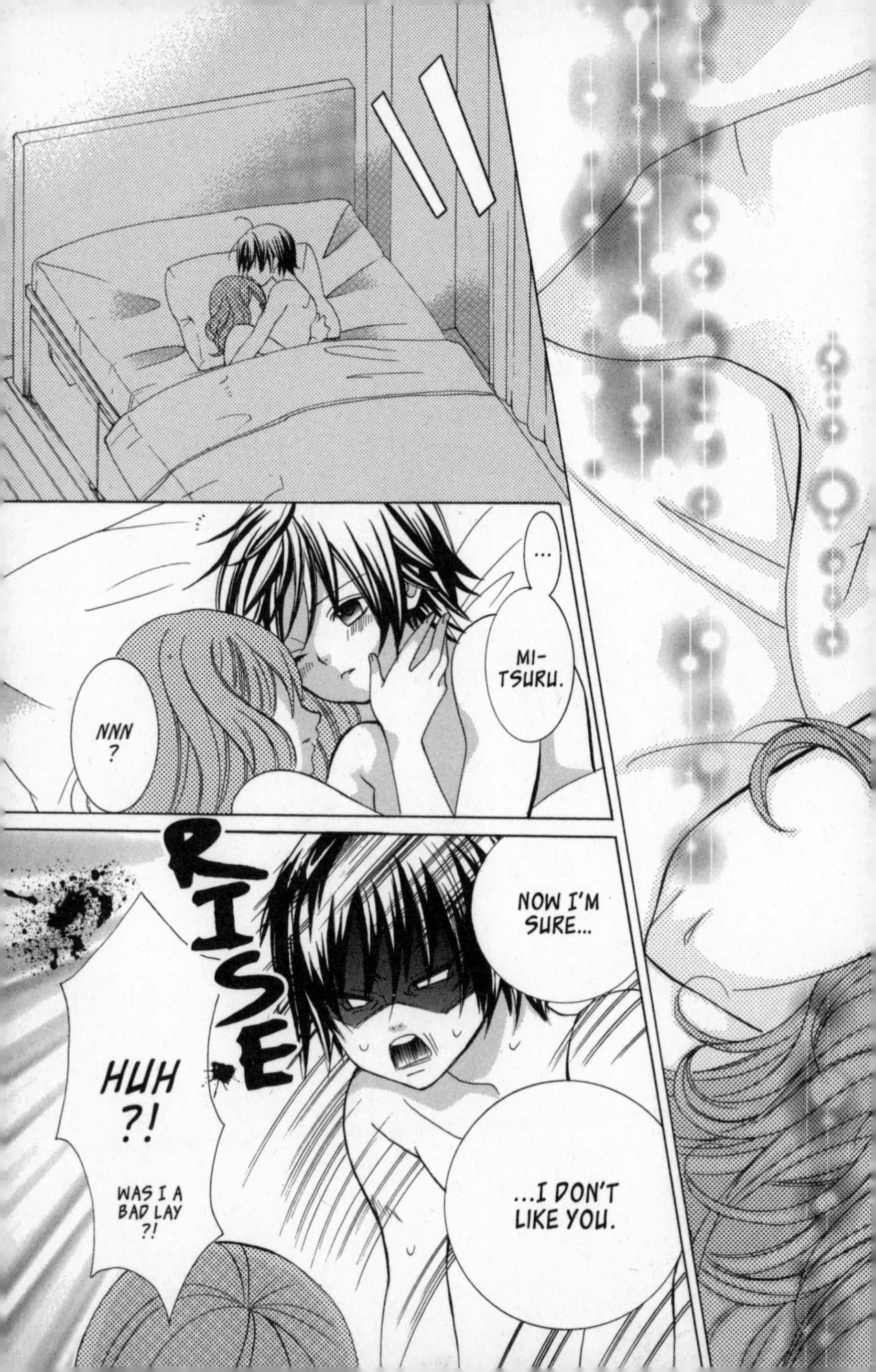
...
MI-TSURU.
NNN?
NOW I'M SURE...
RISE
...I DON'T LIKE YOU.
HUH?!
WAS I A BAD LAY?!

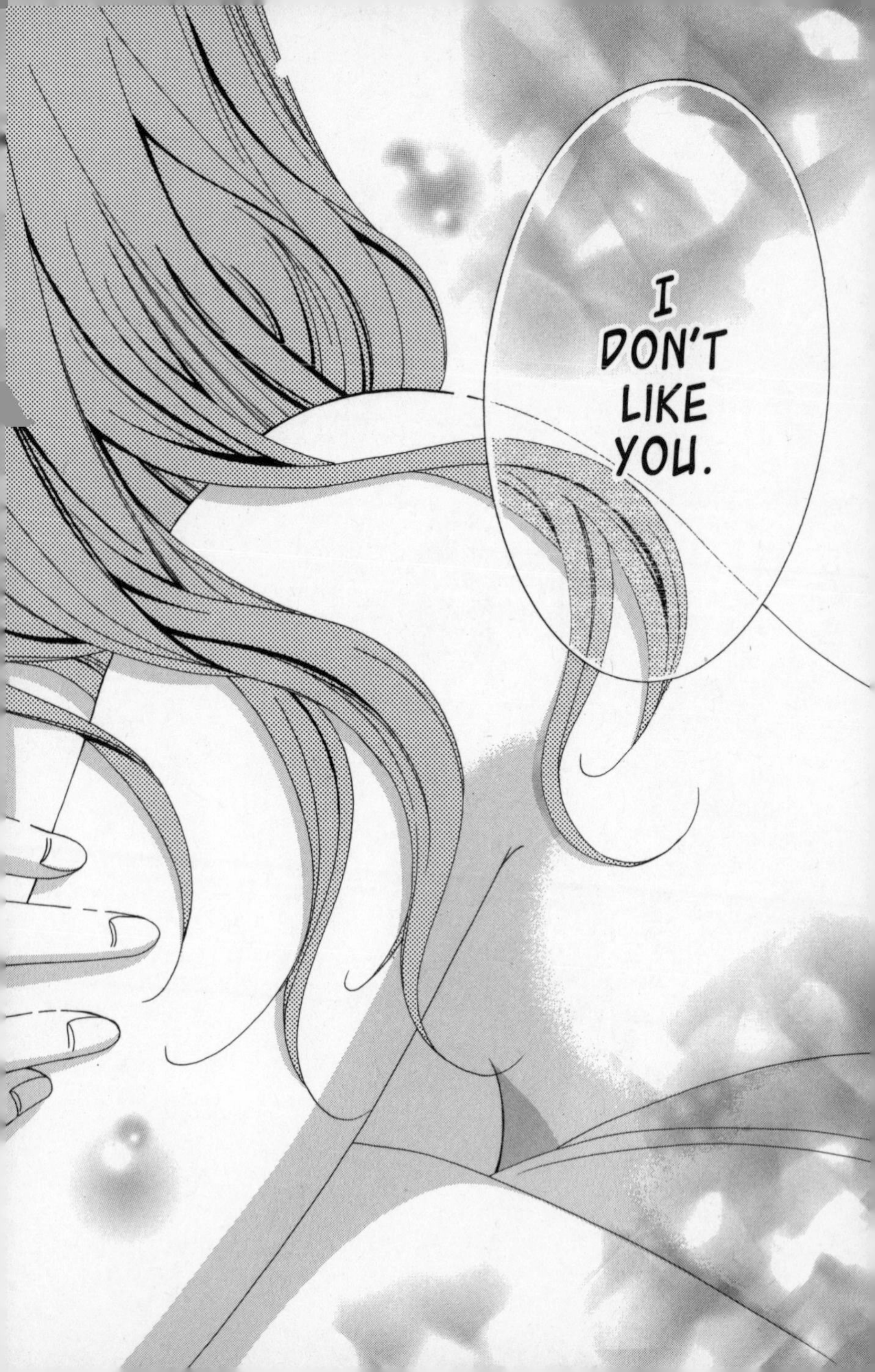
I DON'T LIKE YOU.

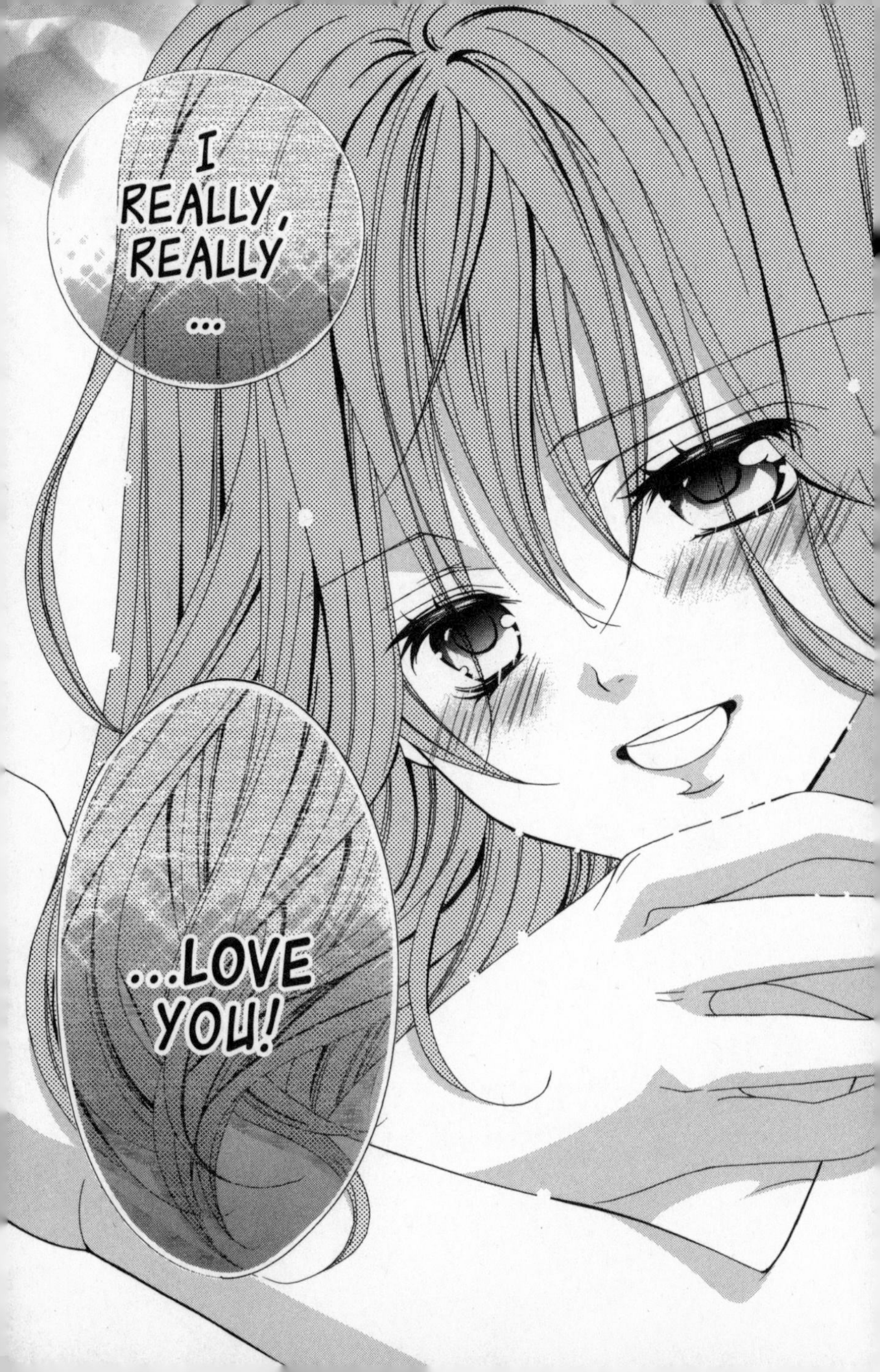
I REALLY, REALLY ...
...LOVE YOU!

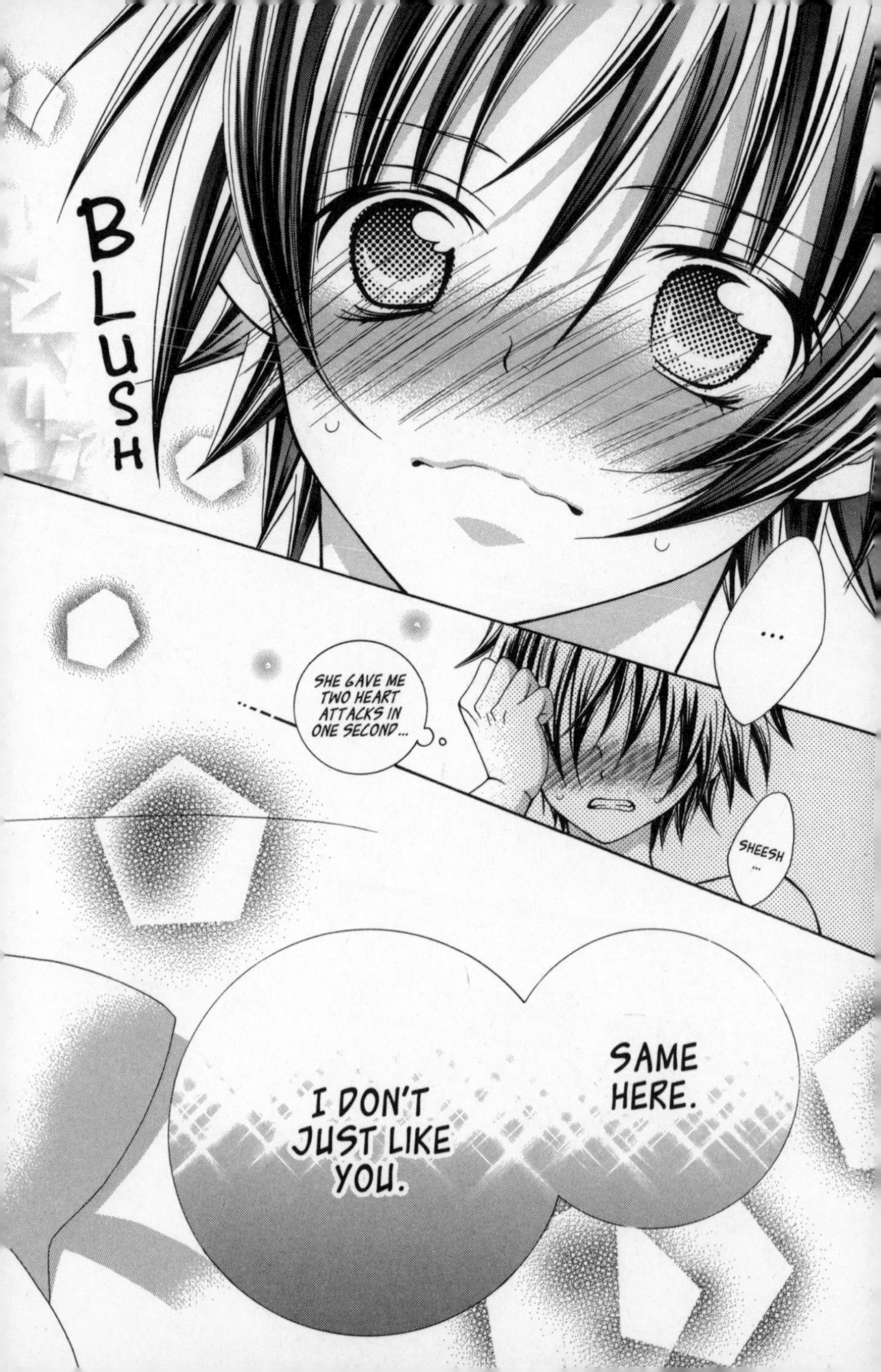
BLUSH
...
SHE GAVE ME TWO HEART ATTACKS IN ONE SECOND...
SHEESH...
SAME HERE.
I DON'T JUST LIKE YOU.

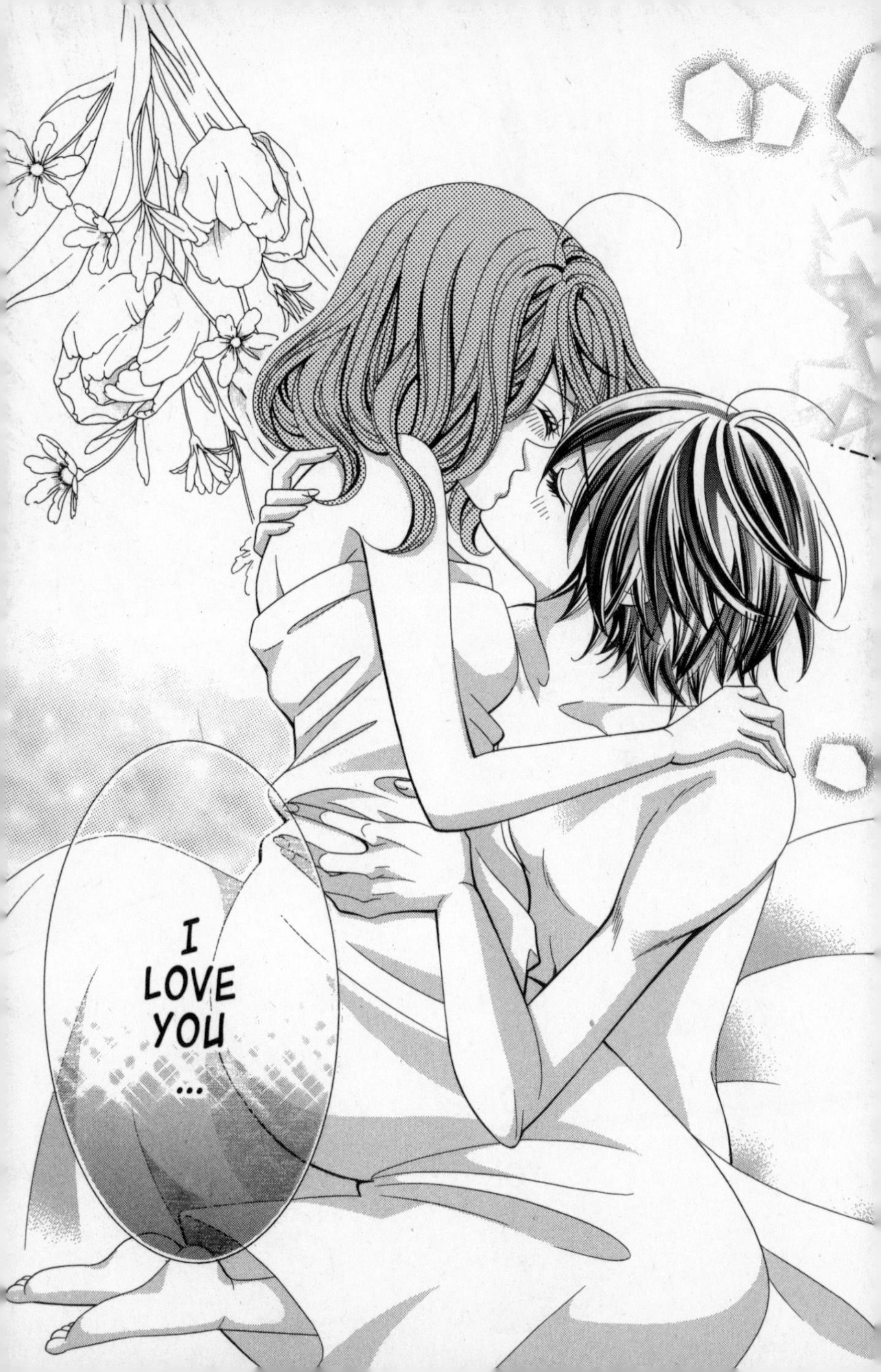
I LOVE YOU ...

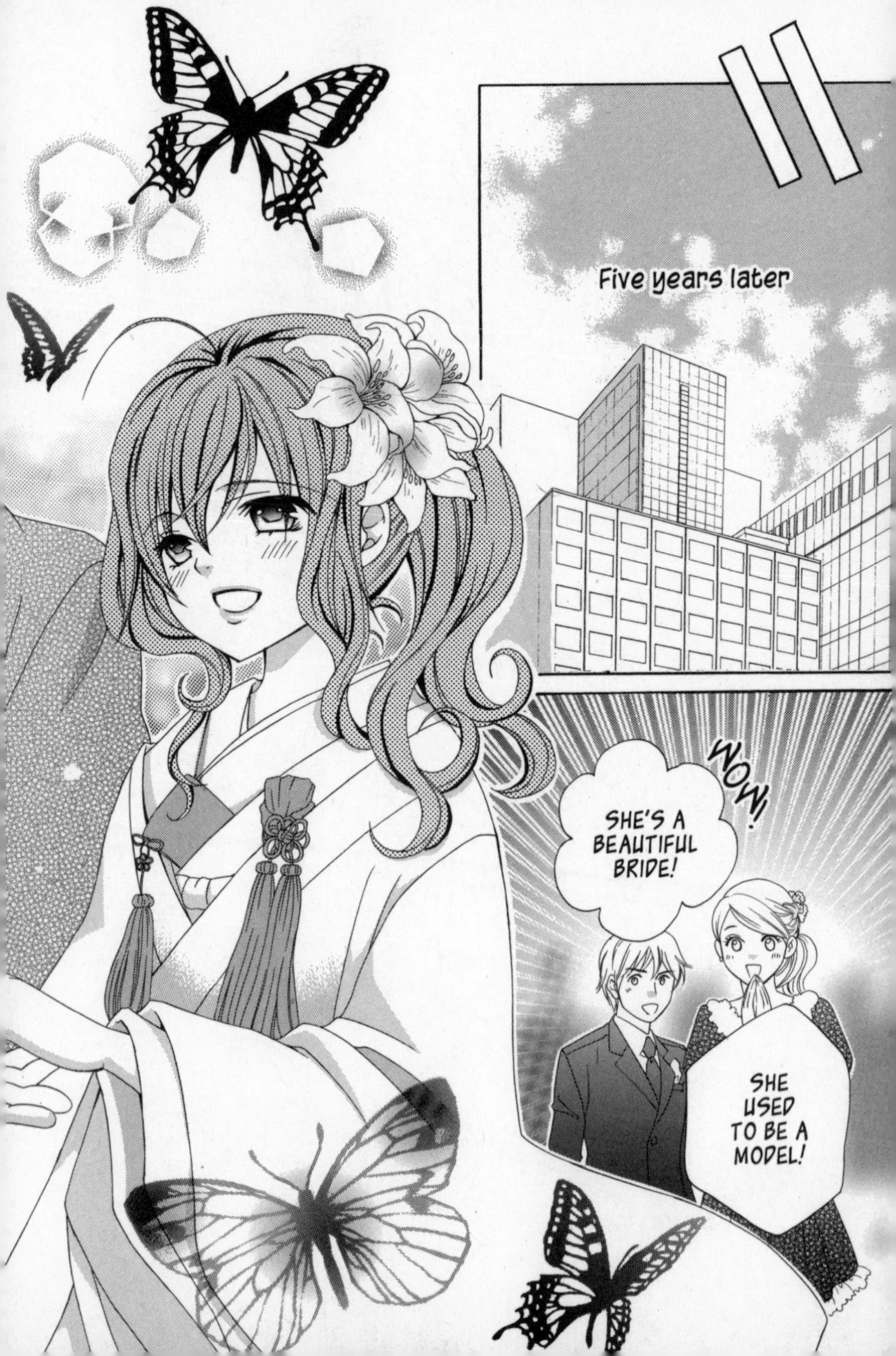
Five years later
WOW!
SHE'S A BEAUTIFUL BRIDE!
SHE USED TO BE A MODEL!

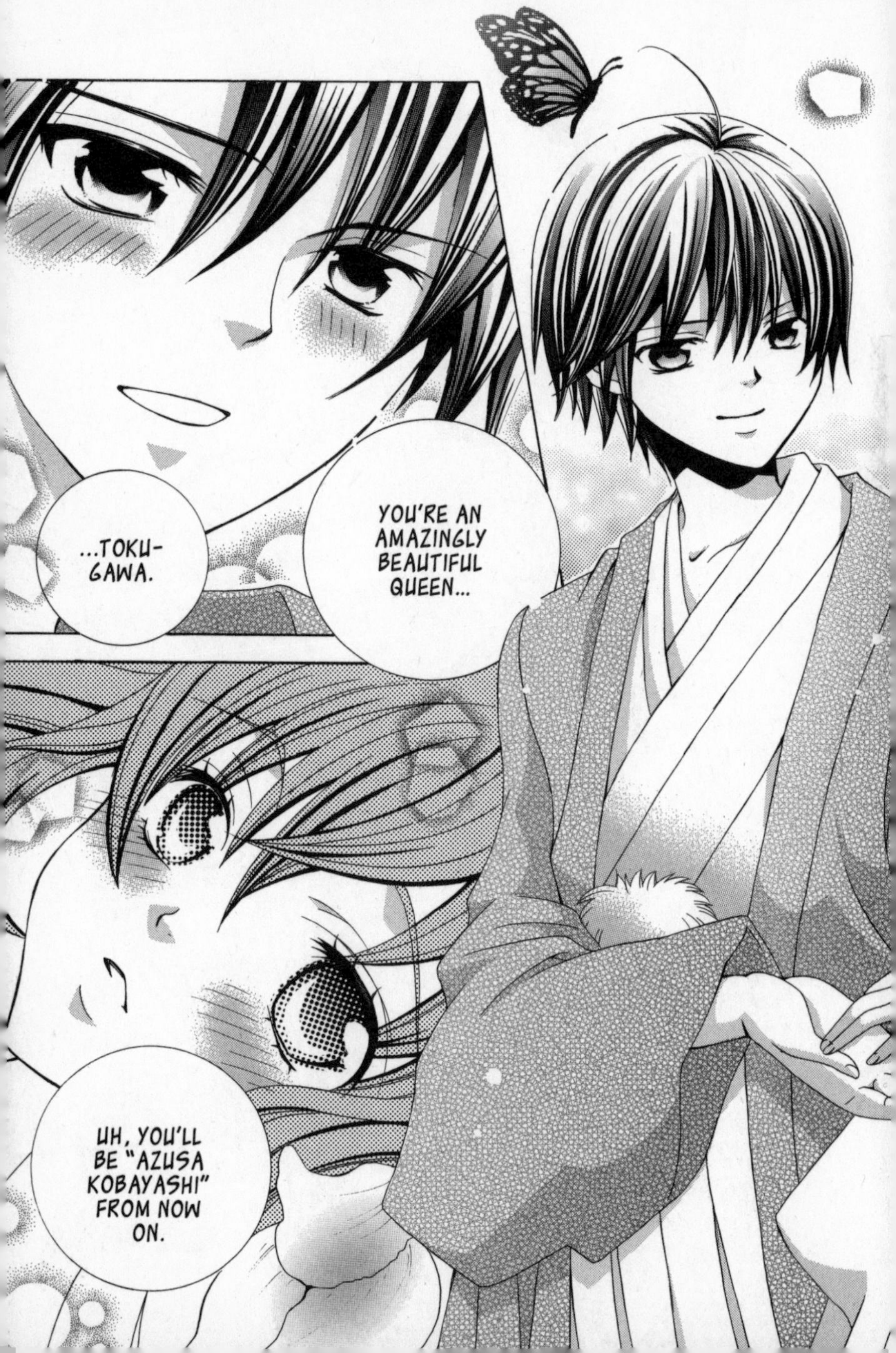
YOU'RE AN AMAZINGLY BEAUTIFUL QUEEN...
...TOKU-GAWA.
UH, YOU'LL BE "AZUSA KOBAYASHI" FROM NOW ON.

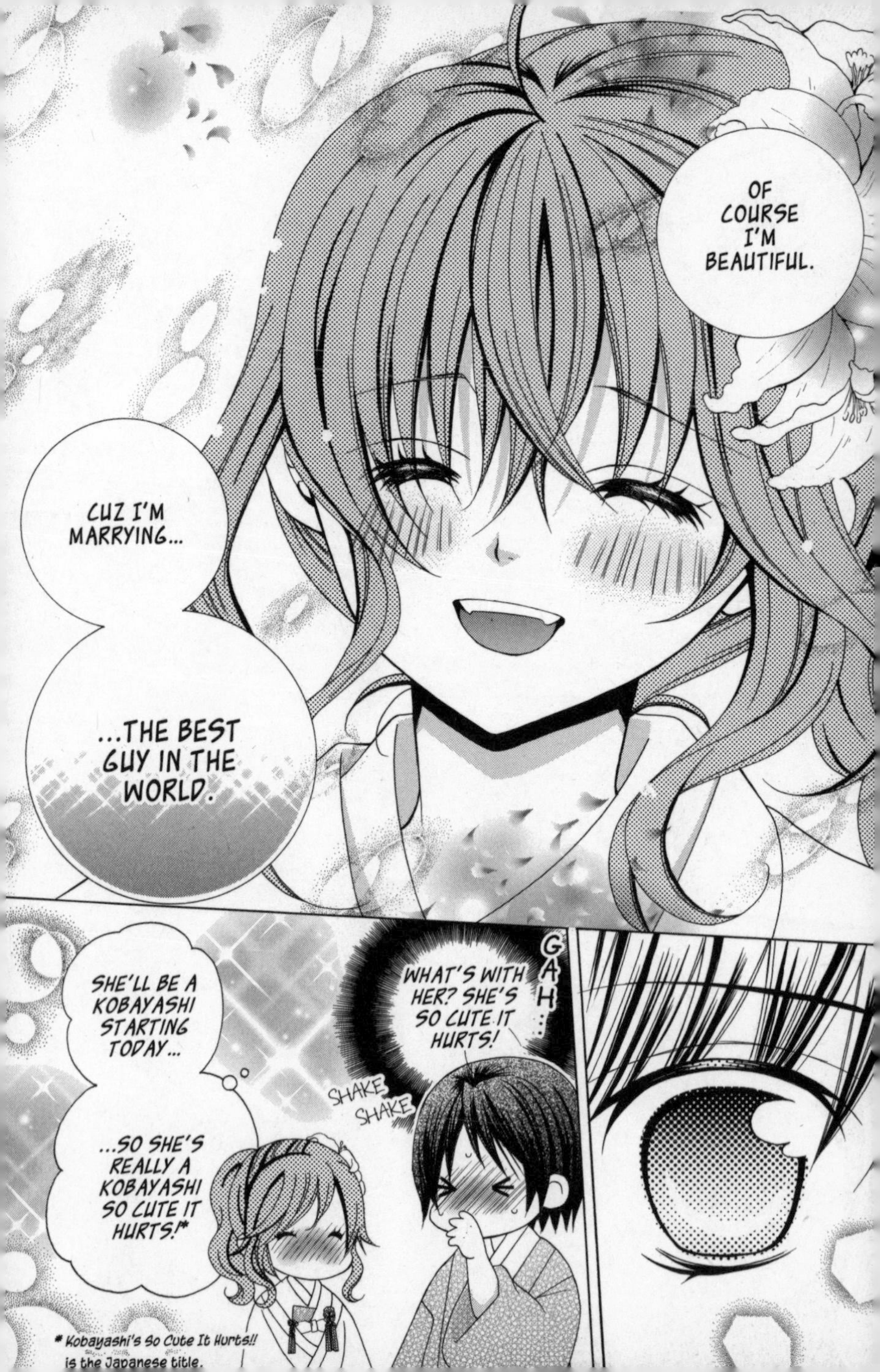
OF COURSE I'M BEAUTIFUL.
CUZ I'M MARRYING...
...THE BEST GUY IN THE WORLD.
GAH...
WHAT'S WITH HER? SHE'S SO CUTE IT HURTS!
SHE'LL BE A KOBAYASHI STARTING TODAY...
SHAKE SHAKE
...SO SHE'S REALLY A KOBAYASHI SO CUTE IT HURTS!*

* Kobayashi's So Cute It Hurts!! is the Japanese title.

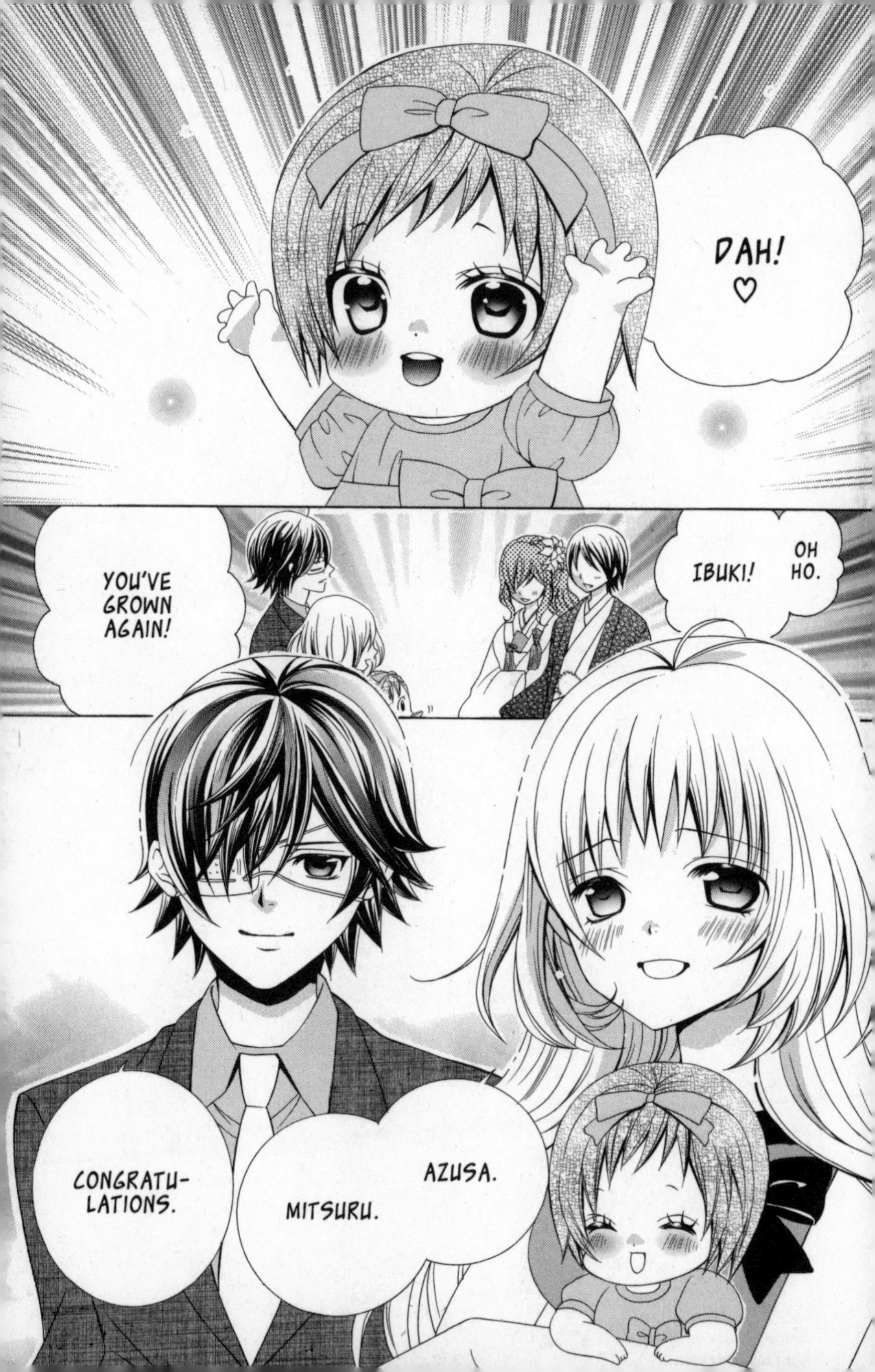
DAH! ♡
OH HO.
IBUKI!
YOU'VE GROWN AGAIN!
AZUSA.
MITSURU.
CONGRATU-LATIONS.

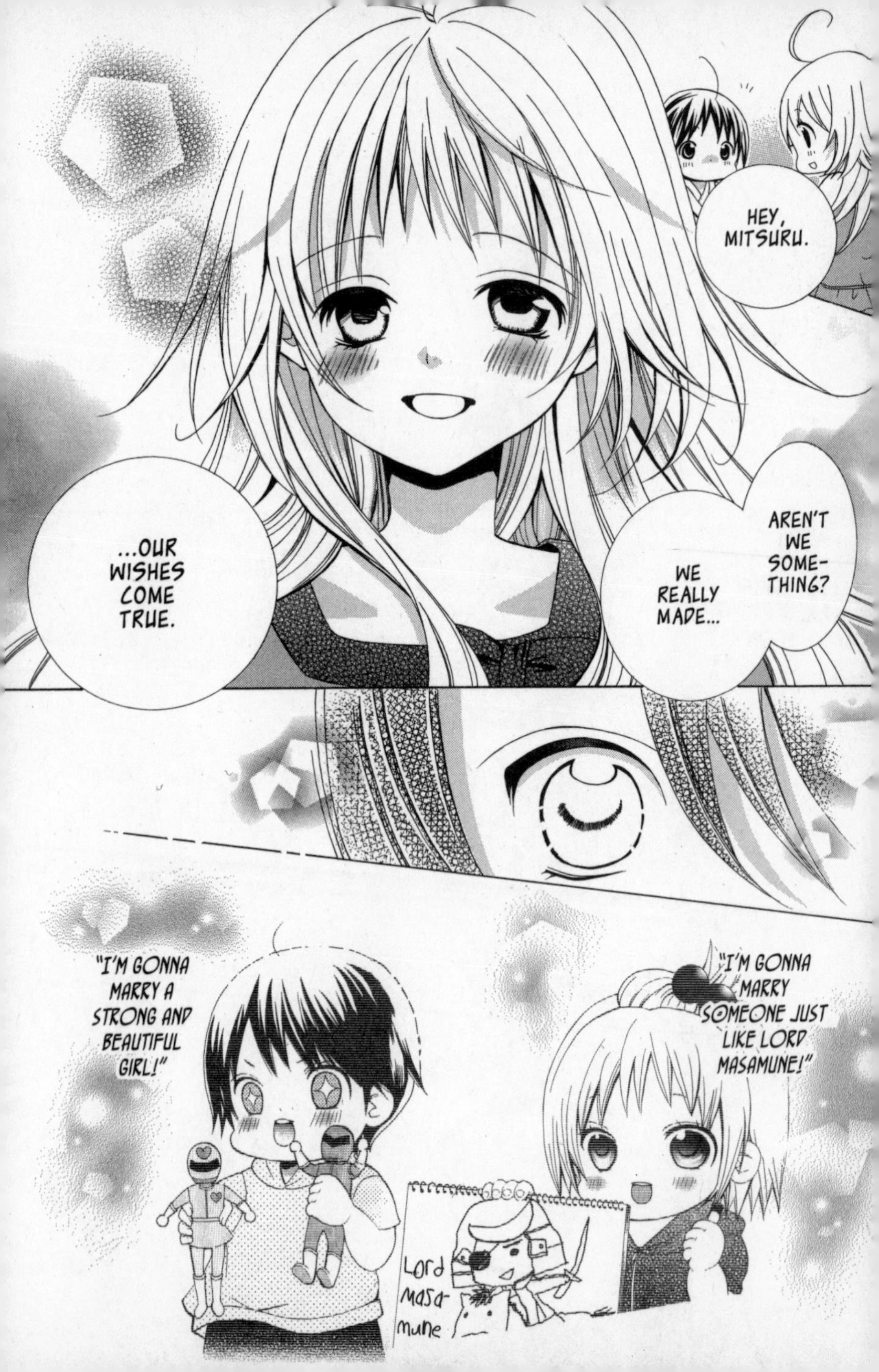
HEY, MITSURU.
AREN'T WE SOMETHING?
WE REALLY MADE...
...OUR WISHES COME TRUE.
"I'M GONNA MARRY SOMEONE JUST LIKE LORD MASAMUNE!"
Lord Masa-mune
"I'M GONNA MARRY A STRONG AND BEAUTIFUL GIRL!"

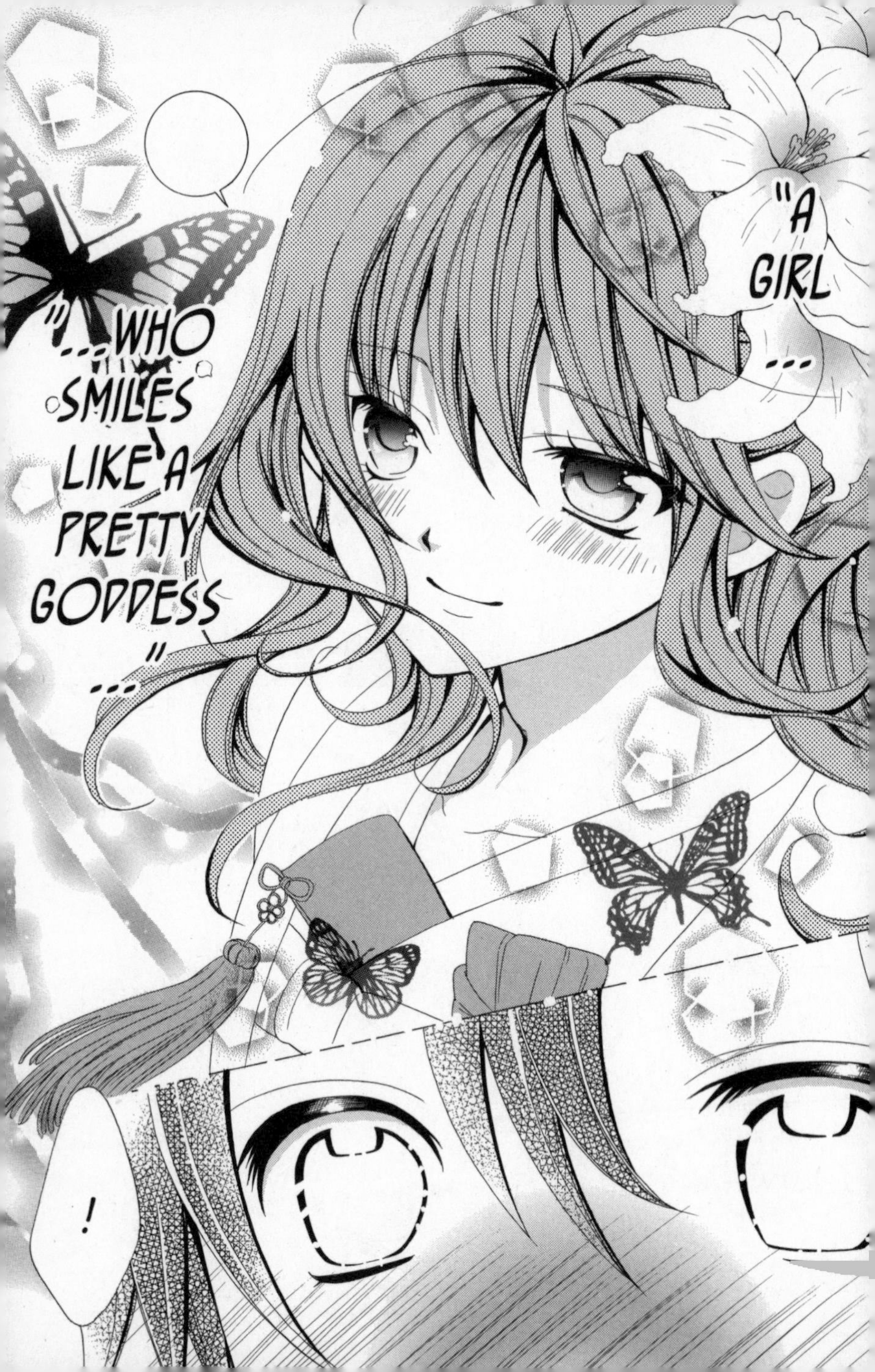
"A GIRL ...
"...WHO SMILES LIKE A PRETTY GODDESS ..."
!

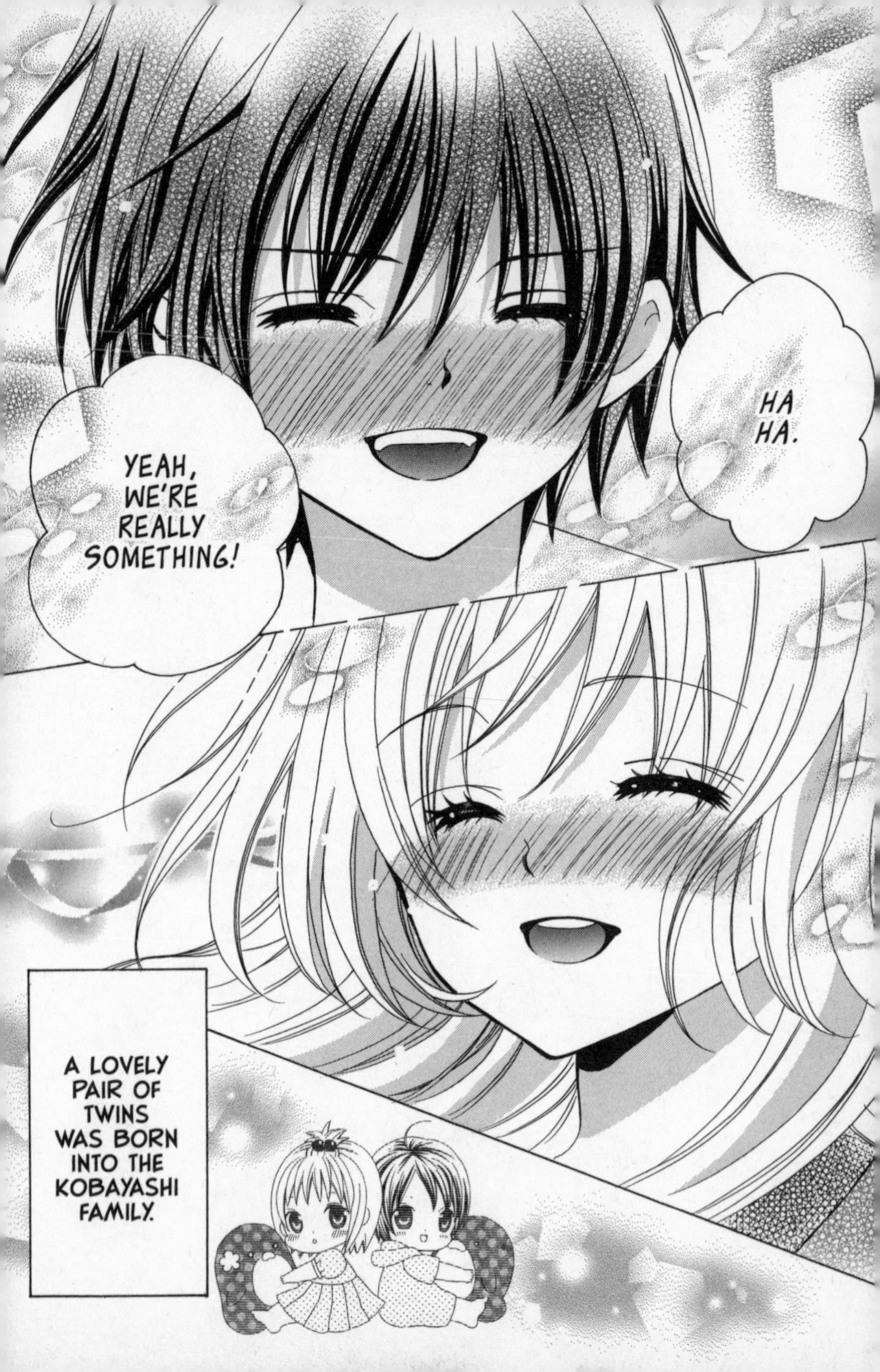
HA HA.
YEAH, WE'RE REALLY SOMETHING!
A LOVELY PAIR OF TWINS WAS BORN INTO THE KOBAYASHI FAMILY.

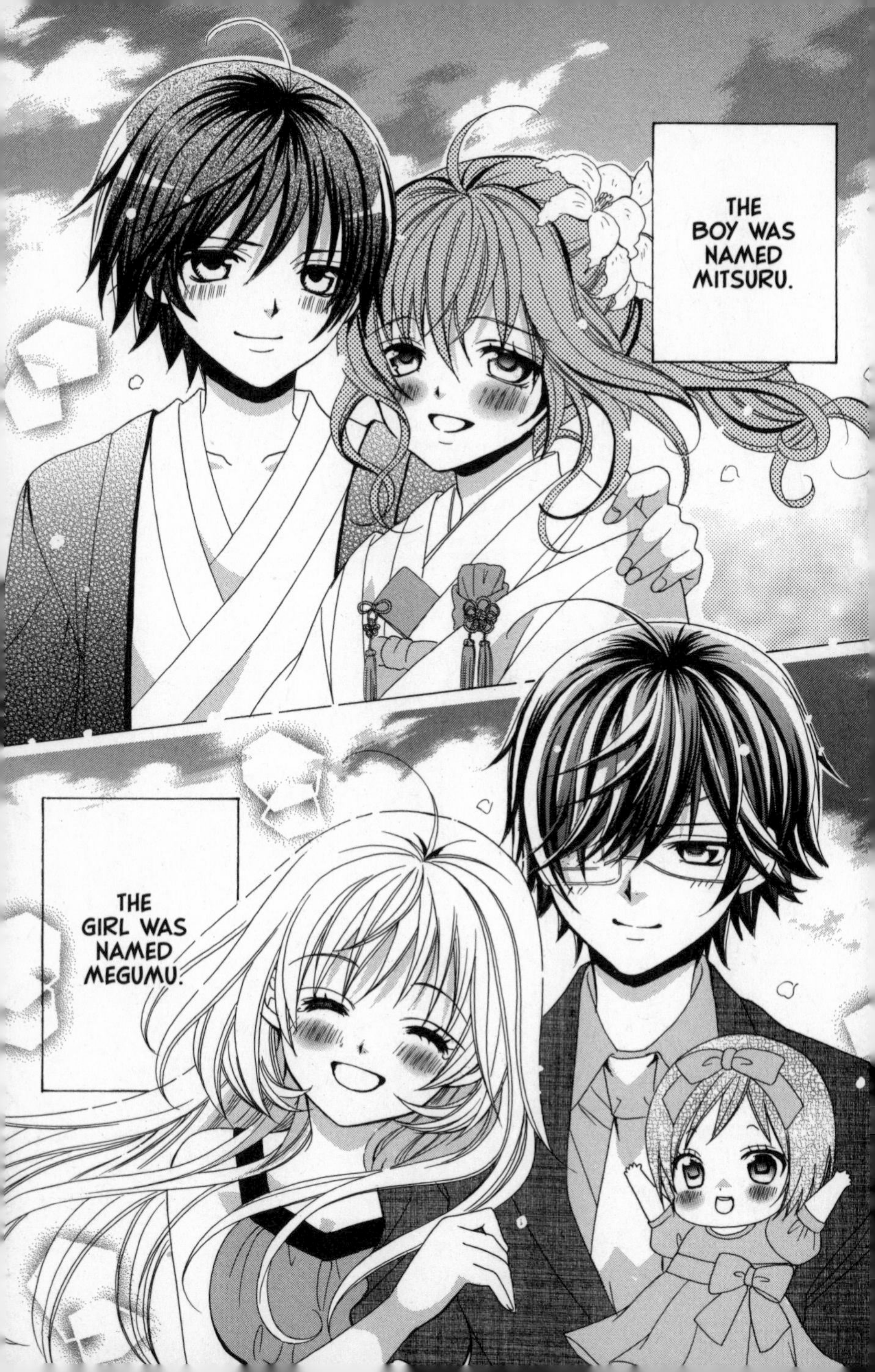
THE BOY WAS NAMED MITSURU.
THE GIRL WAS NAMED MEGUMU.

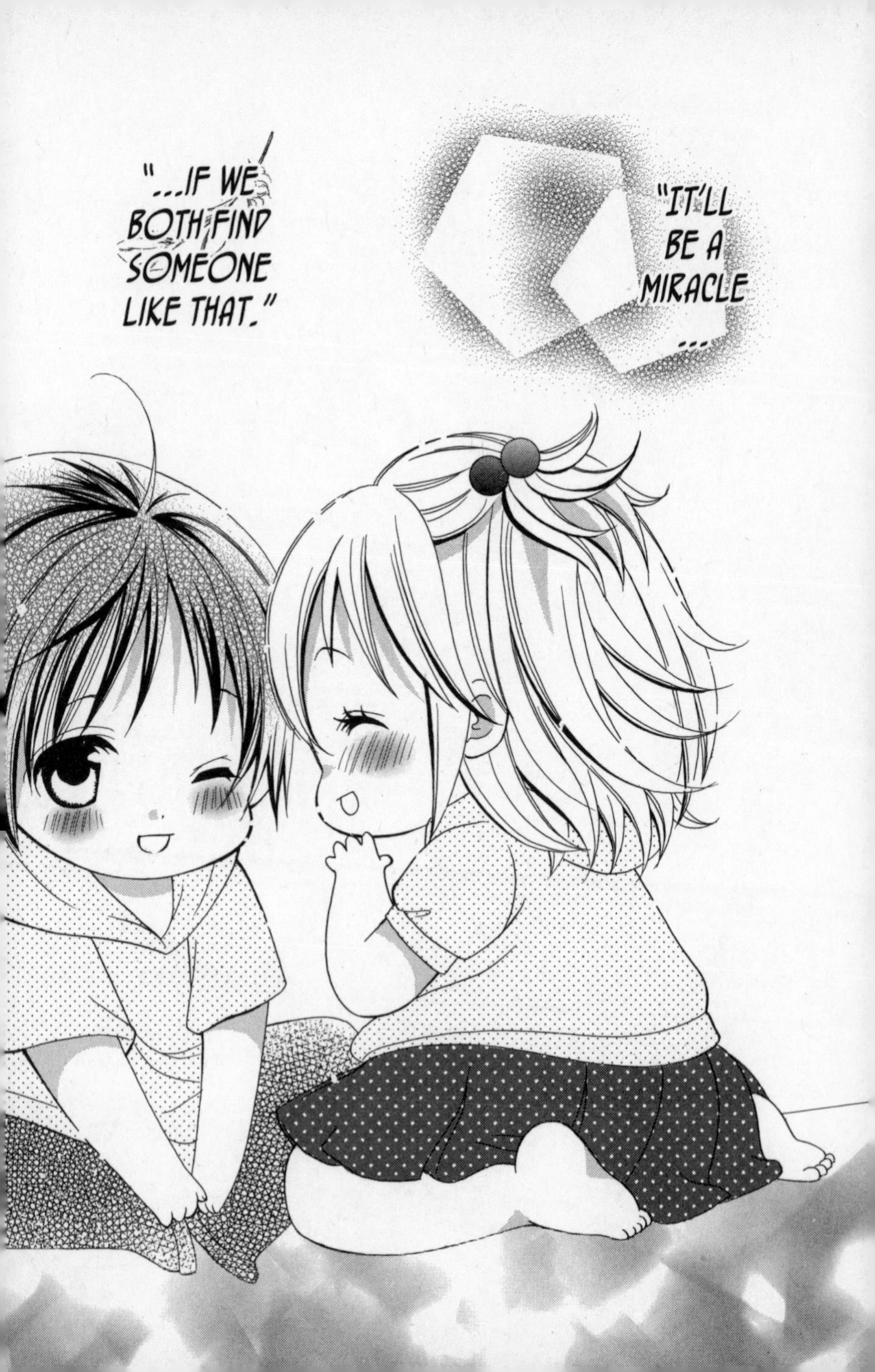
"IT'LL BE A MIRACLE ...
"...IF WE BOTH FIND SOMEONE LIKE THAT."

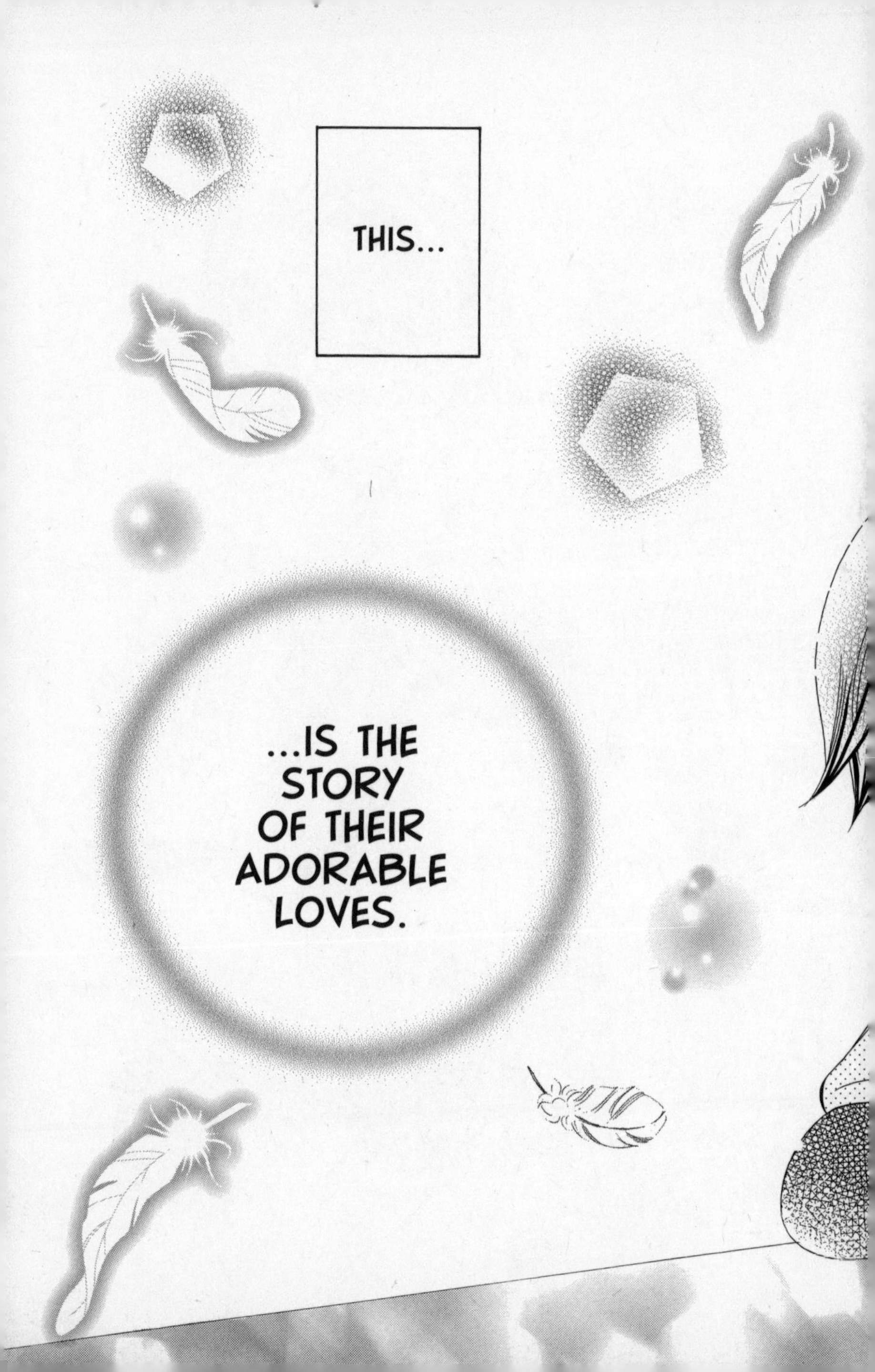
THIS...
...IS THE STORY OF THEIR ADORABLE LOVES.

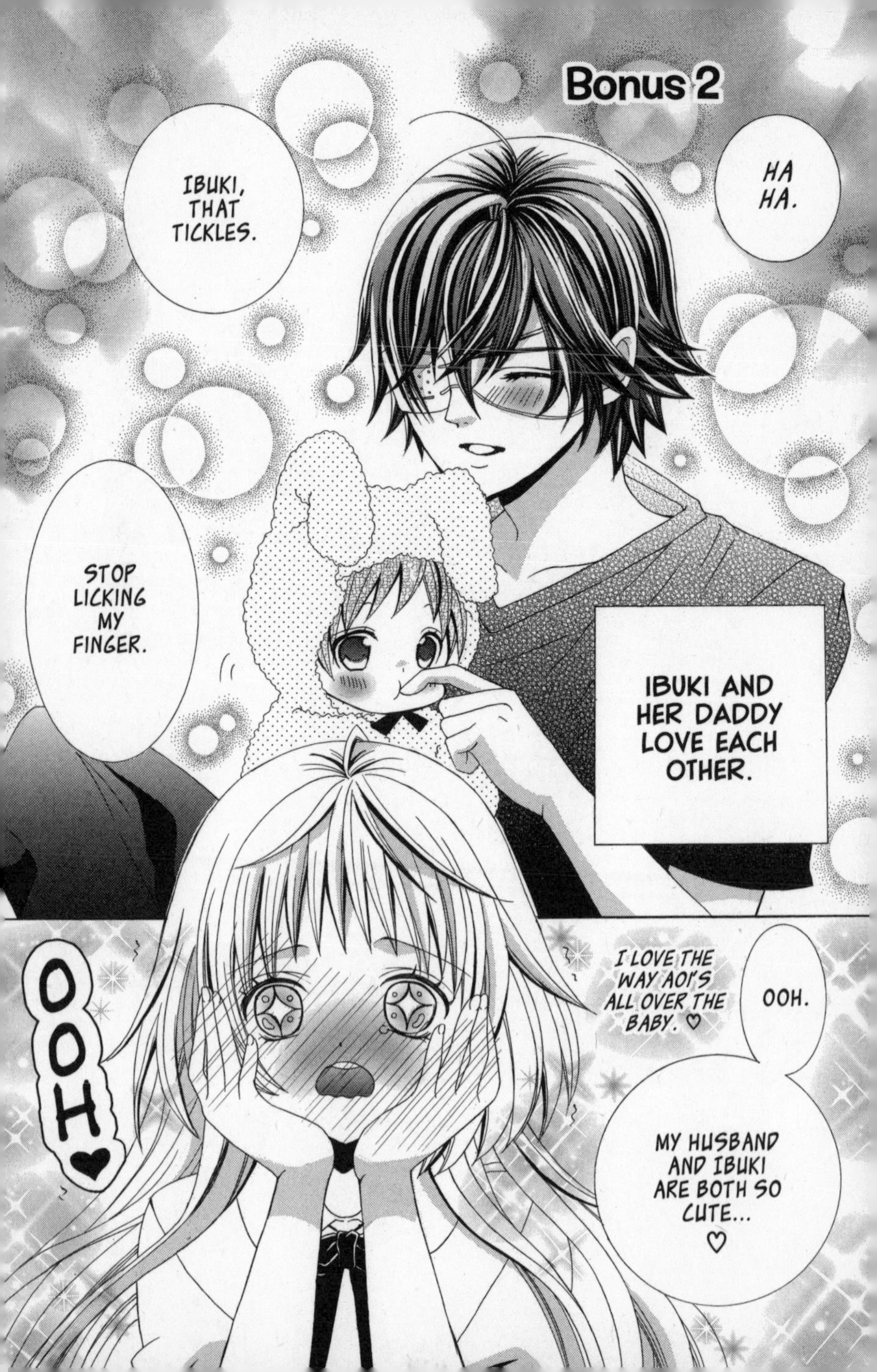
Bonus 2
HA HA.
IBUKI, THAT TICKLES.
IBUKI AND HER DADDY LOVE EACH OTHER.
STOP LICKING MY FINGER.
OOH.
I LOVE THE WAY AOI'S ALL OVER THE BABY. ♡
MY HUSBAND AND IBUKI ARE BOTH SO CUTE... ♡
OOH OOH♥

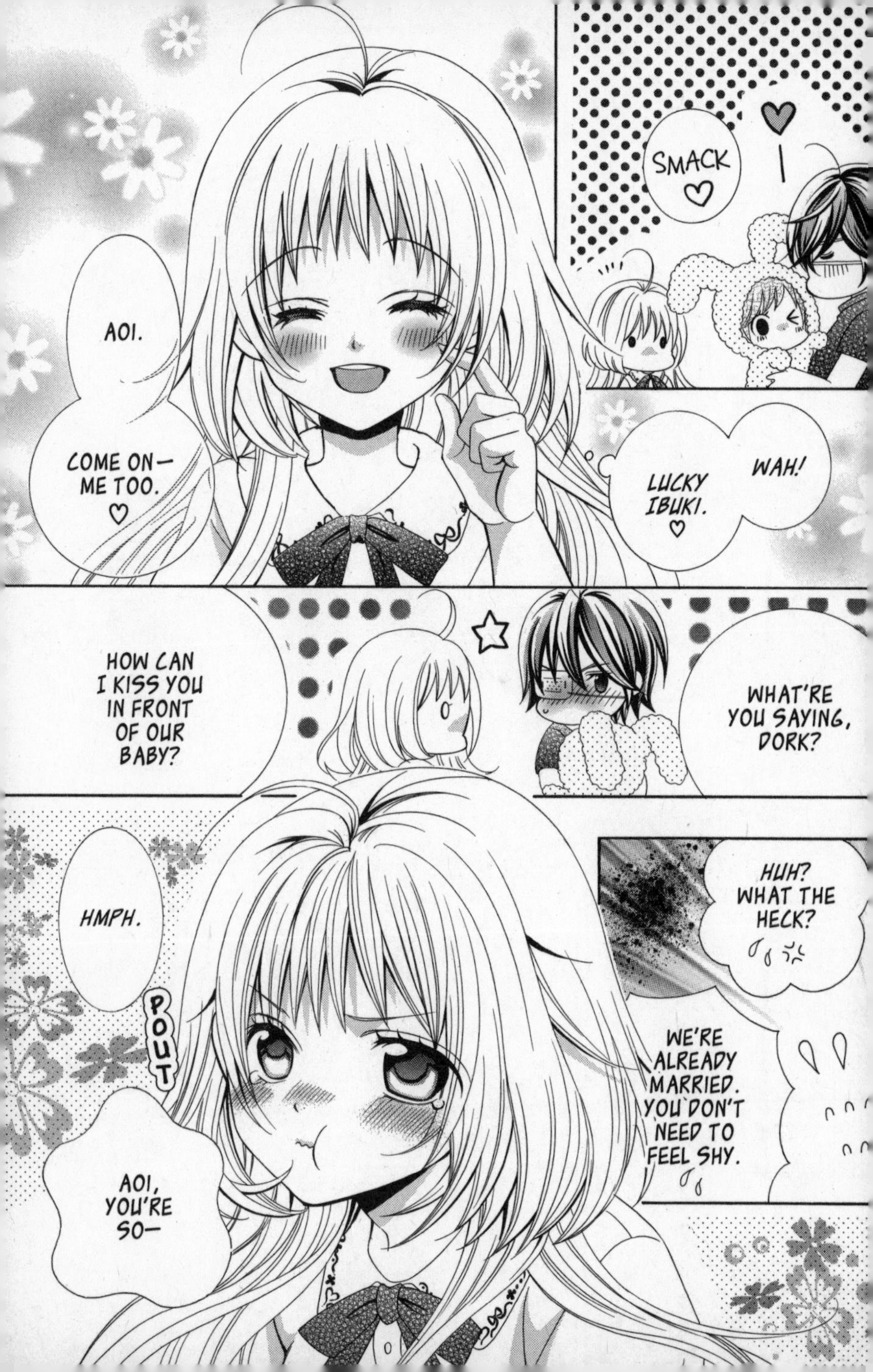

SMACK ♡
WAH!
LUCKY IBUKI. ♡
AOI.
COME ON— ME TOO. ♡
WHAT'RE YOU SAYING, DORK?
HOW CAN I KISS YOU IN FRONT OF OUR BABY?
HUH? WHAT THE HECK?
WE'RE ALREADY MARRIED. YOU DON'T NEED TO FEEL SHY.
HMPH.
POUT
AOI, YOU'RE SO—

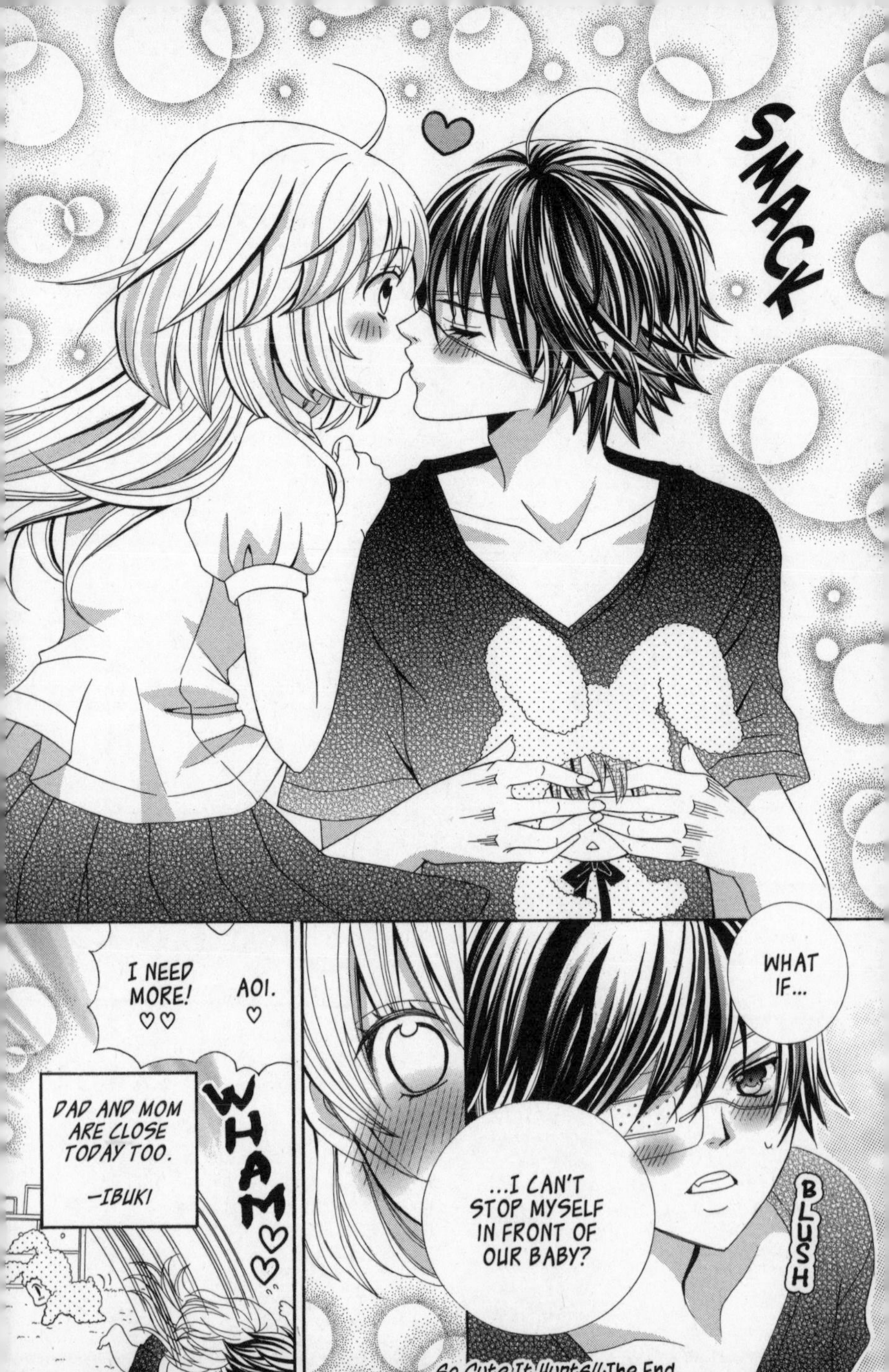
SMACK
WHAT IF...
...I CAN'T STOP MYSELF IN FRONT OF OUR BABY?
BLUSH
AOI. ♡
I NEED MORE! ♡♡
WHAM ♡♡
DAD AND MOM ARE CLOSE TODAY TOO.
—IBUKI

So Cute It Hurts!! The End

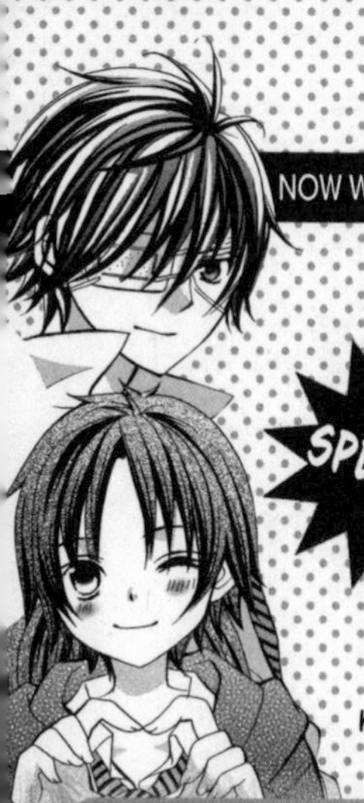

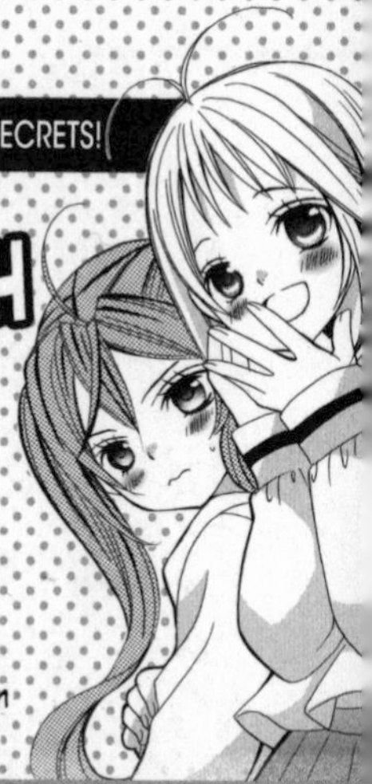

NOW WE CAN SHARE ALL THE *SO CUTE!* BEHIND-THE-SCENES SECRETS!

SPECIAL INTERVIEW WITH GO IKEYAMADA

After running for three years, *So Cute!* reached its happy ending. We asked Go about *So Cute!* production secrets and all the thought she put into the series!

I FIT IN EVERYTHING I WANTED!

How did you come up with the idea for *So Cute!*?

BEFORE I BEGAN THIS SERIES, I WAS THINKING ABOUT DOING A THREE-CHAPTER STORY ABOUT **TWINS SWITCHING PLACES** THAT I'D THOUGHT UP WHEN I WAS A NEWBIE. THEN I STARTED THINKING, **"WHAT ELSE DO I WANT TO INCLUDE?"** I WANTED TO DRAW A STORY THAT INCLUDED EYE PATCHES, SIGN LANGUAGE AND TWINS. INITIALLY I WAS TOLD THAT A BOY WITH AN EYE PATCH WAS NOT ACCEPTABLE, BUT I PLEADED, **"I WANT TO DRAW AN EYE-PATCH BOY!"** (*SMILE*)

How did you decide what Mego and Mitsuru would be like?

I WANTED TO MAKE MEGO AND MITSURU BOUNDLESSLY CHEERFUL BECAUSE ALL THE OTHER CHARACTERS **HAD HEARTBREAKING BACKSTORIES.** (*SMILE*) I'VE ALWAYS LIKED STORIES WHERE **THE HEROINE'S LOVE NEVER WAVERS, NO MATTER WHO HER HERO IS.**

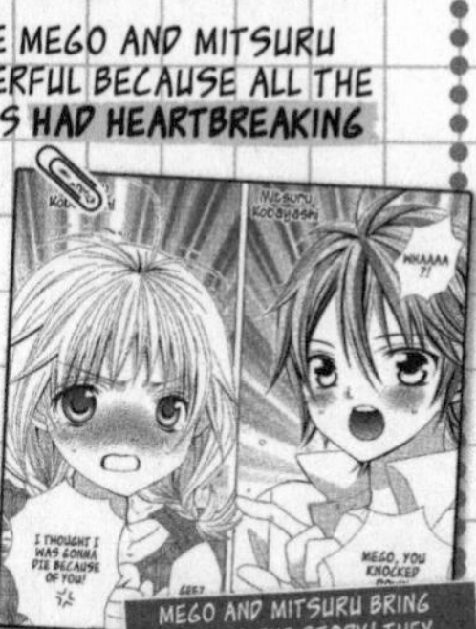

MEGO AND MITSURU BRING LIGHT TO THE STORY! THEY REALLY ARE STARS!

Was there anything you found difficult with this series?

THAT **AOI COULDN'T WINK** BECAUSE OF THE EYE PATCH, AND THAT **READERS COULDN'T SEE HIS EXPRESSION** WHEN I DREW HIM FROM HIS RIGHT SIDE. HE COULDN'T PLAY AN ACTIVE ROLE IN THE STORY EITHER, SINCE HE COULDN'T BE AROUND OTHER WOMEN.

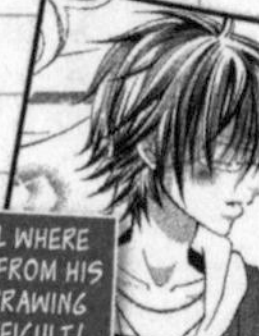

A RARE PANEL WHERE AOI IS DRAWN FROM HIS RIGHT SIDE. DRAWING THIS WAS DIFFICULT!

But didn't that make Mego's goodness stand out?

SHE WAS SUPPOSED TO BE CUTER AND MORE MODEST, BUT SHE TURNED OUT TO BE STRONG. (*SMILE*) AND READERS HATED AZUSA IN THE BEGINNING! **I WANTED AZUSA'S CHARACTER TO MAKE A STRONG IMPACT, AND I WANTED TO DRAW A KIND OF CHARACTER I'D NEVER DRAWN BEFORE.** SHE WAS THE **"MOST HATED CHARACTER** IN *SHO-COMI*" UNTIL CHAPTER 4. (*SMILE*) HOWEVER, THE READERS REACTED POSITIVELY WHEN SHE TOLD MITSURU SHE LIKED HIM IN VOLUME 3.

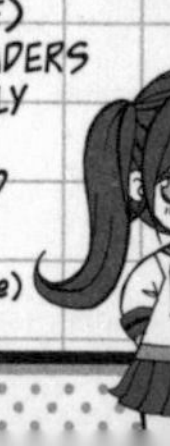

(continued on next page)

(continued from previous page)

THEN THE READERS STARTED LIKING AZUSA, AND I THOUGHT, **"GOOD JOB, AZUSA!"** (*SMILE*) THOSE WERE THE THINGS I WAS MOST WORRIED ABOUT WHEN THE SERIES BEGAN.

Azusa was a very expressive and lovable character.

I ENJOYED DRAWING AZUSA THE MOST. MY ASSISTANT DREW THE BIRD THAT IS WITH UESUGI WHEN HE FIRST APPEARS. I HAD A WHITE BIRD LIKE A DOVE IN MIND, BUT IT TURNED OUT TO BE A ROUND SPARROW. (*SMILE*) **IT WAS CUTE, SO I SAID, "LET'S GO WITH THIS."** THEN IT STARTED APPEARING REGULARLY, SO WE DECIDED TO NAME IT. WE THOUGHT UESUGI WOULD NAME IT LIKE A DELUSIONAL TEENAGER, SO WE CALLED IT **KYOYA ("CRAZY" + "NIGHT")** IN THE STUDIO. (*SMILE*)

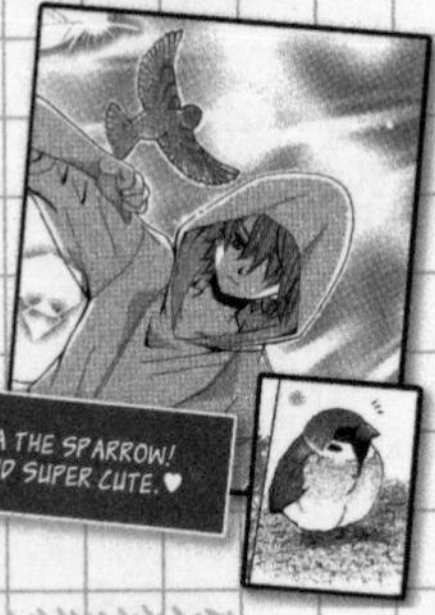

THIS IS KYOYA THE SPARROW! IT'S ROUND AND SUPER CUTE.♥

Which scenes were you excited about drawing?

MEGO'S LOVE CONFESSION USING SIGN LANGUAGE. I NEED TO HAVE THE ENTIRE PLOT READY BEFORE I CAN START DRAWING A SERIES, AND THE FIRST HIGH POINT IN THIS SERIES FOR ME WAS THE CONFESSION SCENE. **THE SECOND HIGH POINT WAS WHEN MEGO KISSES AOI'S EYE THAT HAS BEEN HIDDEN BY HIS EYE PATCH.** I WAS HAPPY WHEN I FINISHED DRAWING BOTH SCENES, BECAUSE I'D REACHED BOTH MY GOALS.

NOW THAT SO CUTE! IS FINISHED...

How are you feeling now that you've finished *So Cute!*?

I WAS ABLE TO DRAW IT TO THE VERY END. THERE WERE MANY THEMES IN THIS SERIES THAT MADE ME THINK, "WILL I REALLY BE ABLE TO DRAW THIS?" BECAUSE THE STORY FEATURES SENSITIVE TOPICS LIKE SIGN LANGUAGE, THE SCAR BENEATH AOI'S EYE PATCH AND THE EARTHQUAKE. IT WAS VERY DIFFICULT TO THOROUGHLY PORTRAY SIGN LANGUAGE, SO I FELT LIKE I WOULDN'T BE ABLE TO DRAW EXACTLY WHAT I WANTED. BUT I HOPE THIS WORK MADE READERS **WANT TO LEARN MORE ABOUT SIGN LANGUAGE** AND **FEEL COMPASSION.**

(continued on next page)

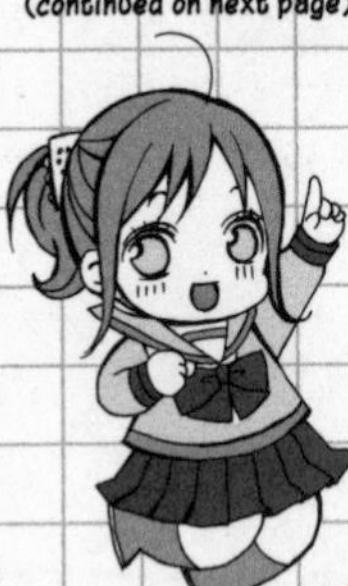

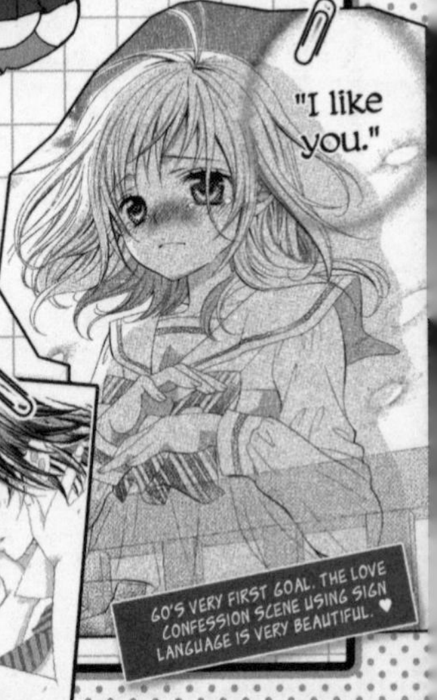
"I like you."

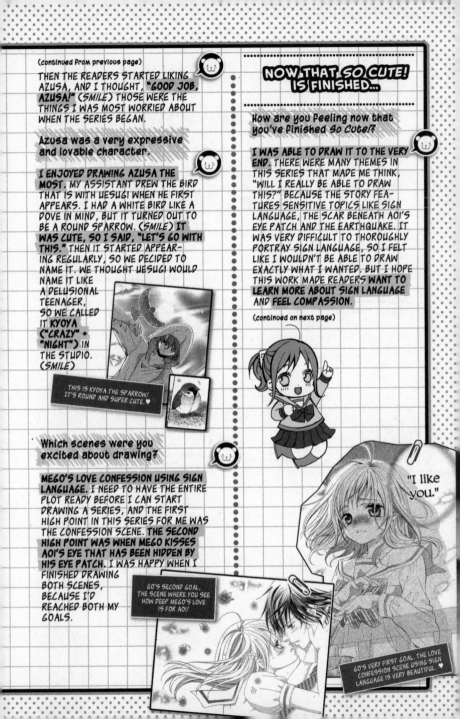

GO'S VERY FIRST GOAL. THE LOVE CONFESSION SCENE USING SIGN LANGUAGE IS VERY BEAUTIFUL.♥

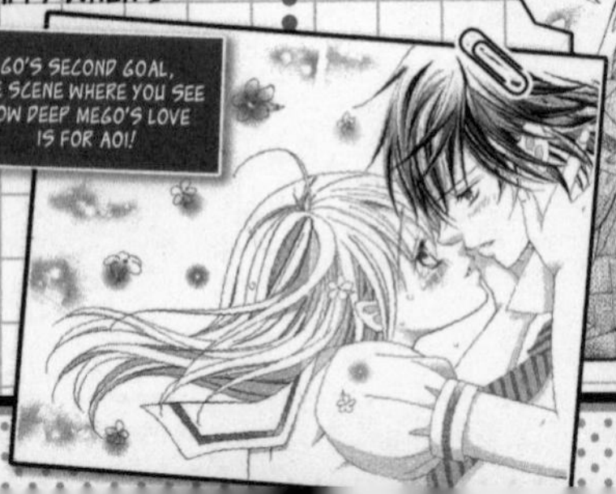

GO'S SECOND GOAL. THE SCENE WHERE YOU SEE HOW DEEP MEGO'S LOVE IS FOR AOI!

(continued from previous page)

Why did you decided to include sign language? How did you come up with the idea for *So Cute!*?

I'VE ALWAYS WANTED TO DRAW IT. THERE WAS A TV DRAMA CALLED *HOSHI NO KINKA* THAT FEATURED SIGN LANGUAGE, AND MY FRIENDS AND I TRIED COMMUNICATING WITH SIGN LANGUAGE AFTER WE SAW IT. SO I FELT THAT FEATURING SIGN LANGUAGE IN THE MANGA MIGHT BE A CATALYST FOR OTHERS. PEOPLE WHO SERIOUSLY FEATURE SIGN LANGUAGE IN THEIR WORKS MIGHT FEEL LIKE I WASN'T REALLY ABLE TO PORTRAY IT... BUT WHILE I WAS DRAWING, MY HEART AND MIND WORKED AS ONE.

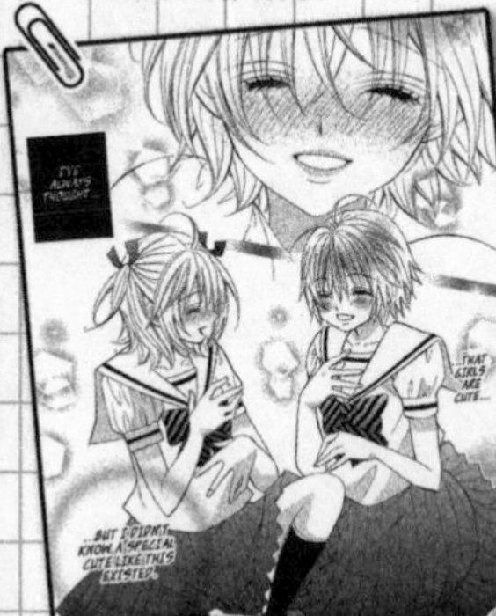
I'VE ALWAYS THOUGHT...
...THAT GIRLS ARE CUTE...
...BUT I DIDN'T KNOW A SPECIAL CUTE LIKE THIS EXISTED.

THE SCENE WHERE MITSURU AND SHINO ENJOY TALKING IN SIGN LANGUAGE MAKES YOU SMILE!

PORTRAYING THE EARTHQUAKE

You must've gotten huge reactions when you portrayed the earthquake in the climax.

I WAS THINKING ABOUT SUPPORTING RECONSTRUCTION OF THE AFFECTED AREAS THROUGH THIS WORK EVEN BEFORE I BEGAN THE SERIES. BUT I HAD MY DOUBTS BECAUSE I WASN'T SURE WHETHER I'D REALLY BE ABLE TO DRAW IT.

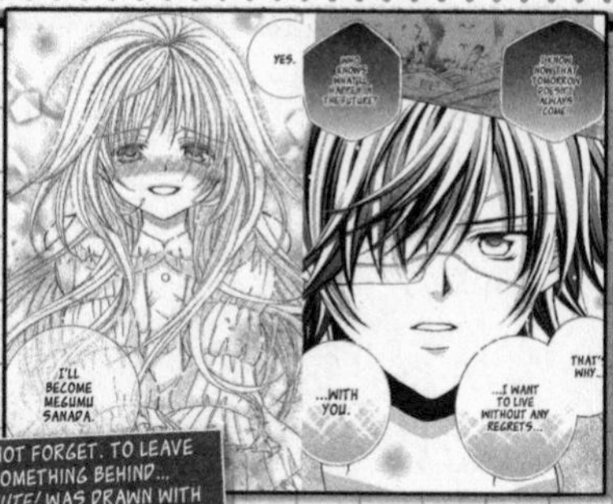
I KNOW NOW THAT TOMORROW DOESN'T ALWAYS COME
WHO KNOWS WHAT'LL HAPPEN IN THE FUTURE?
THAT'S WHY...
...I WANT TO LIVE WITHOUT ANY REGRETS...
...WITH YOU.
YES.
I'LL BECOME MEGUMU SANADA.

TO NOT FORGET. TO LEAVE SOMETHING BEHIND... *SO CUTE!* WAS DRAWN WITH THAT IN MIND.

What made you decide to draw it then?

I HADN'T BEEN ABLE TO FORGET THE VIDEO OF THE TSUNAMI AT NATORI, MIYAGI PREFECTURE, FOR MANY YEARS... ONE REASON IS THAT SOMEONE WHO TOOK CARE OF ME WHEN I WAS LITTLE PASSED AWAY THEN. SO I JUST COULDN'T SAY "LET'S DO OUR BEST!" WHEN EVERYONE WAS SENDING MESSAGES AFTER THE EARTHQUAKE... SO I KEPT THINKING, "SHOULDN'T I DRAW ABOUT IT?" THEN I HEARD ABOUT AN ARTIST WHO SURVIVED THE TOKYO AIR RAID AND WAS PAINTING HIS EXPERIENCES. THAT MADE ME FEEL LIKE I MIGHT BE ABLE TO LEAVE SOMETHING BEHIND BY DRAWING ABOUT THE EARTHQUAKE. *SO CUTE!* IS PUBLISHED OUTSIDE OF JAPAN TOO, SO I FELT THAT MAYBE PEOPLE OVERSEAS WOULD READ THIS IF I DREW ABOUT IT AND THAT EVEN IF I RECEIVED CRITICISM FOR DRAWING ABOUT IT NOW, I MIGHT STILL BE ABLE TO LEAVE SOMETHING FOR THE FUTURE. I ALSO FELT THAT IF I DREW ABOUT THE EARTHQUAKE IN A ROMCOM, READERS WOULD BE ABLE TO FEEL SOMETHING EVERY TIME THEY READ IT. BUT I WORRIED THAT I MIGHT MAKE THE READERS WHO HAD BEEN THROUGH THE EARTHQUAKE REMEMBER THEIR PAINFUL EXPERIENCES, SO I AGONIZED OVER WHETHER I SHOULD REALLY DRAW IT OR NOT.

I felt like this series was saying, "This is how we'll live our lives. How will you live yours?" There are people who are still suffering, so we understand it could be difficult for your message to get through...

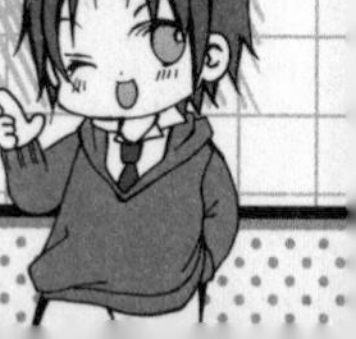

(continued on next page)

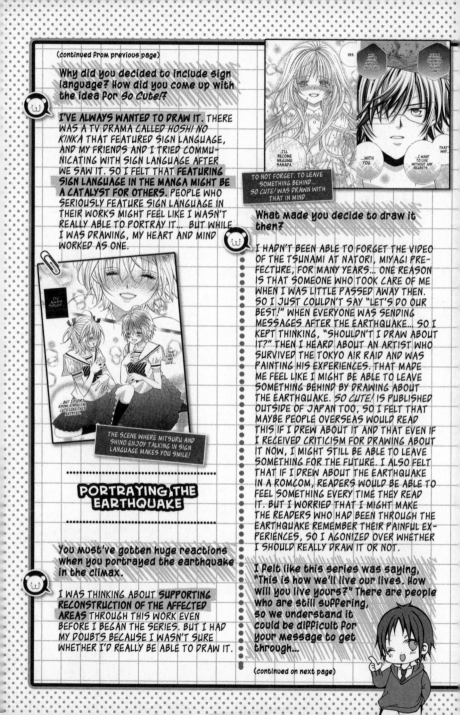

(continued from previous page)

PEOPLE READ THIS SERIES AND WARMLY ACCEPTED WHAT I'D DRAWN, SO I WAS VERY GRATEFUL FOR THAT. BEFORE I STARTED DRAWING, I I DISCUSSED THINGS WITH MY MIDDLE SCHOOL TEACHER, WHO SAID, "THERE ARE PEOPLE WHO WANT TO FORGET AND PEOPLE WHO ARE UNABLE TO FORGET, SO YOU SHOULD DRAW BOTH PERSPECTIVES." THAT'S WHY I LEFT IT UP TO THE READERS.

What sort of reactions did you receive from the readers?

WHEN I DREW THE CHAPTER WHERE THE EARTHQUAKE HITS, I RECEIVED A LETTER FROM A GIRL WHO LIVES IN FUKUSHIMA. SHE WROTE, "THE EARTHQUAKE IS A PAINFUL MEMORY, SO TO BE HONEST, I DIDN'T WANT YOU TO DRAW IT IN THE MANGA. BUT I BELIEVE YOU WILL GIVE A HAPPY ENDING TO MEGO AND AOI." I COULDN'T HELP CRYING WHEN I READ THAT... SO WHILE I WAS DRAWING, I KEPT THINKING, "I PROMISE I'LL MAKE THEM HAPPY!"

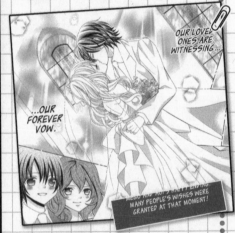

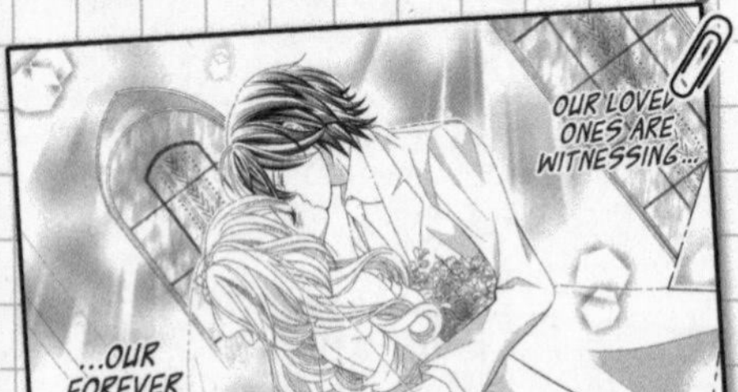
OUR LOVED ONES ARE WITNESSING...
...OUR FOREVER VOW.
MEGO AND AOI'S HAPPY ENDING. MANY PEOPLE'S WISHES WERE GRANTED AT THAT MOMENT!

First published in *Sho-Comi* 2015, issue 23 supplement.

We hope the happy ending was read by readers like her. Is there anything that has changed for you because of this series?

I FELT LIKE I WAS GIVEN AN OPPORTUNITY WITH THIS SERIES. EVEN WHEN I WAS HAVING A HARD TIME WITH STORY DEVELOPMENT, I WAS TOLD "NOT THAT WAY, THIS WAY" AND WAS ABLE TO MAKE CHOICES THAT SOMEHOW CONNECTED EVERYTHING. IT WAS A LOT OF WORK, BUT SOMETHING ALWAYS HELPED ME ALONG THE WAY AND I WAS ABLE TO DRAW MORE CLEARLY THAN I WOULD HAVE OTHERWISE.

Is there anything you'd like to do now that the series is over?

I'D LIKE TO GO TO SENDAI, SINCE I HAVEN'T GONE BACK IN A WHILE. THE CHRISTMAS PAGEANT OF STARLIGHT IS REALLY BEAUTIFUL.

Finally, a message to the readers, please.

THANK YOU SO MUCH FOR READING THIS SERIES FOR THREE YEARS! I'M VERY GRATEFUL THAT A WONDERFUL GAME AND DRAMA CDS WERE MADE. ISSUE 24 OF *SHO-COMI* WILL COME WITH A LOVEY-DOVEY PHOTO CARD OF MEGO AND AOI, AND I'LL DRAW A FUN BONUS STORY FEATURING MITSURU AND AZUSA FOR ISSUE 2 IN THE NEW YEAR! I'M ALSO PLANNING MY NEW SERIES. A HEROINE YOU'VE NEVER SEEN BEFORE WILL SHINE GORGEOUSLY, SO LOOK FORWARD TO IT!

We'll look forward to it! Thank you so much!

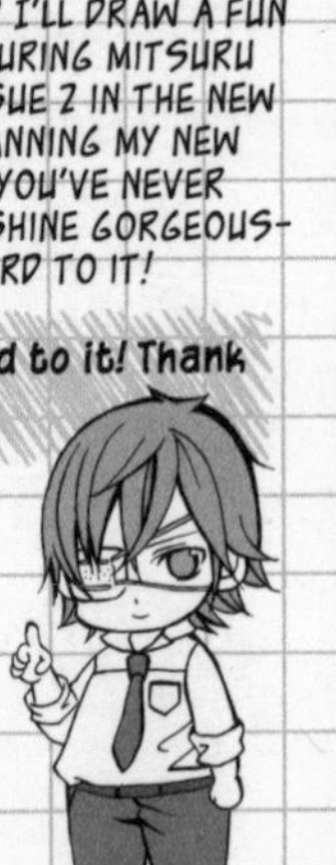

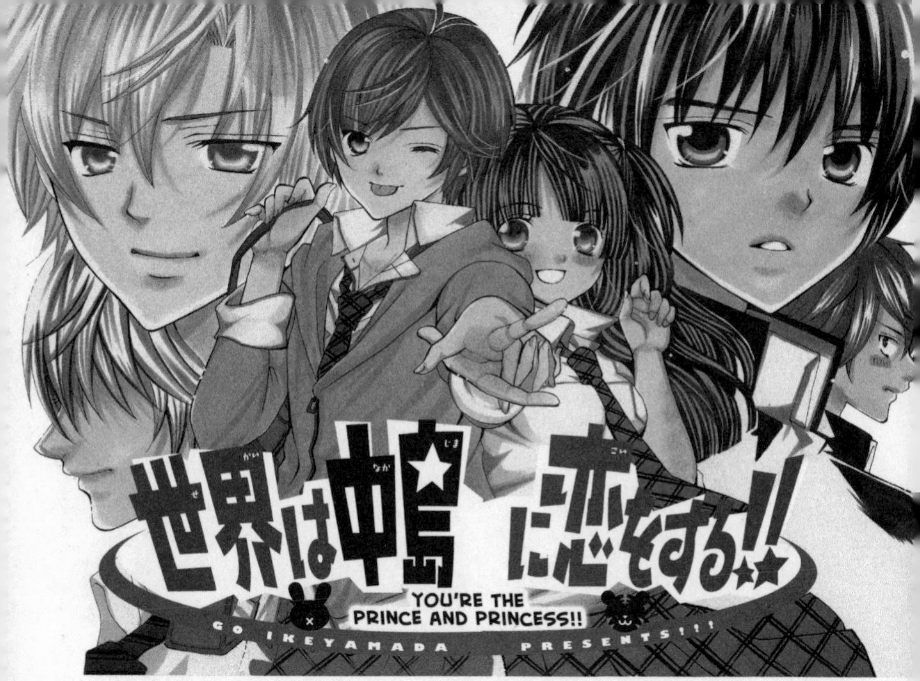
世界は中島に恋をする!!
YOU'RE THE PRINCE AND PRINCESS!!
GO IKEYAMADA PRESENTS!!!

MY NEW SERIES IS TITLED ***SEKAI WA NAKAJIMA NI KOI O SURU!!***

(SUZUKI → KOBAYASHI → NAKAJIMA, SO I'M STILL USING NAMES IN MY SERIES TITLES. LOL.)
SEKACHUU!! FOR SHORT. LOL. PLEASE READ IT!!

THE SERIES IS ALREADY RUNNING IN *SHO-COMI* MAGAZINE. IT'S A ROMCOM WITH A VERY UNIQUE HEROINE AND HER PRINCE. IT BREAKS NEW GROUNDS FOR BOTH ME AND *SHO-COMI*, SO I'M WONDERING HOW READERS WILL REACT!!

THE FIRST CHAPTER CONTAINS LOTS OF SURPRISES, BUT I'LL DO MY BEST TO MAKE THE CHARACTERS CHARMING AND ATTRACTIVE SO EVERYONE WILL LOVE THEM! I HOPE YOU'LL ENJOY THIS NEW SERIES TOO!

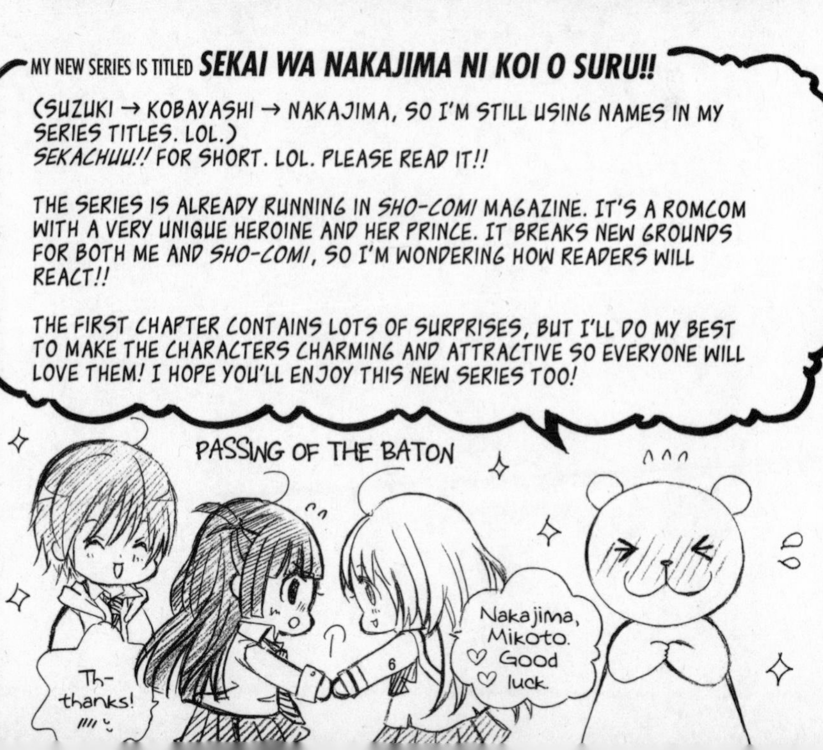
PASSING OF THE BATON
Nakajima, Mikoto. ♡ Good ♡ luck.
Th- thanks!

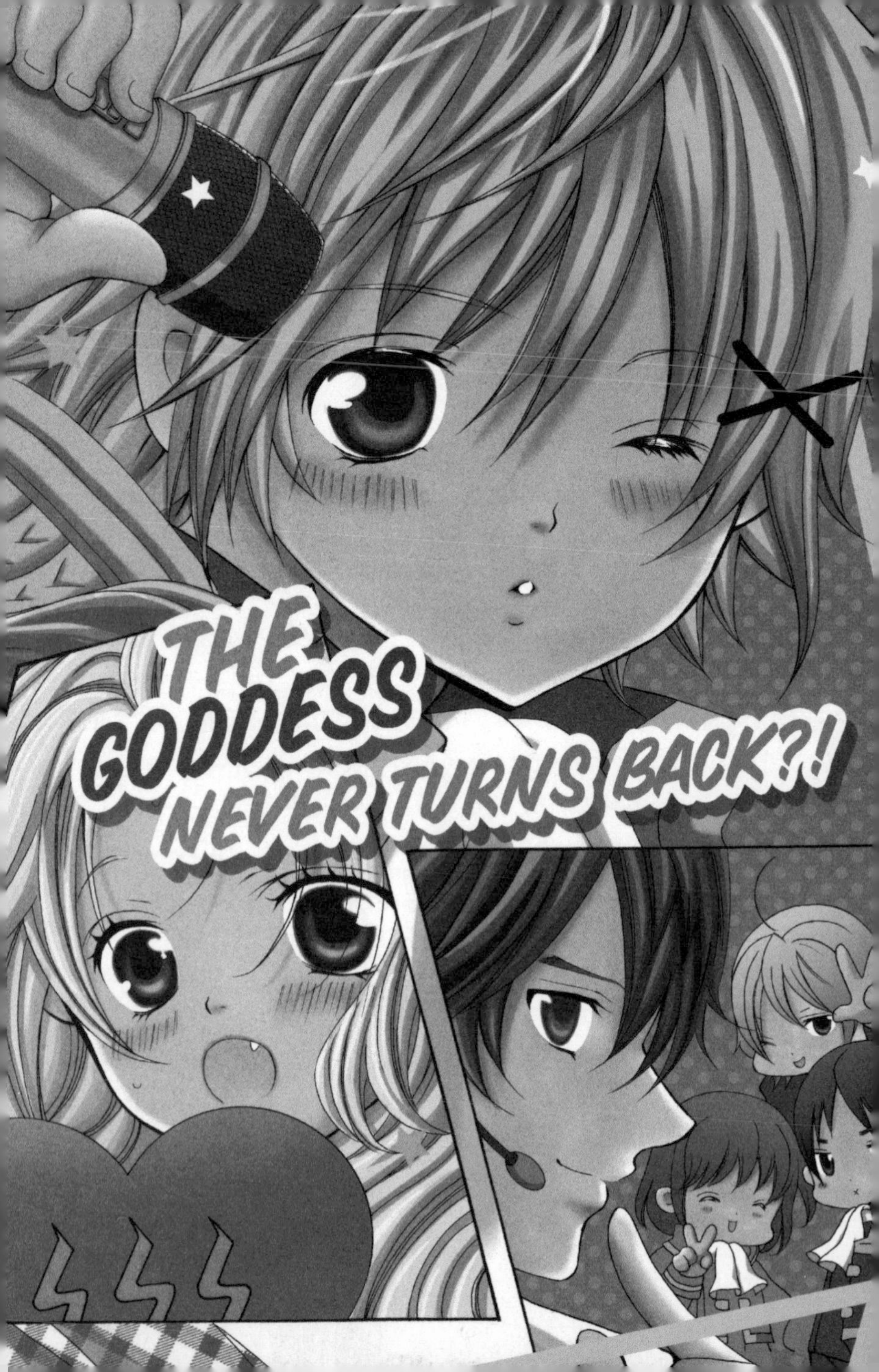
THE GODDESS NEVER TURNS BACK?!

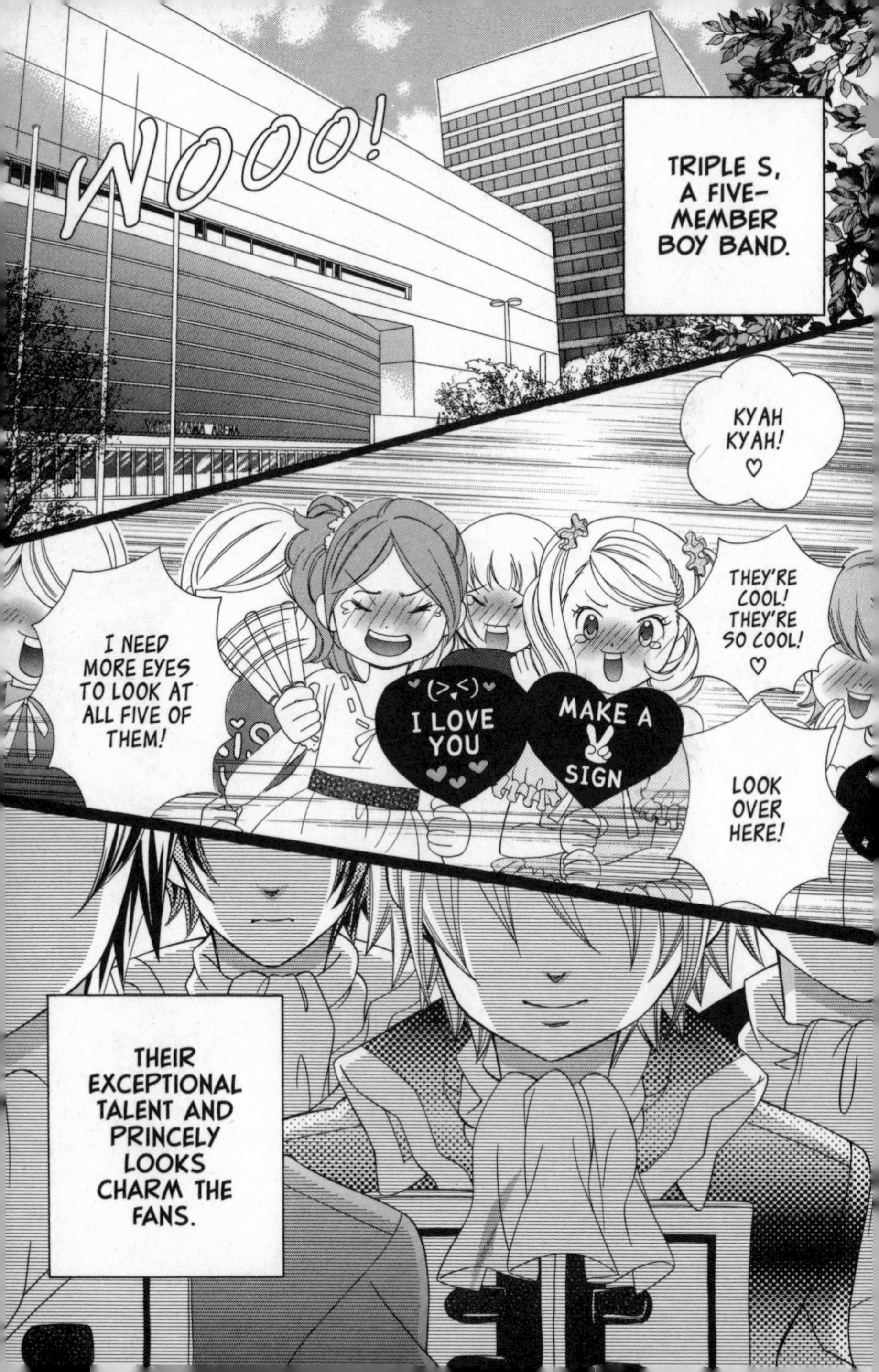

TRIPLE S, A FIVE-MEMBER BOY BAND.
WOOO!
KYAH KYAH! ♡
THEY'RE COOL! THEY'RE SO COOL! ♡
LOOK OVER HERE!
MAKE A ✌ SIGN
(>.<) I LOVE YOU
I NEED MORE EYES TO LOOK AT ALL FIVE OF THEM!
THEIR EXCEPTIONAL TALENT AND PRINCELY LOOKS CHARM THE FANS.

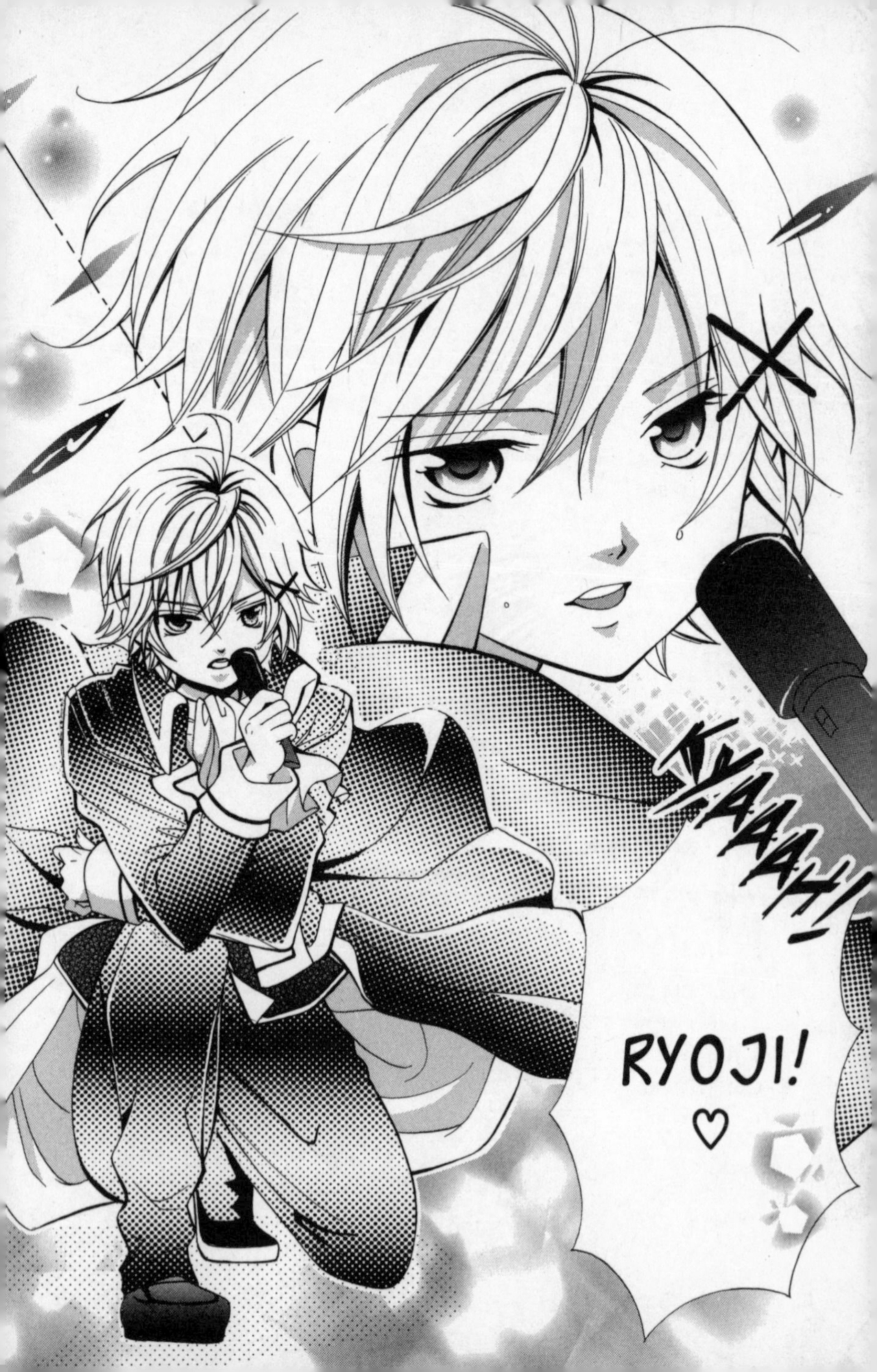
KYAAAH!
RYOJI! ♡

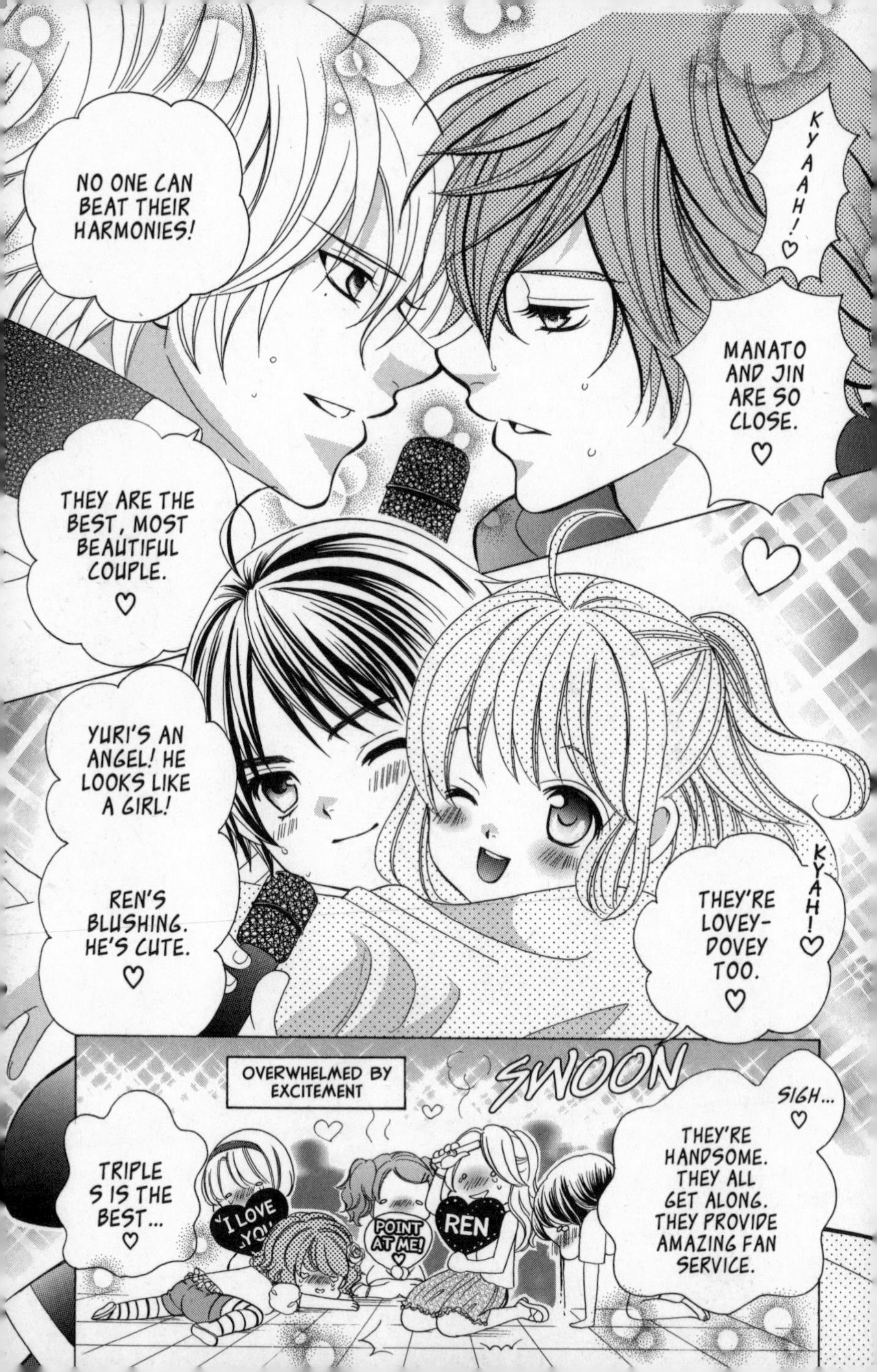
KYAAH! ♡
MANATO AND JIN ARE SO CLOSE. ♡
NO ONE CAN BEAT THEIR HARMONIES!
THEY ARE THE BEST, MOST BEAUTIFUL COUPLE. ♡
KYAH! ♡
THEY'RE LOVEY-DOVEY TOO. ♡
YURI'S AN ANGEL! HE LOOKS LIKE A GIRL!
REN'S BLUSHING. HE'S CUTE. ♡
SIGH... ♡
SWOON
OVERWHELMED BY EXCITEMENT
THEY'RE HANDSOME. THEY ALL GET ALONG. THEY PROVIDE AMAZING FAN SERVICE.
REN
POINT AT ME!
I LOVE YOU
TRIPLE S IS THE BEST... ♡

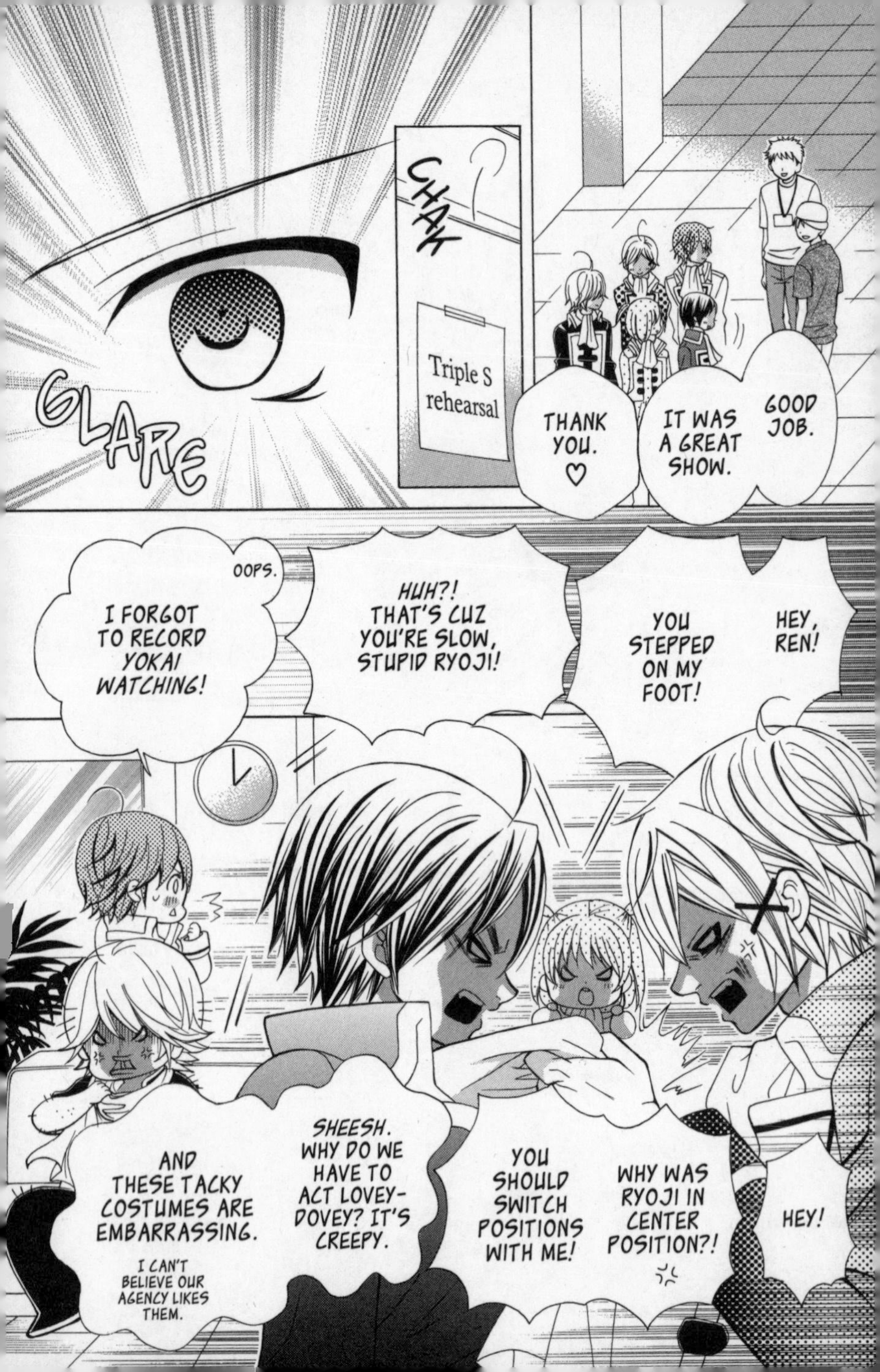
GOOD JOB.
IT WAS A GREAT SHOW.
THANK YOU. ♡
Triple S rehearsal
CHAK
GLARE
HEY, REN!
YOU STEPPED ON MY FOOT!
HUH?! THAT'S CUZ YOU'RE SLOW, STUPID RYOJI!
OOPS.
I FORGOT TO RECORD YOKAI WATCHING!
HEY!
WHY WAS RYOJI IN CENTER POSITION?!
YOU SHOULD SWITCH POSITIONS WITH ME!
SHEESH. WHY DO WE HAVE TO ACT LOVEY-DOVEY? IT'S CREEPY.
AND THESE TACKY COSTUMES ARE EMBARRASSING.
I CAN'T BELIEVE OUR AGENCY LIKES THEM.

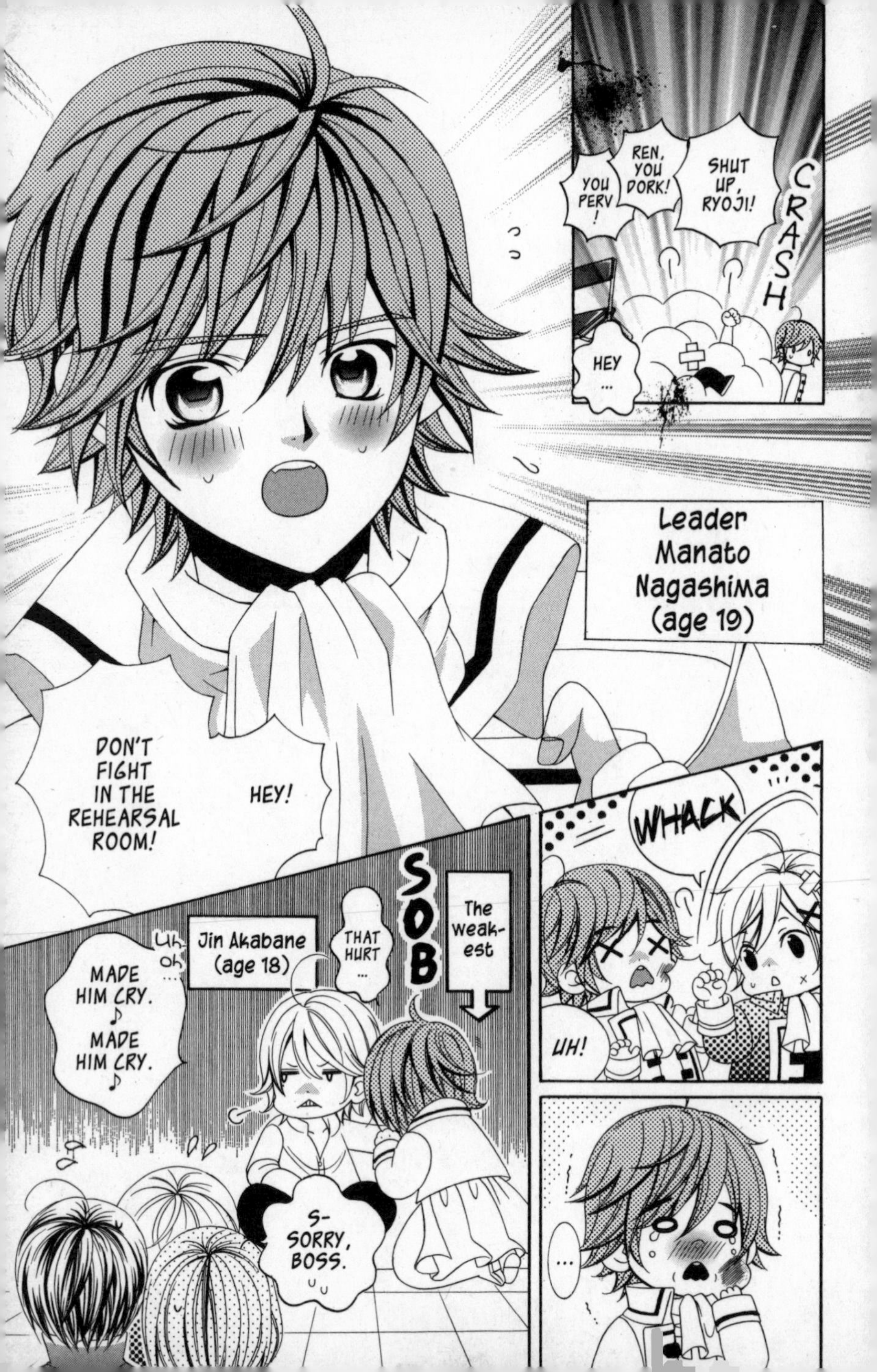
SHUT UP, RYOJI!
REN, YOU DORK!
YOU PERV!
CRASH
HEY...
Leader Manato Nagashima (age 19)
HEY!
DON'T FIGHT IN THE REHEARSAL ROOM!
WHACK
UH!
...
The weak-est
SOB
THAT HURT...
Jin Akabane (age 18)
Uh oh...
MADE HIM CRY. ♪ MADE HIM CRY. ♪
S-SORRY, BOSS.

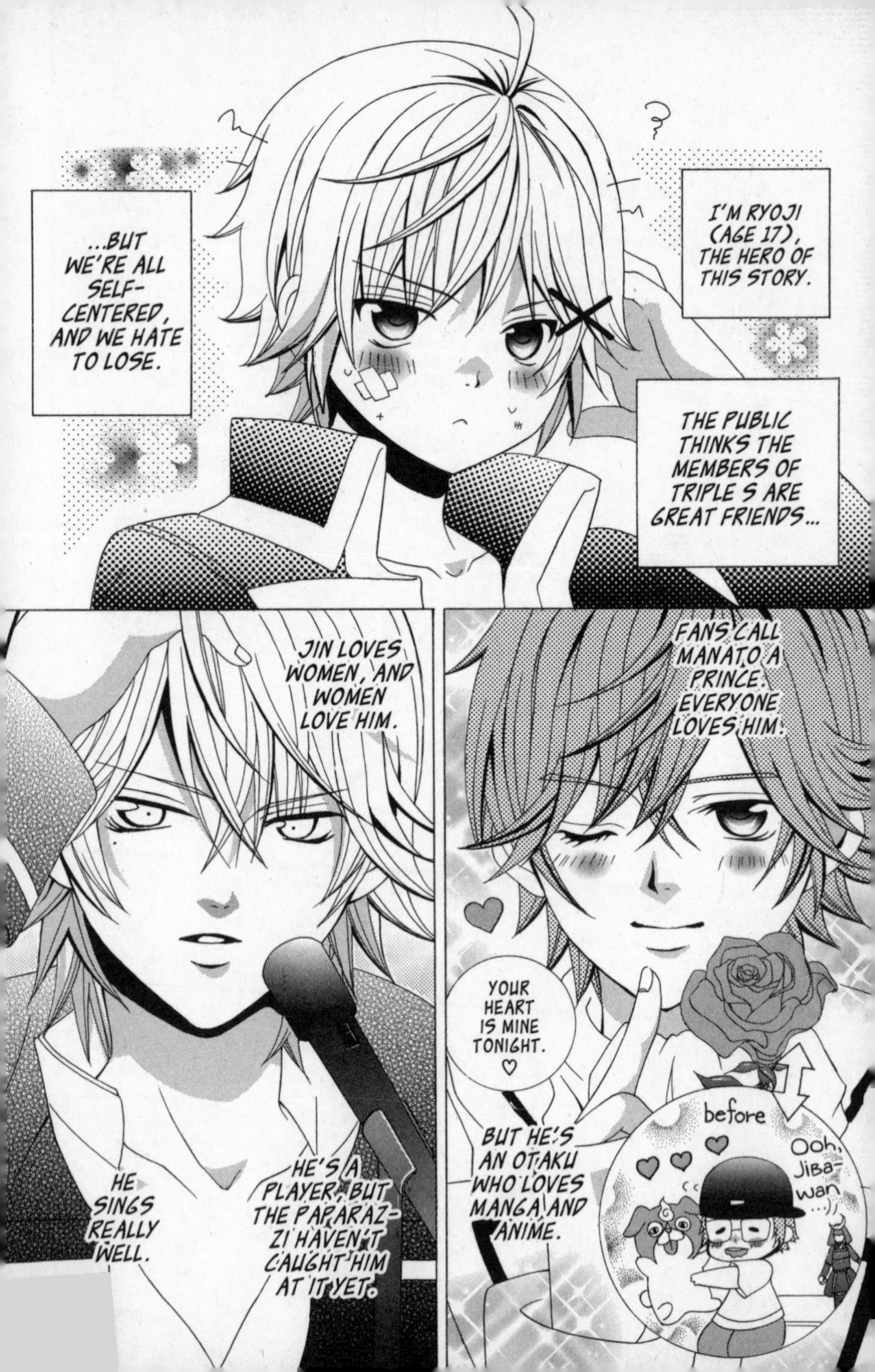
I'M RYOJI (AGE 17), THE HERO OF THIS STORY.
THE PUBLIC THINKS THE MEMBERS OF TRIPLE S ARE GREAT FRIENDS...
...BUT WE'RE ALL SELF-CENTERED, AND WE HATE TO LOSE.
FANS CALL MANATO A PRINCE. EVERYONE LOVES HIM.
YOUR HEART IS MINE TONIGHT. ♡
before
Ooh, Jiba-wan...
BUT HE'S AN OTAKU WHO LOVES MANGA AND ANIME.
JIN LOVES WOMEN, AND WOMEN LOVE HIM.
HE'S A PLAYER, BUT THE PAPARAZZI HAVEN'T CAUGHT HIM AT IT YET.
HE SINGS REALLY WELL.

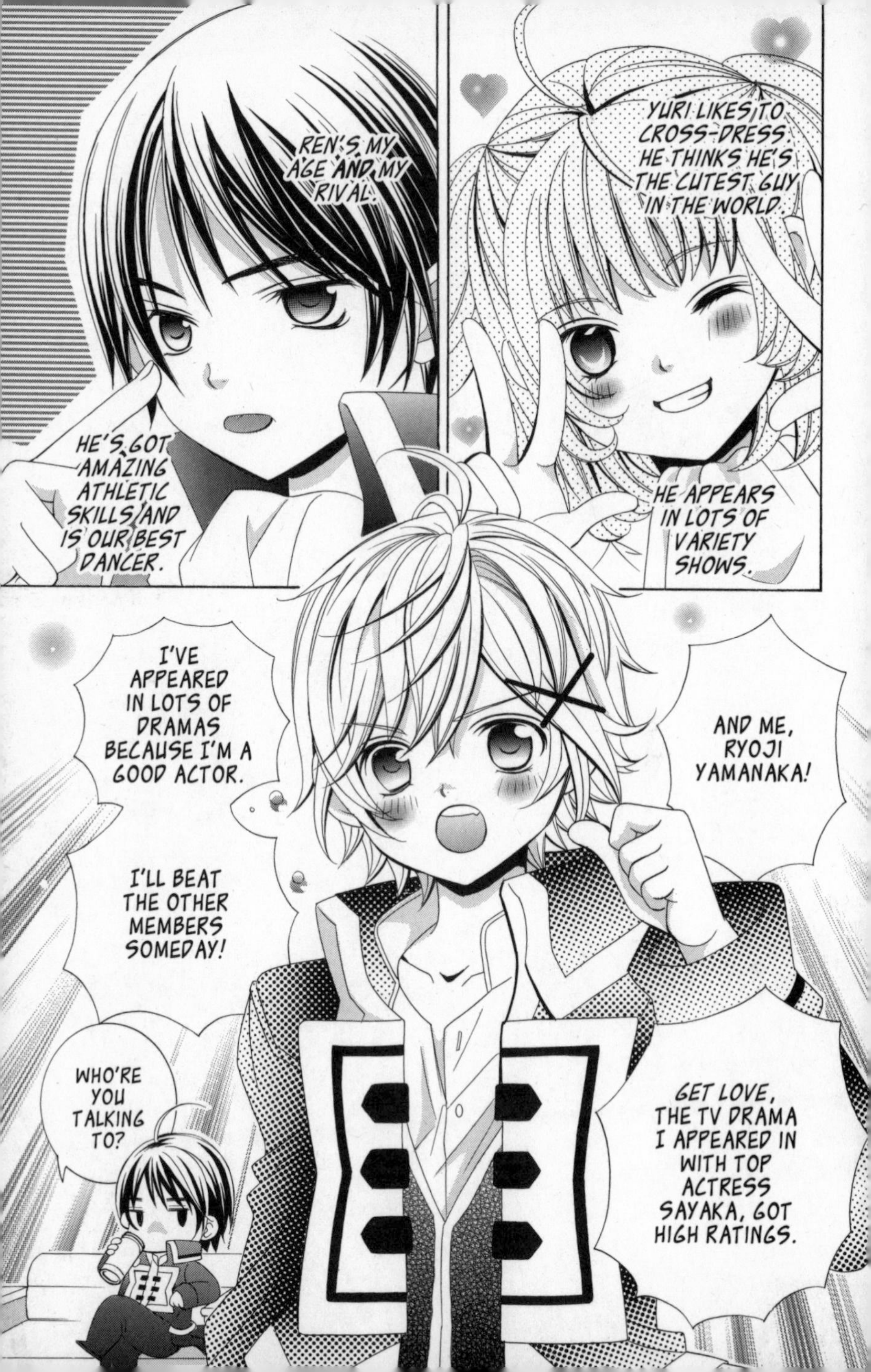
YURI LIKES TO CROSS-DRESS. HE THINKS HE'S THE CUTEST GUY IN THE WORLD.
HE APPEARS IN LOTS OF VARIETY SHOWS.
REN'S MY AGE AND MY RIVAL.
HE'S GOT AMAZING ATHLETIC SKILLS AND IS OUR BEST DANCER.
AND ME, RYOJI YAMANAKA!
I'VE APPEARED IN LOTS OF DRAMAS BECAUSE I'M A GOOD ACTOR.
GET LOVE, THE TV DRAMA I APPEARED IN WITH TOP ACTRESS SAYAKA, GOT HIGH RATINGS.
I'LL BEAT THE OTHER MEMBERS SOMEDAY!
WHO'RE YOU TALKING TO?

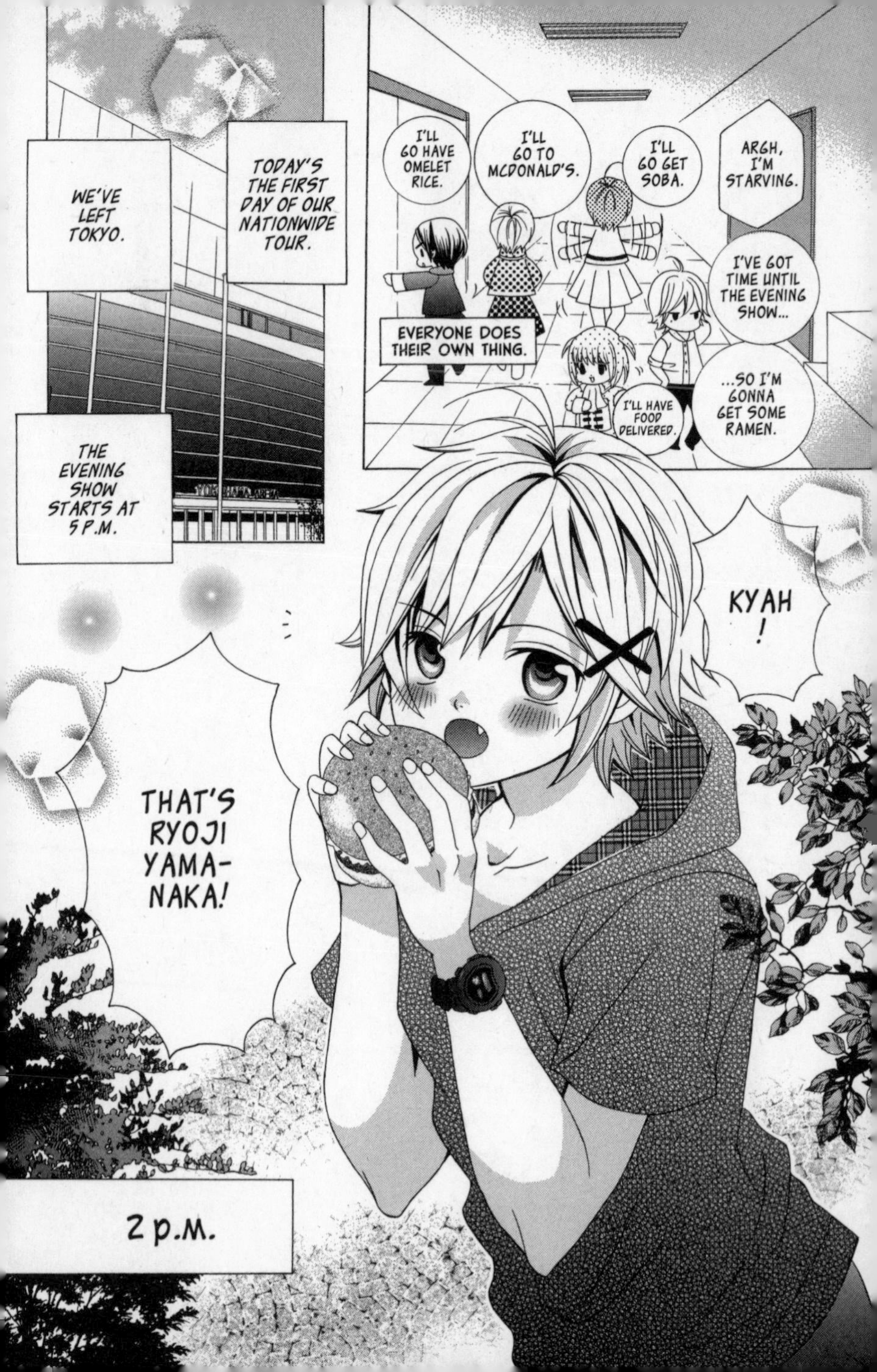
ARGH, I'M STARVING.
I'LL GO GET SOBA.
I'LL GO TO MCDONALD'S.
I'LL GO HAVE OMELET RICE.
I'VE GOT TIME UNTIL THE EVENING SHOW...
...SO I'M GONNA GET SOME RAMEN.
I'LL HAVE FOOD DELIVERED.
EVERYONE DOES THEIR OWN THING.
TODAY'S THE FIRST DAY OF OUR NATIONWIDE TOUR.
WE'VE LEFT TOKYO.
THE EVENING SHOW STARTS AT 5 P.M.
KYAH!
THAT'S RYOJI YAMANAKA!
2 p.m.

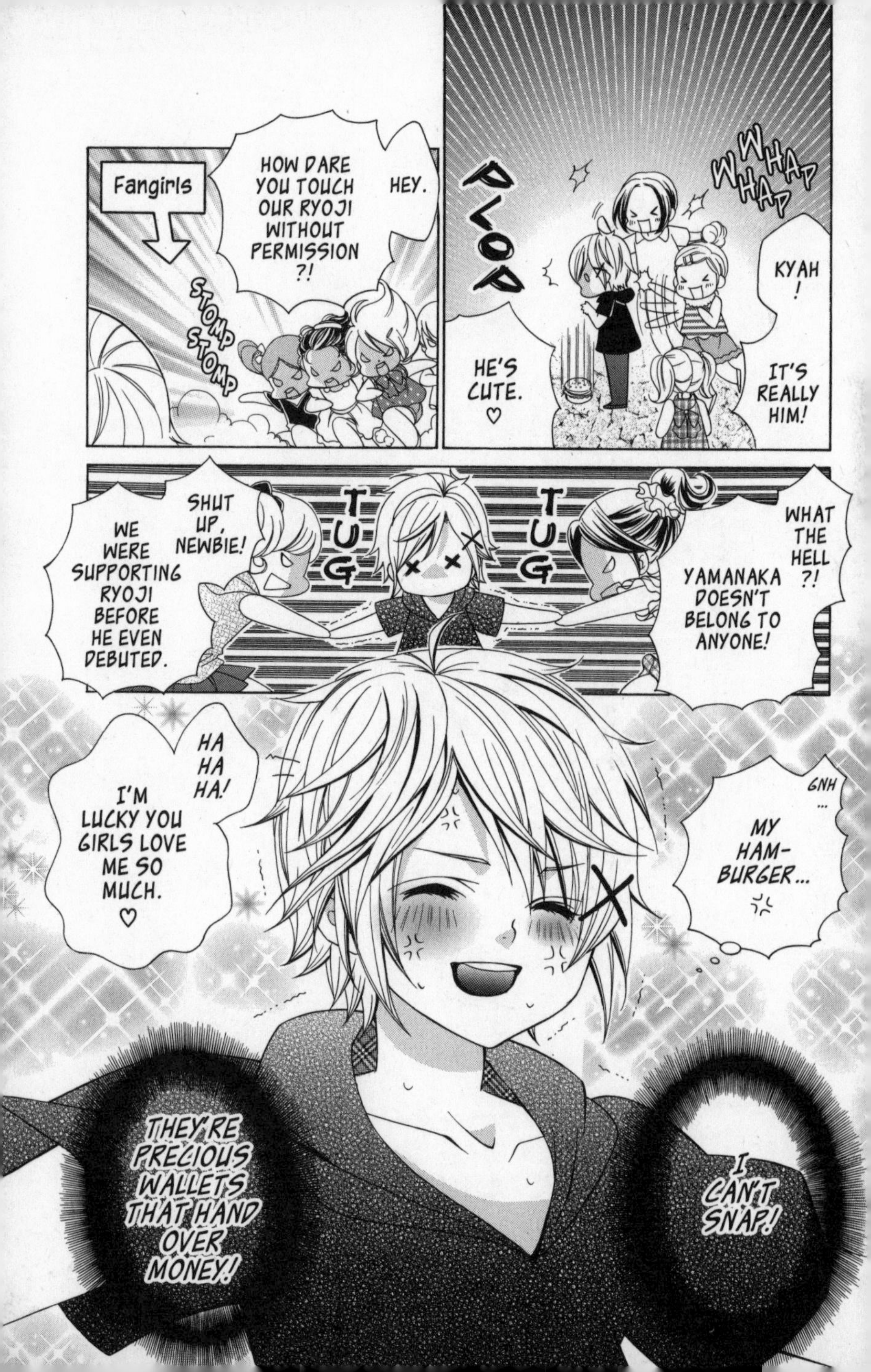
WHAP WHAP
PLOP
KYAH!
IT'S REALLY HIM!
HE'S CUTE. ♡
HEY.
HOW DARE YOU TOUCH OUR RYOJI WITHOUT PERMISSION?!
Fangirls
STOMP STOMP
WHAT THE HELL?!
YAMANAKA DOESN'T BELONG TO ANYONE!
TUG
TUG
SHUT UP, NEWBIE!
WE WERE SUPPORTING RYOJI BEFORE HE EVEN DEBUTED.
GNH...
MY HAMBURGER...
HA HA HA!
I'M LUCKY YOU GIRLS LOVE ME SO MUCH. ♡
I CAN'T SNAP!
THEY'RE PRECIOUS WALLETS THAT HAND OVER MONEY!

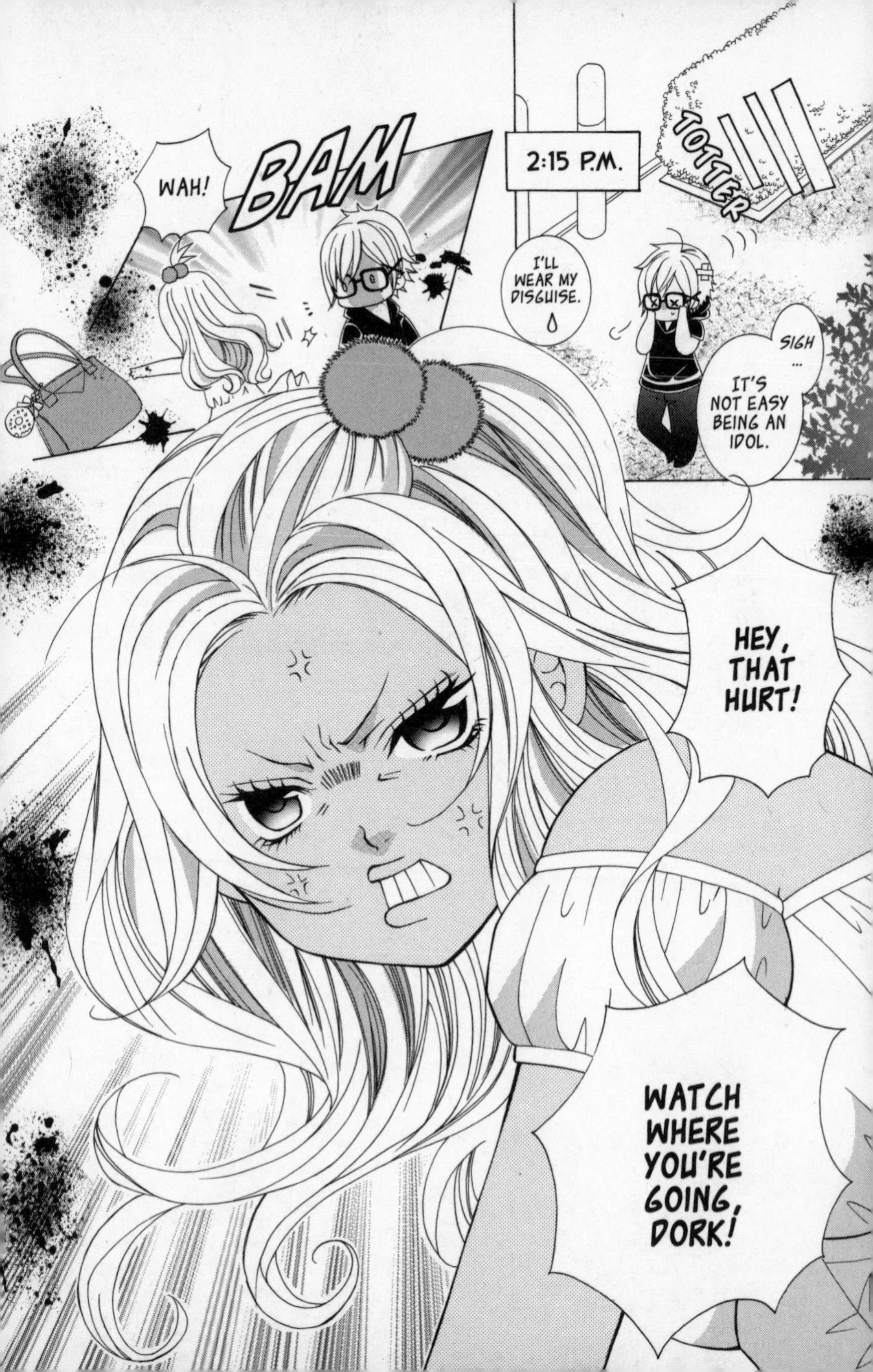
2:15 P.M.
TOTTER
SIGH... IT'S NOT EASY BEING AN IDOL.
I'LL WEAR MY DISGUISE.
BAM
WAH!
HEY, THAT HURT!
WATCH WHERE YOU'RE GOING, DORK!

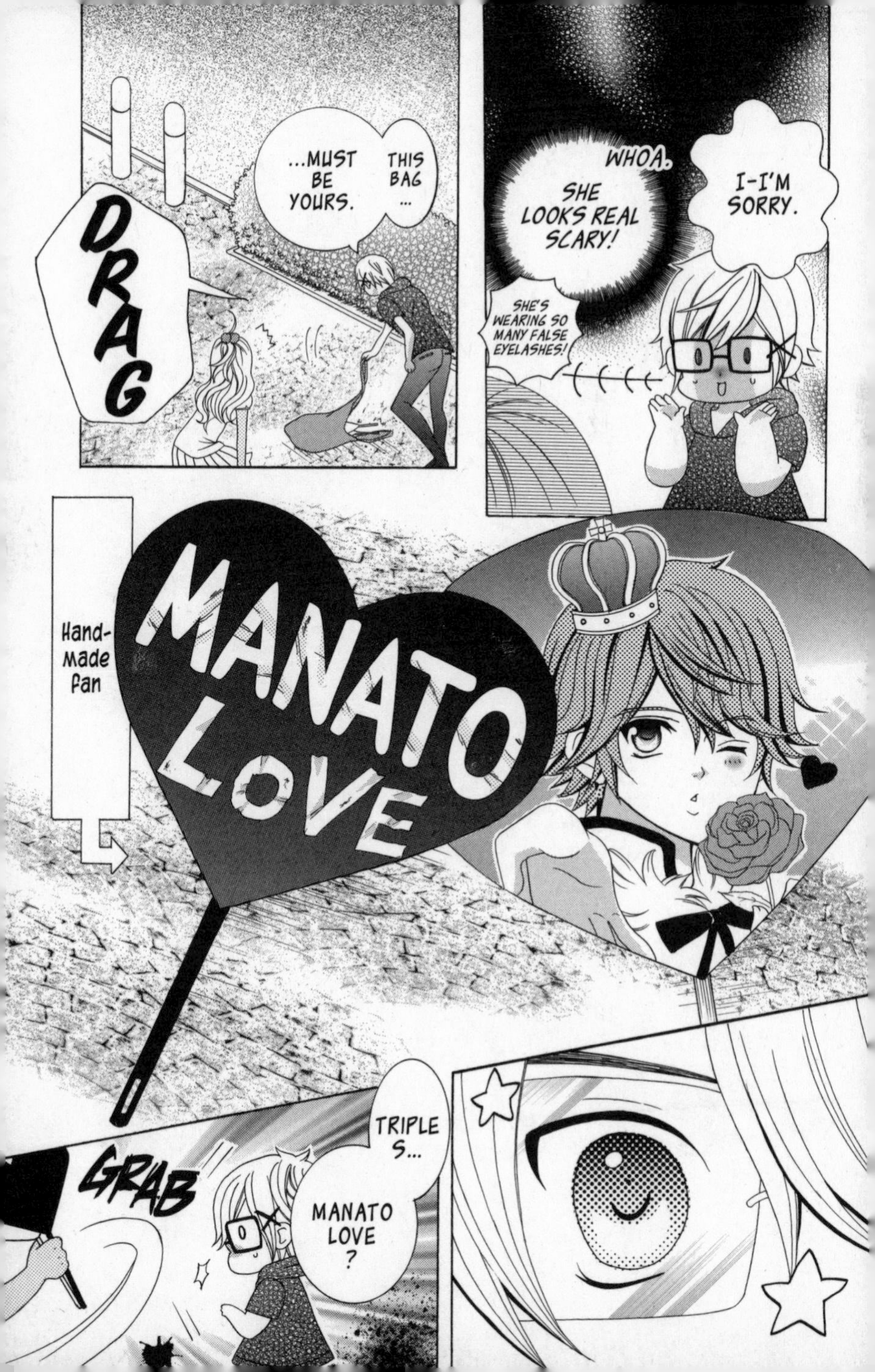
I-I'M SORRY.
WHOA.
SHE LOOKS REAL SCARY!
SHE'S WEARING SO MANY FALSE EYELASHES!
THIS BAG...
...MUST BE YOURS.
DRAG
Hand-made fan
MANATO LOVE
TRIPLE S...
MANATO LOVE?
GRAB

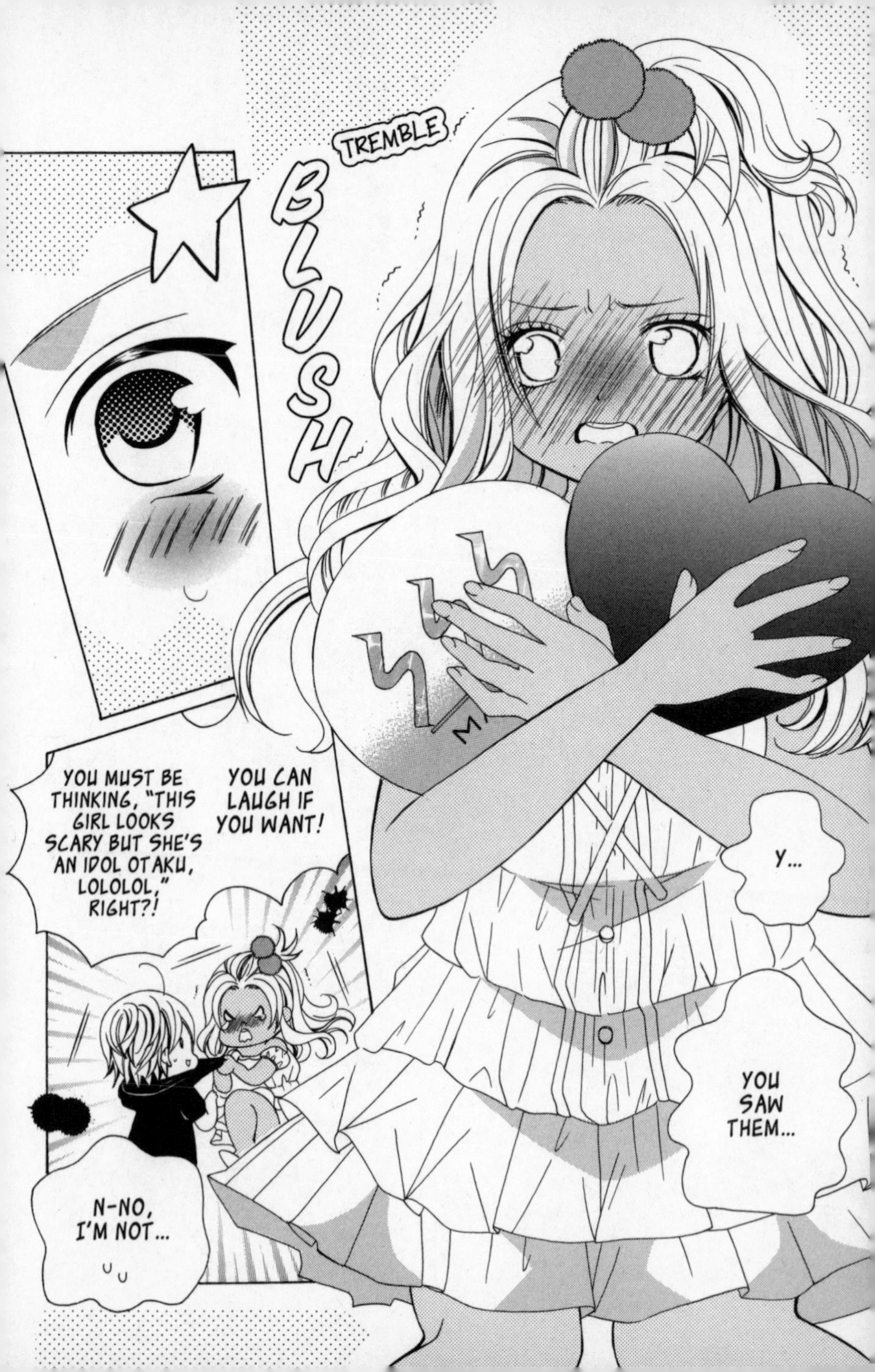
TREMBLE
BLUSH
Y...
YOU SAW THEM...
YOU CAN LAUGH IF YOU WANT!
YOU MUST BE THINKING, "THIS GIRL LOOKS SCARY BUT SHE'S AN IDOL OTAKU, LOLOLOL," RIGHT?!
N-NO, I'M NOT...

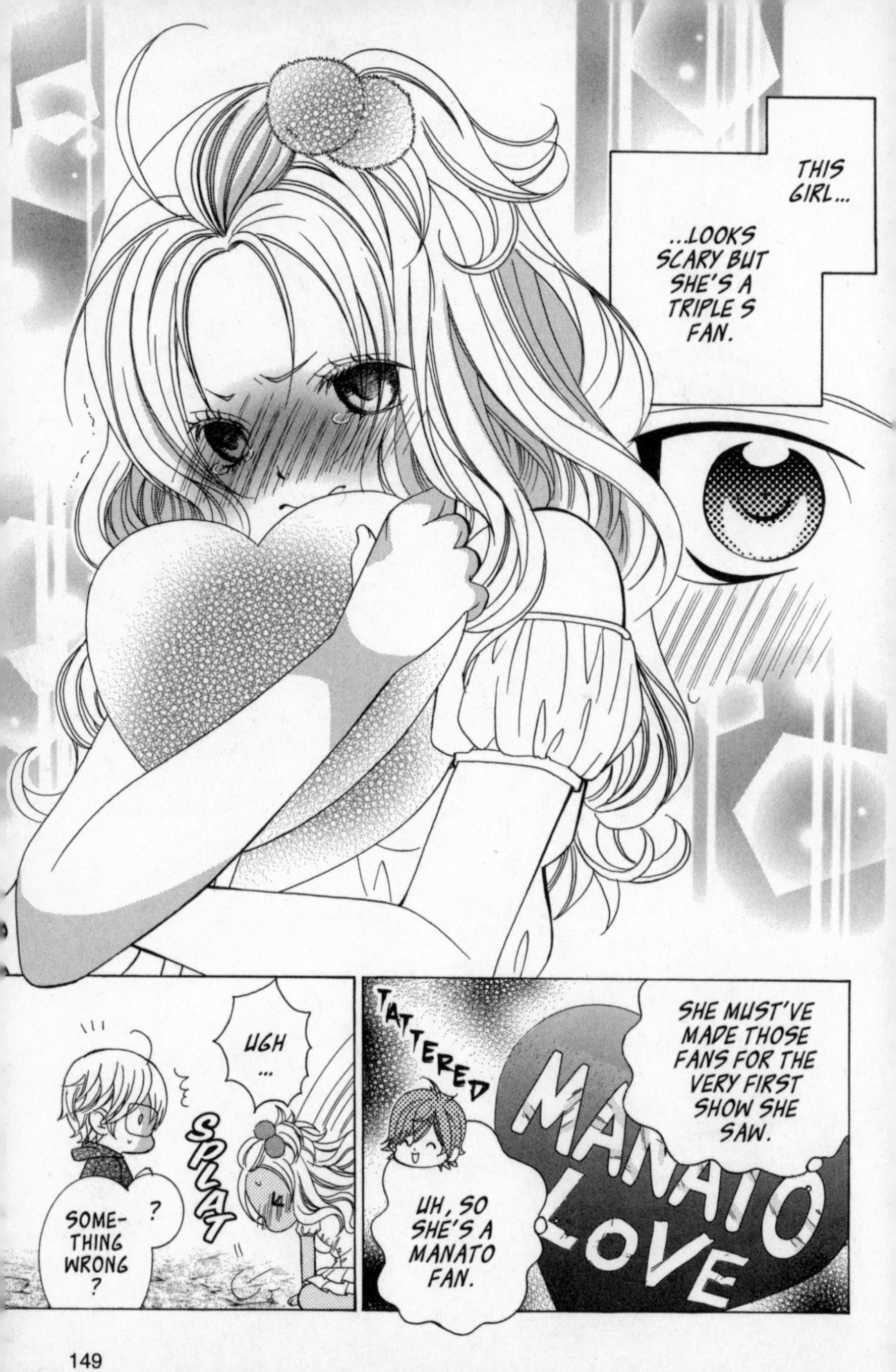
THIS GIRL...
...LOOKS SCARY BUT SHE'S A TRIPLE S FAN.
SHE MUST'VE MADE THOSE FANS FOR THE VERY FIRST SHOW SHE SAW.
TATTERED
MANATO LOVE
UH, SO SHE'S A MANATO FAN.
UGH ...
SPLAT
SOME-THING WRONG ?

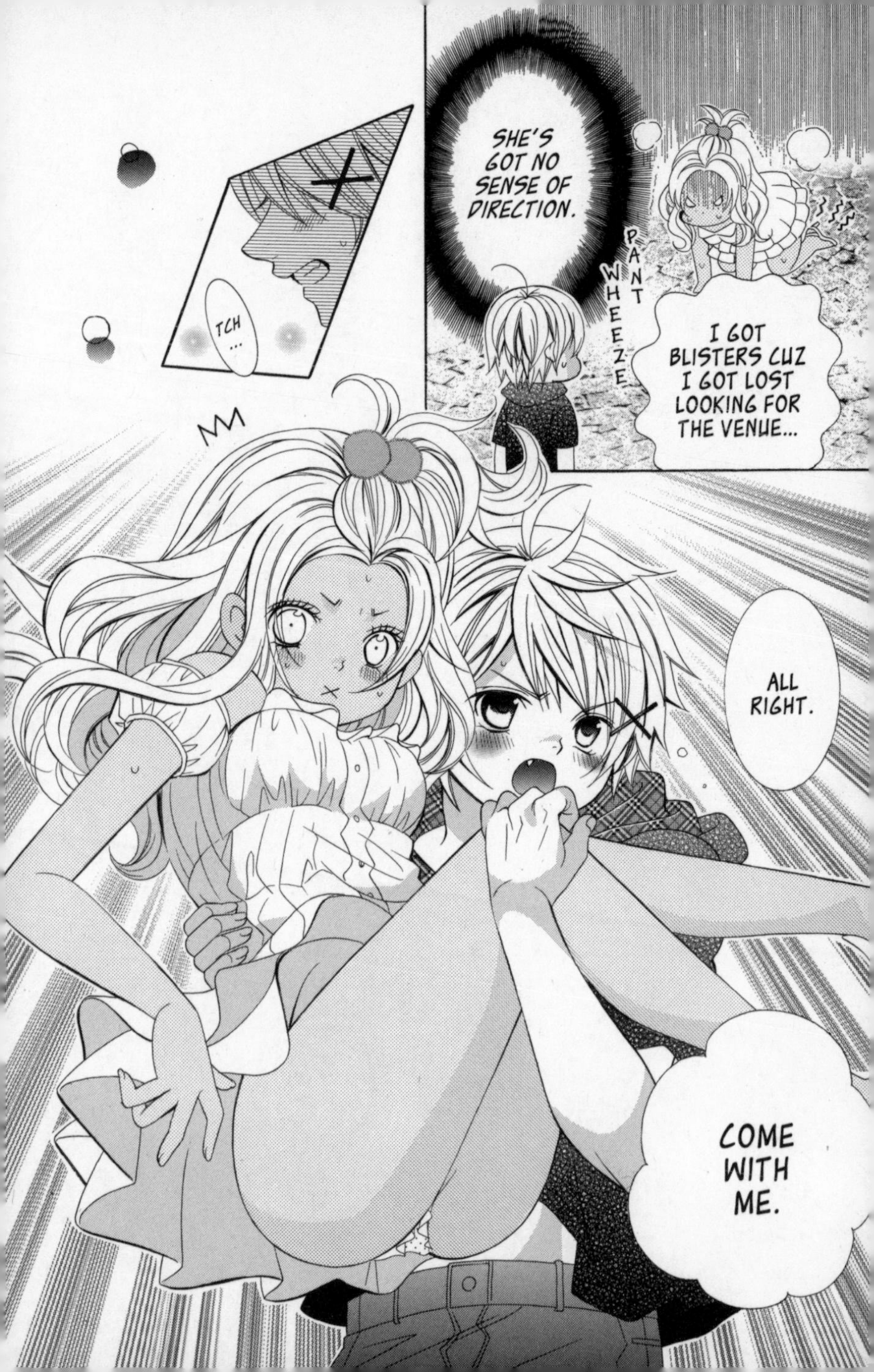
PANT
WHEEZE
I GOT BLISTERS CUZ I GOT LOST LOOKING FOR THE VENUE...
SHE'S GOT NO SENSE OF DIRECTION.
TCH ...
ALL RIGHT.
COME WITH ME.

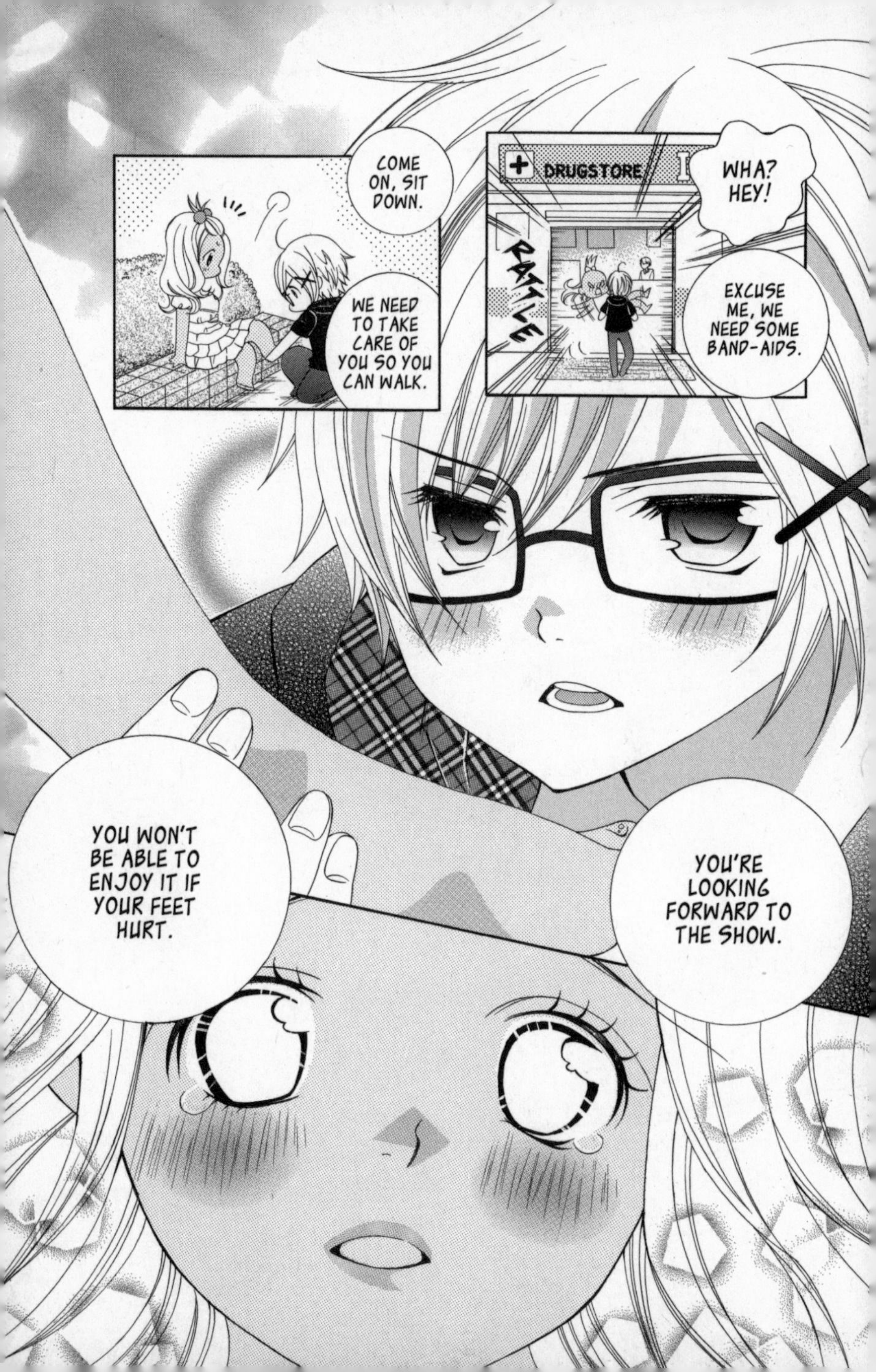
WHA? HEY!
DRUGSTORE
EXCUSE ME, WE NEED SOME BAND-AIDS.
RATTLE
COME ON, SIT DOWN.
WE NEED TO TAKE CARE OF YOU SO YOU CAN WALK.
YOU'RE LOOKING FORWARD TO THE SHOW.
YOU WON'T BE ABLE TO ENJOY IT IF YOUR FEET HURT.

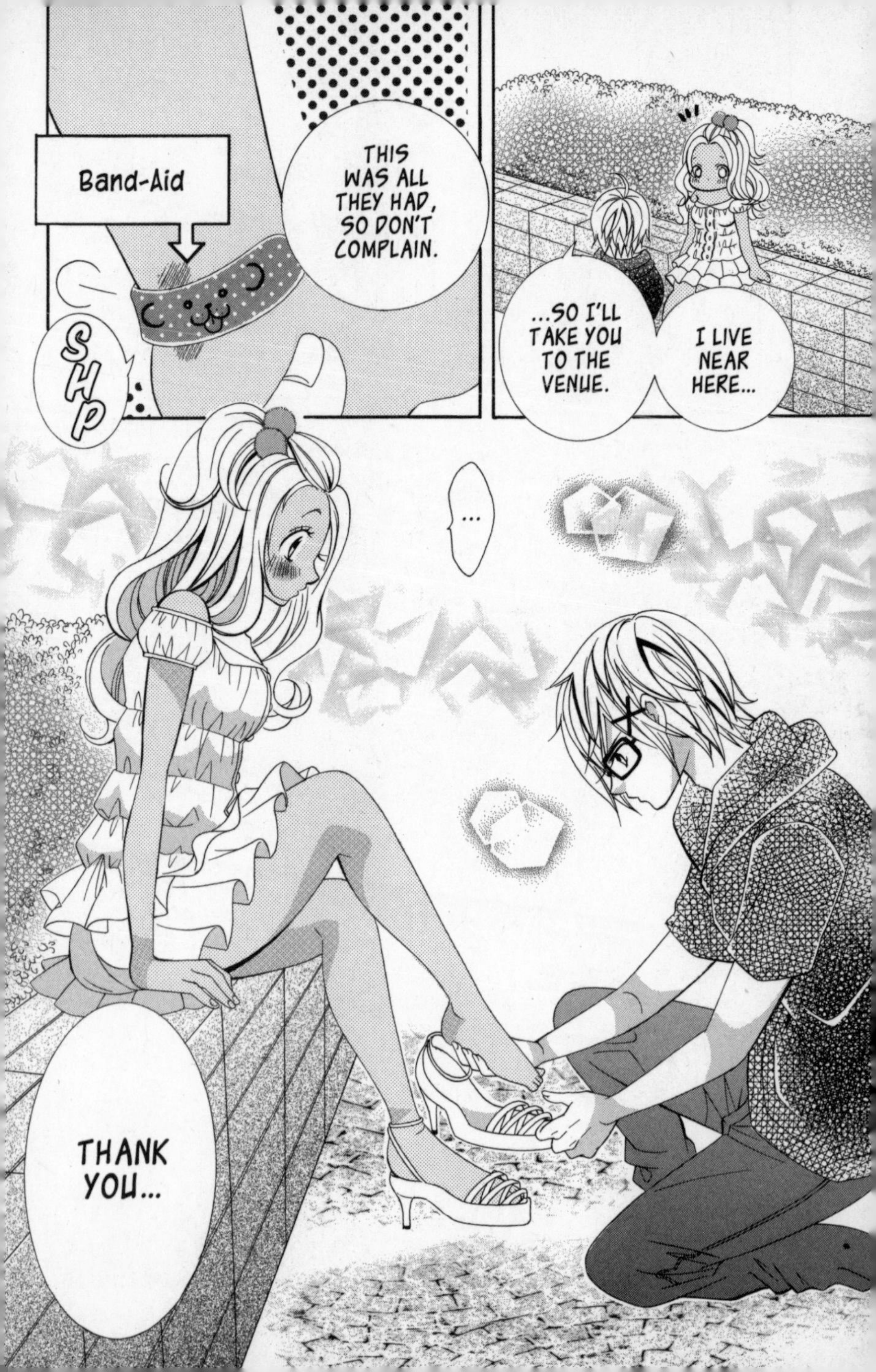
I LIVE NEAR HERE...
...SO I'LL TAKE YOU TO THE VENUE.
THIS WAS ALL THEY HAD, SO DON'T COMPLAIN.
Band-Aid
SHP
...
THANK YOU...

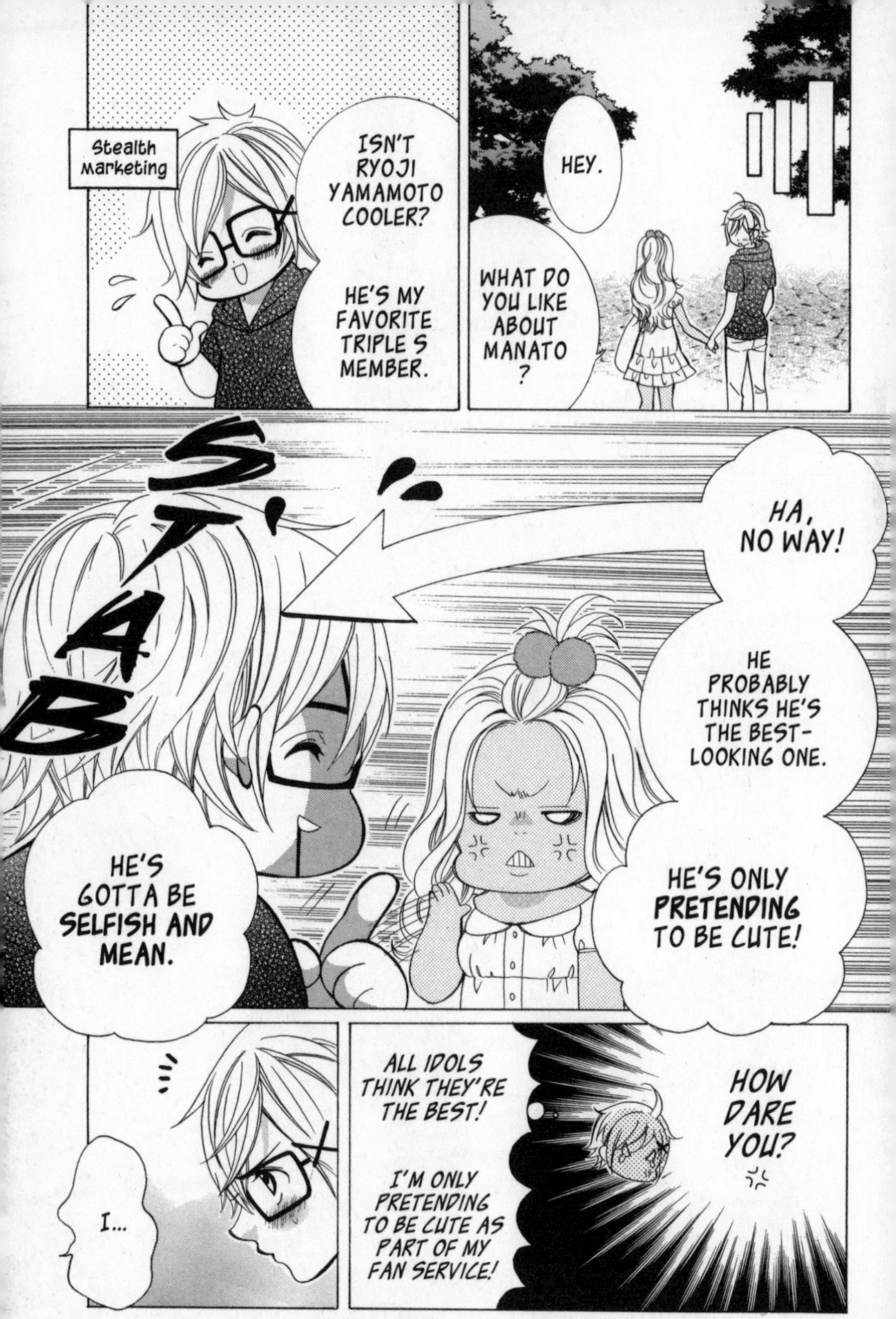
HEY.
WHAT DO YOU LIKE ABOUT MANATO?
Stealth Marketing
ISN'T RYOJI YAMAMOTO COOLER?
HE'S MY FAVORITE TRIPLE S MEMBER.
HA, NO WAY!
HE PROBABLY THINKS HE'S THE BEST-LOOKING ONE.
HE'S ONLY PRETENDING TO BE CUTE!
STAB
HE'S GOTTA BE SELFISH AND MEAN.
HOW DARE YOU?
ALL IDOLS THINK THEY'RE THE BEST!
I'M ONLY PRETENDING TO BE CUTE AS PART OF MY FAN SERVICE!
I...

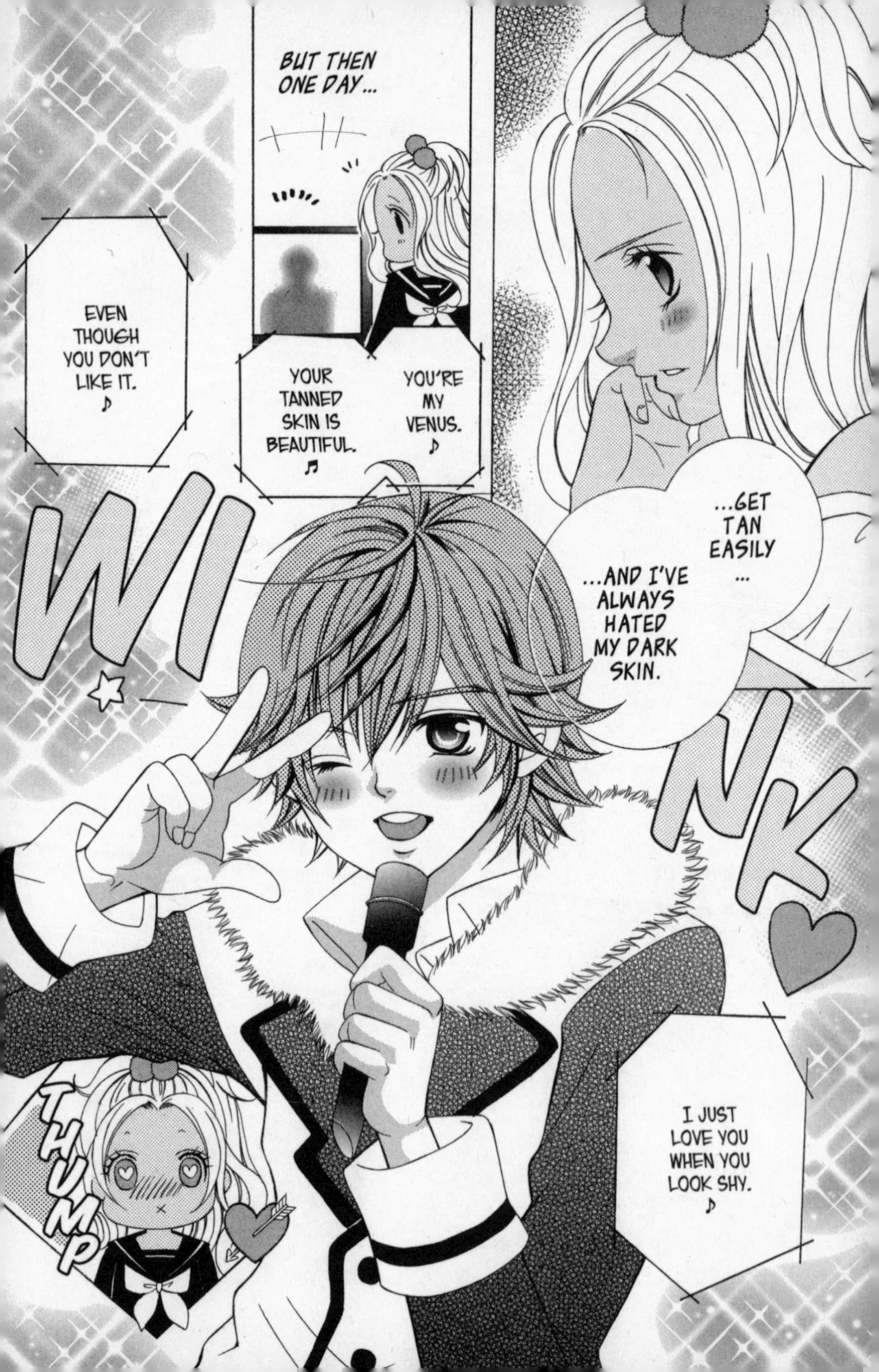
...GET TAN EASILY...
...AND I'VE ALWAYS HATED MY DARK SKIN.
BUT THEN ONE DAY...
YOU'RE MY VENUS. ♪
YOUR TANNED SKIN IS BEAUTIFUL. ♫
EVEN THOUGH YOU DON'T LIKE IT. ♪
WINK
I JUST LOVE YOU WHEN YOU LOOK SHY. ♪
THUMP

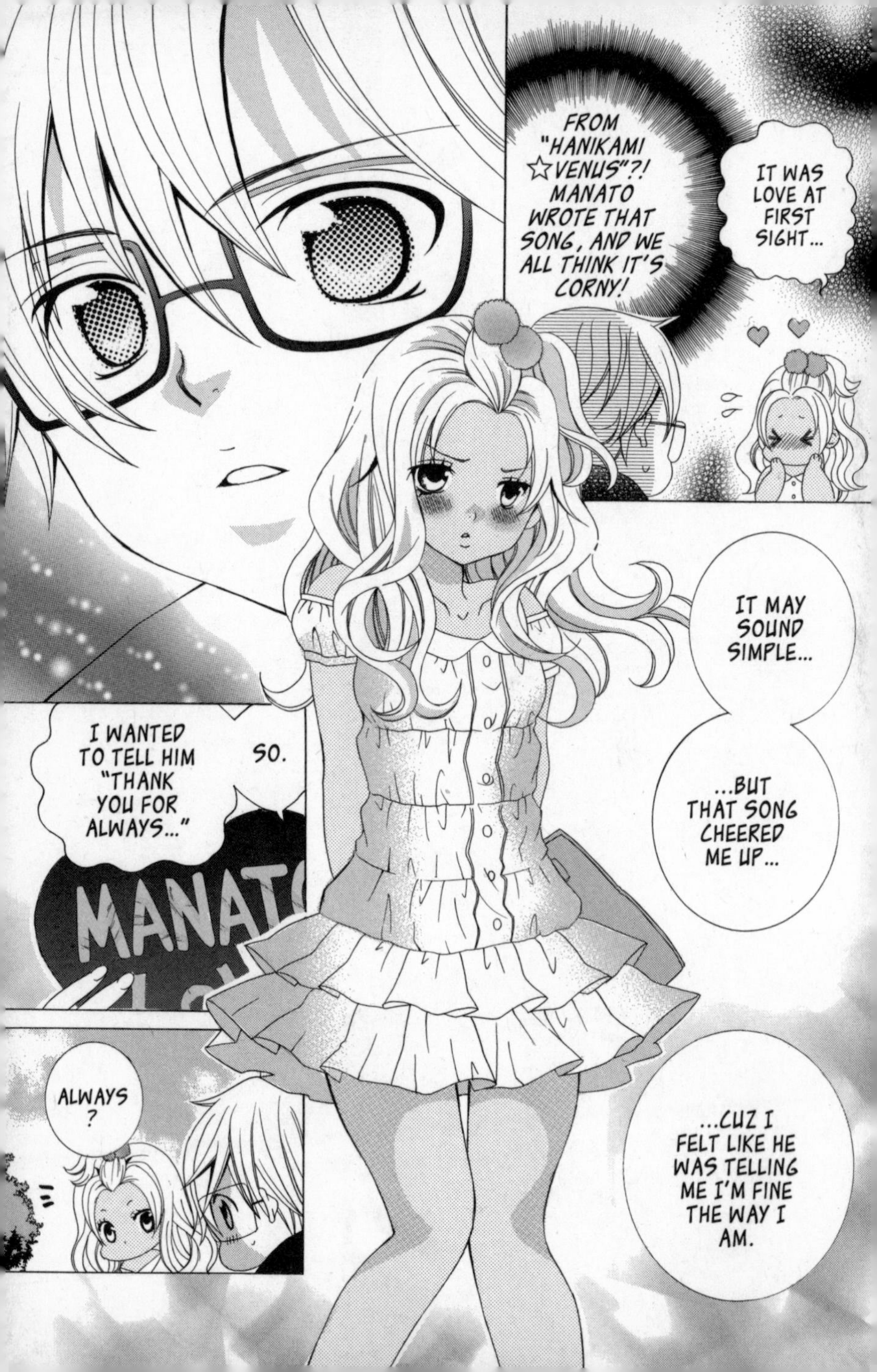

IT WAS LOVE AT FIRST SIGHT...
FROM "HANIKAMI ☆VENUS"?! MANATO WROTE THAT SONG, AND WE ALL THINK IT'S CORNY!
SO.
I WANTED TO TELL HIM "THANK YOU FOR ALWAYS..."
MANATO
ALWAYS ?
IT MAY SOUND SIMPLE...
...BUT THAT SONG CHEERED ME UP...
...CUZ I FELT LIKE HE WAS TELLING ME I'M FINE THE WAY I AM.

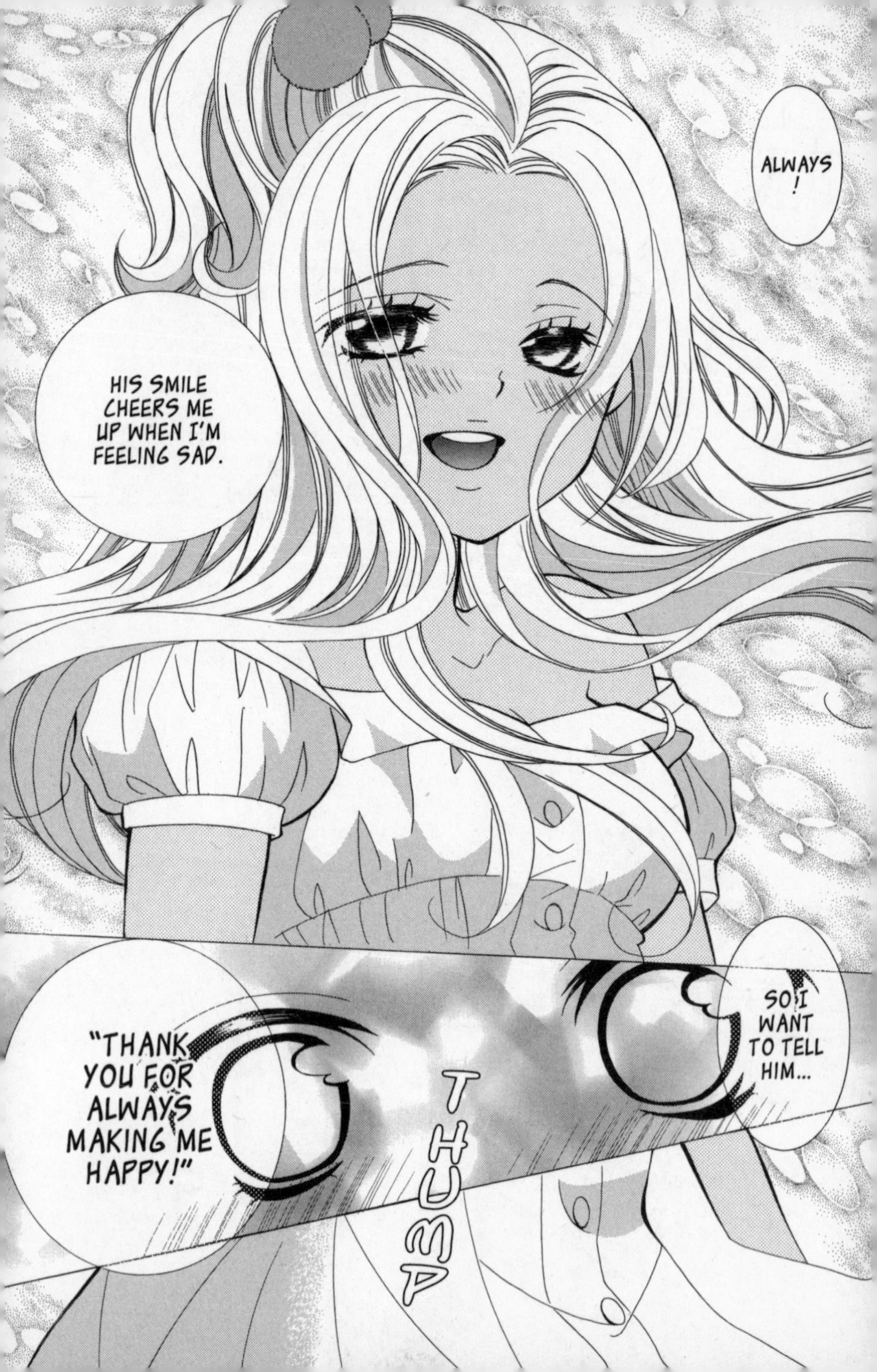
ALWAYS!
HIS SMILE CHEERS ME UP WHEN I'M FEELING SAD.
SO I WANT TO TELL HIM...
THUMP
"THANK YOU FOR ALWAYS MAKING ME HAPPY!"

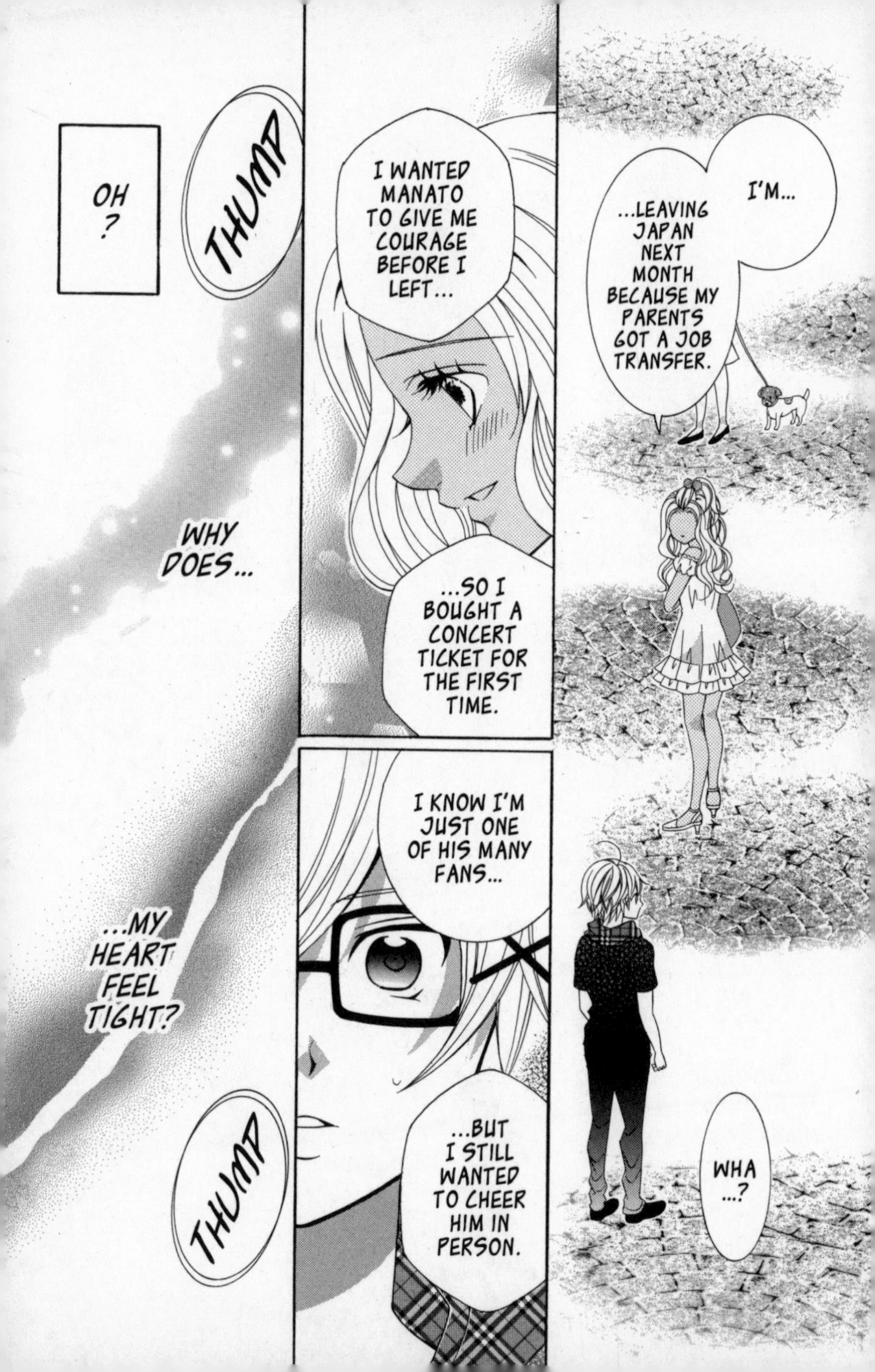
I'M...
...LEAVING JAPAN NEXT MONTH BECAUSE MY PARENTS GOT A JOB TRANSFER.
WHA ...?
I WANTED MANATO TO GIVE ME COURAGE BEFORE I LEFT...
...SO I BOUGHT A CONCERT TICKET FOR THE FIRST TIME.
I KNOW I'M JUST ONE OF HIS MANY FANS...
...BUT I STILL WANTED TO CHEER HIM IN PERSON.
THUMP
OH?
WHY DOES...
...MY HEART FEEL TIGHT?
THUMP

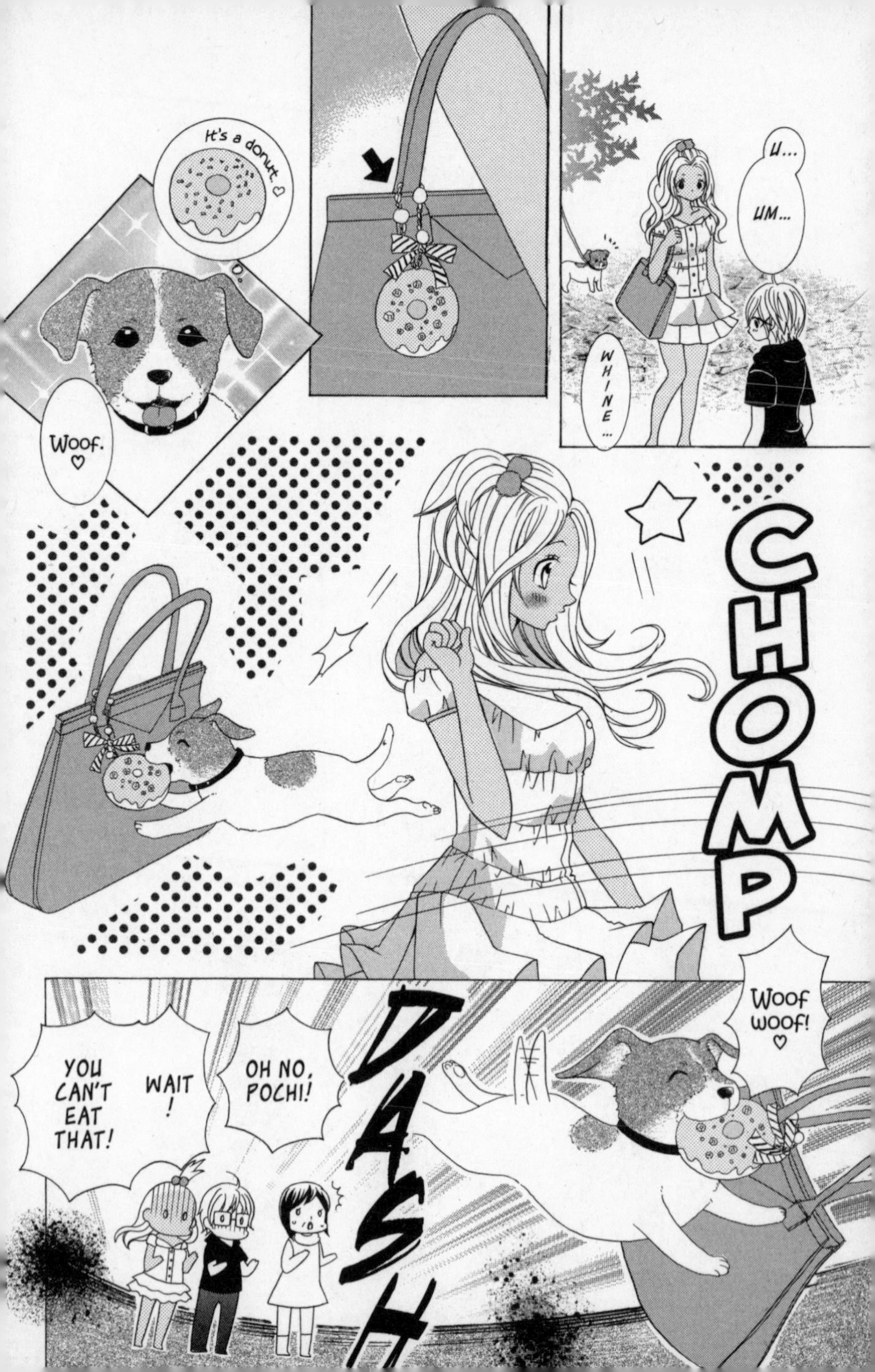
U...
UM...
WHINE...
It's a donut ♡
Woof. ♡
CHOMP
Woof woof! ♡
DASH
OH NO, POCHI!
WAIT!
YOU CAN'T EAT THAT!

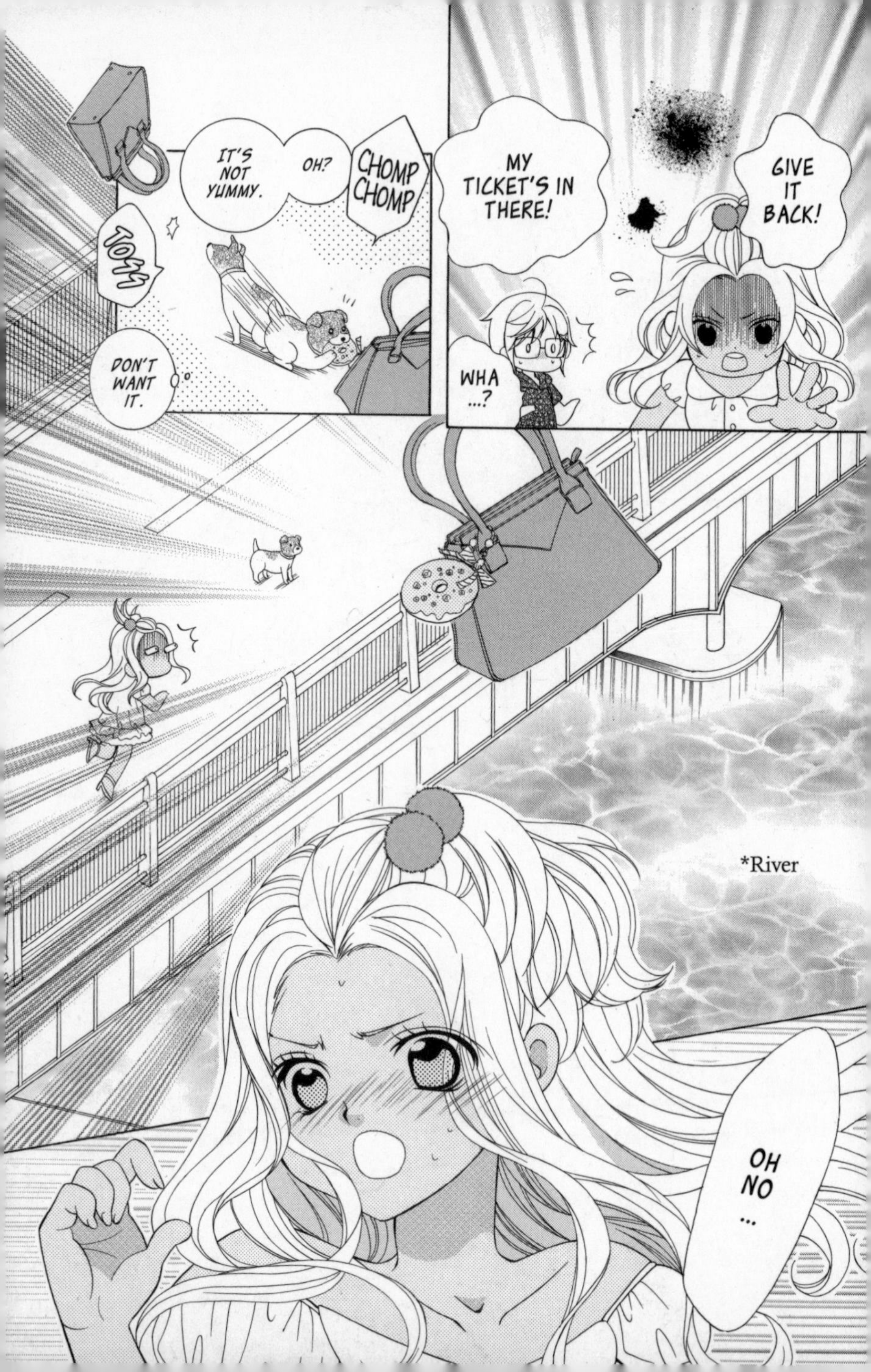
GIVE IT BACK!
MY TICKET'S IN THERE!
WHA ...?
CHOMP CHOMP
OH?
IT'S NOT YUMMY.
TOSS
DON'T WANT IT.
*River
OH NO ...

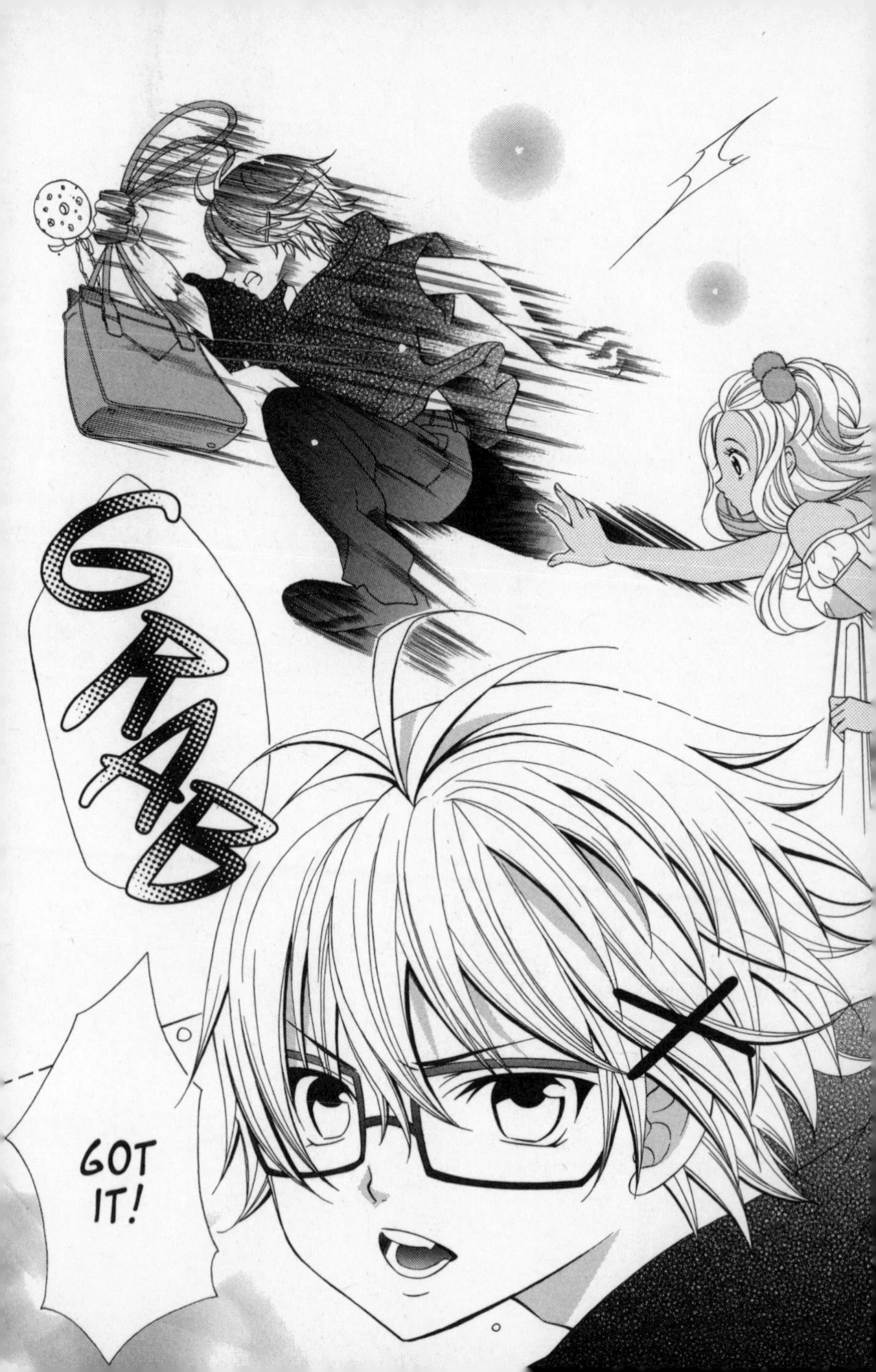
GRAB
GOT IT!

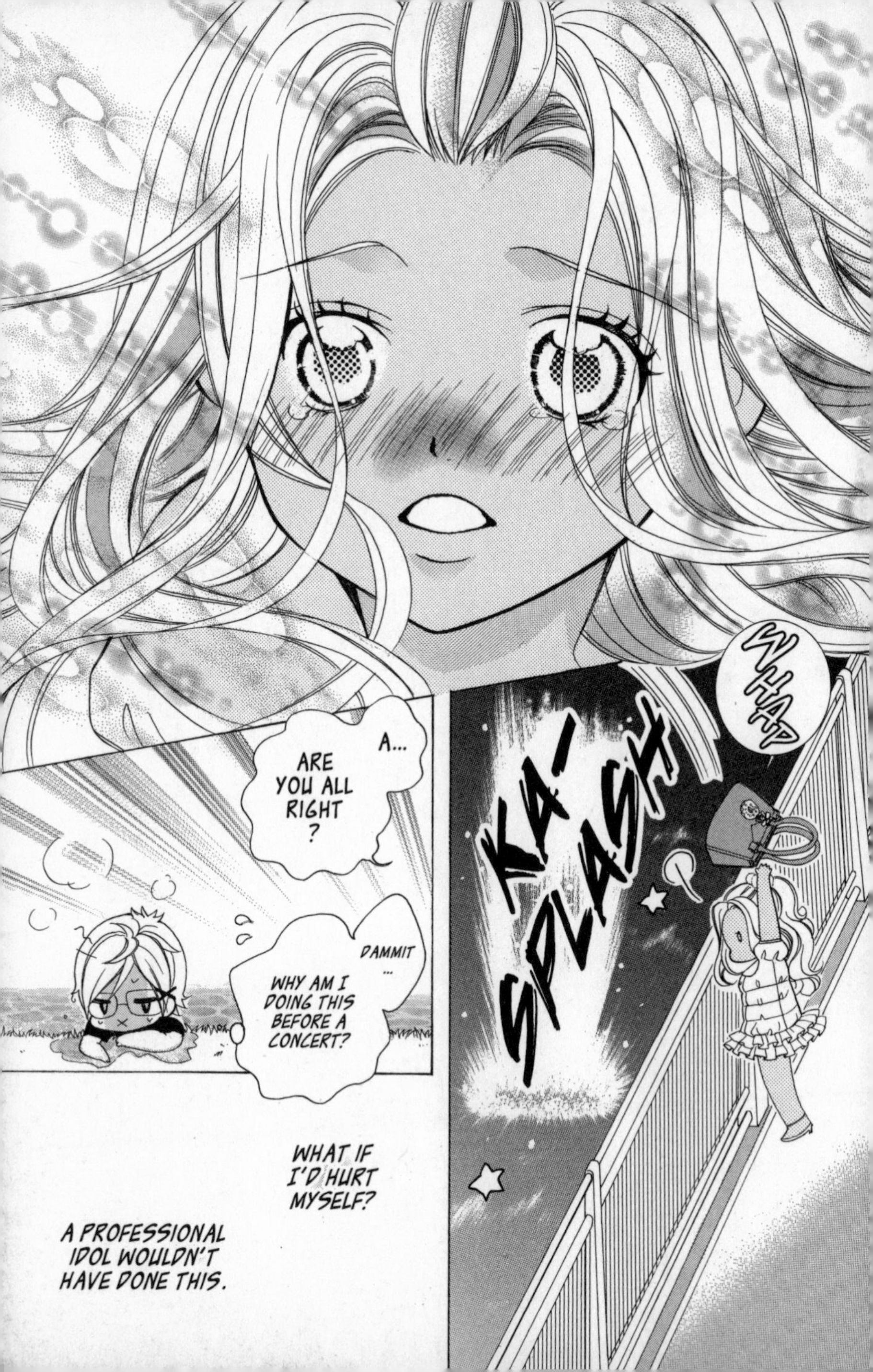
WHAP
KA-SPLASH
A...
ARE YOU ALL RIGHT?
DAMMIT...
WHY AM I DOING THIS BEFORE A CONCERT?
WHAT IF I'D HURT MYSELF?
A PROFESSIONAL IDOL WOULDN'T HAVE DONE THIS.

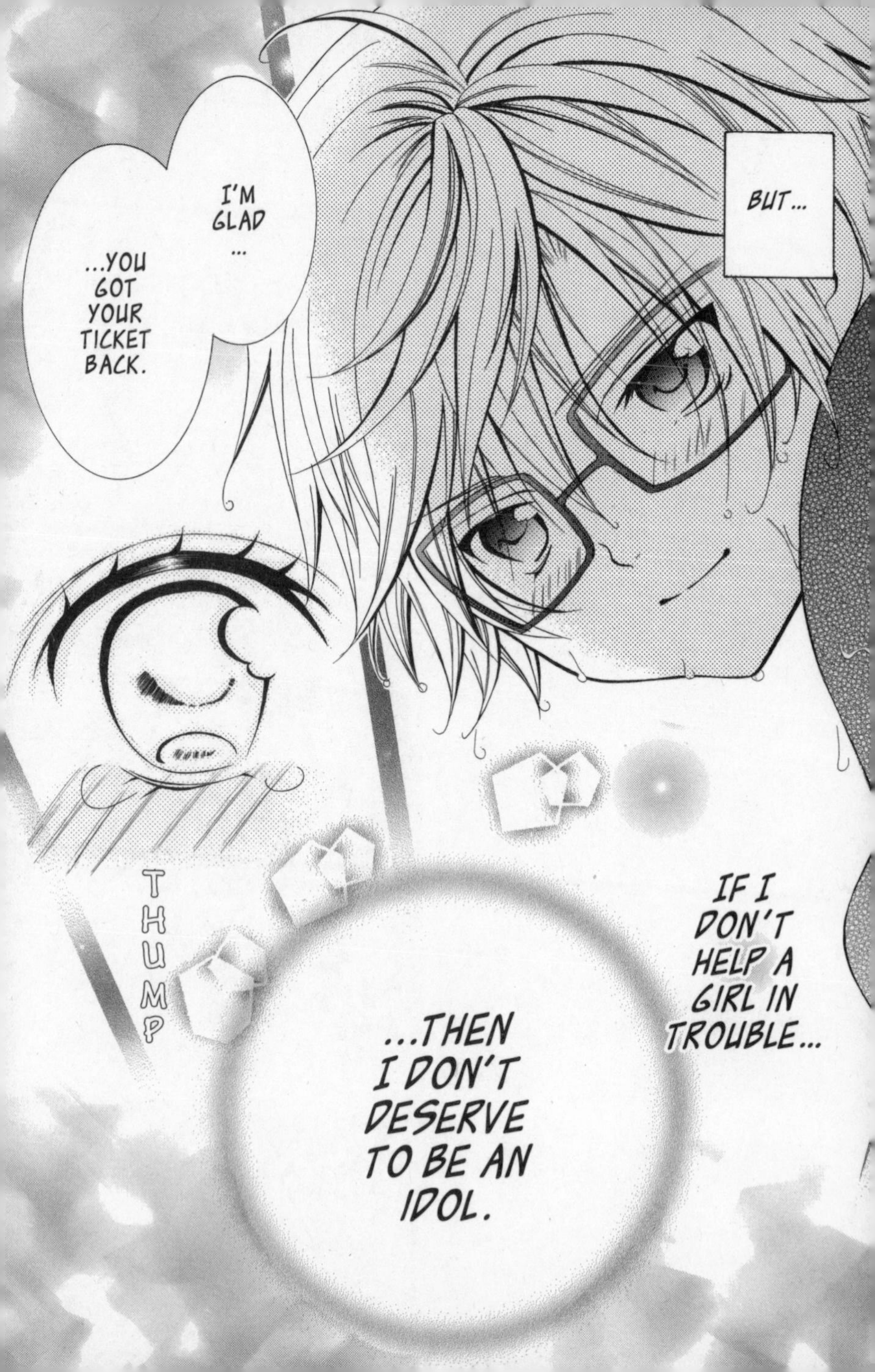
BUT...
I'M GLAD...
...YOU GOT YOUR TICKET BACK.
IF I DON'T HELP A GIRL IN TROUBLE...
...THEN I DON'T DESERVE TO BE AN IDOL.
THUMP

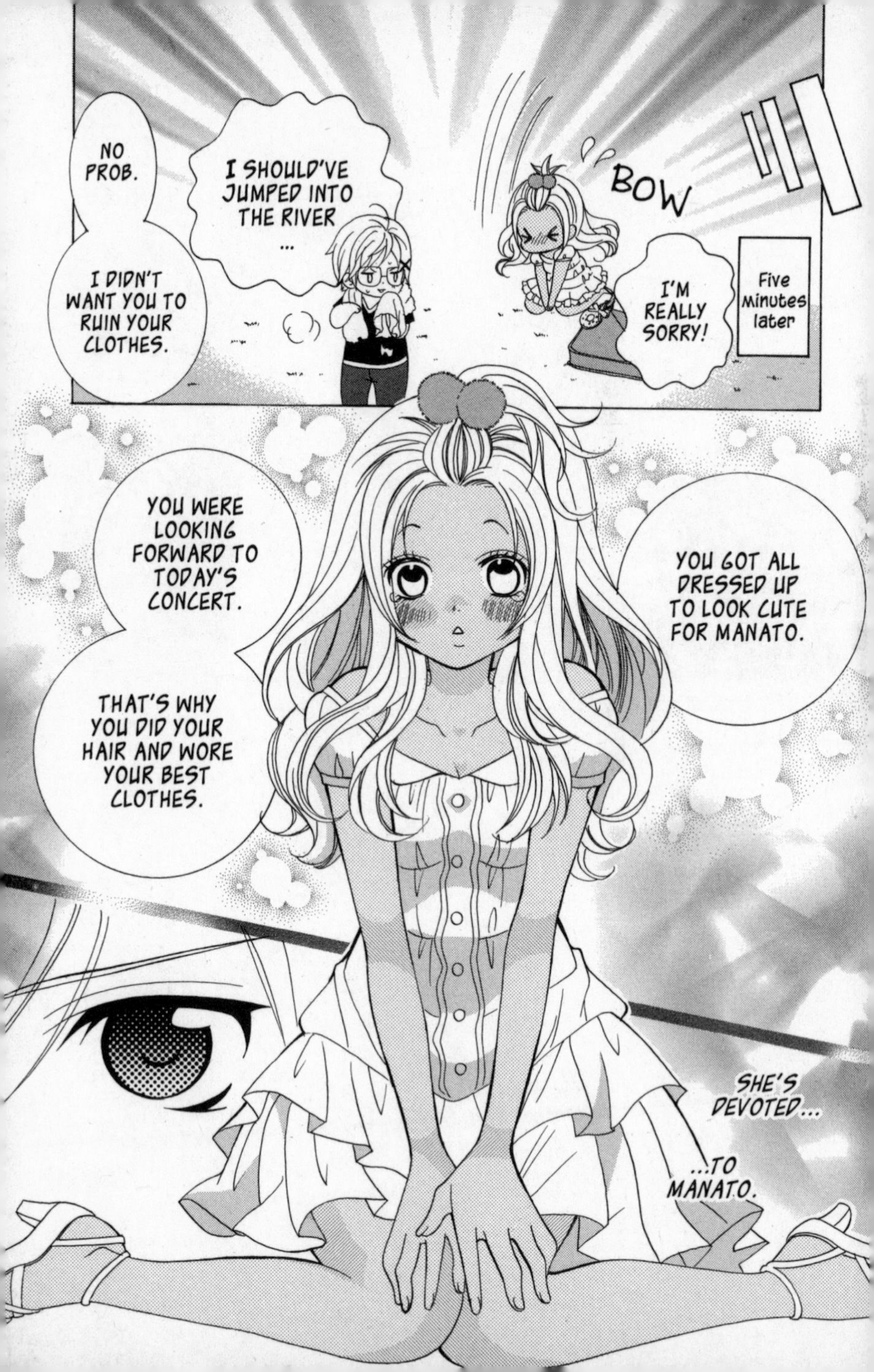
Five minutes later
I'M REALLY SORRY!
BOW
I SHOULD'VE JUMPED INTO THE RIVER ...
NO PROB.
I DIDN'T WANT YOU TO RUIN YOUR CLOTHES.
YOU GOT ALL DRESSED UP TO LOOK CUTE FOR MANATO.
YOU WERE LOOKING FORWARD TO TODAY'S CONCERT.
THAT'S WHY YOU DID YOUR HAIR AND WORE YOUR BEST CLOTHES.
SHE'S DEVOTED...
...TO MANATO.

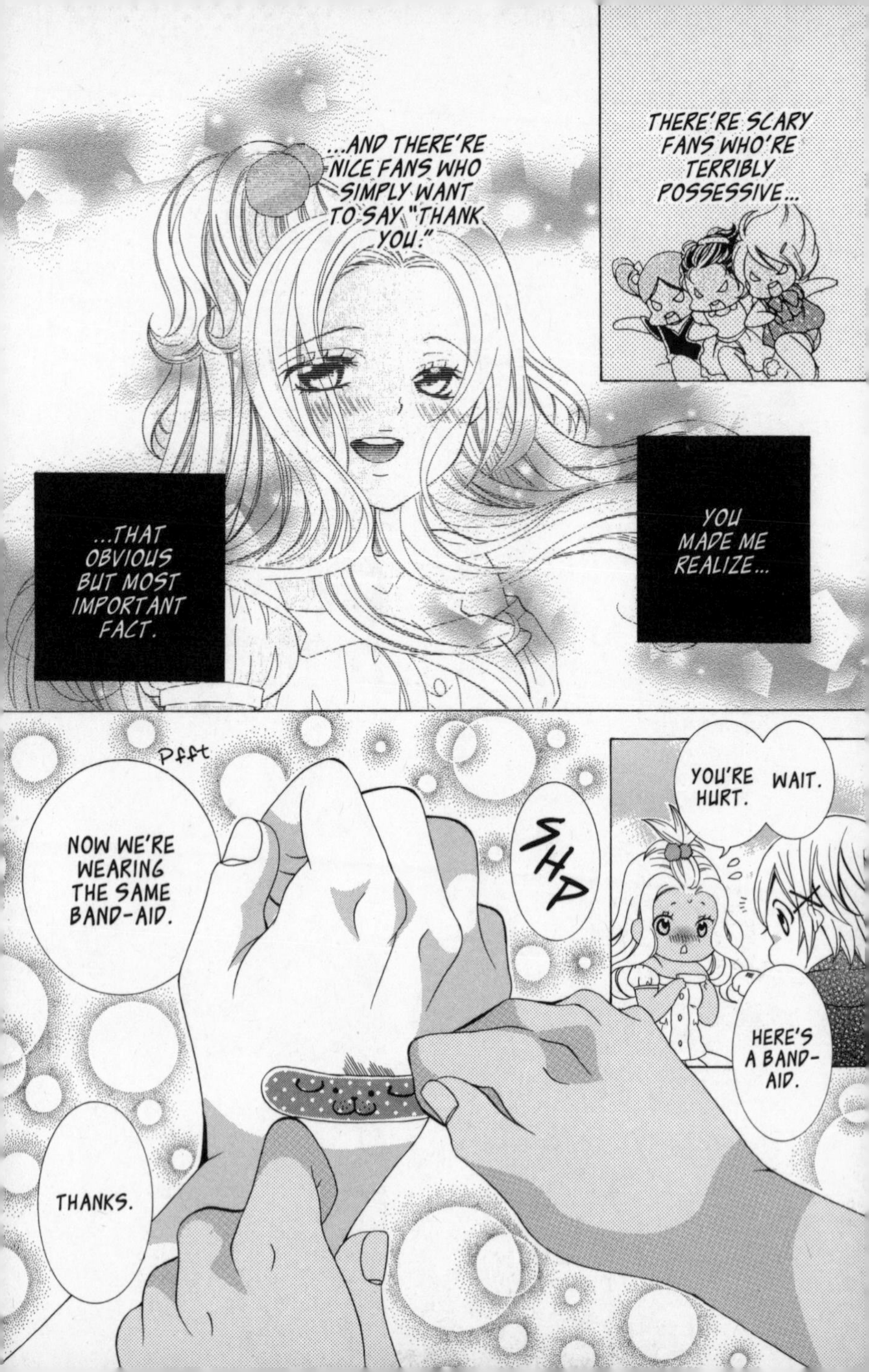
THERE'RE SCARY FANS WHO'RE TERRIBLY POSSESSIVE...
...AND THERE'RE NICE FANS WHO SIMPLY WANT TO SAY "THANK YOU."
YOU MADE ME REALIZE...
...THAT OBVIOUS BUT MOST IMPORTANT FACT.
WAIT.
YOU'RE HURT.
HERE'S A BAND-AID.
SHP
Pfft
NOW WE'RE WEARING THE SAME BAND-AID.
THANKS.

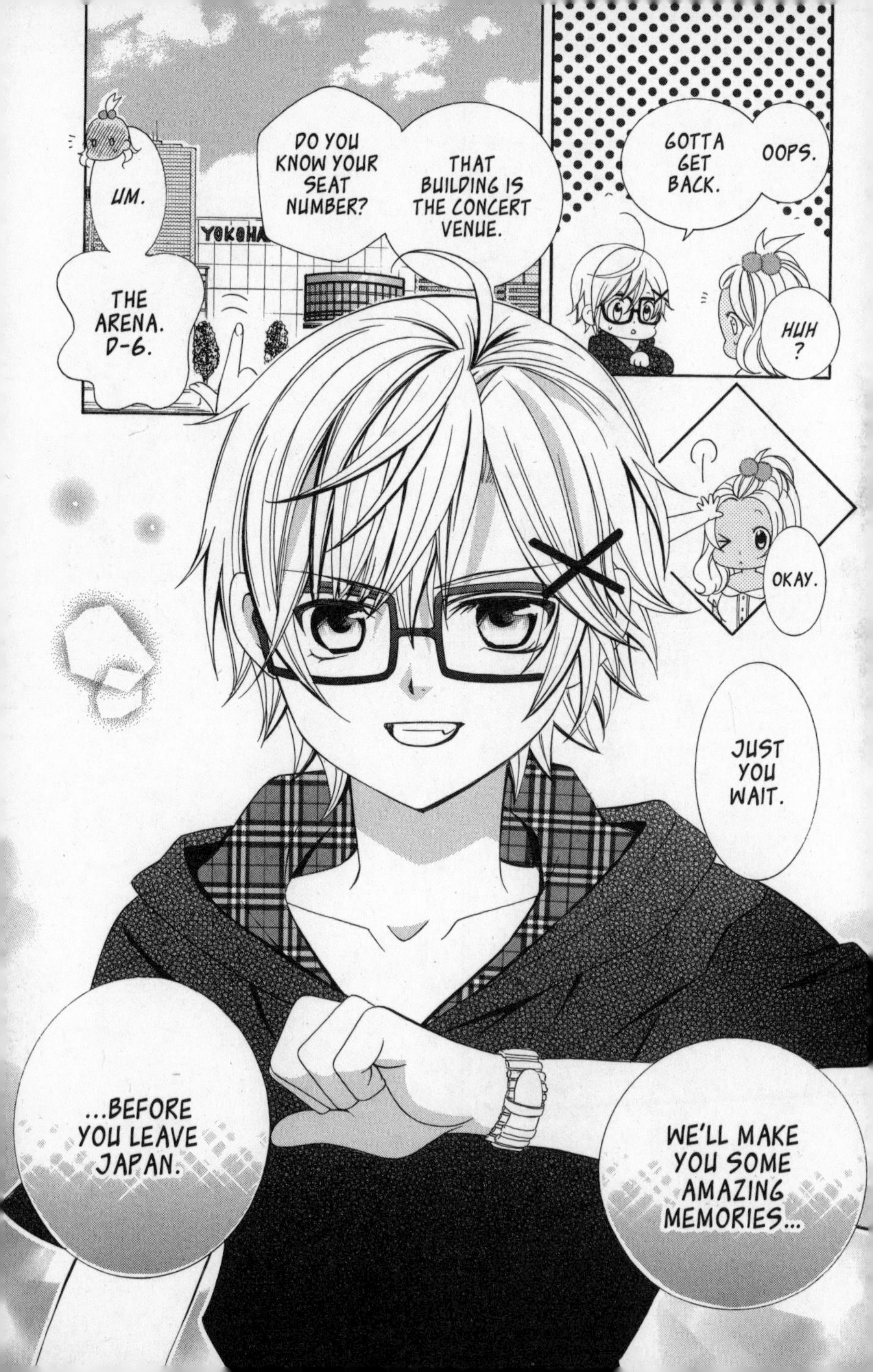
OOPS.
GOTTA GET BACK.
HUH?
THAT BUILDING IS THE CONCERT VENUE.
DO YOU KNOW YOUR SEAT NUMBER?
UM.
THE ARENA. D-6.
OKAY.
JUST YOU WAIT.
WE'LL MAKE YOU SOME AMAZING MEMORIES...
...BEFORE YOU LEAVE JAPAN.

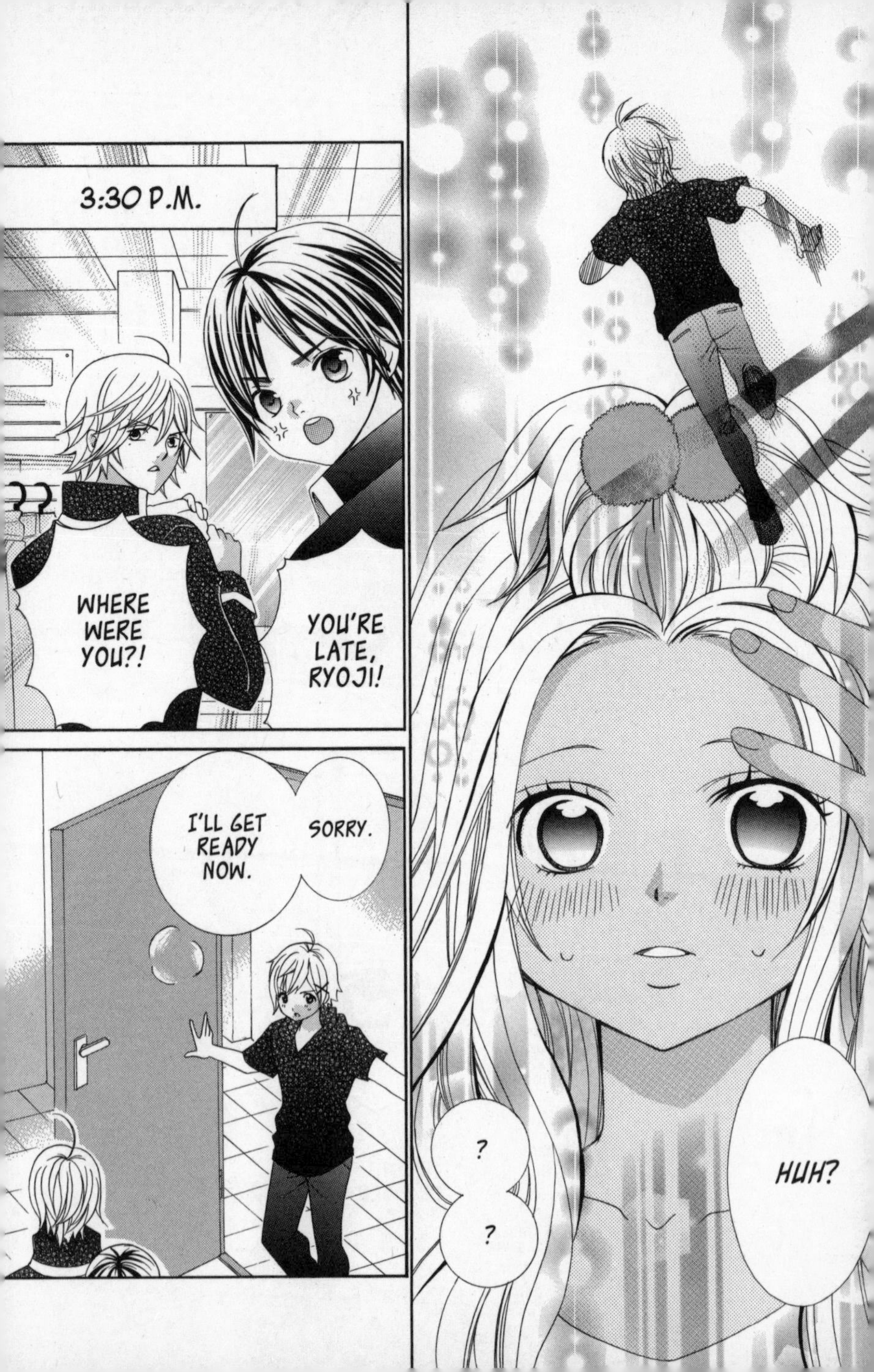
HUH?
?
?
3:30 P.M.
YOU'RE LATE, RYOJI!
WHERE WERE YOU?!
SORRY.
I'LL GET READY NOW.

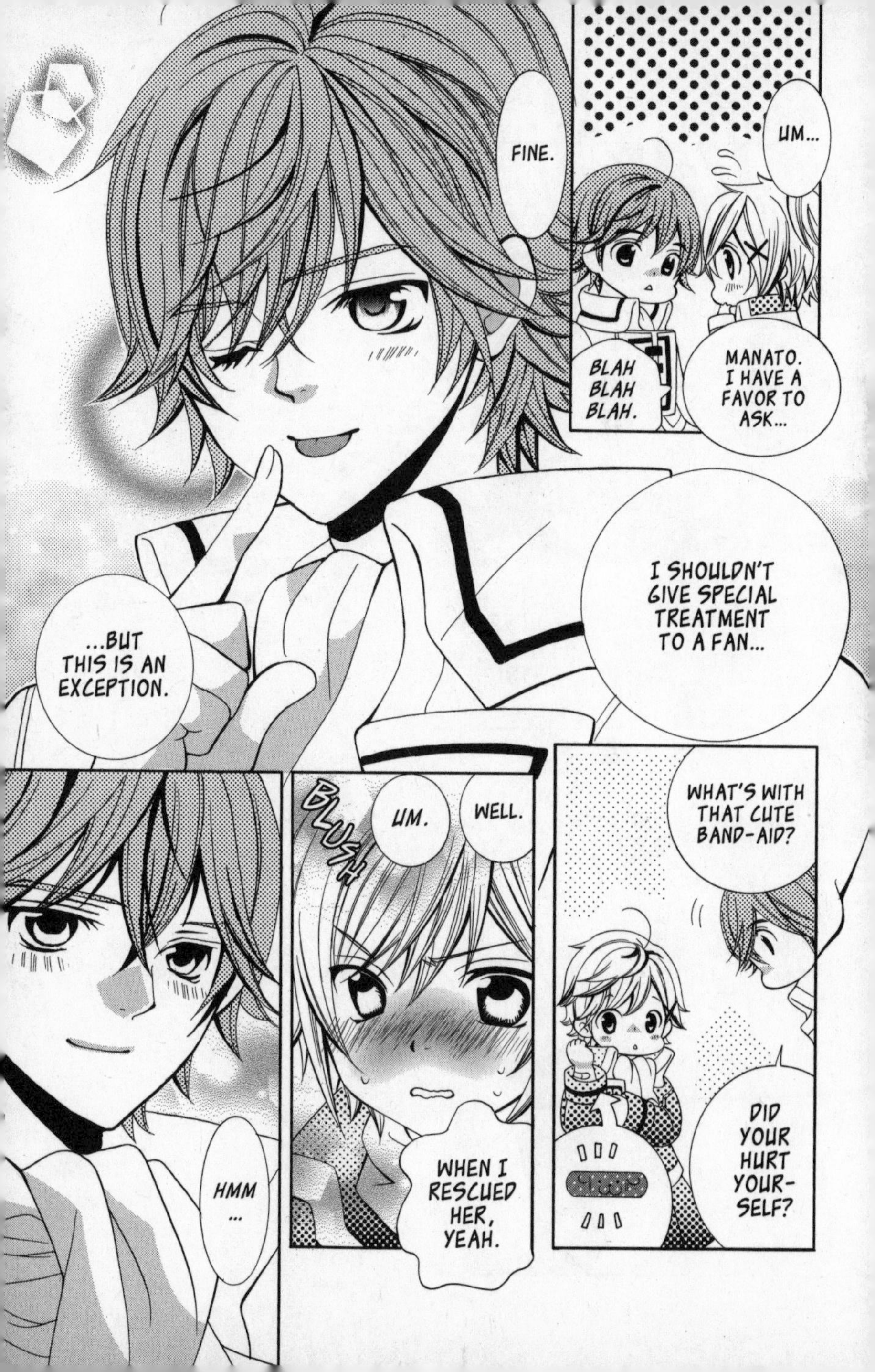
UM...
MANATO. I HAVE A FAVOR TO ASK...
BLAH BLAH BLAH.
FINE.
I SHOULDN'T GIVE SPECIAL TREATMENT TO A FAN...
...BUT THIS IS AN EXCEPTION.
WHAT'S WITH THAT CUTE BAND-AID?
DID YOUR HURT YOUR-SELF?
WELL.
UM.
BLUSH
WHEN I RESCUED HER, YEAH.
HMM ...

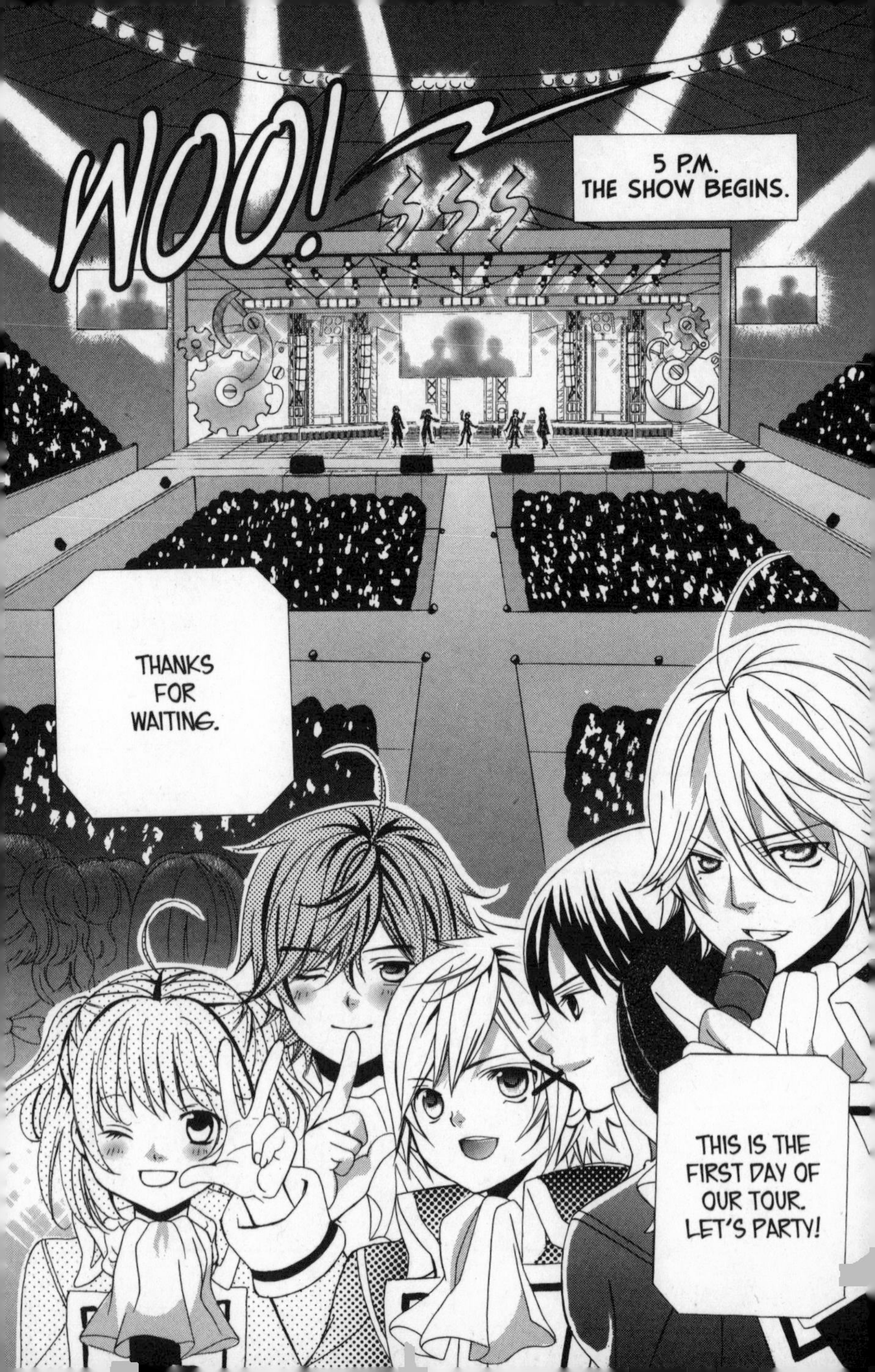
WOO!
5 P.M. THE SHOW BEGINS.
THANKS FOR WAITING.
THIS IS THE FIRST DAY OF OUR TOUR. LET'S PARTY!

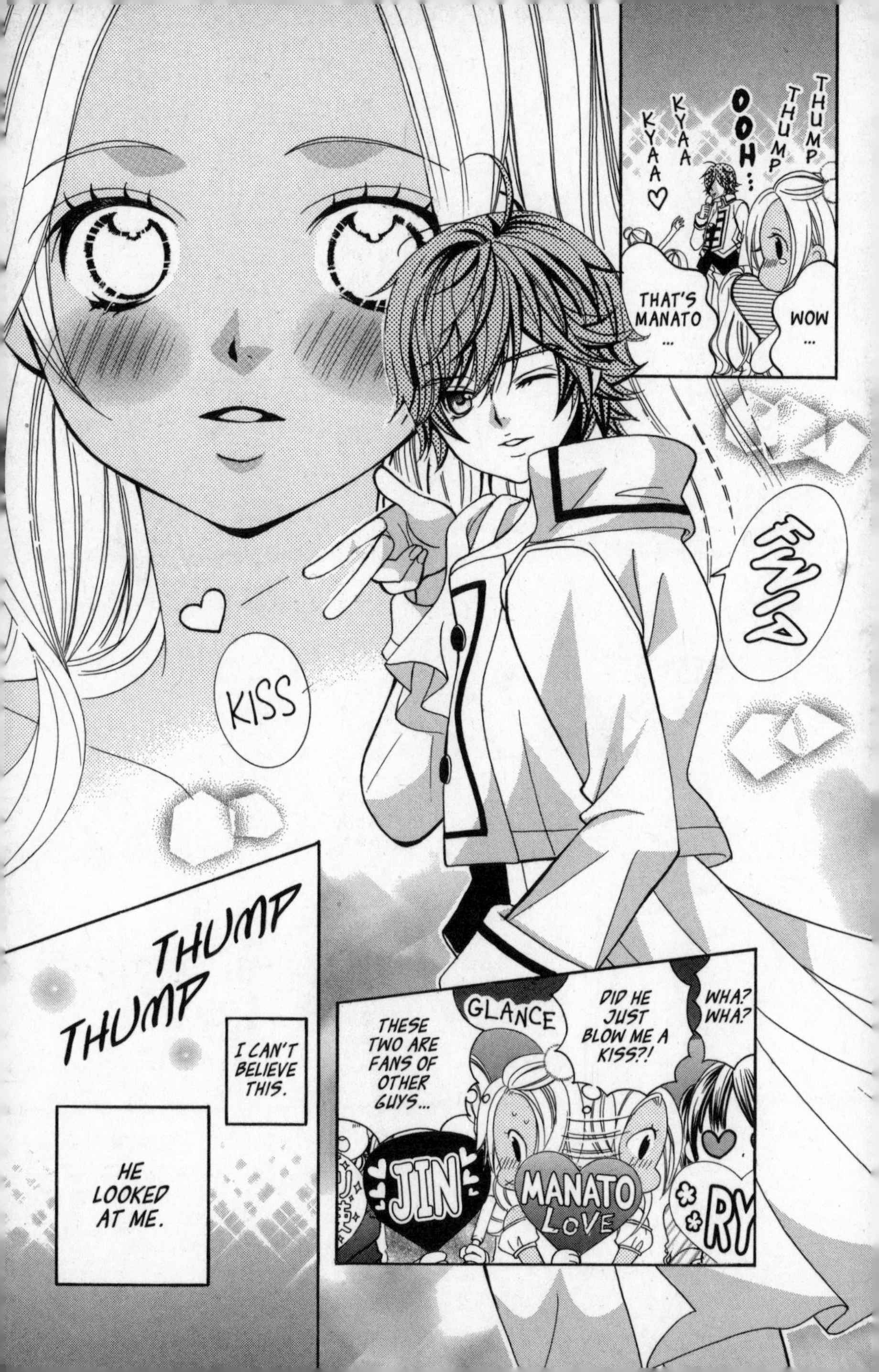
THUMP THUMP
OOH...
KYAA KYAA ♡
WOW...
THAT'S MANATO...
FWIP
KISS
WHA? WHA?
DID HE JUST BLOW ME A KISS?!
GLANCE
THESE TWO ARE FANS OF OTHER GUYS...
RY
MANATO LOVE
JIN
THUMP THUMP
I CAN'T BELIEVE THIS.
HE LOOKED AT ME.

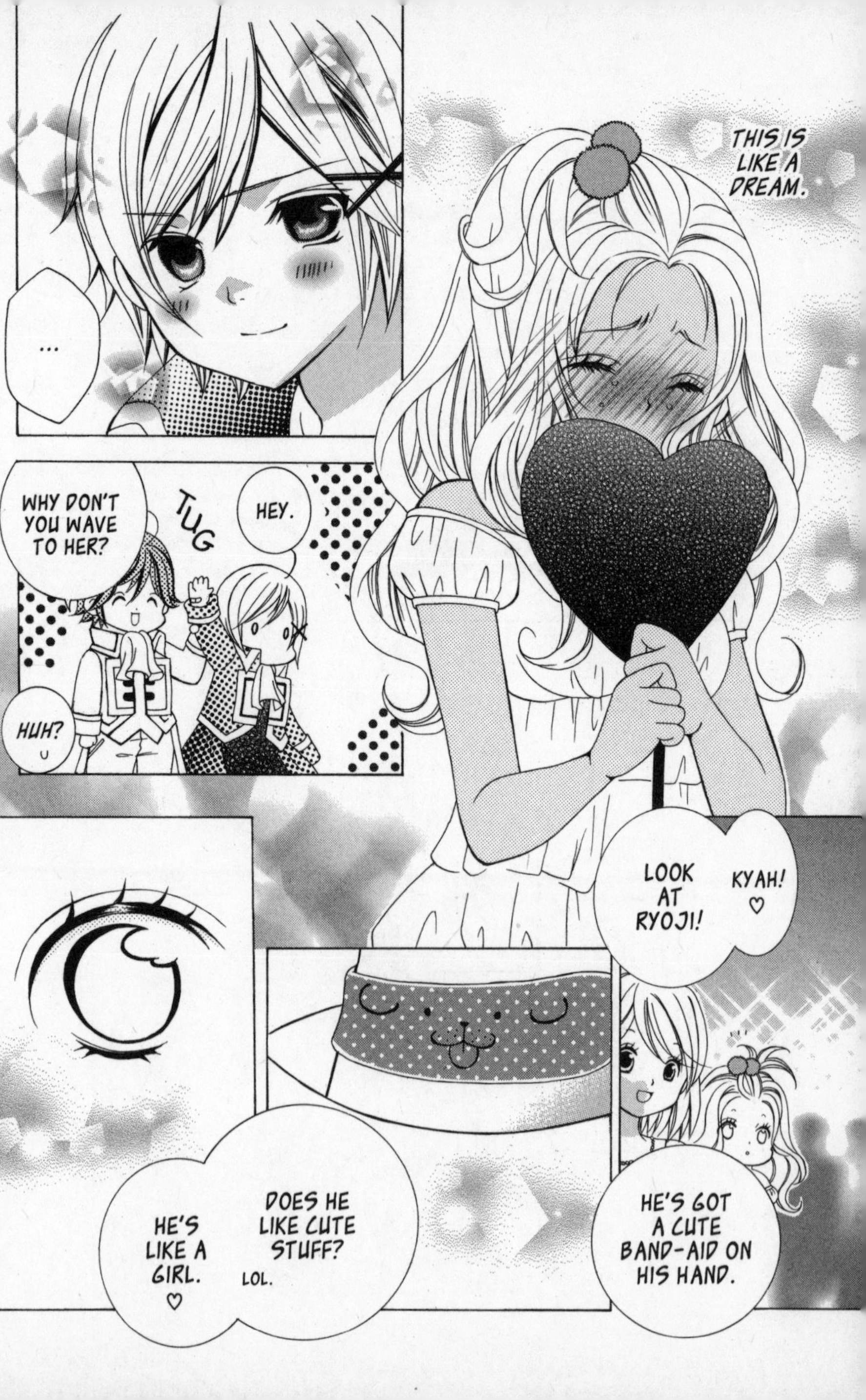
THIS IS LIKE A DREAM.
...
HEY.
TUG
WHY DON'T YOU WAVE TO HER?
HUH?
KYAH! ♡
LOOK AT RYOJI!
HE'S GOT A CUTE BAND-AID ON HIS HAND.
DOES HE LIKE CUTE STUFF?
LOL.
HE'S LIKE A GIRL. ♡

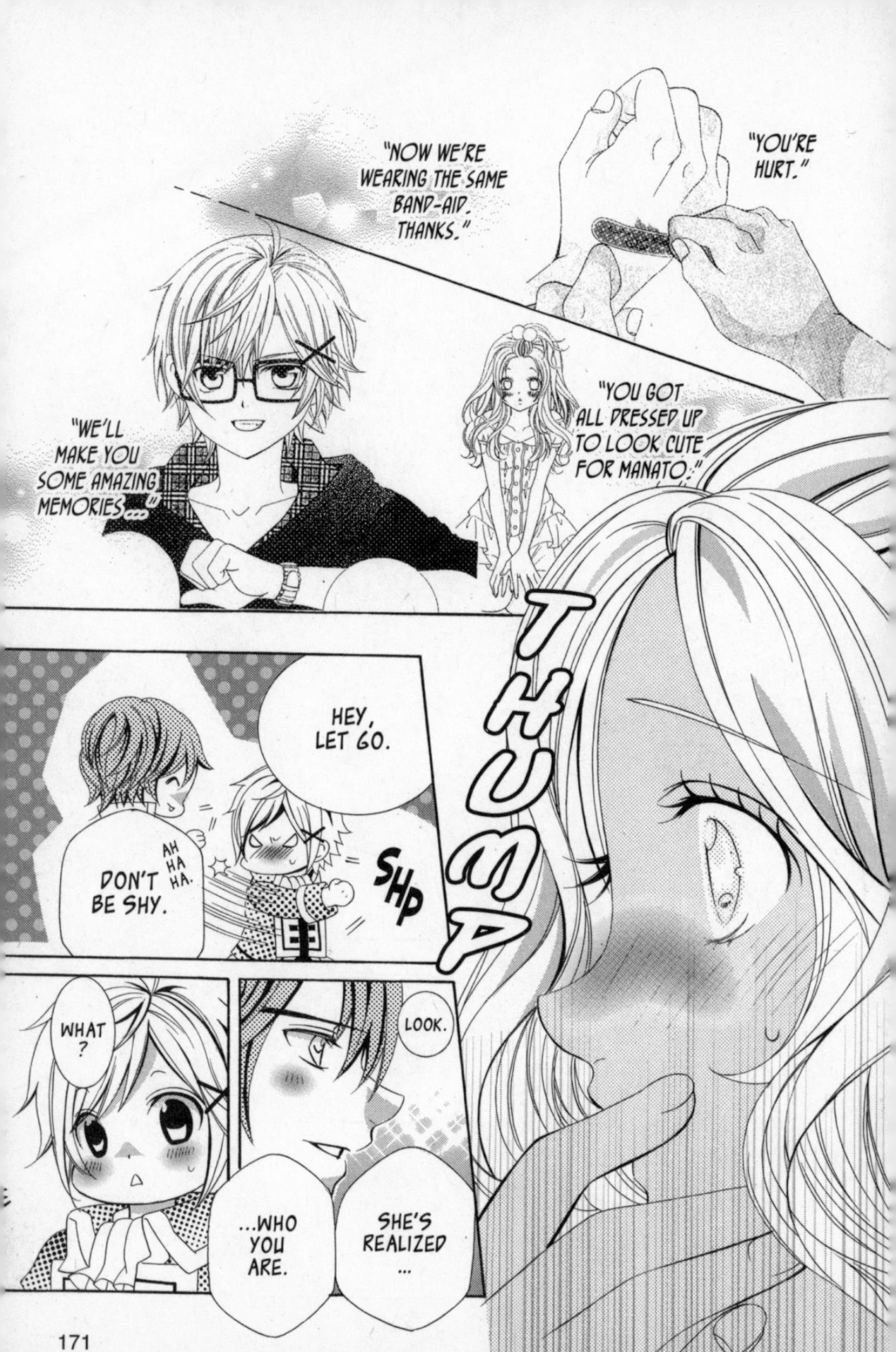
"YOU'RE HURT."
"NOW WE'RE WEARING THE SAME BAND-AID. THANKS."
"YOU GOT ALL DRESSED UP TO LOOK CUTE FOR MANATO."
"WE'LL MAKE YOU SOME AMAZING MEMORIES..."
THUMP
HEY, LET GO.
SHP
AH HA HA.
DON'T BE SHY.
LOOK.
SHE'S REALIZED...
...WHO YOU ARE.
WHAT?

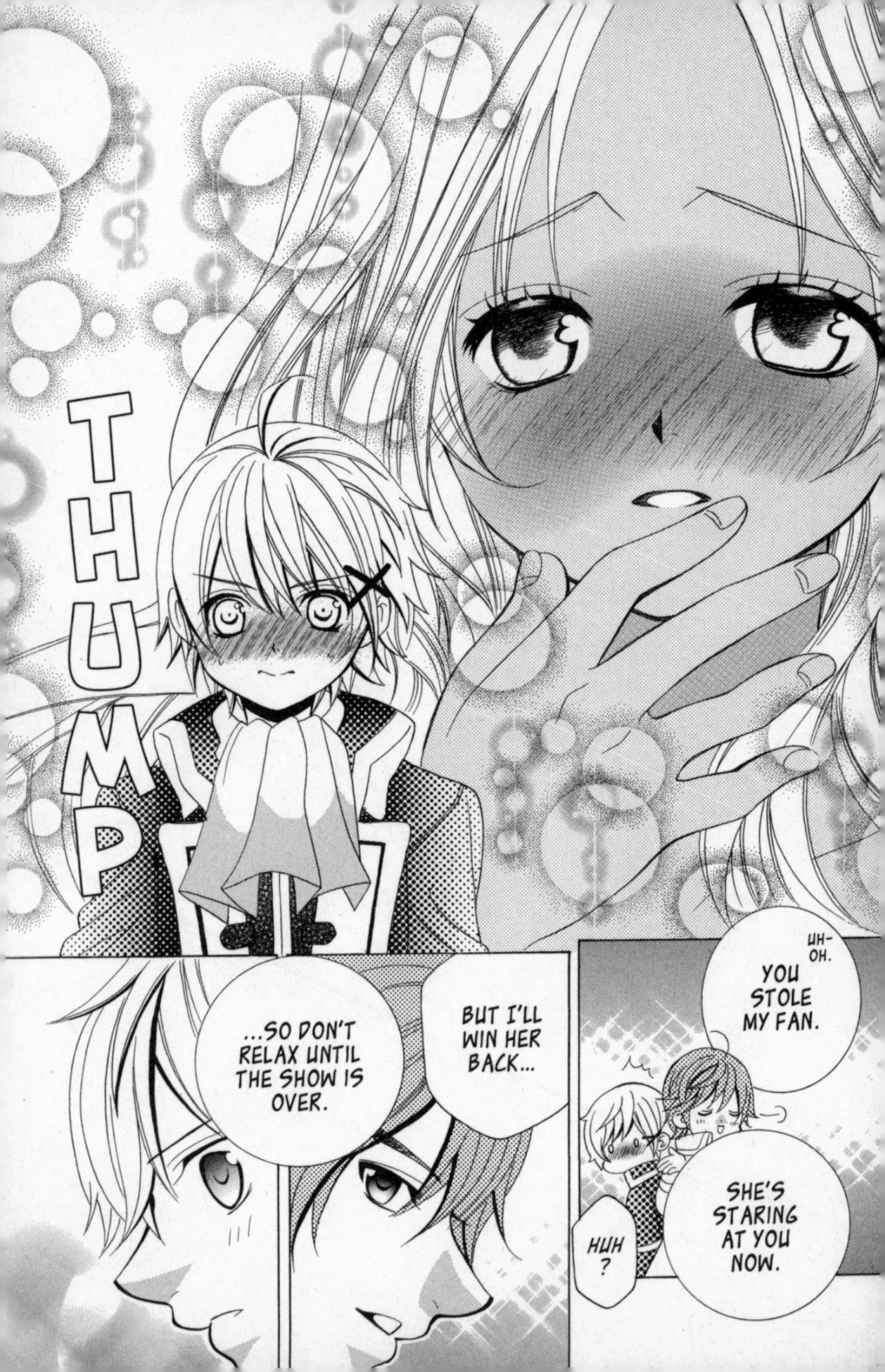
THUMP
UH-OH.
YOU STOLE MY FAN.
SHE'S STARING AT YOU NOW.
HUH?
BUT I'LL WIN HER BACK...
...SO DON'T RELAX UNTIL THE SHOW IS OVER.

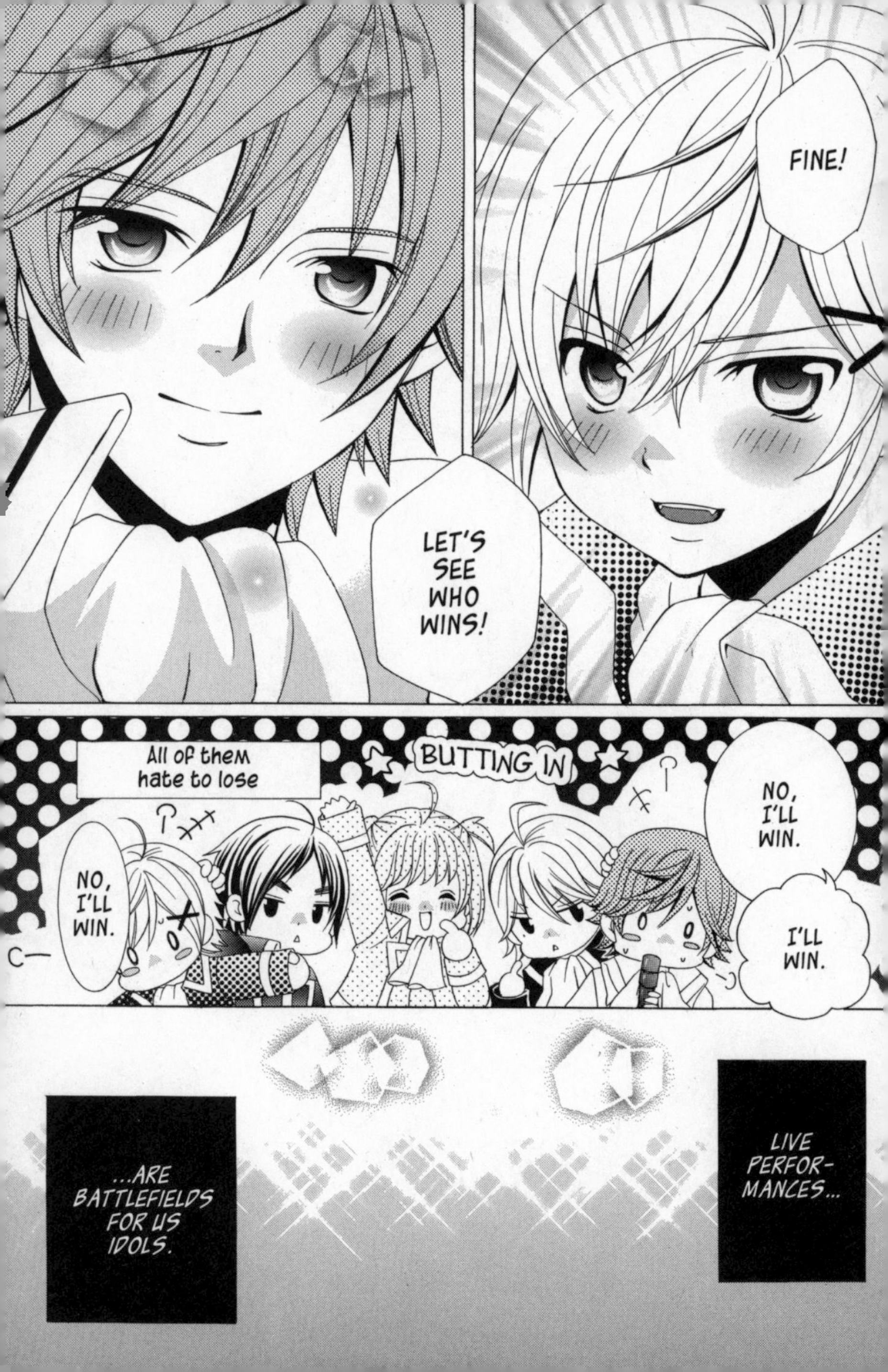
FINE!
LET'S SEE WHO WINS!
BUTTING IN
NO, I'LL WIN.
I'LL WIN.
All of them hate to lose
NO, I'LL WIN.
LIVE PERFOR-MANCES...
...ARE BATTLEFIELDS FOR US IDOLS.

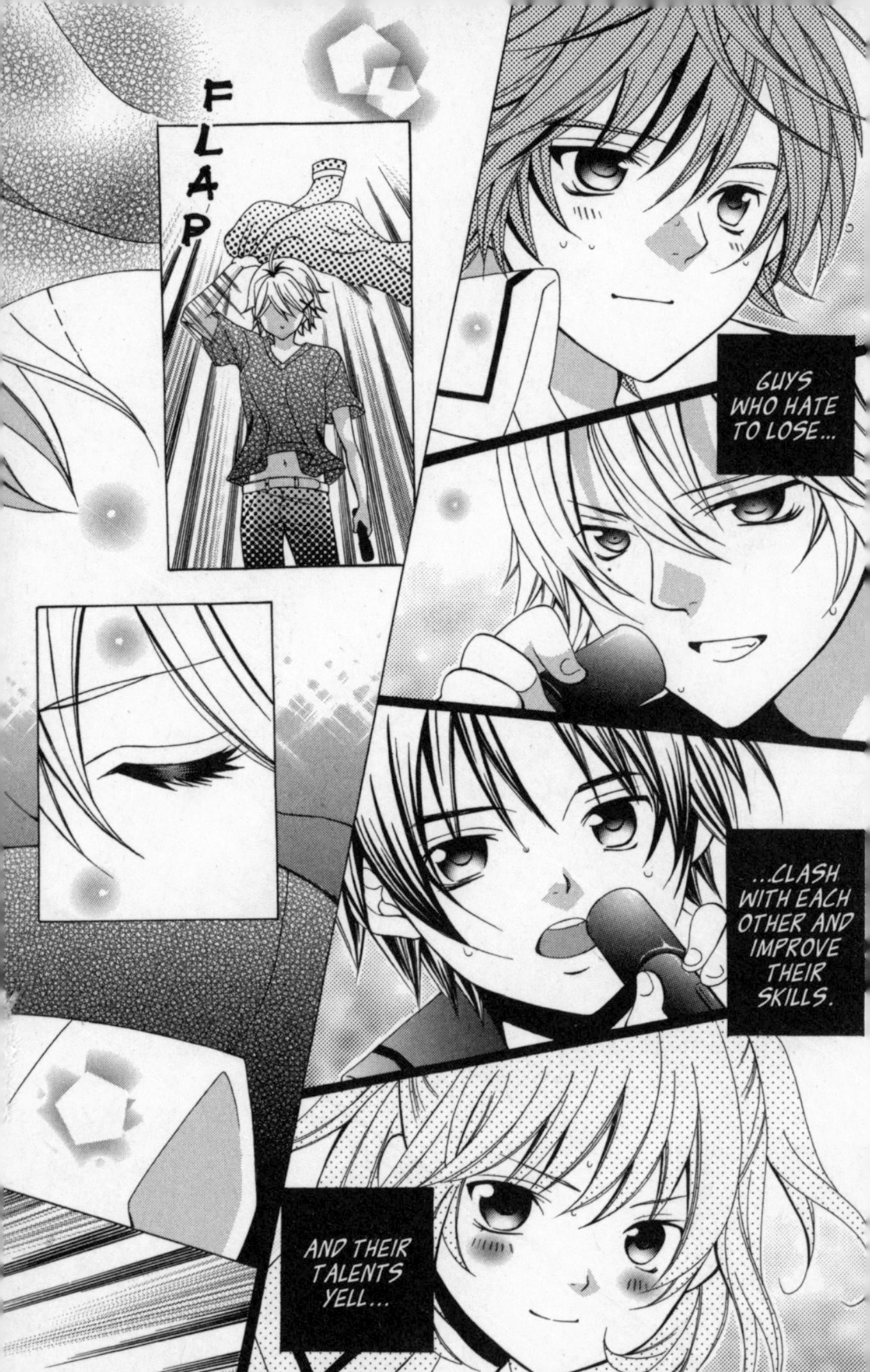

GUYS WHO HATE TO LOSE...
...CLASH WITH EACH OTHER AND IMPROVE THEIR SKILLS.
FLAP
AND THEIR TALENTS YELL...

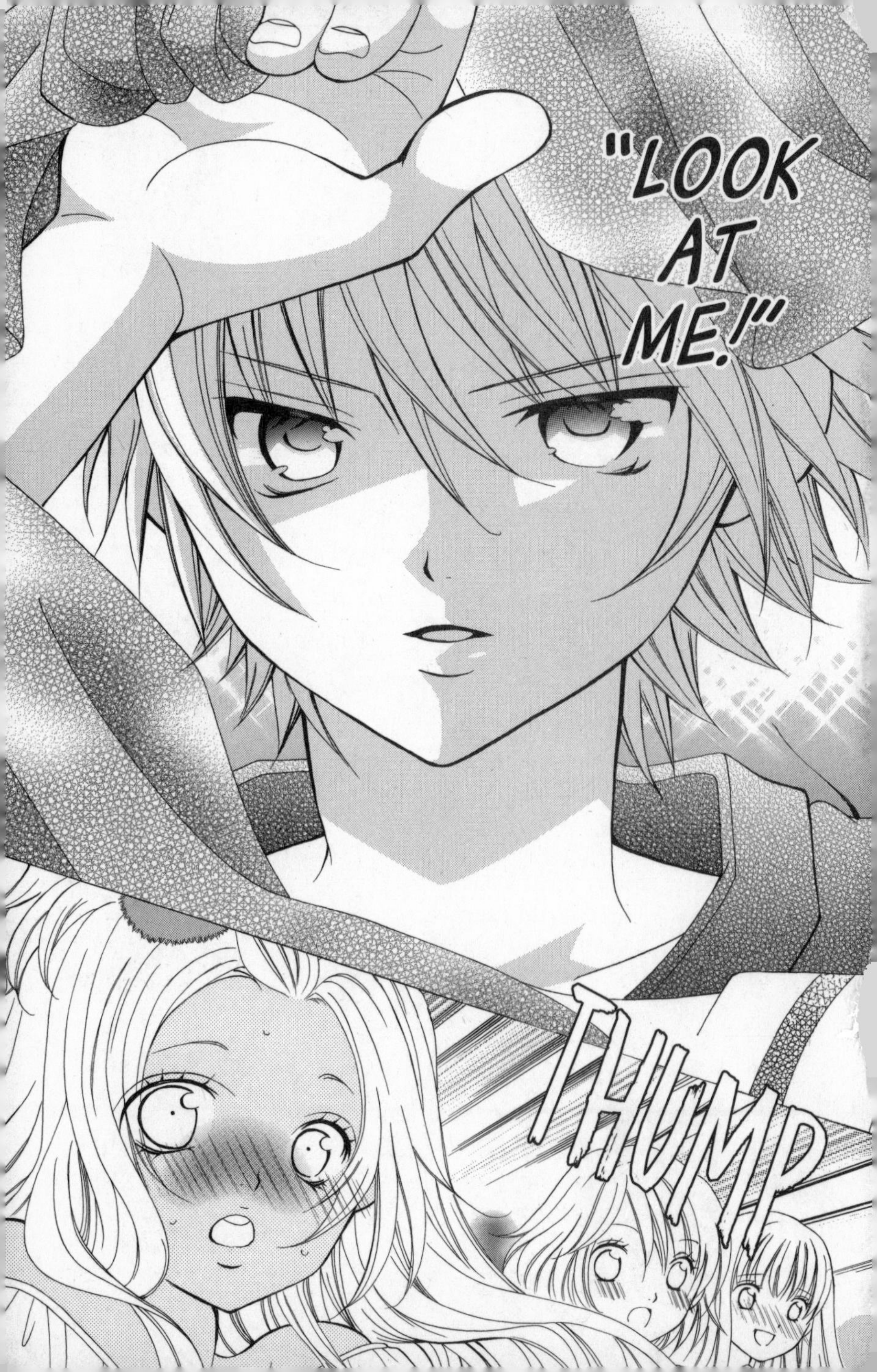
"LOOK AT ME!"
THUMP

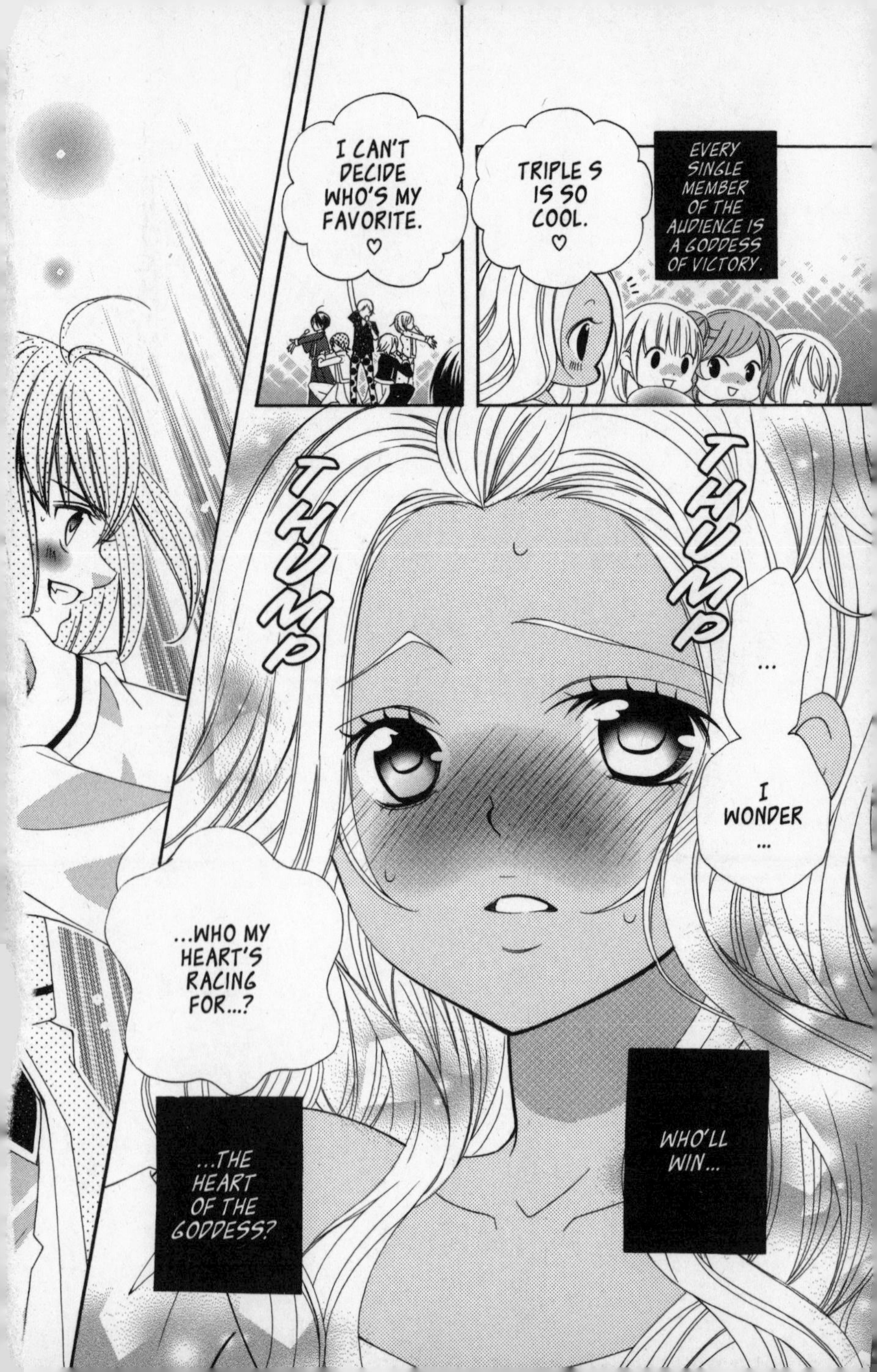
EVERY SINGLE MEMBER OF THE AUDIENCE IS A GODDESS OF VICTORY.
TRIPLE S IS SO COOL. ♡
I CAN'T DECIDE WHO'S MY FAVORITE. ♡
THUMP
THUMP
... I WONDER ...
...WHO MY HEART'S RACING FOR...?
WHO'LL WIN...
...THE HEART OF THE GODDESS?

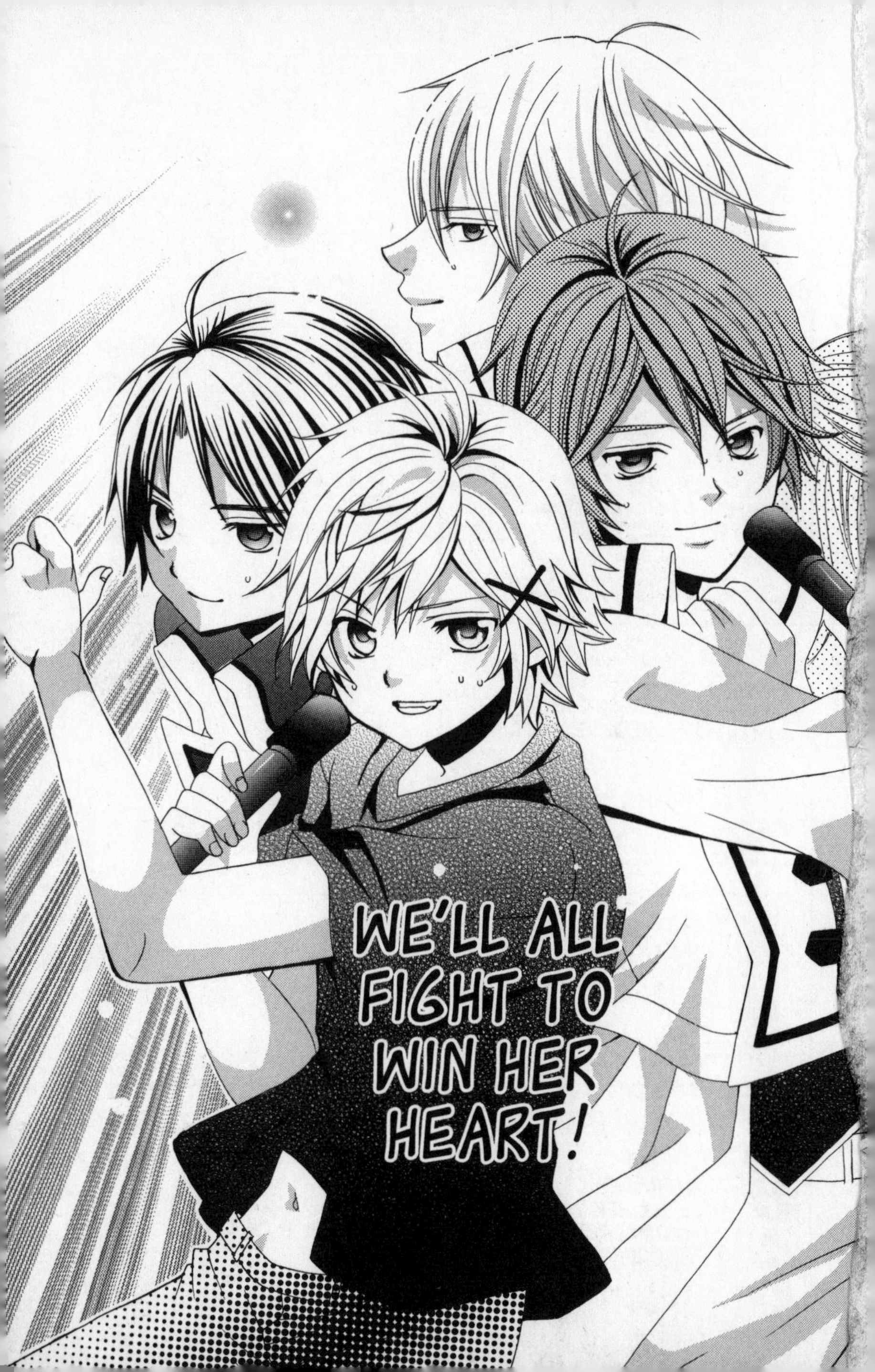
WE'LL ALL FIGHT TO WIN HER HEART!

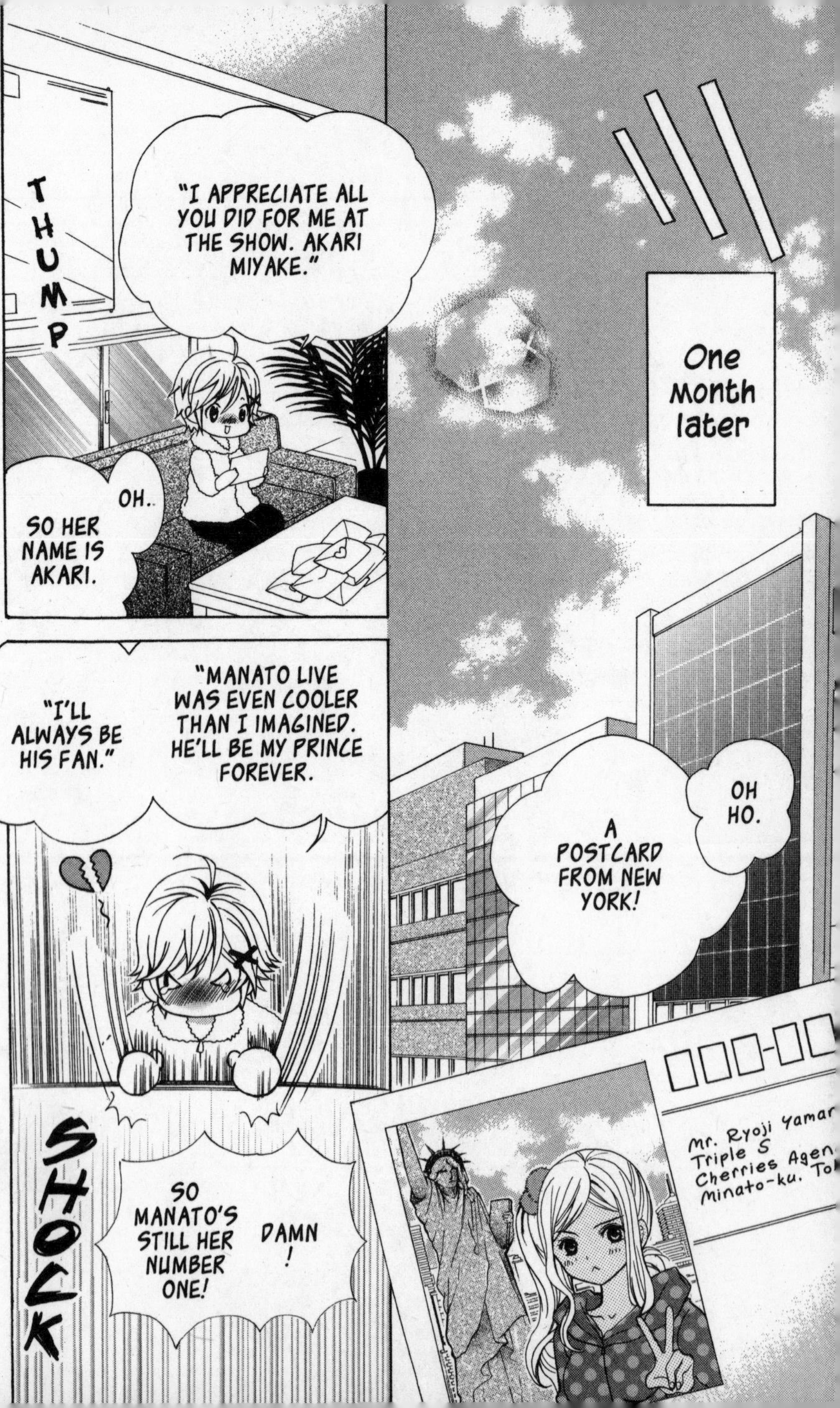
One Month later
OH HO.
A POSTCARD FROM NEW YORK!
Mr. Ryoji Yamar
Triple S
Cherries Agen
Minato-ku. To
"I APPRECIATE ALL YOU DID FOR ME AT THE SHOW. AKARI MIYAKE."
THUMP
OH..
SO HER NAME IS AKARI.
"MANATO LIVE WAS EVEN COOLER THAN I IMAGINED. HE'LL BE MY PRINCE FOREVER.
"I'LL ALWAYS BE HIS FAN."
SHOCK
SO MANATO'S STILL HER NUMBER ONE!
DAMN!

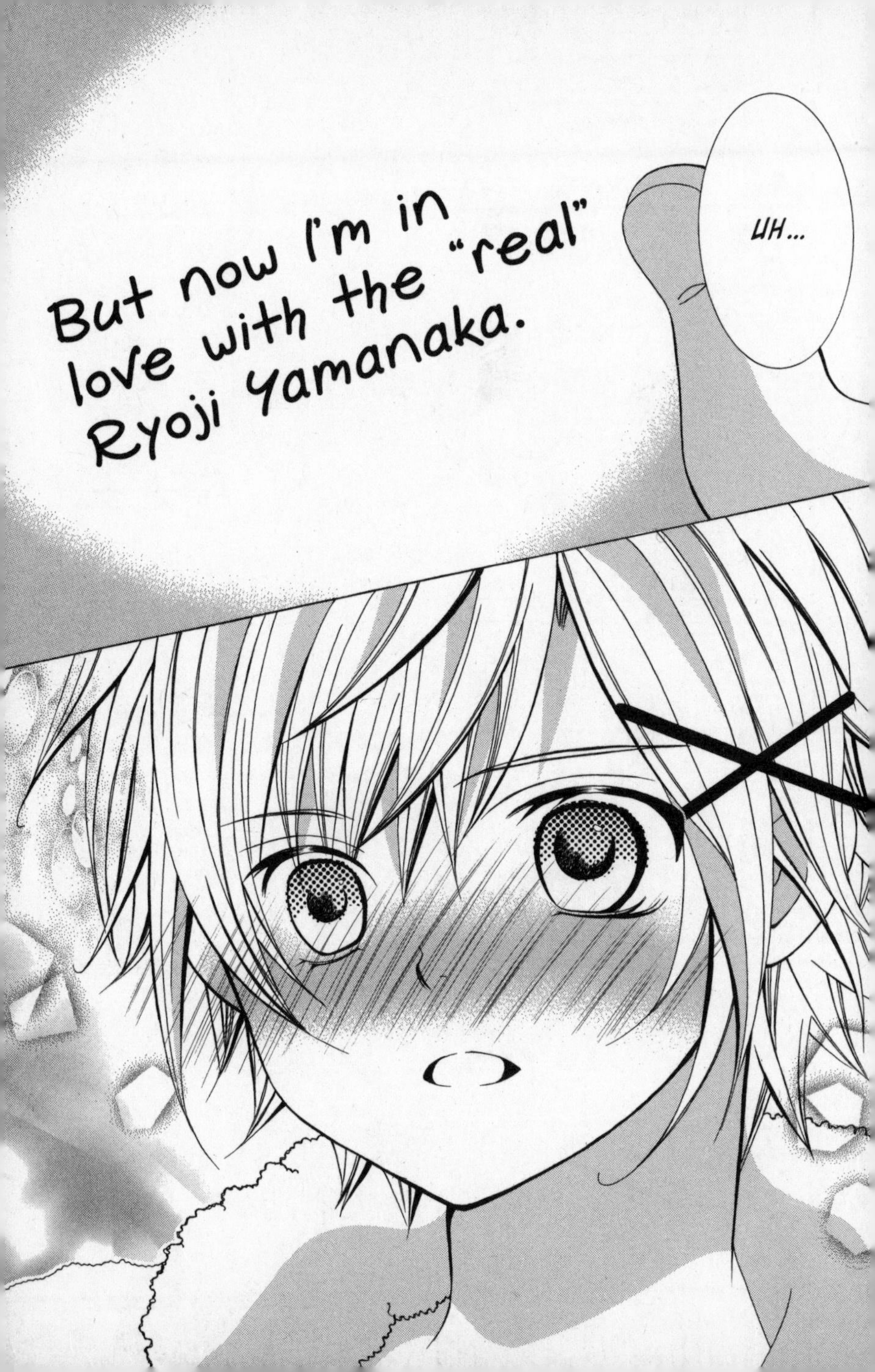
UH...
But now I'm in love with the "real" Ryoji Yamanaka.

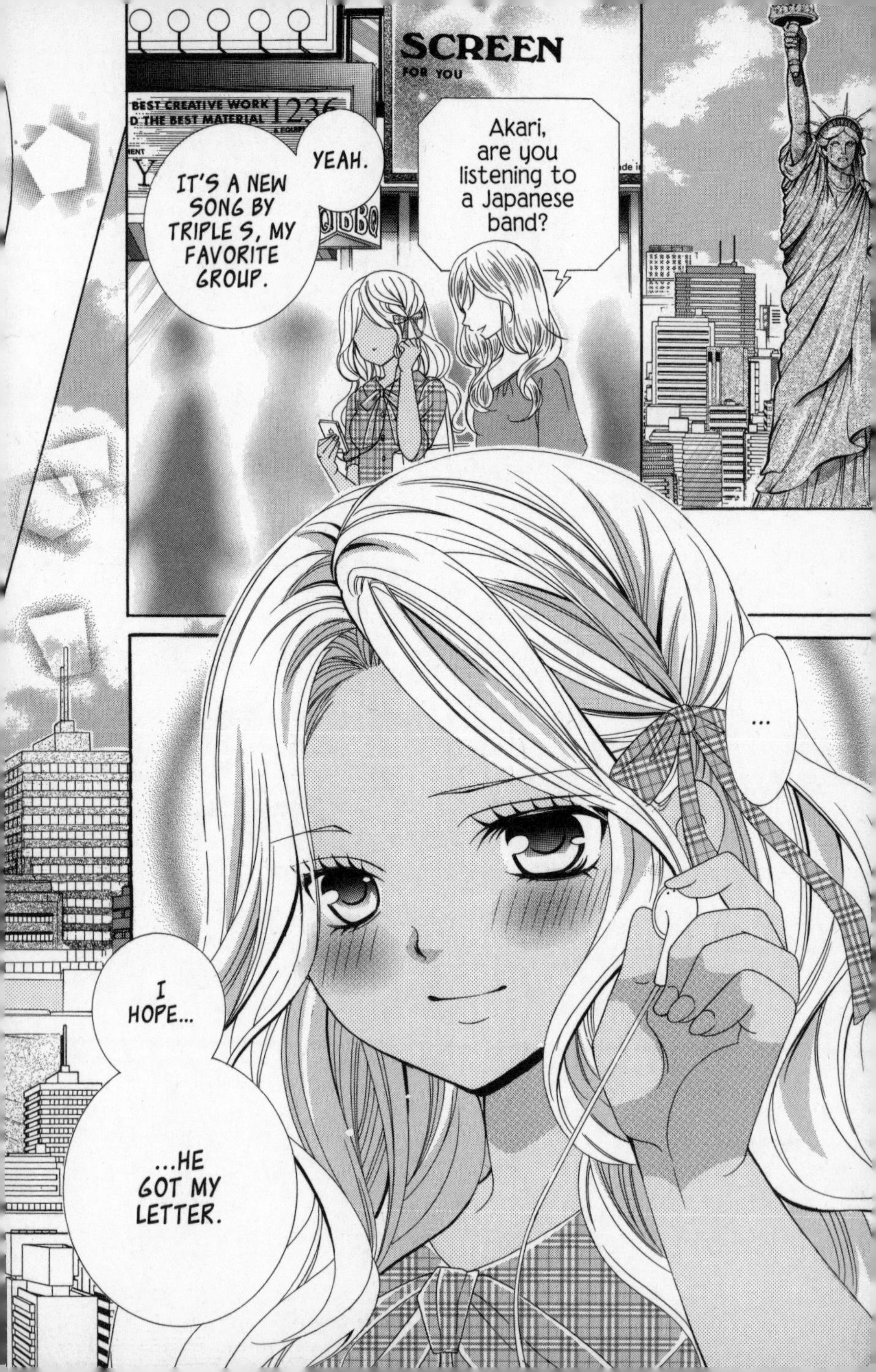
SCREEN
FOR YOU
BEST CREATIVE WORK 1236
Akari, are you listening to a Japanese band?
YEAH.
IT'S A NEW SONG BY TRIPLE S, MY FAVORITE GROUP.
...
I HOPE...
...HE GOT MY LETTER.

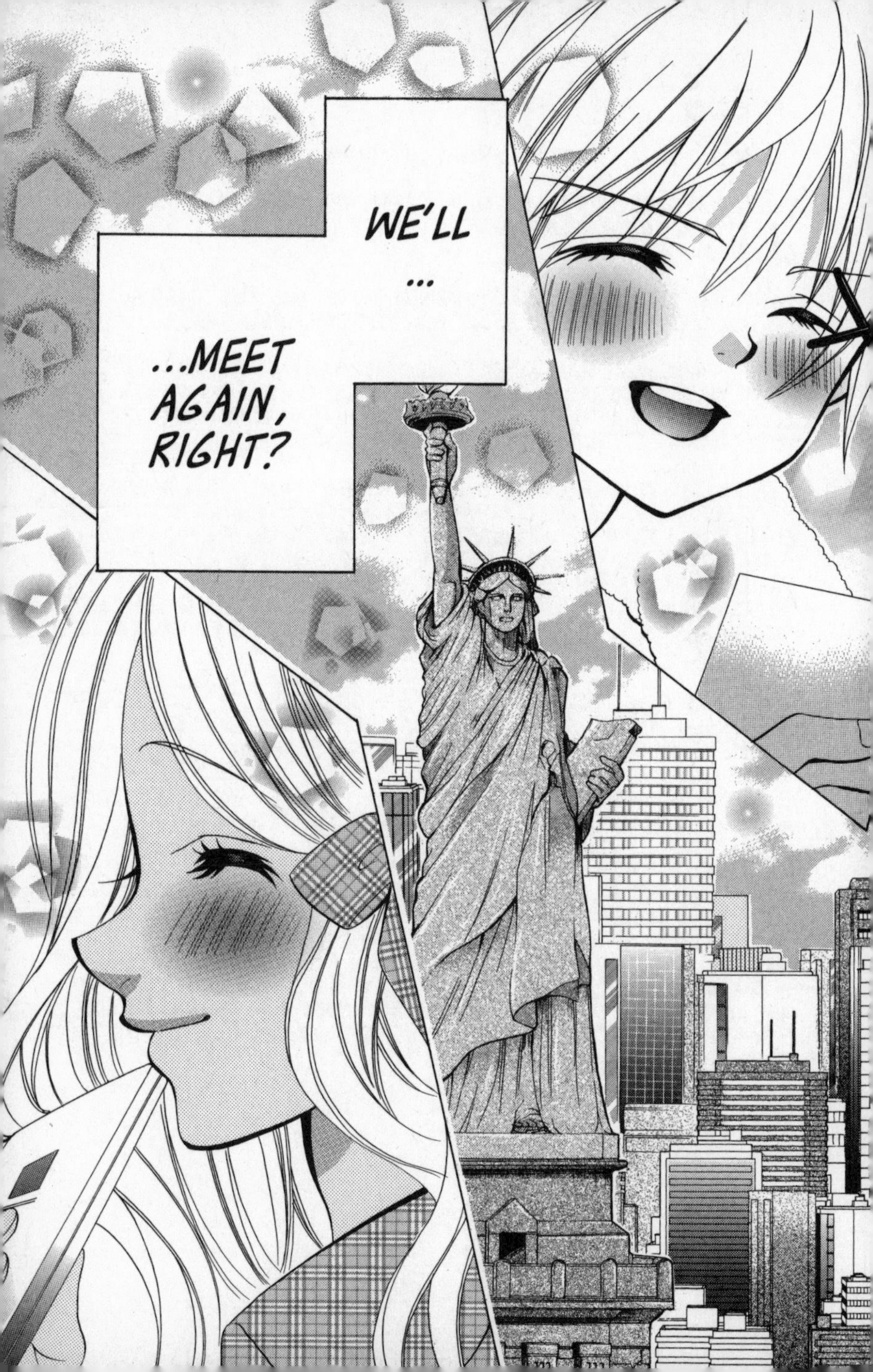
WE'LL
...
...MEET AGAIN, RIGHT?

AFTERWORD

THANK YOU SO MUCH FOR READING ALL 15 VOLUMES OF *SO CUTE IT HURTS!*

THE CLIMAX (VOLUMES 13-15) MAINLY FEATURED THE TOHOKU EARTHQUAKE, SO I APOLOGIZE FOR KEEPING LOVE SCENES (THE BEST PART OF SHOJO MANGA) TO A MINIMUM.

I THOUGHT I WAS PREPARED TO DRAW THE FINAL ARC, BUT I WAS ACTUALLY VERY SCARED AND WORRIED ABOUT HOW READERS WOULD REACT.

I THINK THERE WERE MANY READERS WHO FELT SAD AND ANGRY BECAUSE THEY DIDN'T WANT TO BE REMINDED OF THEIR PAINFUL MEMORIES. I WAS READY TO ACCEPT ANY CRITICISMS. HOWEVER, I RECEIVED MORE WARM WORDS OF SUPPORT THAN I'D EXPECTED, AND I COULDN'T STOP CRYING.

I RECEIVED LETTERS FROM ALL OVER JAPAN. EVERYONE WROTE ABOUT WHAT HAPPENED AFTER THE QUAKE, THAT THEY WANTED TO FIGURE OUT WHAT THEY COULD DO, THAT THEY DIDN'T WANT TO SEE IT AS SOMEONE ELSE'S PROBLEM, SINCE SOMETHING SIMILAR MIGHT HAPPEN TO THEM ONE DAY... I RECEIVED SINCERE WORDS FROM READERS WHO WERE VERY YOUNG WHEN THE EARTHQUAKE OCCURRED, WORKING WOMEN IN THEIR TWENTIES AND MALE READERS OLD ENOUGH TO BE THE FATHERS OF READERS. I WAS VERY ENCOURAGED BY THEIR WORDS.

THE STORY DEVELOPMENT WAS VERY SERIOUS, SO I THOUGHT READERS' RESPONSES TO *SHO-COMI'S* QUESTIONNAIRES MIGHT BE NEGATIVE. SURPRISINGLY, WE RECEIVED OUR BEST RESPONSES STARTING WITH THE EARTHQUAKE CHAPTER TO THE FINAL CHAPTER. I WAS REALLY MOVED THAT GRADE SCHOOL AND MIDDLE SCHOOL STUDENTS, WHO ARE *SHO-COMI'S* TARGET AUDIENCE, THOUGHT ABOUT THE EARTHQUAKE SO SERIOUSLY.

I FELT LIKE IT WAS FATE THAT MY FIRST EDITOR, EDITOR S, WAS ALSO FROM SENDAI. THE SCENE WHERE MEGO AND HER MOTHER HEAD FOR SENDAI TO LOOK FOR AOI IS ACTUALLY BASED ON THE EXPERIENCE OF EDITOR S'S MOTHER.

(EDITOR S'S MOTHER WAS VISITING TOKYO WHEN THE EARTHQUAKE OCCURRED. SHE WAS WORRIED ABOUT HER FAMILY, SO SHE PROCURED FOOD AND RETURNED TO SENDAI FROM HANEDA AIRPORT VIA YAMAGATA AIRPORT, SINCE SENDAI AIRPORT WAS CLOSED DUE TO THE TSUNAMI. HER FAMILY WAS SAFE, AND THEY STILL LIVE IN SENDAI.)

I WAS REALLY SURPRISED THAT THE *SHO-COMI* EDITORIAL DEPARTMENT ALLOWED ME TO DRAW THE EARTHQUAKE, SINCE IT IS A VERY DIFFICULT AND SENSITIVE SUBJECT. I WAS VERY SCARED THE EDITORIAL DEPARTMENT MIGHT BE CRITICIZED DEPENDING ON HOW I DREW IT... EDITOR S LATER TOLD ME, "I'D HAVE SAID NO IF IT WASN'T YOU. THE EDITORIAL DEPARTMENT WOULD NEVER HAVE LET ANYONE ELSE DRAW IT EITHER." I WAS MOVED BY THE GENEROSITY OF THE EDITORIAL DEPARTMENT AND MY EDITOR FOR TRUSTING ME ENOUGH TO DRAW THIS.

I HAD A NEW EDITOR STARTING WITH CHAPTER 68, VERY CLOSE TO THE FINAL ARC (EDITOR S WAS MY EDITOR FOR FOUR YEARS STARTING FROM 2011). EDITOR I IS ALSO FROM THE TOHOKU REGION (AKITA PREFECTURE) AND DID EVERYTHING TO SUPPORT ME THROUGH THE END OF THE SERIES.

THE STAR FESTIVAL IN THE FINAL ARC IS BASED ON A WISH I SAW AT SEN-DAI'S STAR FESTIVAL FIVE MONTHS AFTER THE EARTHQUAKE. THE PAPER STRIP SAID "I HOPE EARTHQUAKES NEVER HAPPEN AGAIN" IN A SMALL CHILD'S HANDWRITING. I FELT VERY SAD WHEN I READ IT.

DISASTERS ALWAYS HAPPEN, BUT WE MIGHT BE ABLE TO MINIMIZE DAM-AGES IF WE REMEMBER THE WISDOM AND KNOWLEDGE THAT OUR ANCES-TORS LEFT US. I PRAY THAT THIS SERIES WILL BECOME AN OPPORTUNITY FOR READERS TO SEEK OUT MORE ABOUT WHAT HAPPENED.

"THE MIRACLE OF KAMAISHI" REFERRED TO THE FACT THAT 99 PERCENT OF GRADE SCHOOL AND MIDDLE SCHOOL STUDENTS SURVIVED THE TSUNAMI. THEY SURVIVED BECAUSE THEY KNEW ABOUT THE TSUNAMI CODE (RUN FOR HIGH GROUND AND SAVE YOURSELF) THAT HAS BEEN HANDED DOWN IN THE KAMAISHI AREA FOR GENERATIONS.

WE HAND DOWN OUR SAD MEMORIES AND NEVER FORGET THEM. WE LEAVE THEM AS PHOTOGRAPHS, DRAWINGS AND RELICS. I BELIEVE ALL OF THEM WILL SOMEDAY SAVE THE LIVES OF FUTURE CHILDREN.

(I BELIEVE WE, WHO WERE BORN AFTER WWII, ARE ABLE TO UNDERSTAND THAT WARS ARE TERRIFYING BECAUSE SURVIVORS PASSED DOWN THEIR MEMORIES IN PAINTINGS AND STORIES. THEY'VE ALSO LEFT RELICS SUCH AS THE ATOMIC BOMB DOME SO WE CAN SEE THE TRAGEDIES OF WAR.)

I WAS DRAWING *SUZUKI-KUN* WHEN THE EARTHQUAKE HIT. I WAS VERY SCARED BECAUSE AFTERSHOCKS ALSO KEPT HITTING IN TOKYO... I FELT LIKE MY ASSISTANTS WOULD BE IN DANGER IF MY STUDIO COLLAPSED. I COULDN'T AFFORD TO HAVE SOMETHING HAPPEN TO THEM AT MY STUDIO. I TOLD MY ASSISTANTS OVER AND OVER TO RETURN HOME BECAUSE I THOUGHT I SHOULD SEND THEM TO THEIR FAMILIES SINCE WE DIDN'T KNOW WHAT MIGHT HAPPEN THE NEXT DAY. BUT THEY SAID "WE'RE FINE! CALM DOWN, SENSEI!" AND CONTINUED WORKING. I OWE THEM A DEBT OF GRATITUDE FOREVER.

MY ASSISTANTS DREW REALISTIC BACKGROUNDS FOR THE *SO CUTE!* FINAL ARC AFTER DOING RESEARCH. I THINK THEY WERE SCARED WHEN THEY REMEMBERED THE EARTHQUAKE, BUT I'M GRATEFUL ONCE AGAIN THAT THEY BRACED THEMSELVES AND DID GREAT WORK.

IT'S BEEN FIVE YEARS SINCE THE QUAKE. I THINK IT'S A MIRACLE I'M LIVING MY LIFE. I'D NEVER THOUGHT ABOUT WHERE ELECTRICITY CAME FROM UNTIL THE EARTHQUAKE. I DIDN'T KNOW THE KANTO AND TOKYO AREA WAS USING ELECTRICITY GENERATED BY NUCLEAR POWER PLANTS IN THE TOHOKU REGION. I WANT TO REMEMBER ALWAYS THAT OUR DAILY LIVES ARE PROTECTED BECAUSE THERE WERE WORKERS AND RESCUE TEAMS WHO RISKED THEIR LIVES TO MINIMIZE THE DAMAGE, AND BECAUSE THERE ARE PEOPLE WHO'RE STILL FIGHTING NOW.

I MADE MEGO AND MITSURU'S FATHER A MEMBER OF THE SELF-DEFENSE FORCE (SDF) BECAUSE I WANTED TO FEATURE SDF MEMBERS WHO PARTICIPATED IN RESCUE OPERATIONS AFTER THE EARTHQUAKE AND PORTRAY WHAT THEIR FAMILIES WENT THROUGH. I FOUND OUT THAT CHILDREN AND THE SDF MEMBERS WHO WERE USING SCHOOLS AS THEIR BASE OF OPERATIONS DID INTERACT WITH EACH OTHER. CHILDREN SAW SDF MEMBERS LEAVING THEIR SCHOOLS EVERY DAY TO GO RESCUE PEOPLE AND THOUGHT OF THEM AS HEROES. SDF MEMBERS WHO WERE GOING THROUGH UNSPEAKABLE EXPERIENCES WERE SAVED AND ENCOURAGED BY THESE CHILDREN'S WORDS.

I WAS DEEPLY MOVED WHEN I SAW THAT A TEENAGE BOY WHO HAD BEEN RESCUED DECIDED HE WANTED TO BECOME A RESCUE WORKER. I CAN'T HELP BUT PRAY THAT THE SDF MEMBERS WHO RESCUED SO MANY PEOPLE STAY SAFE AND THAT THERE'S PEACE IN THIS WORLD.

I ALSO HOPE SOCIETY AS A WHOLE WILL SUPPORT CHILDREN WHO WERE ORPHANED BY THE EARTHQUAKE... I DREW AOI'S BROTHER AKANE WITH THAT THOUGHT IN MIND. YOUNG AKANE REALLY DID HIS BEST IN THE STORY, AND HE MOVED THE STORY FORWARD IN THE FINAL CHAPTER, PULLING AOI AND MEGO WITH HIM.

I HAD ALREADY DECIDED WHEN THE SERIES STARTED THAT THE STORY WOULD END WITH SHINO'S WEDDING AND THE PENGUIN PICTURE BOOK THAT SHINO AND MEGO CREATED TOGETHER. MY HEART FELT SAVED WHEN I DREW AN OLDER AKANE READING THE PICTURE BOOK TO MEGO'S CHILDREN. I THINK AKANE BECAME A SYMBOL OF HOPE AT THE VERY END OF THE STORY.

I DID MY ABSOLUTE BEST WITH THIS STORY. MY SINCERE GRATITUDE TO ALL MY READERS WHO WARMLY SUPPORTED THE SERIES UNTIL THE VERY END, PEOPLE WHO LET US INTERVIEW THEM, ALL MY DEPENDABLE ASSISTANTS WHO SUPPORTED ME AT ALL TIMES, THE EDITORIAL DEPARTMENT, AND MY PREVIOUS EDITOR S AND CURRENT EDITOR I. THANK YOU SO MUCH.

THIS HAS BECOME A LONG AFTERWORD, BUT I'D LIKE TO TALK ABOUT THE CHARACTERS. INITIALLY I'D PLANNED FOR MEGO TO BE MORE TIMID AND TO HAVE AOI PROTECT HER. BUT AOI'S BACKSTORY WAS MORE SERIOUS THAN I'D IMAGINED, AND IT TURNED OUT HE COULDN'T PLAY AN ACTIVE ROLE IN THE STORY. SO MEGO BECAME TOUGH, AND THE HEROINE BECAME MORE OF A HERO. SHE WAS SMALL, BUT SHE WAS POWERFUL AND DID HER BEST, AND SHE WAS SO DEVOTED TO AOI THAT EVEN I WAS SURPRISED. I WAS VERY SORRY I MADE AOI SHOULDER SUCH A HEAVY PAST, BUT I PRAY THAT HE LIVES HIS FUTURE LIFE HAPPILY WITH MEGO AND THEIR CHILDREN, SURROUNDED BY AKANE, SHINO, KAGETSUNA, UESUGI AND ALL THE PEOPLE WHO LOVE HIM.

MITSURU AND AZUSA: I REALLY ENJOYED DRAWING THESE TWO! THEY WERE VERY UNIQUE AND STUBBORN, SO I WAS ALWAYS ABLE TO INCLUDE SOME COMEDY IN THEIR FIGHT SCENES AND LOVE SCENES WITHOUT WORRYING TOO MUCH. I WAS RELIEVED AZUSA'S FATHER AND MOTHER REACHED AN UNDERSTANDING WITH EACH OTHER AT THE END OF THE BONUS CHAPTER.

MITSURU AND SHINO: I WANTED TO END THE INTRO AND THE CONCLUSION OF THE STORY WITH THEIR "THANK YOU." I WAS VERY HAPPY *SHO-COMI* READERS LOVED THE BONUS FEATURING MITSURU AND AZUSA'S WEDDING WHEN THE STORY WAS PUBLISHED IN THE MAGAZINE.

MAMI KOIDE SENSEI WROTE THE NOVEL *MAINICHI GA AISHISUGITE ITAI!* AFTER THE SERIES WAS COMPLETED. THE NOVEL IS AVAILABLE FOR SALE THROUGH *SHO-COMI* MAGAZINE AND FEATURES AOI AND MEGO AFTER THEY'RE MARRIED AND AZUSA, WHO CONTINUES TO SUPPORT THE TOHOKU REGION THROUGH THE TOKUGAWA GROUP. THE STORY IS VERY HEARTWARMING AND LOVELY, SO I HOPE EVERYONE READS IT.

THANK YOU FOR THESE THREE YEARS!
GO IKEYAMADA
JANUARY 2016

AUTHOR BIO

This is the final volume of *So Cute It Hurts!!* My sincerest gratitude to each and every one of you who have rooted for *So Cute!* for all 15 volumes. Thank you for your warm support!!

I'm very nervous right now because my new series, *Sekai wa Nakajima ni Koi o Suru!!*, has just started in *Sho-Comi* magazine, but I always have been, and always will be, supported by your warm feelings.

Please keep reading my manga.

Go Ikeyamada is a Gemini from Miyagi Prefecture whose hobbies include taking naps and watching movies. Her debut manga *Get Love!!* appeared in *Shojo Comic* in 2002, and her current work *So Cute It Hurts!!* (*Kobayashi ga Kawai Suguite Tsurai!!*) is being published by VIZ Media.

SO CUTE IT HURTS!!
Volume 15

Shojo Beat Edition

STORY AND ART BY
GO IKEYAMADA

English Translation & Adaptation/Tomo Kimura
Touch-Up Art & Lettering/Joanna Estep
Design/Izumi Evers
Editor/Pancha Diaz

KOBAYASHI GA KAWAISUGITE TSURAI!! Vol.15
by Go IKEYAMADA
© 2012 Go IKEYAMADA
All rights reserved.
Original Japanese edition published by SHOGAKUKAN.
English translation rights in the United States of America, Canada,
the United Kingdom and Ireland arranged with SHOGAKUKAN.

Printed in the U.S.A.

Published by VIZ Media, LLC
P.O. Box 77010
San Francisco, CA 94107

10 9 8 7 6 5 4 3 2 1
First printing, October 2017

www.viz.com   www.shojobeat.com

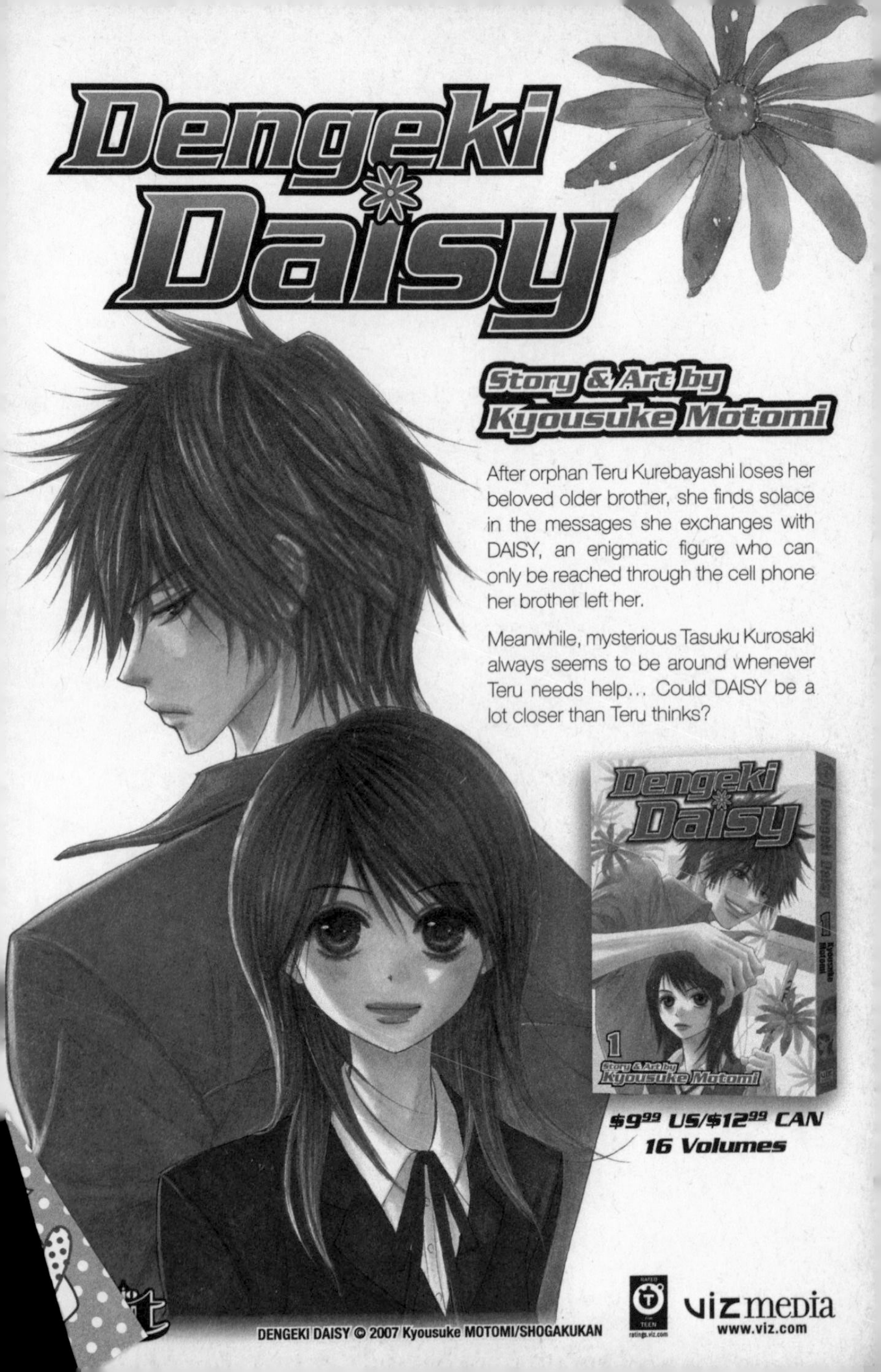
Dengeki Daisy
Story & Art by
Kyousuke Motomi
After orphan Teru Kurebayashi loses her beloved older brother, she finds solace in the messages she exchanges with DAISY, an enigmatic figure who can only be reached through the cell phone her brother left her.
Meanwhile, mysterious Tasuku Kurosaki always seems to be around whenever Teru needs help… Could DAISY be a lot closer than Teru thinks?
Dengeki Daisy
1
Story & Art by
Kyousuke Motomi
$9.99 US/$12.99 CAN
16 Volumes
DENGEKI DAISY © 2007 Kyousuke MOTOMI/SHOGAKUKAN
RATED T TEEN
ratings.viz.com
viz media
www.viz.com

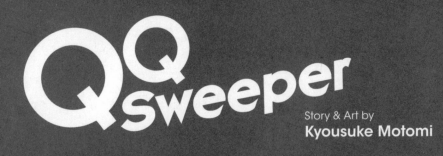

QQ Sweeper

Story & Art by
Kyousuke Motomi

By the creator of *Dengeki Daisy* and *Beast Master*!

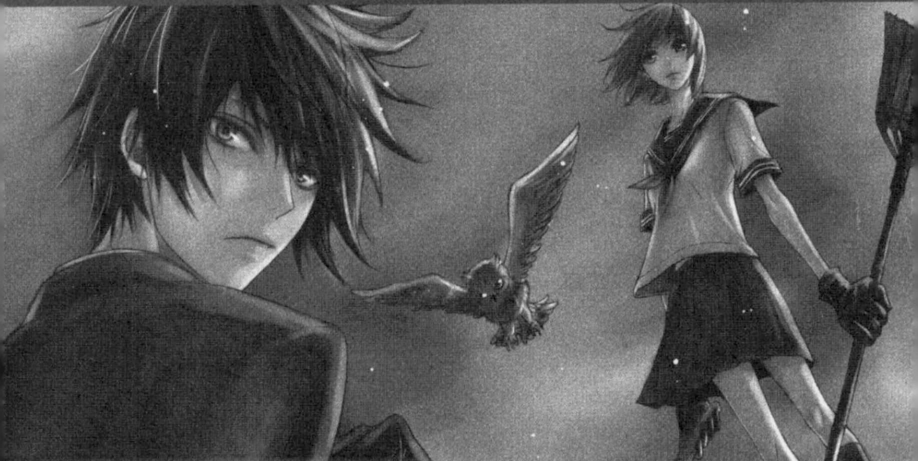

One day, Kyutaro Horikita, the tall, dark and handsome cleaning expert of Kurokado High, comes across a sleeping maiden named Fumi Nishioka at school... Unfortunately, their meeting is anything but a fairy-tale encounter! It turns out Kyutaro is a "Sweeper" who cleans away negative energy from people's hearts—and Fumi is about to become his apprentice!

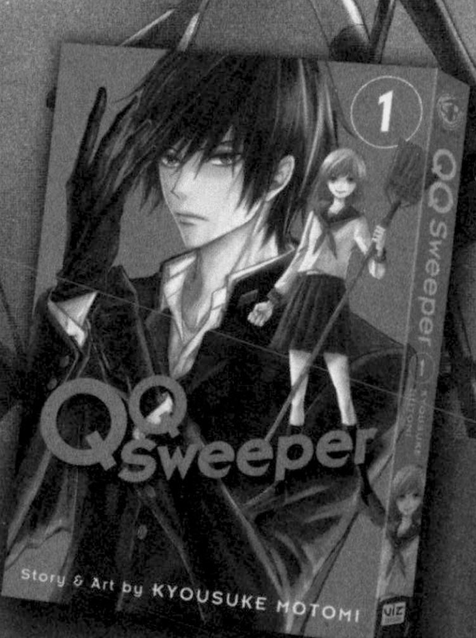
1
QQ Sweeper
QQ Sweeper
Story & Art by KYOUSUKE MOTOMI
VIZ

Shojo Beat VIZ media
viz.com

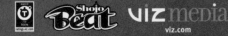

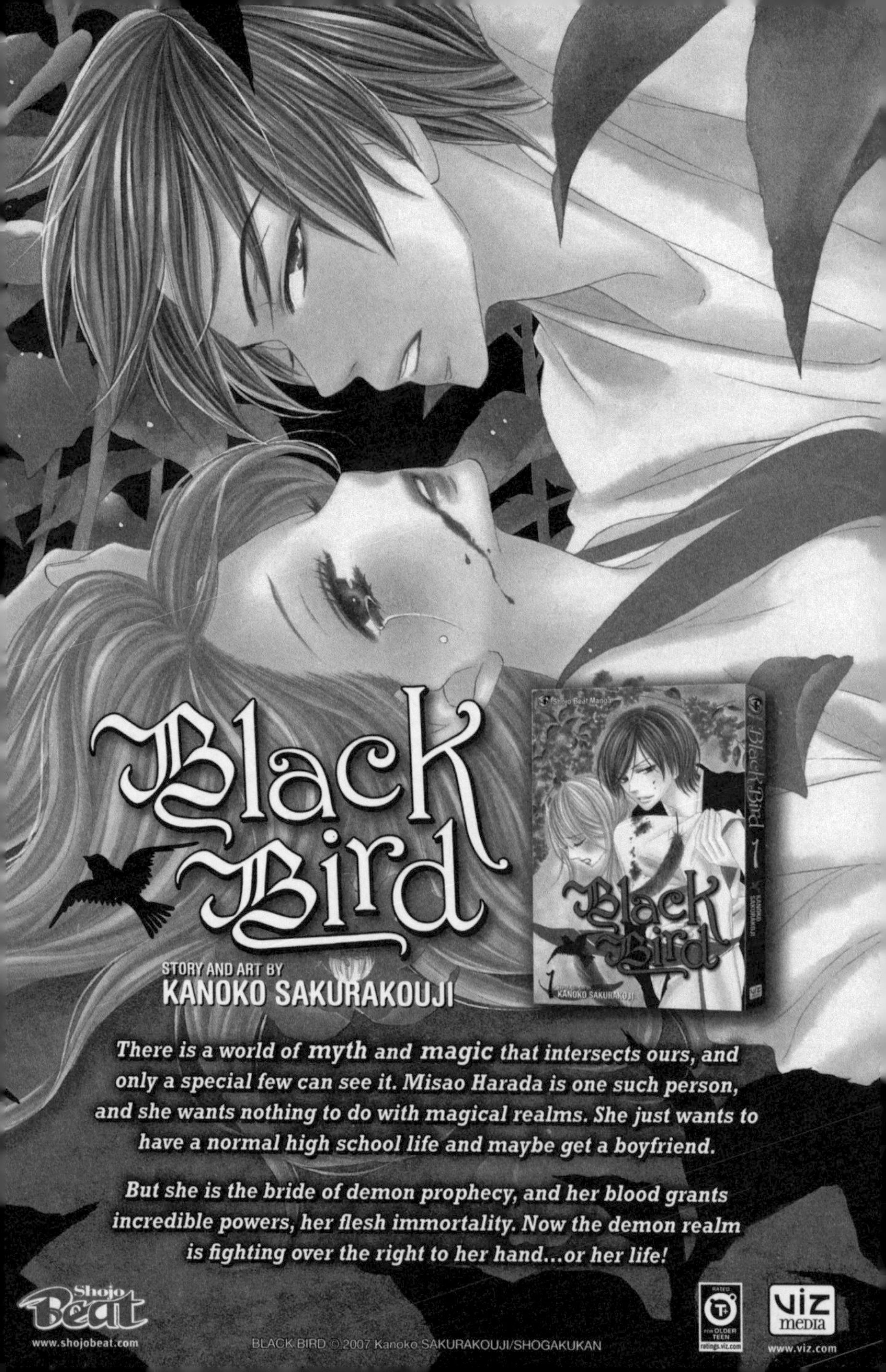
Black Bird
STORY AND ART BY
KANOKO SAKURAKOUJI
Shojo Beat Manga
Black Bird
1
KANOKO SAKURAKOUJI
There is a world of myth and magic that intersects ours, and only a special few can see it. Misao Harada is one such person, and she wants nothing to do with magical realms. She just wants to have a normal high school life and maybe get a boyfriend.
But she is the bride of demon prophecy, and her blood grants incredible powers, her flesh immortality. Now the demon realm is fighting over the right to her hand...or her life!
Shojo Beat
www.shojobeat.com
BLACK BIRD © 2007 Kanoko SAKURAKOUJI/SHOGAKUKAN
RATED
T+
FOR OLDER TEEN
ratings.viz.com
VIZ media
www.viz.com

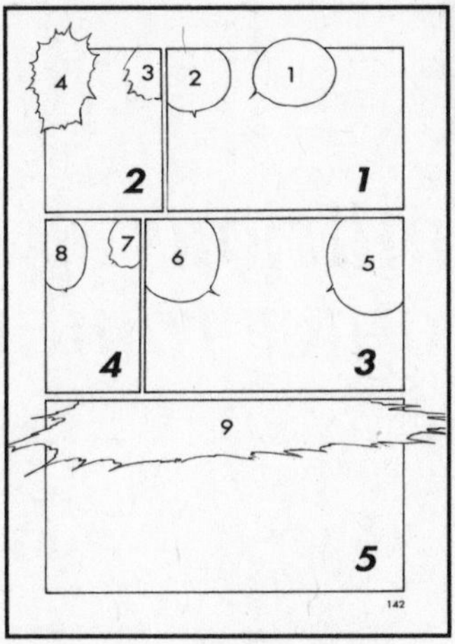

This is the last page.

In keeping with the original Japanese comic format, this book reads from right to left—so action, sound effects and word balloons are completely reversed. This preserves the orientation of the original artwork—plus, it's fun! Check out the diagram shown here to get the hang of things, and then turn to the other side of the book to get started!

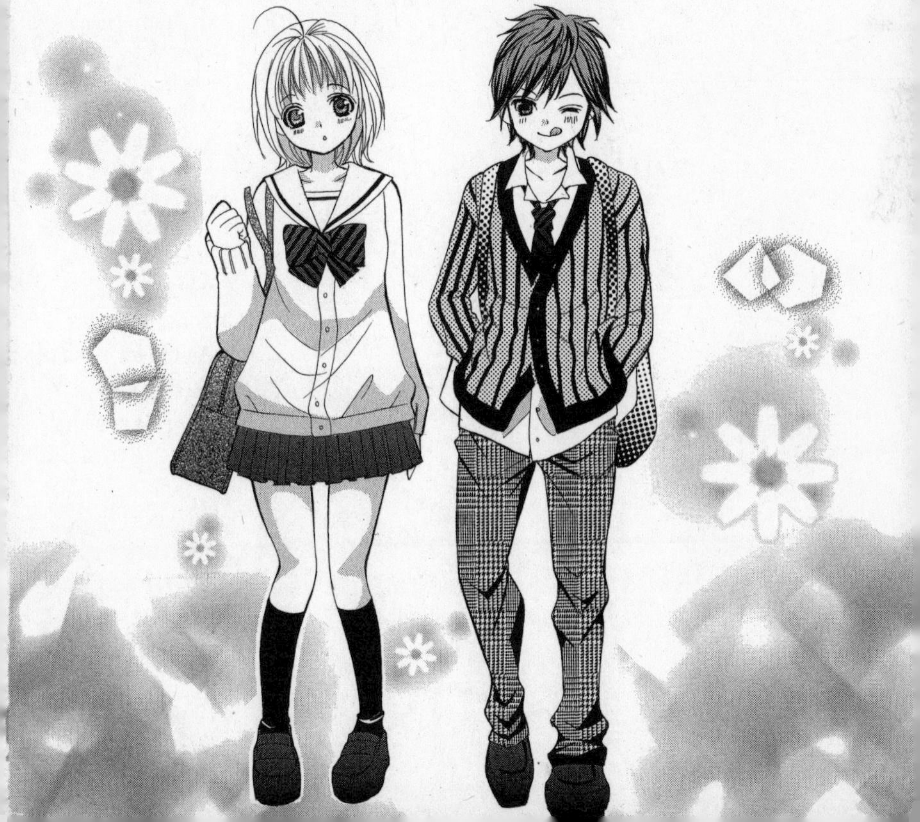

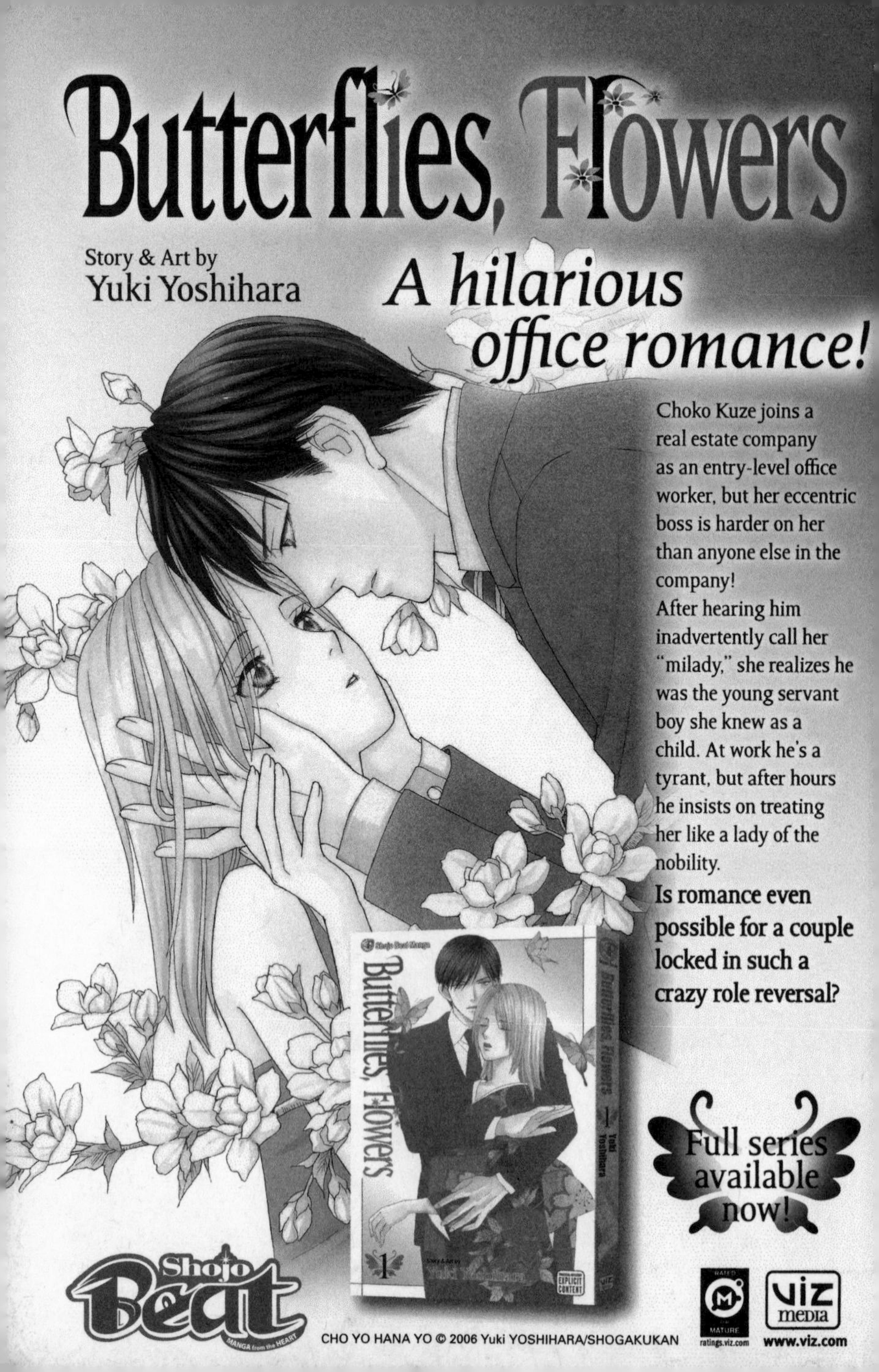
Butterflies, Flowers
Story & Art by
Yuki Yoshihara
A hilarious office romance!
Choko Kuze joins a real estate company as an entry-level office worker, but her eccentric boss is harder on her than anyone else in the company!
After hearing him inadvertently call her "milady," she realizes he was the young servant boy she knew as a child. At work he's a tyrant, but after hours he insists on treating her like a lady of the nobility.
Is romance even possible for a couple locked in such a crazy role reversal?
Butterflies, Flowers
1
Yuki Yoshihara
EXPLICIT CONTENT
Full series available now!
Shojo Beat
MANGA from the HEART
CHO YO HANA YO © 2006 Yuki YOSHIHARA/SHOGAKUKAN
RATED M MATURE
ratings.viz.com
VIZ media
www.viz.com